D1540851

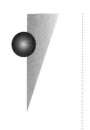

The Cybrarian's Manual

P AT E N S O R

Editor

American Library Association

Chicago and London 1997

The paper used in this publication meets the minimum requirements of American National Standard for Information Sciences—Permanence of Paper for Printed Library Materials, ANSI Z39.48-1992.∞

Project editor: Joan A. Grygel

Cover and text design: Image House

Compositor: Clarinda in Garamond and Universe Condensed on Penta DeskTopPro

Printed on 50-pound Welcome Recycled, a pH-neutral stock, and bound in 10-point coated Bristol cover stock by Victor Graphics, Inc.

Library of Congress Cataloging-in-Publication Data

The cybrarian's manual / Pat Ensor, editor.
     p. cm.
   Includes bibliographical references and index.
   ISBN 0-8389-0693-1
    1. Internet (Computer network)—United States. 2. Library information networks—United States. I. Ensor, Pat.
   Z674.75.I58C93 1996
   025.04—dc21   96-47711

01 00 99 98 97   5 4 3 2 1

CONTENTS

PREFACE

Welcome to *The Cybrarian's Manual,* the librarian's guide to cyber-space. The cyberspace that many librarians move in today, and more will occupy tomorrow, is anywhere, everywhere, and nowhere. It is the collective virtual space created by the operations of millions of computers linked together. At least, that is what it is today—who knows what it will be tomorrow or the day after?

I think most librarians would agree that it has revolutionized our work lives and the information-seeking experiences of many of our patrons and of many people who never enter a library. A couple of short years ago, we in academia wondered when the rest of the world would discover the Internet; today, it seems one can scarcely find a printed advertisement that doesn't list a Web site. Seeing a URL (Uniform Resource Locator) rendered on one of those temporary, press-on-letter signs by the road is quite an experience. Where did they get all those slashes, for one thing?

You might wonder if you really need a guidebook for exploring cyber-space; what does this book do that is so different? Its aims are to cover many of the practical, day-to-day aspects of a librarian's travels in cyber-space as well as to take a peek at some things to come. It does not aim to cover management, political, or social aspects of the cyberspace journey. And one of the main aims is to provide a manual that is truly readable—the tone is light, and in many places, we have even aimed for, yes, humor! It is structured so that you, the reader, can dip into it here and there or sit down and read it straight through. It is not a resource aimed at the complete beginner, but it can be useful to a beginner who is willing to use the references given to read up on many of the topics. It is aimed at a more intermediate audience—those of us who aren't really beginners but aren't ready, and may never be, to read books about how to set up Internet firewalls.

Why read a book when you could just head out on the Web on your own? And isn't this going to get out of date fast? I believe when you read these pieces, you'll see that the authors have something unique to add to coverage of the topics included here. More to the point, who heads out on the road with no map and no guidebook? That guy back at the turnoff asking directions at the service station, that's who. This book includes many signposts to points of interest on the Web that should help keep you moving down the road. These references will undoubtedly date quickly, but wher-ever possible, you are provided with ongoing references to topics, such as the relevant area on Yahoo, that should include new sources and updates of old ones. Best of all, we have set up Cyberlib.net on the ALA Editions home page *(http://www.ala.org/alaeditions.html)* for up-to-date features and resources around the themes of this ink-and-paper edition.

Some housekeeping details: You will find many URLs in this book. Some of them are given at the ends of sentences, and there are periods after them. These periods are never included at the end of a URL! The only thing at the end of a URL would be a letter or a "/"; don't include anything else when you enter the URL into your browser.

Any pieces in this book with no author attribution were written by me for this work. For contributions from journals and periodicals, I have retained the original style of notes, which will appear at the end of the pieces. Original pieces do not include notes, though references, sources, or a bibliography often follow the piece. The citations for these articles use a modification of the APA style.

Finally, I would like to thank a number of people connected with the production of this book: all my wonderful contributors; Patrick Hogan at ALA Editions; Shannon M. Cunningham, American Productivity and Quality Center; and Torina Rogers, Hayde Hernandez, Rob Spragg, Charles Bailey, and Pamela Adame at University of Houston Libraries.

Cyberlib.net

Cyberlib.net is the Web presence of *The Cybrarian's Manual*, where Pat Ensor and editorial colleagues will post new features and timely updates. To visit, go to the ALA Editions home page:

http://www.ala.org/alaeditions.html

1

The Internet—The Basics

THE USUAL INTERNET GENERAL INFORMATION AND HISTORY

No one needs yet another chapter that starts "The Internet was born when . . . and grew up in a log cabin . . . ," etc., so you're going to need to do some reading elsewhere if you have been living in a cave and have no idea what the Internet is, what you can do with it, and where it came from. Here are some pointers as to what to read/access from your no-doubt fully wired (and charming) cave home.

Bibliography

Ballard, Terry. (1994). "The Missing Dragon, or Stumbling through the Internet." *American Libraries, 25*, 988–9.

> Brief, readable personal account of the pitfalls of using the Internet. Might raise your comfort level by letting you know others have encountered the same problems you have.

Bruce, Harry. (1994). "The Internet as New Information Infrastructure." *LASIE, 24*, 77–83.

> Although dated, this article gives a very good brief introduction to Internet history from the library point of view. It also includes a bibliography of what some librarians had written as introductions to the Internet to that point.

Lankes, R. David. (1994). "The Internet Model." *Information Searcher, 7*, 3–6.

> Excellent explanation of the different levels that constitute the Internet—hardware, software, and resources. Has clear explanations of Transmission Control Protocol/Internet Protocol (TCP/IP), clients and servers, and Internet addresses.

Lomarcan, Diana L. (1995, March). "Networks: The Basics." *Computers in Libraries*, 19–24.

> Actually, this is not the basics of networks but, rather, of the Internet. It really gets down to basics, telling you in simple terms about the hard-

ware and software involved in the Internet, how you get connected, and what you can do when you get on. Very good introduction for those who really know nothing about the Internet but are embarrassed to admit it.

Shaw, Debora. (1994). "Libraries of the Future: Glimpses of a Networked, Distributed, Collaborative, Hyper, Virtual World." *Libri, 44,* 206–23.
Terrible subtitle, and it's not strictly about the Internet, but this is an excellent review of many issues that have implications for the Internet—networks, hypermedia, collaboratories, virtual reality, knowbots, and more. Also has a long list of references.

Swain, Leigh, and Cleveland, Gary. (1994). "Overview of the Internet: Origins, Future, and Issues." *IFLA Journal, 20,* 16–21.
A bit out of date, but a great brief overview of history, structure, and issues.

URLography

General Guides to the Internet. [Online]. Available: *http://lcweb.loc.gov/global/internet/guides.html*
This page is a product of the Library of Congress. It provides the "author's" name for the guides it lists, so if someone tells you to find Brendan Kehoe's guide, you'll be able to find it from this list.

Life on the Internet: Starting Out. [Online]. Available: *http://www.screen.com/understand/startingout.html*
This is notably good because of its annotations; covers a broad range of topics.

SoloTech's Resources for the Internet Novice. [Online]. Available: *http://www.execpc.com/~wmhogg/beginner.html*
No annotations, but, wow, is this extensive! Lists numerous resources under just about any topic a beginner might want to locate.

These are only a few of the possibly helpful sites. To stay up to date, look at Yahoo as follows: *http://www.yahoo.com/Computers_and_Internet/Internet/Information_and_Documentation/* This is where you'll find beginner's guides, books on the Internet (some full-text copies and some sites), and introductions to the World Wide Web.

CHECK THESE OUT REGULARLY

What follows is a list that was compiled from various sources and recommendations. I have tried to include a selection of periodicals with Internet news, substantive reviews of Internet sites, thoughtful commentary, or library approaches to the Internet. Pick out some to try, then decide what you want to look at regularly.

You may find that you, like most of the rest of humanity, don't read things unless they're right in your face. Some of the Web resources listed here have e-mail subscription options; that might be something to consider, assuming you check your e-mail regularly! Some are posted to certain discussion lists by their publishers, and you automatically get them if you're on that list. Of course, you can always bookmark the ones you're interested in and even create your own page of resources!

Electronic Sources

The Ariadne Newsletter. Available: *http://ukoln.bath.ac.uk/ariadne/*

College & Research Libraries News Internet Resources. Available: *http://library.byu.edu/crln/*

Current Cites. Available: *http://sunsite.berkeley.edu/CurrentCites/*

D-Lib Magazine. Available: *http://www.dlib.org/magazine.html*

Edupage. Available: *http://educom.edu/web/edupage.html*

HotWired. Available: *http://www.hotwired.com/*

InfoWorld. Available: *http://www.infoworld.com/*

Interactive Age Home Page. Available: *http://techweb.cmp.com:80/techweb/ia/current/*

iWORLD: Internet News and Resources. Available: *http://www.mecklerweb.com/*

NetGuide Magazine. Available: *http://techweb.cmp.com/techweb/ng/current/*

Public Access Computer Systems Review. Available: *http://info.lib.ub.edu/pacsrev.html*

SIMBA Media Daily: Internet. Available: *http://netday.iworld.com/simba/*

Print Sources

Database
  Online
  Online, Inc.
  462 Danbury Road
  Wilton, CT 06897
  $110 each

Internet World
  Mecklermedia Corp.
  20 Ketchum Street
  Westport, CT 06880
  $29

21C
  International Publishers Distr.
  820 Town Center Drive
  Langhorne, PA 19047-9357
  $24

WEBWEEK
  Mecklermedia Corp.
  20 Ketchum Street
  Westport, CT 06880
  $50

Wired
  Wired Ventures, Ltd.
  Box 191826
  San Francisco, CA 94119-9866
  $39.95

Want More?

There are more periodical publications in print and out on the Web than any one person could possibly assess, so in addition to the previous recommendations, make sure you check out the following sites for more listings and insightful reviews of Web publications about the Internet. (See also Judi Copler's section on "Browsers, Extensions and the Kitchen Junk Drawer" for additional recommendations.)

Global Network Navigator. (1996). *GNN Select Internet: Magazines.* [Online]. Available: *http://gnn-e2a.gnn.com/gnn/wic/wics/internet.imag.html*

InterNIC. *Staying Current.* [Online]. Available: *http://rs.internic.net/scout/toolkit/current.html*

Point Communications Corp. (1995). *Internet News.* [Online]. Available: *http://www.pointcom.com/text/reviews/ciinnn.htm*

Organizations Cybrarians Should Know About

American Library Association at *http://www.ala.org/*
> Yes, the venerable organization is getting involved in the cyber-age. ALA makes statements, files suits, and creates partnerships, all having to do with the new electronic age. Check its site for more information.

Coalition for Networked Information at *http://www.cni.org/CNI.homepage.html*
> "The Coalition for Networked Information was founded in March 1990 with a mission to help realize the promise of high performance networks and computers for the advancement of scholarship and the enrichment of intellectual productivity. The Coalition is a partnership of the Association of Research Libraries, CAUSE, and EDUCOM." It had lots of interesting projects going.

Electronic Frontier Foundation at *http://www.eff.org/*
> "The Electronic Frontier Foundation: A non-profit civil liberties organization working in the public interest to protect privacy, free expression, and access to online resources and information." This is a pioneering organization, fighting for your rights to privacy and free expression on the Internet.

International Federation of Library Associations and Institutions at *http://www.nlc-bnc.ca/ifla/*
> "The International Federation of Library Associations and Institutions, or IFLA, is a worldwide, independent organization created to provide librarians around the world with a forum for exchanging ideas, promoting international cooperation, research and development in all fields of library activity."

Internet Engineering Task Force at *http://www.ietf.cnri.reston.va.us/home.html*
> "The Internet Engineering Task Force (IETF) is the protocol engineering and development arm of the Internet." You know how they tell you no one is in charge of the Internet? Well, they're right. But the people in-

volved with IETF are the ones who decide what protocols and standards are followed to perform many functions on the Internet.

National Information Standards Organization at *http://www.niso.org/*
"The National Information Standards Organization is a nonprofit association accredited as a standards developer by the American National Standards Institute, the national clearinghouse for voluntary standards development in the US." NISO is the source for American information standards; unfortunately, it doesn't link to information on its most famous standard Z39.50. Not to worry; you can check it out at *http://ds. internic.net/z3950/z3950.html.*

World Wide Web Consortium at *http://www.w3.org/hypertext/WWW/ Consortium/*
"The W3 Consortium exists to develop common standards for the evolution of the World Wide Web." Check its site out for information about HyperText Markup Language (HTML) standards, the HyperText Transfer Protocol (HTTP), and the Platform for Internet Content Selection (PICS) specification to indicate Web site content as well as much more.

For more organizations, see IFLA's "Organizations and Companies Serving the Library Community" at *http://www.nlc-bnc.ca/ifla/II/orgs.htm.*

INTERNET SIZE AND GROWTH

Patrick Flannery

Patrick Flannery is network and systems analyst at the Texas Medical Center Library in Houston, and chair of the Legislation and Regulation Committee of the Library and Information Technology Association. He has written and spoken widely about library legislative and electronic topics.

> If we enlarge the penguin to the size of a man, its brain is still smaller.
> But—and here's the point—*it's bigger than it was!*
>   —from *Monty Python's Flying Circus,* series III, episode 12

OK, here's the short version: The Internet is much, much bigger than it was and getting more so all the time. And, let's face it, articles about this phenomenon tend to be as interesting as counting how many breaths the average person exhales in a lifetime or measuring how fast planetary matter is receding into outer space.

So why should the already overburdened librarian care about the size and growth of the Internet? Isn't it enough that we must struggle daily with new sites, new techniques, new possibilities? The skillful surfer doesn't need to measure the ocean to ride the wave.

Or does he? Well, he certainly doesn't measure out water in a cup, but he does recognize the relationship between wave size and a variety of factors—tides, winds, storm proximity. He sees the wave in a context of change and rides with a healthy respect for that context. Likewise, librarians should develop a healthy respect for the context of the Internet—its sheer enormity, breathtaking expansion, and almost daily redefinition. It takes as much humility as skill to ride the wave.

Consider that, in physics, a state of rapid expansion can render a fact obsolete within an extremely short time. The concept of a fact's life span seems counterintuitive to many of us, but it is what underlies much of modern physics; this notion in turn has had a profound impact on twentieth-century philosophy and literary theory. Why does this matter? Well, librarians often define themselves in terms of facts: facts that answer patron questions, facts about our professional goals, facts about our place in the information world. At the very least, the Internet's rapid expansion should cause us to ask the question: Are the "facts" of our profession still valid?

Likewise, we are all aware of the close relationship between the goals of our profession and the tools that we employ to achieve those goals. Librarians are increasingly aware of the wisdom in the saying: "When your only tool is a hammer, everything looks like a nail." We naturally choose tools that we think will best help us meet our goals, but somewhere along the way, our goals begin to fit the shape of our tools, subtly redefining what we achieve.

Throughout our professional history, the book has been a valued tool. Like all tools it not only served a purpose, it also defined how we went about our jobs and thought about our profession. The book has been a remarkably stable tool over four centuries, despite a constant linear growth pattern. But over the past several years librarians have acquired a range of new tools, and we've noticed that they have one remarkable property in common: in the expanding world of the Internet, they mutate constantly. Tools that worked last year are collapsing under the weight of the rising numbers of users, applications that exceed available network bandwidth, and database search algorithms that cannot scale up to meet the needs of increasingly large data sets. New tools arise daily to meet these challenges, and we put energy into acquiring, learning, and employing these tools. We struggle to reshape data to conform to the shape of our new tools, worrying constantly that this year's decisions will return to haunt us next year. (At the time this piece was written, as our profession rushes to HyperText Markup Language (HTML)-encode everything in sight, renowned futurist Paul Saffo was already declaring the World Wide Web "dead").* The very way we see our professional reality shifts constantly in such an environment of explosive growth.

So perhaps it is worth the working librarian's time to look up from the flood of Internet details and consider the beast itself: its scope, shape, size, and continual growth. Let's examine this phenomenon once more, recognizing that, clichéd though it may already be to say it, the Internet is *the* critical factor for librarians interested in moving into the next century professionally intact. (A simple caveat to those of you reading this chapter: do not trust these facts. Names, URLs, and other seeming truths may no longer be relevant, existent, or true. We are stepping through the Looking Glass that is any human revolution; expect the unexpected.)

---

*Nee, E. (1996, February). "Paul Saffo: An interview by Eric Nee." *Upside*, p. 26: "The Web as we know it is already dead. It's dead in two ways: because it's going to mutate into something else very quickly and be unrecognizable within 12 months, and secondly, it's dead because all it's got on it is dead information. . . . Sure, there are links, but the links just lead to more dead information. It's a big information mausoleum."

So, How Big Is Big?

> "Space" it says "is big. Really big. You just won't believe how vastly hugely mind bogglingly big it is. I mean you may think it's a long way down the road to a chemist, but that's just peanuts to space."
> —Douglas Adams, *The Hitchhiker's Guide to the Galaxy*

So how big is the Internet?

Why not answer the question for yourself in real time? As of this writing, a simple keyword search of any of the commercial Internet indexers (including Yahoo, Excite, Lycos, and Alta Vista—names that may or may not mean something to you in the future) reveals dozens of online sources of information about the size, growth rate, and demographics of the Internet. Yahoo employs a useful hierarchical subject list (see: *http://www.yahoo. com/Computers_and_Internet/Internet/Statistics_and_Demographics/*). It's almost impossible *not* to find information about the size of the Internet on the Internet—like many new technologies, the Internet is almost comically self-referential. Hyperlinks to maps, charts, surveys, conference proceedings, and articles will quickly answer the question—or at least leave you swimming in data. (One of the most interesting aspects of the Internet is its ability to transport data, regardless of its tactile format. As a representative example, see Bell, G. (1995), *Mapping the Internet, Part II: Tracking Internet Growth*. [Online]. Available: *http://www.uvc.com/gbell/2transcript. html.*

Of course the Internet wasn't always big. From its simple beginnings in 1969 as the U.S. government funded Advanced Research Projects Agency Network (ARPANET), the Internet grew slowly but steadily until the mid-1980s. (An essential source in matters of Internet history is *Hobbes' Internet Timeline,* lovingly compiled over the years by Robert Hobbes Zakon of the MITRE Corporation, and widely available on the Internet through *http:// info.isoc.org/guest/zakon/Internet/History/HIT.html.*) Various markers along this road are still recognizable today: the first sketches of an Ethernet network on a piece of paper in 1972, the development of the Transmission Control Protocol (TCP) in 1974, and the inauguration of Because It's Time Network (BITNET) in 1981. With the creation of the National Science Foundation Network (NSFNET) in 1986, however, the Internet as we think of it today came into being.

NSFNET, high-speed data lines linking university, research, and military networks, provided the academic world with a conceptual focus that could easily be understood as the Internet. After 1986 it became easy to use data generated by the National Science Foundation to answer (at least in a sense) the question of Internet size. That growth from 1986 to the present is now legendary; as Christopher Anderson wrote in *Economist,*

> Whatever the number is today [1995] . . . it will be at least half as big again a year from now. No communications medium or consumer

electronics technology has ever grown as quickly; not the fax machine, not even the PC. At this rate, within two years the citizens of cyberspace will outnumber all but the largest nations.

But, Is It Really That Big?

Such statistical overkill normally produces one of two reactions in the average librarian: MEGO (My Eyes Glaze Over) and skepticism. The more we hear that the Internet is huge, the more we are likely to wonder whether it really is that big. Such a backwash of skepticism washed over the news media in 1995.

In July 1995 a survey of Internet domains was conducted by Network Wizards, Menlo Park, California. This survey was typical of a number of surveys done that year, and nicely demonstrates the Internet growth curve we have come to accept as normal. Table 1 illustrates the growth pattern of the Internet over a period of two and one half years. (A current URL for the Internet Domain Survey is *http://www.nw.com/zone/WWW/top.html*.)

But this chart also drew attention to an interesting side phenomenon. Of the large number of machines registered as being connected to the Internet (hosts), a surprisingly small number replied when electronically "pinged" (addressing an Internet post with a query as to its identity). This small response suggested that the size of the Internet, and hence the number of users (a best-guess estimate arrived at by extrapolating from the host figure), had been grossly overestimated. Almost overnight, estimates of actual Internet usage in the United States tumbled precipitously.

Another statistical fiasco occurred later in 1995 when businesses eager to reach new customers on the Internet began to discover that estimates of the number of such customers had been based incorrectly on the number of hits recorded on Net servers. In Internet jargon, a *hit* indicates that one computer has requested information, generally in the form of a file, from

TABLE 1

Number of Hosts, Domains, and Nets

Date	Hosts	Domains	Replied to Ping*	Network Class[†]		
				A	B	C
Jul '95	6,642,000	120,000	1,149,000	91	5,390	56,057
Jan '95	4,852,000	71,000	970,000	91	4,979	34,340
Oct '94	3,864,000	56,000	1,024,000	93	4,831	32,098
Jul '94	3,212,000	46,000	707,000	89	4,493	20,628
Jan '94	2,217,000	30,000	576,000	74	4,043	16,422
Oct '93	2,056,000	28,000		69	3,849	12,615
Jul '93	1,776,000	26,000	464,000	67	3,728	9,972
Apr '93	1,486,000	22,000	421,000	58	3,409	6,255
Jan '93	1,313,000	21,000		54	3,206	4,998

*estimated by pinging 1 percent of all hosts
[†]See page 48 for definitions of network classes.

another computer. Many early sites on the World Wide Web proudly displayed the numbers of times a page was requested—without mentioning that, depending on the actual composition of an HTML-encoded page, one user retrieving one page might generate multiple hits. Again, estimates of the size of the Internet tumbled when Web log files were reanalyzed to determine the actual number of users behind those hits. Those being charged for advertising space on Web sites were quick to seize on this evidence of size inflation because the rates quoted them were often based on inflated log-file analyses.

Not surprisingly, the ferocity of these debates about the Internet's actual size increased at about the same rate as its degree of commercialization. The more money involved, the more Net citizens (or, perhaps more realistically, Net property owners) wanted data that accurately reflected their hopes and aspirations for their financial future—and if those data didn't reflect those aspirations, well, they could always dispute that accuracy.

Models of Internet Expansion

These wars of statistical interpretation leave the average Internet user scratching her head and wondering whether it is even safe to pose the question "How big is the Internet?" In the future it could also benefit librarians to focus on the *models* used to tell the story of Internet growth.

So after looking at the "facts" of Internet growth, I'd like to examine a related question: *How* has the Internet grown? More precisely, how has this growth been modeled in the information that librarians are likely to find presented on the issue? In the past several years, authors have struggled to draw the exponential curve that is the Internet's size without leaving readers glassy-eyed and unconcerned. To do so, they have employed a variety of models, each with its own assumptions and biases. In examining each of these three models in turn, we will focus on how each model tends to distort the information on which it is based and how this distortion in turn affects the mental picture each of us acquires of the Internet.

Model One: The Internet as Story

The wise storyteller knows that stories often succeed in conveying meaning to people when numbers fail to do so. Numbers about the Internet frequently leave us dazed and disoriented; stories about its size, ubiquity, and impact can quickly and easily impress us.

In December 1993 Win Treese published the first of his *Internet Index* series *(http://pubs.iworld.com/iw-online/intindex.html)*. Based on the highly popular and often-imitated "Harper's Index" published monthly in *Harper's Magazine,* the *Internet Index* describes itself as "an occasional collection of facts and statistics about the Internet and related activities." As does its parent, the Treese index presents reality selectively, juxtaposing seemingly related facts as in the following example.

Number of Internet-related events (conferences, workshops, etc.) already
scheduled for 1996: 95
Number scheduled to take place in Slovenia: 1
Number already scheduled for 1999: 1

The sequencing of these facts is all important, and it conveys a message:
in this case, that of the geographic and temporal pervasiveness of the
Internet.

As in the tale of the elephant and the blind men, Treese attempts to
convey the meaning of something very large by touching it at various locations and from various angles. Those perspectives never yield a comprehensive picture, but that very failure is the point: The Internet is so big that
we can only ever see it from an angle. A perhaps unintentional side message of this model of Internet growth concerns the innate limits of human
comprehension: We will never understand the Internet because it is beyond
human comprehension. Mere mortals should stand aside, chastened and
humble, in the face of this enormous beast.

But Treese's method also fits a broader pattern of attempts by the news
media to describe the Internet's scale and scope. The "Internet as story"
model uses unconnected stories to impress upon readers something that it
cannot otherwise make understandable: explosive growth. The sudden appearance of the Internet in a July 5, 1993, *New Yorker* cartoon (with the
famous caption "On the Internet, no one knows you're a dog") said more
to most people about the Internet's cultural pervasiveness than did the
charts and graphs of the Internet Society. Similarly the launching of the
Vatican's World Wide Web site in January 1996 made headlines around
the world: The story eloquently conveyed the infiltration of Internet technology in a world seemingly distant from it.

How big is the Internet? Well, once upon a time . . .

Model Two: The Internet as Unity

The collective noun is one of language's dirtier tricks, leading us to see a
unified whole where none actually exists. The word "Internet" is a wonderful example of the collective noun and one of those remarkable English
neologisms whose singular form obscures its collective nature. In this second model of Internet growth, we find that the concept of the Internet as
unity is critical.

Unlike the other two models, we can actually pin down the day this one
stopped working: April 30, 1995. Until that day, the NSF-regulated Internet
backbone, high-speed data lines that provided the uppermost level of connectivity among the various networks comprising the Net, was the property
of the U.S. government. On May 1 the backbone, or more properly *back-
bones,* became the commercial property of several major telecommunications corporations who had worked with NSF to reposition the last remnants
of the National Research and Education Network to commercial platforms
such as SprintNet and MCINet.

One thing lost in that transition was a monthly data set generated by the
NSF from 1988 until 1995: backbone packet counts. Regardless of the nature

of the information passed on the Internet, all of it had to be broken down and transmitted in uniformly sized and structured electronic packets that could be easily counted as a by-product of monitoring network perform-ance. Collected and maintained for the NSF by the Merit Network *(ftp:// nic.merit.edu/nsfnet/statistics/README)*, these data came to symbolize for many the Internet as a whole.

> NSFNET performance statistics have been collected, processed, stored, and reported by the Merit Network since 1988, in the early stages of the NSFNET project. During December 1994, the numbers contained in Merit's statistical reports began to decrease, as NSFNET traffic began to migrate to the new NSF network architecture. In the new architec-ture, traffic is exchanged at interconnection points called NAPs (Net-work Access Points). Each NAP provides a neutral interconnection point for U.S.-based and international network service providers. On April 30, 1995, the NSFNET Backbone Service was successfully tran-sitioned to the new network architecture. Although the reports are inclusive through the end of the NSFNET service, the November 1994 reports were the last to reflect the nature of the NSFNET backbone traffic in its entirety.

With the NSFNET backbone as a common upper level, Internet users had a strong impression of the Internet as unity. Users could generate charts based on the numbers of packets of electronic data that passed over various nodes of the Internet during those years, the steadily increasing numbers of packets yielding ever more dramatic curves on graphs. The Internet was countable, able to be visualized, and to a certain degree predictable.

The trouble with this statistical approach to the Internet should be ob-vious to anyone familiar with the work of the Yale-based political scientist Edward Tufte. Tufte has pointed out in his excellent volumes on graphical portrayals of data that we can make data say what we want by fiddling with the graphs. To put it another way: any revolution looks dramatic on a graph when the coordinates of that graph are scaled by the revolution's partisans; if the graph is rescaled by more-objective observers, the results are often much less visually dramatic, or at the very least, much more in keeping with long-range historical data. The Internet "revolution" looks much more in keeping with historical trends when viewed as an extension of the communications revolution of the twentieth century or the scientific revolution of the nineteenth century. Just as we fail to be impressed by tales of our great-grandparents struggling to place their first long-distance phone call, so our children will roll their eyes in boredom as we labor to impress upon them the miracle that was the HyperText Transfer Protocol (HTTP).

The second problem with this model of Internet growth is, oddly enough, that it actually *underestimated* the facts. The Internet never was a unity, and NSFNET backbone traffic was never more than synecdoche: the part standing for the whole. Uncounted were the thousands of subnetworks beneath the NSFNET backbone. In a way, the unity model of the Internet served to diminish the size and complexity of the very thing it sought to highlight. How big is the Internet? Well, it always was bigger than this model could portray.

Model Three: The Internet as Accepted Environment

By 1996 a new model of Internet size and growth had begun to emerge: the Internet as an operating environment that, love it or hate it, we simply have to accept. How big is the Internet? Big enough, we are told, to serve as the backdrop to all we do as a profession, as a culture, as a world. In some ways a throwback to the unity model with its view of the Internet as a thing that could be understood solely by counting, the environment model instead serves a different purpose. Writers (myself included) have abandoned attempts to forge a common understanding of the Internet; now particular writers try to make the Internet comprehensible to particular groups of users. The consequences of this approach are predictable: The Internet of the business person is not that of the librarian; it looks different to the media executive and the research chemist; the school child and the political organizer see two different Internets. But regardless of these differences in perspective, each user is asked to see the Internet as the backdrop for all she does. The Internet medium is the message, so get with the program.

Of course we recognize that this last proposition is highly questionable. Librarians recognize the Internet as a context for their work, a highly valuable tool in their tool bag. Librarians also recognize that the Net does not solve our professional problems of acquiring, organizing, and retrieving information; if anything, it seriously exacerbates them (while paradoxically facilitating new solutions to them). At the very least, librarians should examine the hidden assumptions of this perspective on the Internet.

Examples of this model abound. Internet access providers stress the Internet as consumer appliance to the home market (with the important subtext, "those who don't buy in will be left out"); these same providers stress the Internet as an essential marketing and sales tool to the business market. Educators labor to impress upon funding bodies that education itself is increasingly network based. During the protracted debates over the revision of the U.S. 1934 telecommunications law, lobbyists from hundreds of groups agreed on only one thing: that the Internet was the sine qua non of the discussion. So who benefits from the "Internet as environment" model? As they say in Washington, follow the money. By presenting a selective group of facts as a holistic view of the environment, one can sell Internet technology to ever more-diverse groups of new users, keenly anxious not to be left out.

And *Therefore . . . ?*

OK, I'll be the first to admit I'm avoiding the question. The real answer is this: No one knows how big the Internet is. Part of the problem lies in defining our terms. What is this Internet that we are measuring? As the technologies of computer, telephone, and television continue to merge, should statistics for these technologies likewise merge? If I can regulate the temperature of my home over the Net from my office PC, is my home on the Internet? These and similar questions will continue to plague Net stat-isticians in the coming years.

But term-quibbling simply evades the deeper question. What does the Internet's size mean? We've seen in the models examined that it can mean different things in different contexts. The numbers, in a very important sense, don't matter—what we, as professionals, make of these numbers does. If we see the Internet as a tool that changes what we as librarians ultimately seek to do, then the Internet, big or small, has voided our future. If we see it, however, as a context for achieving what have always been our professional goals, then the Internet, whatever its size, becomes a tool in our professional hands.

References

Frook, J. E. (1995). "Web-Hit Audit System Called into Question." *Communications Week,* 589: 1.

———. (1995). "Web Survey Usage Disparity Alarms Businesses." *Communications Week* 584: 5.

Treese, Win. *Internet Index.* [Online]. Available: *http://pubs.iworld.com/iw-online/intindex.html*

Tufte, E. R. (1983). *The Visual Display of Quantitative Information.* Cheshire, CT: Graphics Press.

2

Are You Wired In?

The American Public, the Public Library, and the Internet

An Ever-Evolving Partnership

Karen Starr

Karen Starr is the director of network information at the PORTALS regional library network based in Portland, Oregon. She has written and spoken widely about networking, including having a column with *CD-ROM Professional* magazine. She may be reached as *KSTARR@PORTALS. PDX.EDU*. The project discussed in this article was done while Starr was networking consultant at the Idaho State Library.

Picture yourself on a beach or in a mountain cabin in some exotic location. You take out your computer and hook it up to the Internet to do your job, contact a colleague, or find a piece of information that you need for a project. Has the information superhighway arrived? Television commercials and the politicians would have us believe so. What are we being offered? In reality, it is a vision of where some of the players on the information superhighway see American society going, of what these players think the future will look like to the public.

Where are libraries in this picture that is being painted for the public by commercial companies through the mass media? Let's take a look at the

- role that the public library can and should play on the Internet
- expectations of the public
- issues that need to be addressed to provide Internet access for the public through the library
- opportunities to help shape the emerging information infrastructure

The Role of the Public Library on the Internet

Library roles are profiles of services a library chooses to provide to its public. McClure, Owen, Zweizig, Lynch, and Van House in their book *Planning and Role Setting for Public Libraries* define eight roles for public libraries.

- Community Activities Center: The library is a central focus point for community activities, meetings, and services.
- Community Information Center: The library is a clearinghouse for current information on community organizations, issues, and services.
- Formal Education Support Center: The library assists students of all ages in meeting educational objectives established during their formal courses of study.
- Independent Learning Center: The library supports individuals of all ages pursuing a sustained program of learning independent of any educational provider.
- Popular Materials Library: The library features current, high-demand, high-interest materials in a variety of formats for persons of all ages.
- Preschoolers' Door to Learning: The library encourages young children to develop an interest in reading and learning through services for children and for parents and children together.
- Reference Library: The library actively provides timely, accurate, and useful information for community residents.
- Research Center: The library assists scholars and researchers in conducting in-depth studies, investigating specific areas of knowledge, and creating new knowledge.

Each role is a shorthand way of describing what a library is trying to do, who the library is trying to serve, and what resources the library needs to achieve these ends. The Internet is becoming increasingly significant as the prototype for the emerging information superhighway. None of the public library roles as we currently know them directly address electronic information services. The authors suggest that libraries need to reevaluate their roles in the community given the rapidly changing information infrastructure.

Should a public library develop a "new" role in the community as an electronic information service? Will libraries disappear as we now know them? Will they become clusters of electronic databases staffed by automation specialists? Is this where the Internet will take the library community? Should librarians assume that electronic information will ultimately be the only information medium?

Traditionally libraries have been a focal point for the public to gain access to information regardless of form, including print, records, videos, microforms, and electronic databases. Librarians formalized decisions about the kinds of information they collected through their collection development policies and plans. The equipment they purchased to house and deliver the information depended on its format and included bookshelves, microform readers, VCRs and computers.

Providing access to electronic information is not a new role for libraries or librarians. We have been doing so since the early 1970s. But now the Internet has arrived out of a cloistered past where it was used primarily by academics, the research community, and the Department of Defense for communications purposes. What does the Internet really do? One might suggest that the Internet is nothing more than a technical infrastructure. The Internet is not equal to information. It gives users the means to access information provided by a variety of suppliers. The producers and distributors of electronic information now have direct access to the general public and can market their products to their public when before they had libraries, bookstores, information database vendors, and computer stores as their delivery system. The library community can no longer take for granted that it is one of a few key players in the information arena.

Librarians and their boards of trustees need to take a hard look at the roles of their libraries in their communities. Should libraries take on the role as a primary Internet service provider like the private companies that provide Internet access? In some communities, perhaps. In all communities? Probably not. There is a significant need in society for a one-stop shopping center of cultural and educational services related to the product of information in whatever form it might appear. Access to electronic information that happens to be housed on the Internet necessarily must be part of the information potpourri offered by the library. The library that chooses to ignore the Internet as a communications mechanism to access information for its public does so at risk to its viability and vitality as an ever-evolving cultural and educational center of the community.

The Public's Expectations

In early 1994 the Idaho State Library's Library Development Division co-sponsored a series of eight Internet focus groups statewide in cooperation with local public libraries. A total of 179 people participated in the focus groups, which were held in Salmon, Idaho Falls, Twin Falls, Nampa, Cascade, Moscow, Orofino, and Sandpoint. The State Library provided the facilitator and the meeting content. The public library directors identified key stakeholders in their communities and made a meeting room available. The key stakeholders included city officials, engineers, local business people, educators, Forest Service personnel, legislators, artists, and college students, among others.

Participants in the focus groups were asked several questions. One of them was aimed at discovering the types of information the community members would like to see on an electronic information network (the Internet). The results of the focus groups illustrated the public's interest in

- expert advice on a variety of topics including medicine, law, car repair, computer technology, animal husbandry, and gardening
- economic development, investment, bank rates, consumer product safety, and insurance
- community-based information such as events, volunteers, local classified advertisements, special interest groups, housing information, public meetings, transportation schedules, and local employment opportunities
- computer training, foreign language programs, homework service, teacher recertification, school activities, school scheduling, and adult education

- electronic mail and the ability to transfer files locally as well as worldwide
- access to public records, voting records of legislators, absentee voting, the ability to renew a driver's license, the rules and regulations from governmental agencies, and taxes
- information about hunting and fishing, environmental quality, the local weather, road advisories, sports, recreation, law enforcement and public safety, and social services available in the community
- access to electronic encyclopedias, local libraries' catalogs, full-text articles online, and document delivery

It was obvious from the results of the focus groups that the public is interested in a wide spectrum of information resources. Libraries currently providing access to the Internet soon discover their systems can be quickly overwhelmed by members of the public who want access to Multiple User Dungeons (MUDs) or chat rooms. This use conflicts with librarians' expectations that the public will use the Internet for research purposes. A creative adolescent using a MUD might argue that she or he *is* engaged in research.

Is it the role of the library to serve as a free entertainment center? Does not the popular reading room role suggest just that? Is tying up a modem line, public access work station or bandwidth for several hours to play on a MUD or chat the best use of limited resources? It is apparent that such a use can interfere with the ability of others to efficiently and effectively retrieve the information they need to solve a research question.

How does a library meet the demands of its public for Internet access within the constraints of its available resources? It does so by learning about what is available on the Internet, surveying the needs of the public, and then developing a plan to meet those needs. The library staff can then effectively deal with the wide and varied demands for access to electronic information including MUDs and chat rooms.

In 1995 the Idaho State Library used a combination of state and federal funds to support access by public libraries to the Internet on a statewide basis. Currently 54 percent of the public libraries in Idaho have some form of access to the Internet (dial-up access to an Internet provider or dedicated Internet nodes) covering 69 percent of the state's population. The State Library designed the project so that the libraries would have up to a year to evaluate the use of the Internet for their patrons, determine how they would make that access available to the public, and incorporate Internet access into the libraries' long-range plans.

At no time during the project were the libraries expected to give the public open access to the Internet. If a library chose to do so, that was a local decision. The libraries were expected to involve their boards of trustees and members of their community in the evaluation and planning process. One public library director commented in her evaluation of the project that

We have had such a positive response by patrons, staff, and friends of the library that there was no doubt that we would continue our Internet program. We are fortunate enough to have a local server, so this makes our plans even more possible. We had many work sessions for students, adults, and staff with a large attendance and great enthusiasm. We look forward to this [coming] year mostly because we know more and the fear is gone!

Implementation Issues

The day has not yet arrived when all libraries can be automatically wired to the Internet by plugging in computer equipment and playing immediately. Telephone companies, television cable companies, and the entertainment industry are working toward creating an environment that would allow Internet users to do just that. Such is the vision, but it certainly is not the reality with which most of us must deal.

What must a library do to make Internet access happen in the library for its public? The actual technical details of installing access are addressed in Marshall Breeding's chapter. What are the issues that came to light as a result of Idaho's public library Internet access project? What have other public libraries in the country discovered? The following comments only touch the surface of the issues. A bibliography at the end of the chapter provides further information. In addition, it is important to stay current by using your skills as a librarian and searching the current literature, attending conferences that showcase how others are dealing with the same concerns, and joining listserv discussion groups on the Internet such as *PUBLIB@NYSERNET.ORG* (Public Libraries Listserv) and *PUBLIB-NET@NYSERNET.ORG* (Public Libraries on the Internet).

Types of Access

How a library accesses the Internet will be affected by the size of its legal-population service area, budget, and membership in a regional or statewide library network. If your library is a member of a regional or statewide library network, then it is likely the library will automatically obtain access to the Internet through the network. Generally most libraries acquire either a Serial Line Internet Protocol (SLIP) or Point-to-Point-Protocol (PPP) account with an Internet provider or implement their own dedicated Internet access nodes. (See the following article, "Internet Access Options for Libraries," for a description of access methods.)

A library with an operating income of $500,000 or more will likely implement its own dedicated Internet node, which allows it to be connected to the Internet twenty-four hours per day and seven days per week. If your library has an operating income of less than that amount, you may choose to implement a dedicated Internet node, but you more likely will obtain a SLIP or PPP account from a local Internet provider.

What does a SLIP account allow a library to do? When the library dials into the Internet provider the library becomes an Internet node so long as it is connected to the provider. When the library disconnects from the provider, then it is no longer an Internet node. The library can use the full range of Internet programs such as File Transfer Protocol (FTP), Telnet, a World Wide Web browser, Gopher, and e-mail. The library needs a computer, a modem, access to a telephone line, software such as Internet Chameleon or Internet in a Box, and one or more accounts with an Internet provider.

Computer technology changes so rapidly that to suggest hardware specifications would be an unnecessary use of space. Computer vendors will often recommend less-capable technology than a library should purchase. Libraries notoriously under buy technology for budgetary reasons. Frankly, doing so is a poor investment of taxpayers' dollars. That does not mean that a library should buy the ultimate in technology; rather it means that good business decisions should be made. Read the current computer magazines, visit local computer stores, ask what the Internet provider recommends, and contact the state library's technology consultant.

Internet access project participants definitely reacted when the Idaho State Library insisted in the fall of 1994 that the libraries invest in 486 computers with 16 megabytes (MB) of random access memory (RAM) running at a minimum of 66 megahertz (MHz) and with at least 500 MB on the hard disk for a budgeted amount of roughly $2,000 to $2,300. Some felt that this was just too much computing power! Others thought it was not enough. A year later such computers were no longer made by most computer companies. That same price range buys a giant leap in computing power. Most project libraries will not be able to buy new equipment any time soon nor will they be able to upgrade the memory on their project computer. The project participants are still able to use the computers with the newest software and should be able to move to Windows 95 with minimal problems. The lesson is that, if possible, the library should buy the level of technology it will need a year from actual purchase date. This ultimately will save money and staff frustration.

The quality of phone lines in America seriously hampers libraries that use dial-up access to the Internet. Whether it is downtown Seattle, Washington, or isolated and rural Salmon, Idaho, the problems are the same. Packets of information traveling between the library and an Internet provider at times become so scrambled by line noise that sessions leave library staff and patrons frustrated with the search process. It does not seem to matter that fiber optics have been run to a community, as they have even in many remote parts of the United States. Local telephone service personnel who actually work in the field will admit that the lines are noisy. Unfortunately, telephone company management and public utilities commissions seem to find it difficult to resolve line-quality problems. In some cases it is beyond their control. If you must make a telephone call beyond a local dialing area, the call will travel through more than one carrier. Packets can drop at any of the switching stations. Therefore, when purchasing a modem, invest in the best possible technology. Voice-grade telephone lines are not designed to handle speeds faster than 28.8 kilobits/second (Kbps), which is the fastest regular modem currently available. If a faster speed or better line quality is important, explore data-quality phone lines.

Security Issues

Access to the Internet brings with it susceptibility to attack by individuals who have a need to spend their time invading other people's computers and computer networks. Bruce Newell (public and network services librarian, Lewis and Clark Library, Helena, Montana) indicated the following in a note about network and computer security mailed to Montana libraries connecting to the Internet as part of the Wiring Montana project.

> You should have a comprehensive security strategy in place. Not planned, implemented. This usually takes the form of installed hardware or software firewalls, that is, specially configured routers and/or software programs designed to control traffic in and out of your site. Firewalls allow the traffic you want while denying access or certain types of access which would be destructive.
>
> Designing and implementing firewalls is a technically demanding task. You'd be smart to ask your online catalog vendor or LAN (Local Area Network) administrator for the name of a consultant specializing in firewalls and familiar with libraries and your network environment. Costs vary from $5,000 to $10,000 or greater. Whatever the cost, within reason, it's probably worth it.
>
> Consider the following ugly scenarios next time you're getting ready to drop off into blissful sleep. What happens if a hacker comes in and pops open patron records? "I see" says he, "that Thelma Sue has checked out the *Joy of Sex* again!" The word gets around . . . then Thelma Sue can and probably will sue the library because Montana law requires libraries to protect our patrons' privacy. With Internet access and without a firewall, we have neglected our lawful duty to our public.
>
> Alternatively, what if some lout blasts into your UNIX system and tosses away your operating system. Voila, no operating system! Voila, no transaction records from yesterday. What would it cost your library to fly someone in and rebuild your operating system from the ground up? This kind of operation costs $100 an hour, a good week's work plus untold angst.

I am reminded of the old saying that locks are just for keeping the honest people out of your home. Those interested in reading more about current Internet security issues may find Tsutomu Shimomura's book *Takedown,* which describes the pursuit and capture of Kevin Mitnick, the internationally famous hacker, an interesting study. All libraries providing access to the Internet should have a reasonable and responsible information-protection plan. Newell's suggestion to hire experienced, well-qualified consultants, preferably with library applications knowledge, to help you is a valid point. By following the plan, a library will have long-term, effective protection at a justifiable cost.

Yes, security on the Internet is an issue. No, we shouldn't avoid the Internet because security is an issue. "The real secret of computer security is to be aware, to watch the systems carefully, something most people don't do," writes Shimomura. It takes a whole community to raise a child. It takes the entire interconnected country to create a safe environment on the Internet in an ethical and professional manner without violating the rights of its citizens under the U.S. Constitution.

Budgeting

Start-up costs for Internet access, which include equipment, training, and line costs, can often be subsidized with grant monies from state and federal sources. After the grant money runs out, funding Internet access becomes a local concern. If a library has established a dedicated Internet node or a SLIP or PPP account with a local provider, Internet access costs become identifiable and fixed on a monthly basis. These costs can be incorporated into the library's budget.

If the Internet provider has a local telephone number, libraries with dial-up access can purchase a set number of hours per month with their membership fee. If no local phone number is available, the library must pay for use of the vendor's 800 telephone number, which costs between $4 and $10 per hour. Budgeting for open access to the Internet by the public in such a situation becomes problematic. If the public wanted to access the Internet all the hours the library is open, the resulting telecommunications bill would exceed the library's operating budget in some cases. Consequently those who must dial an 800 number for access to the Internet will often choose to obtain information from the Internet for their public. Certainly this is not an ideal solution, but it is a practical one until the time comes when more of the country is locally wired for Internet access. In some cases these libraries can obtain more economical access to the Internet if they cooperate with other local units of government and local businesses to bring a centralized Internet node to the community.

Library budgets are notoriously finite. Libraries may need to reallocate their resources to support access to the Internet. Such decisions are affected by local circumstances and should be made by library staff and members of the board of trustees in cooperation with their local communities. On the other hand, budgets do not have to be insufficient. If staff and trustees have laid the appropriate groundwork with the community, it is highly likely the library will receive the support it needs to incorporate Internet access into the library's infrastructure.

Training

Many people spend time surfing the Internet and seem happy with their results. Did they find the best results possible? Probably not. Searching thoroughly for information on the Internet requires an expertise in using searching software such as InfoSeek, Lycos, and WebCrawler. It also requires an understanding of what constitutes information on the Internet, how it is stored, and how to ask the computer for what is needed. To effectively and efficiently search the Internet for information, users need many of the skills librarians learned in searching online systems like Dialog or in using indexes published on CD-ROM discs.

Both staff and patrons need training. Before a library provides Internet access to the public, the library management needs to make sure that the staff members know how to effectively use the Internet. This means the staff will be comfortable with the software and resources and can teach the public how to use the system.

In many communities, people in the computer industry have started to provide Internet training. These individuals are good at providing an overview of the Internet and teaching others how to use Internet software. Librarians provide the best training on how to retrieve appropriate information for a specific research topic. Learning from one's colleagues in the library field is invaluable. Workshops are offered at local, state, regional, and national library conferences. Some state libraries make library continuing education workshops available to the library community. Where library schools are locally available, they are a good resource. Teleconferences are also offered on a national basis.

Resources on the Internet

From a public library research perspective what types of information are available on the Internet? Both state and federal agencies are making government information accessible. Most states have home pages with links to public information produced by their state agencies. Weather information is available. Foundations have home pages describing whom they serve. Research and training hospitals make articles available about medical research conducted by their institutions. Also offered is information on recreation and consumer product safety . . . the topics are endless. What the public asked for in the focus groups sponsored by the Idaho State Library already exists, scattered across many networks throughout the country.

However, all the information available on the Internet is not free. The Internet is a telecommunications infrastructure that allows people to access information. Some of the long-time information companies that used dial-up access or direct hard-wired telephone lines in the past have switched to Internet access. Their information still costs money. Any material that is copyrighted is unlikely to be accessible via the Internet for free. (See the Web sites *Copyright Fundamentals, http://www.benedict.com/fund.htm,* and U.S. Copyright Office Home Page, *http://lcweb.loc.gov/copyright/,* for information about copyright.) Texts of fiction books available at bookstores are not likely to appear on the Internet until publishers find a way to charge for their use.

What about all the useful information out there that is currently not in machine-readable form? How do you access it via the Internet unless it is mentioned in an accessible indexing service? You don't. For example, a crop scientist doing research on new crops at a land grant university in the Pacific Northwest was approached by the timber industry and environmentalists to study the viability of hemp as an alternative to trees for the production of paper. The last time this country did research with hemp was during the 1940s. The research was published by the U.S. Department of Agriculture as part of its bulletins. The easiest way for that individual to find the information is to look through the boxes in the attic of the university's research farm that were left behind by faculty who worked at the university. The reports are not available in electronic format, and they are not likely to be available any time soon.

In an era of shrinking resources, much of this country's published literature will not be converted to electronic format. America's taxpayers and the publishing industry simply cannot afford to support the cost of conversion. As a country, are we to deny the existence of valuable information just because it is not computerized and, therefore, not available via the Internet? I certainly hope not. Libraries can help identify such resources and sometimes use the Internet to make them accessible to the public.

Censorship and Intellectual Freedom

Information of questionable value and taste has existed for centuries. Traditionally people have had to consciously look to find that information by seeking out red-light districts, adult bookstores and adult movie theaters. Today, with access to the Internet that kind of information can reach you at your desktop computer. The American culture does not do a particularly good job of addressing inappropriate behavior. Often, the rights of the majority are curtailed to take care of the problems created by a few individuals.

Should libraries restrict Internet access because of the questionable material that is easily available? That is a hard question to answer, especially in light of the passage of the Communications Decency Act. Libraries have a long tradition of providing equal access to all types of information and all issues. They provide a cornerstone upon which our democracy has been built.

Recently, a consumer online information company restricted the use of the word *breast* in their discussion groups. That meant people who wanted to talk about breast cancer and who were members of this information company's discussion groups were effectively muzzled. Is this a realistic response on the part of the online company? Not really. Given the current climate in this country, libraries that provide public access to the Internet should have an electronic information access policy that has been carefully reviewed by a lawyer. There are numerous sites on the World Wide Web that provide information useful for developing such policy statements including the following:

American Library Association at *http://www.ala.org/*

Armadillo's WWW Server *Acceptable Use Policies* at *http://chico.rice.edu/armadillo/acceptable.html*

Applying Library Intellectual Freedom Principles to Public and Academic Computers at *http://www.eff.org/CAF/cfp94.kadie.html*

Censorship and Intellectual Freedom Page at *http://ezinfo.ucs.indiana.edu/~quinnjf/censor.html*

Freedom to Read Foundation at *http://www.ala.org/ftrf.html*

Freedom of Expression Links at *http://insight.mcmaster.ca/org/efc/pages/chronicle/censor.html*

Karen's Kitchen: The Freedom Pages at *http://www.intac.com/~kgs/ freedom/*

Please see the section "The Communications Decency Act" for references to Web sites relating to it. In addition, also see "Access to Electronic Information, Services, and Networks: An Interpretation of the *Library Bill of Rights.*"

Ultimately it should not be the library's responsibility to make decisions about what a patron reads. In a democracy, that is supposed to be an individual's choice, and in the case of children it is ultimately the responsibility of their parents.

Opportunities

Has the vision of an information superhighway painted in the mass media arrived? Not really. Will it come? Highly likely. There are some who project that books will no longer be published in print form within 10 to 15 years. I am not certain that assumption will come to fruition. It may be that the book you hold in your hand will be made out of a different plant fiber than wood within 10 to 15 years.

Will an information infrastructure be built? Most assuredly. What role will public libraries play in the development of the infrastructure? Librarians and libraries can no longer afford to fulfill their stereotypical destiny of being one of the country's best-kept secrets. They must step up to the table and ensure that the public understands the information-related services that can be found at the local library. Librarians bring a sophisticated understanding of information and how people use it to that table. There are numerous examples in which librarians and libraries have served as leaders as well as partners in the development of local and regional information networks. As a part of these networks, libraries can provide the means for an organized approach to retrieving information from the Internet by the public.

Librarians need to understand their role and their libraries' role as equal partners in the emerging information infrastructure alongside the telecommunications companies, entertainment companies, and the computer industry. In an era of ever-shrinking resources, libraries cannot and should not compete with these groups but, rather, join them as equals in the information arena. Above all, librarians should be playing a significant role in information policy development on a local, state, regional, and national level as representatives of the public interest.

Bibliography

Barnett, Andy. (1995, July). "Here to Stay; Ten Reasons Why the Internet Will Not Replace the Public Library." *School Library Journal, 41,* 32.

Boehning, Julie. (1995, August). "Should Libraries Have the Ability to Block Internet Sites?" *Library Journal, 120,* 12.

Cohen, Frederick B. (1995). *Protection and Security on the Information Superhighway.* New York: Wiley.

Cole, Timothy W. (1995, January). "Mosaic on Public-Access PCs: Letting the World-Wide Web into the Library." *Computers in Libraries, 15,* 44–50.

Commings, Karen, Cullings, Karen, and Webster, Connie. (1995, April). "Community Information Goes Online in Central Pennsylvania." *Computers in Libraries, 15,* 22–4.

Doran, Kirk. (1995, June). "The Internot: Helping Library Patrons Understand What the Internet Is Not (Yet)." *Computers in Libraries, 15,* 22–6.

Dysart, Jane I., and Jones, Rebecca J. (1995, January). "Tools for the Future: Recreating or 'Renovating' Information Services Using New Technologies." *Computers in Libraries, 15,* 16–19.

Hauptman, Robert, and Motin, Susan. (1994, March). "The Internet, Cyberethics, and Virtual Morality." *Online, 18,* 8–9.

Hernon, Peter. (1995). "Disinformation and Misinformation through the Internet: Findings of an Exploratory Study." *Government Information Quarterly, 12,* 133–9.

———. (1994). "Privacy Protection and the Increasing Vulnerability of the Public." *Government Information Quarterly, 11,* 241–4.

Hert, Carol A. (1994). "A Learning Organization Perspective on Training: Critical Success Factors for Internet Implementation." *Internet Research: Electronic Networking Applications and Policy, 4,* 36–44.

Lago, Karen Nadder. (1993, October). "The Internet and the Public Library: Practical and Political Realities." *Computers in Libraries, 13,* 65–70.

McClure, Charles R. (1994, June). "Network Literacy: A Role for Libraries?" *Information Technology and Libraries, 13,* 115–25.

McClure, Charles R., Owen, Amy, Zweizig, Douglas L., Lynch, Mary Jo, and Van House, Nancy A. (1987). *Planning and Role Setting for Public Libraries: A Manual of Options and Procedures.* Chicago: ALA.

Morgan, Candace D. (1995, October 15). "Fighting the War against Censorship: A National Perspective." *Library Journal, 120,* 36–8.

Saunders, Laverna M. (1992, Spring). "The Virtual Library Today." *Library Administration and Management, 6,* 66–70.

Schuyler, Michael. (1995, January). "The Accidental Hacker." *Computers in Libraries, 15,* 28–32.

———. (1995, April). "Prepare to Be Overwhelmed." *Computers in Libraries, 15,* 42–4.

Shimomura, Tsutomu, with John Markoff. (1995). *Takedown: The Pursuit and Capture of Kevin Mitnick, America's Most Wanted Computer Outlaw— by the Man Who Did It.* New York: Hyperion.

Tenopir, Carol. (1995, October 1). "Internet Issues in Reference." *Library Journal, 120,* 23–30.

Valauskas, Edward J., and John, Nancy R. (1995). *The Internet Initiative: Libraries Providing Internet Services and How They Plan, Pay, and Manage*. Chicago: ALA.

Wiencko, J. A., Jr. (1993). "The Blacksburg Electronic Village." *Internet Research: Electronic Networking Applications and Policy, 3,* 31–40.

INTERNET ACCESS OPTIONS FOR LIBRARIES

Kate Wakefield

Kate Wakefield is the Western Library Network (WLN) network services manager. She is a director-at-large on the Executive Board of Directors of the Library and Information Technology Association of the American Library Association and has been a member of the Internet Room Steering Committee. She may be reached at *WAKE@WLN.COM*.

The essentials of Internet access include deciding upon a mode of access, selecting an Internet Services Provider (ISP), and choosing interface software. Additional information about various software packages you may select to give your Internet connection a friendly front end is included in Marshall Breeding's essay on connecting to the Internet using Serial Line Internet Protocol (SLIP) or Point-to-Point Protocol (PPP). This chapter describes Internet access methods, contrasting their advantages and disadvantages and presenting criteria that will help you select an appropriate ISP.

Currently there are three main types of Internet access. To connect your library to the Internet, you need to determine which of the following access methods meets your needs at an affordable price. The three options to be examined in more detail are dedicated access, basic "shell" dial access, and SLIP or PPP dial access.

Although technically it is not a separate form of access, using special SLIP or PPP software with your personal computer when connecting to the Internet provides specific advantages, described below. The type of interaction this software offers is different enough to justify discussing it as an alternative type of connection. The comparison opens with a high-end solution (dedicated access); next, discussion moves to the simplest type of connection (shell dial access). Finally, a method is offered that allows you to have some of the benefits of dedicated access without its costs (SLIP/ PPP access).

Dedicated Access

Although dedicated access was formerly the province of educational institutions and large business enterprises, many libraries now connect to the Internet through this method. High-speed leased phone lines transmit information directly to desktop work stations through Ethernet or token-ring Local Area Networks (LANs). Large library systems may already be running telecommunications networks to make their libraries' online public access catalogs available to branches. These networks can be upgraded to handle Transmission Control Protocol/Internet Protocol (TCP/IP), the protocol that connects all Internet hosts to each other, enabling libraries to offer Internet-based services to their patrons.

Even many single-location libraries are finding it cost effective to connect to the Internet with a dedicated connection. Depending on how many individuals require access simultaneously and whether there are sufficient computers with modems and phone lines available when needed, dedicated LAN access may be more efficient. If your library has data it would like to make available constantly on the Internet (such as an online public access catalog or a World Wide Web site) or remote online services it needs to access frequently (traditional reference search services such as DIALOG, WestLaw, or newer services such as IAC's full-text databases), then dedicated Internet connections may be your best option.

Annual charges for dedicated connections vary widely, depending on the speed of the connection, its distance from the backbone network's nearest "point of presence," and whether hardware rental or support services are included in the cost of the connection. Various ISPs charge widely disparate prices for identical services. (See the section on comparing ISPs later in this article for questions to ask your potential Internet supplier.) Libraries should expect several thousand dollars in start-up costs for the necessary hardware to set up their own dedicated Internet connection, ongoing monthly fees ranging from $300 to $800 per month for a 56 kilobits per second (Kbps) connection, and $1,500 to $2,500 per month for a T1 connection (capable of transmitting 1.44 megabits per second).

Advantages

It provides high speed data transmission—56 Kbps is the slowest connection; many large library systems use T1 lines.

Many work stations share one leased line—when connected to a LAN and dedicated Internet connection, each work station does not require separate modems and phone lines.

Libraries choose what software to run and what services to provide to patrons and staff.

You may make your online public access catalog or other local data available on the Internet (while taking proper precautions to protect sensitive data).

It's possible to seamlessly connect to remote online databases from your library catalog.

Disadvantages

The main disadvantage of dedicated access is its higher cost from the service provider. In addition, you will need specialized staff to ensure that the connection performs properly. Many vendors are selling "turnkey" Internet hardware packages, but these products still require frequent attention from knowledgeable staff or outside consultants.

Basic "Shell" Dial Access

Smaller libraries and individuals usually choose dial access as their preferred means of accessing the Internet. Dial access can be accomplished with nearly any computer with a modem, using inexpensive software or shareware that may be distributed with your modem or installed on the computer when you purchase it. Many libraries begin a trial Internet connection through dial access and "graduate" to a dedicated connection once staff have convinced their board or management that there is valuable information to be found on the Internet.

There are two types of dial access—this section refers specifically to "shell" or command-based access that is available from most ISPs and that requires no special Internet-related software. Shell access gets its name from the UNIX command shell that forms the underlying basis of this type of Internet connection and is your means of interacting with various servers and resources. Typically, ISPs will recommend that their customers use VT100 terminal emulation to dial into the provider's modems. This type of emulation allows simple menus with multiple-choice options (you type the number or letter of the menu item desired) or with up and down cursor keys to select individual items. Some menus may be activated with "hot keys" or highlighted letters that perform the menu function.

Shell access should provide all of the basic Internet services: e-mail, Telnet, File Transfer Protocol (FTP), Gopher, World Wide Web (WWW), and Network News. The programs used to work with these services will be determined by your Internet provider and reside primarily on the mainframe or minicomputer "host" at the ISP's central facility. The advantage of centralized processing is that you don't need a high-end computer to use the service—your personal computer is essentially no more than an input device (keyboard) and a monitor. The actual work is being completed by the ISP host. Shell access should be the most inexpensive connection option—typically $20 per month (or less) in most major metropolitan areas.

Advantages

It's inexpensive—requiring low monthly, quarterly, or annual rates from ISPs and no special hardware, just a Mac or IBM-compatible PC, modem, and phone line.

There's no special software to purchase—shareware is readily available if telecommunication software did not come with your modem.

All Internet services should be available, managed by the ISP.
Staff can experiment with the Internet with little risk.

Disadvantages

It is relatively slow (compared with a dedicated connection).
There are a limited number of work stations that can be connected.
Interaction with Internet resources is limited to exchanging text, unless
users learn several UNIX commands.
The World Wide Web is much less visually appealing when viewed solely
through text-based browsers—there are no images, maps, or charts.
Some forms may be difficult to maneuver in. (The same information
should be accessible if the site was well-designed—a big "if.")

SLIP/PPP dial-up corrects some of these deficiencies and simplifies some
of the formerly complex processes.

SLIP/PPP Dial-Up Connections

Connecting to the Internet using special dial-up software that supports either SLIP or PPP allows point-and-click access to Internet resources. SLIP
and PPP are both computer applications that allow your PC or Mac to temporarily become a node on the Internet. This means that you can perform
some Internet functions more easily and directly than you can with a shell
dial-up account and you can take advantage of your knowledge of Windows or the Mac operating system to learn Internet programs more quickly.
With shell access, once you dial into the Internet, your mouse is a dead
appendage—with SLIP or PPP, you can revive your mouse and use it to
select menus, print, and save files.

With SLIP or PPP you must install special telecommunications software
that communicates through one of these protocols. The good news is that
many ISPs now provide this software free to their subscribers and that shareware is readily available in books for those whose providers don't distribute
software. (Examples of such books are listed at the end of this chapter.)
Several commercial software packages also continue to add features and
decrease in cost. Windows 95, OS/2 WARP, and the Mac System 7.5 all
incorporate TCP/IP support into their operating system (although some additional software may be required to make use of this support). Please refer
to Marshall Breeding's chapter for additional information about how SLIP
and PPP software works and how to select a software package that meets
your needs.

All Internet service providers should support SLIP or PPP or both. Some
of the newer providers no longer offer shell access, and some providers
require that you set up a separate user identification to access shell services.
But most ISPs will set up a single user ID that can be used with either

shell or SLIP/PPP, depending on the software installed on the computer that dials into the service. SLIP or PPP access should be inexpensive—from $20 to $30 per month in most metropolitan areas. Your ISP should be able to provide preconfigured software or step-by-step installation instructions to set up the software for use with their service. The configuration information will be different for each ISP, so you must obtain this information from the provider for your software to work properly.

SLIP or PPP dial-up allows users to have several of the advantages of a dedicated Internet connection without the high cost. When your SLIP or PPP software connects, your ISP lends your work station an IP address for the duration of the phone call. This type of connection allows you to run programs locally on your personal computer and interact directly with Internet resources. The difference is most striking in applications such as File Transfer Protocol (FTP). With shell dial access, FTP transfers a copy of the desired file from one mainframe to another. Users must then exit the FTP site and use another program (a download protocol, such as Kermit, Xmodem, or Zmodem) to move the file from their ISP to their own personal computer. With SLIP or PPP dial-up, the desired file is copied directly from the remote site into the user's own hard drive (or floppy) in a single step—often by simply dragging a file icon from one column or part of the window to another. Macintosh FTP programs such as Fetch automatically recognize whether a file is compressed and start a program such as Stuffit Expander to uncompress the file as it is transferred, saving yet another tedious manual step.

Electronic mail is also significantly changed in the SLIP/PPP arena. Rather than storing your mail on a remote host and dialing in to read it, you can choose to have your messages transferred to your desktop personal computer using a "POP mail" package (Post Office Protocol). This can be a disadvantage if you need to access your messages from more than one computer (for instance, from work as well as from home), but you can choose to use your basic mail program for reading mail if this is the case. The advantage of using POP mail packages is that you can read or reply to messages without being dialed into the Internet. You can also create new e-mail messages offline (perhaps several of them), then dial in and send the messages. Working with attachments is a much simplified process for most graphical user interface (GUI) mail programs—you can cut and paste text into the body of the message, insert text files, or attach files directly from the hard drive.

Advantages

They are relatively inexpensive (you can obtain shareware or purchase software).

Hardware requirements are modest when compared to dedicated connections (Mac or PC with Windows, Windows 95, or OS/2 WARP).

Users can select interface software and personally customize it.

Files can be easily saved locally (onto the personal computer's hard drive or floppy) because file transfers move directly from remote sites to the personal computer.

E-mail attachments and text insertion can be done in fewer steps; e-mail messages can be created and viewed offline.

Disadvantages

Disadvantages of SLIP/PPP dial-up connections are primarily those of dial-up access, covered in the next section. In addition, it requires significantly more computing power than shell access (a faster processor chip, more Random Access Memory, a higher speed modem, and Windows instead of DOS).

Dedicated or Dial-Up?

Disadvantages of dial-up when compared with dedicated access revolve around the capabilities of the modem itself. The speeds obtained by modems, though regularly increasing due to new compression algorithms and new standards, are still only half those of high-speed lines. Line quality is also an issue—frame relay or other dedicated connections are guaranteed by phone companies to be able to carry data, but voice-grade lines are not.

Moreover, each dial-up computer will require its own modem, phone line, and Internet account at the ISP if it is to be used simultaneously with other dial-up computers. This can be inconvenient for small libraries that need to use the same phone line to conduct other business. It can also be a problem in larger libraries, where all available phone lines are assigned for other uses. Dedicated access removes these barriers, but it is much more expensive. Remember, if you want to make a Web page or your online public access catalog available on the Internet, dedicated access is necessary. Also, many bandwidth-intensive applications, such as CUSeeMe video conferencing and Internet phone applications, require a minimum of a 56 Kbps connection to perform well.

Newer Types of Access

In major metropolitan areas, new methods of accessing the Internet are becoming available, such as Integrated Services Digital Network (ISDN). ISDN is a special digital phone line and digital modem that allow high-speed dial-up access. ISDN modems typically connect at 64 Kbps or 128 Kbps. Using ISDN requires special hardware to replace your computer's modem as well as an ISP that supports this type of access. Costs for ISDN are still being set in most areas, but rates should be substantially less than frame relay dedicated connections. Unfortunately, this service is currently only being offered where telecommunications equipment has been upgraded to accommodate it. Specific information about ISDN is available through a page maintained by Dan Kegel on the Web at *http:// alumni.caltech.edu/~dank/isdn/*.

Additional high-speed networks are continually being tested and made available to businesses and libraries. Asynchronous Transfer Mode (ATM) is another new network protocol, with its own special hardware, which may become more readily available. Current specifications for ATM are the equivalent of T3 lines (45 Mbps) and much more expensive than other dedicated Internet connections. However, telecommunications providers have recently developed a "slow ATM" that is equivalent in data transmission speed to a T1 line (1.44 Mbps). If this becomes widely available, it could be the protocol that will help libraries make the transition to much higher speed networks capable of supporting live video teleconferencing and other high bandwidth applications.

Who Offers Access?

Unlike some services that are provided by only one company (or a handful of companies that can be easily compared), there are a multitude of Internet service providers. These range from huge national companies to local "mom and pop" shops, each with slightly different features, access options, and pricing. Another wrinkle in the comparison process is determining what you want to do with the Internet, so that you can determine what level of access is appropriate for your needs. For instance, if you plan to integrate multimedia into your network or to access or present audio or video files to your users, you will need to plan for much higher bandwidth.

Historically, Internet access has been available through private networks, regional National Science Foundation (NSF) sponsored networks, and local ISPs. Recent commercialization of the Internet has led to multiple private backbone networks operated by major telecommunications providers, such as Advanced Network and Services (ANS), PSINet, Sprint, MCI, UUNET, and Net99.

Private networks continually improve their Internet service offerings and provide specialized content besides that which is generally available free of charge on the Internet. Examples of these private networks include America Online, CompuServe, Genie, and Prodigy. These services usually include several hours of access to their own content for a monthly subscription fee and a surcharge for Internet access. Typically these companies are not the most cost-effective way to obtain plain vanilla Internet access, but they may be valuable to libraries for the custom services they provide. Examples of specialized content include business news (such as articles from the *Wall Street Journal* or *USA Today*), access to local chat groups, interactive discussions with public personalities, or other proprietary content.

Since the Internet initially grew from federally funded network initiatives, many educational institutions and government agencies obtain their access from regional NSF networks. These networks now sell connections to all types of organizations, including to commercial businesses. Although the federal government is discontinuing support of these networks, they will still be part of the marketplace for the near future. If you are planning to purchase a dedicated Internet connection, you will want to contact your

NSF regional network to provide a price comparison with other vendors in the area. Many local ISPs provide direct Internet connections that may be less expensive than similar connections to Tier 1 (major national backbone) commercial providers or to regional NSF networks.

When purchasing a dedicated connection, check with potential providers to compare services as well as price. Find out whether your connection has guaranteed throughput—this is expressed in terms of Committed Information Rate (CIR) for frame-relay connections. If the service is a local provider, check to see from whom it obtains its Internet connection and how many intermediaries there are before you get to a major national backbone. Some providers may be "dual homed" or connected to more than one national backbone—this will make your connection more reliable. Determine whether your ISP has a disaster recovery plan, regular tape or other media backups, and "hotswap" equipment replacements for key network hardware.

Apart from reliability and prices, compare the services offered by potential providers. If your library is not ready to set up individual Internet servers, does your provider offer access to its mail, news, or WWW servers? Some Internet providers will manage Domain Name Systems (DNS) for your library. DNS identifies your computers to the rest of the Internet and is used by each personal computer and Internet software package when it connects to other Internet hosts. You may want to start by having these services managed by your ISP, then move them in house as you gain expertise. Your ISP may offer other consulting services (such as security or hardware selection advice), various levels of support, or training for your users.

Selecting a Dial Access Provider

When selecting a dial access provider, there are a range of options. Not only is there a range of billing options but the means of accessing the provider, the number of services offered, and the quality of support can vary widely. The services you intend to use may affect your choice of providers. If you plan to frequently use file transfer or would like the capability of downloading your e-mail and working with it offline, select a service that supports SLIP or PPP connections.

Dial access users will want to weigh several factors in their choice of Internet service providers. Although price is always a consideration, additional questions answered before selecting a provider can save hours of headaches later. When comparing costs, be sure to ask if there are set-up fees, what the monthly rates are, and if discounts are available for quarterly or annual subscriptions. It is also important to include telecommunications connection costs in your annual Internet budget.

Using dial access means that someone is paying phone charges, either through monthly fees or hourly rates. If the host machine or terminal server equipment is not local, will phone calls be billed to your long-distance connection, or do the hourly connect fees include phone charges? National service providers may offer 800 number access (at an hourly fee) or may have you dial in through public data networks such as CompuServe, MCI (formerly BT-Tymnet), or SprintNet. If your ISP does not have a local access number, you may wish to opt for a higher priced option that includes tele-communications. If you don't, be sure to include in your budget the hourly long distance charge necessary to reach the service. If you travel, you may wish to select a provider that has nationwide access through many local dial-up sites or through an 800 number that you can use for a fee.

Some ISPs include unlimited access for their monthly or annual subscrip-tion fee, while others include a number of hours and then charge for ad-ditional hours. Before you sign up with a provider, find out how many hours are included in the basic rate and what the rate is for additional hours of access. If peak or off-peak rates are part of the plan, be sure you un-derstand what times are included in each of these categories.

Many Internet access books will recommend that you determine the mo-dem-to-user ratio for your ISP. Typically the figure of one modem per ten users is a target. For ISPs that offer unlimited access accounts, this is a valid measurement. However, if your provider meters access, it may be able to support a higher number of users with the same number of modems. Your ISP should be able to explain how it determines when to add addi-tional modems and should have statistical reporting available on its modem usage. If possible, obtain a demo account and dial in frequently to see whether the phone rings busy and to test whether services perform adequately.

Some ISPs have hidden charges. Be sure to ask whether there are any services that are not included in the basic rate. Are there charges per e-mail message or for use of specific services? There may be additional fees related to use, such as disk storage charges, or for optional services. Is SLIP or PPP offered? Is the cost the same? If you want to use both shell and SLIP or PPP, find out whether your ISP supports both.

ISPs offer various levels of service. If you can obtain a demo account, try requesting help from the support desk for various problems. Try phon-ing the support desk as well as sending e-mail. Find out if there is any documentation specific to the service—is there a manual, or online help, or a WWW page? Some ISPs offer training for new users; check to see whether your ISP offers Internet training or whether it can direct you to online tutorials. If possible, try to determine whether your ISP regu-larly upgrades services offered, and how it communicates changes in services.

Conclusion

Determining how to best access the Internet is a balance of matching your desires with your budget and of locating an ISP that is able to provide you with the desired level of service. Once you have determined whether ded-icated or dial access is more appropriate, be sure to contact as many of the regional ISPs in your area as possible to get prices for several competing options. Prepare a checklist, and ask all of the providers the same questions.

Obtain demo accounts, if possible, to test whether the provider offers the support you may need as a new user. Choose your dial access provider carefully the first time, so you don't have to switch several times—your e-mail address will change each time you change providers.

Electronic Resources for Locating a Provider

Celestin Company. (1996, April). *Providers of Commercial Internet Access.* [Online]. Available: *http://www.celestin.com/pocia/index.html*

Herbison, B. J. (1996, April). *Internet Access Providers Meta-List.* [Online]. Available: *http://www.herbison.com/herbison/ia_meta_list.html*

Kaminsky, Peter. *PDIAL—Public Dial-Up Internet Access List.* [Online]. Available: *http://www.pdial.com/*

Mecklermedia. (1996, April). *The List (Internet Services Providers).* [Online]. Available: *http://www.thelist.com/*

Electronic Resources for Library Internet Access

Bocher, Bob. (1996, April). *On Ramps: Internet Access Options.* [Online]. Available: *http://www.state.wi.us/agencies/dpi/www/on_ramps.html*

McClure, Charles R., Bertot, John Carlo, and Beachboard, John C. (1995, June). *Internet Costs and Cost Models for Public Libraries: Final Report.* [Online]. Available: *http://istweb.syr.edu/Project/Faculty/ McClure.NCLIS.Report.html*

Other Resources

Boardwatch magazine. *Directory of Internet Service Providers.* Littleton, CO. Issued quarterly—more than 5,400 regional providers are listed in the spring 1996 issue.

Butler, Mark. (1994). *How to Use the Internet.* Emeryville, CA: Ziff-Davis.

Engle, Mary. (1995). *Internet Connections: A Librarian's Guide to Dial-Up Access and Use.* Chicago: ALA.

Gilster, Paul. (1995). *The SLIP/PPP Connection: The Essential Guide to Graphical Internet Access.* New York: Wiley.

Hahn, Harley. (1994). *The Internet Complete Reference.* Berkeley, CA: Osborne McGraw-Hill.

Krol, Ed. (1994). *The Whole Internet: User Guide and Catalog* (2nd ed.). Sebastopol, CA: O'Reilly.
    There is also a Windows 95 edition.

Reynolds, Dennis. (1993, September). "Evaluating Dial-Up Internet Access Options." *Computers in Libraries, 13,* 86–94.

Tennant, Roy. (1994). *Crossing the Internet Threshold: An Instructional Handbook* (2nd ed.). Berkeley, CA: Library Solutions.

Start-Up Kits (including SLIP/PPP Software)

Engst, Adam. (1995). *The Internet Starter's Kit for Macintosh* (3rd ed.). Indianapolis: Hayden.

————. (1995). *The Internet Starter's Kit for Windows* (2nd ed.). Indianapolis: Hayden.

Fraase, Michael. (1995). *Macintosh Internet Tour Guide* (2nd ed.). Research Triangle Park, NC: Ventana.

————. (1995). *Windows Internet Tour Guide* (2nd ed.). Research Triangle Park, NC: Ventana.

Netscape Navigator Resources

Kidder, Gayle. (1996). *Netscape Navigator Quick Tour for Macintosh: Accessing & Navigating the Internet's World Wide Web* (2nd ed.). Research Triangle Park, NC: Ventana.

————. (1995). *Netscape Navigator Quick Tour for Windows: Accessing & Navigating the Internets World Wide Web* (2nd ed.). Research Triangle Park, NC: Ventana.

It's Time to Ask [Alternate] Dr. Internet!

N*ote:* This message was subliminally transmitted to me by a document using the Netscape <BLINK> tag.

1. My library wants to get on the Internet. How big a server do I need?

You may have been told otherwise, but a recent study commissioned by Dr. Internet Labs proves that Size Matters. You just can't impress some people with a small server; they want something big and satisfying. Most readers will understand that server quality should rightfully be measured in terms of storage space, memory, or network throughput. Your library director, though, needs visual impact, or you'll never get another nickel for toys.

So don't spend your whole budget on that Alpha box you want. Buy a 486 and rack mount it in a cabinet at least four feet high and three feet wide. Make sure it has blinking lights on the side, and—for good measure— glue a couple of antique tape reels onto it. Then your server will impress anyone, and they won't laugh or throw their drink in your face.

2. Who decides who gets Web pages?

Don't underestimate the degree of control exerted by certain powers over the content, and even the very existence, of Web pages. It is well known, for example, that the National Security Agency has invested heavily in Web indexing software and maintains a list of every Web page. This list is regularly reviewed by agents of the Defense Intelligence Agency and the secret police of several other nations in conjunction with the Men in Grey Suits.

Web pages deemed undesirable have been known to disappear, along with their authors, and sometimes even their Internet Service Providers. I'm not making this up, you know— this is documented. I have proof!

3. I have heard that in the future newspapers will be electronic. Exactly how will this work?

In all cases where a technology migration requires more than 20 cents of retraining (the famous "pair of dimes" shift), it has been demonstrated that users respond best when the new technology works with a familiar delivery mechanism. Early tests of electronic newspapers tried wireless satellite transmissions, delivery via cable television connections, and even home fax machines; none of these proved satisfactory.

Major players in the electronic news industry now plan to hire fleets of adolescents to bicycle around to each neighborhood with a stack of floppy disks. At each subscriber's house, they will either toss the floppy disk into the geraniums or drop it into a puddle in the driveway.

4. Is it true that on the Internet no one can tell you're a dog?

This is no longer true. A start-up company in Cupertino, California, has started marketing a lexical analyzer that examines a number of textual clues (number of modifiers, preference for transitive or intransitive verbs, references to squirrels and rabbits, etc.) and identifies the author's species. This article, for example, would return a result of "human" just for the use of the word "lexical." By way of comparison, any use of the phrase "Make Money Fast" returns a result of "banana slug."

5. Bandwidth is such a fascinating subject. Can you tell us more about it?

Bandwidth is a very simple matter of arithmetic. If I were to append the U.S. Constitution to the end of this post, it would be a much smaller file than if I recorded someone reciting the Constitution as an audio file. But if I sent this post to several thousand people on different lists, then *it* would be bigger, taken as a total of all disk space used up. But if I sent the audio file to everyone on those lists, that would be the biggest.

To appreciate the perfect clarity of this argument, repeat it to people constantly. After a few thousand times, they will tell you to stop. That's bandwidth.

6. **Who is responsible for Alternate Dr. Internet? Where did Alternate Dr. Internet get his degree?**

It is debatable whether "responsible" is the correct term, but Alternate Dr. Internet is a continuum of interdimensional beings who channel their collective wisdom through a librarian in Seattle. They have all been at this far too long. For example, I still vividly remember my first online account, using the locally developed MTS (Michigan Terminal System) operating system, a line editor, and an arcane text formatting program that makes TeX look like Word for Windows. I also had

to walk to school barefoot, through three feet of snow.

I received my Alternate Internet degree from the Granada Correspondence College of Medicine and Information Technology, where my thesis was "Why I Like Internet."

> Tune in next time for Ask Dr. Internet— "I have a master's degree . . . in Internet!"

> Dr. Internet, Master of All Knowledge Benedictine On the Rocks With a Twist No official connection to Dr. Science

Editor's note: [Alternate] Dr. Internet is channeled by Thomas Dowling, who holds copyright on these effusions. You can find his contact information in his chapter on "Multimedia File Formats," which is more serious. At least, I think it is.

Anyway, you can find more wisdom of [Alternate] Dr. Internet at http://chehalis.lib.washington.edu/dri

Your Hardware Platform for Internet Access

LANs and SLIP/PPP Connections

Marshall Breeding

Marshall Breeding *(BREEDING@LIBRARY.VANDERBILT.EDU)* is library networks and microcomputer analyst for the Vanderbilt University Library. He is the editor of *Library Software Reviews;* he also edited *Library LANs: Case Studies in Practice and Application* and wrote *TCP/IP for the Internet.*

So, you want to get connected to the Internet? Whether you plan to connect from the computer at your place of business or from your home, there are a number of options and possibilities. The first question to ask yourself is whether you will connect a single computer or whether you have a group of computers that need Internet access. For home computers and small organizations with only one or two computers, your connection to the Internet can be accomplished with a modem and a telephone line. Larger organizations will likely have a much larger set of computers linked together in some type of network. Rather than connecting each of these computers individually, a single, high bandwidth link can tie the whole network to the Internet. Remember, modem access applies to single computers and network access connects whole groups of computers. In this chapter, I will describe both connection models.

Internet Protocol Suite

For computer networks to connect, they must follow the same communications rules, or protocols. The network protocol used throughout the Internet is called Transmission Control Protocol/Internet Protocol (TCP/IP). In reality, the Internet uses a broader set of protocols, called the Internet

Protocol Suite. For a computer to connect to the Internet it must have software that enables it to use TCP/IP.

Internet Protocol (IP)

For information to be transmitted on the Internet, it must be broken down into small units, called "datagrams" or "packets." Each datagram includes both the raw data to be transmitted and information regarding how it will be used on the network. You can think of the data as residing inside an electronic envelope that contains information such as the originating address, the return address, and various other delivery details.

IP defines basic rules concerning point-to-point delivery of datagrams on the Internet. This protocol involves a specific addressing scheme where each node on the network is assigned a 32-bit binary address. Although computers deal with IP addresses in their native binary form, most humans prefer to see them in a dotted decimal notation, four decimal numbers separated by periods. For example, the binary address 10000001 00111011 10010110 00000101 reads more easily in its dotted decimal representation as 129.59.150.5.

IP networks divide into classes. The class of network sets the limit on the number of permissible nodes. Although other classes theoretically exist, most are either class B networks that support up to 65,536 nodes or class C networks that support only 256 nodes. For class B networks, the first 2 binary digits identify the network type (10), the next 14 digits define the network, and the last 16 digits describe the work station. For class C networks, the first 2 digits identify the network type (11), the next 22 digits identify the network, and only 8 digits describe individual nodes. (Class A networks are the really big ones—there can be up to 126 of them supporting 16,777,214 nodes each.)

Even the decimal representation of IP addresses is much too cumbersome for most. Through another set of protocols, the Domain Name System (DNS), numeric IP addresses are translated into more-meaningful forms such as *breeding.library.vanderbilt.edu*. DNS, though a very simple concept, is implemented through a very large and complex system. For DNS to be useful, any known Internet address name needs to be reliably translated into a numerical IP address. The number of names to be translated is much too large to reside in any one system. DNS operates through the cooperation of name servers throughout the Internet. Each site maintains a table of names and addresses within its local domain. When a DNS request comes for an address outside its domain, it is directed to a higher-level domain name server. DNS operates as a hierarchical database distributed throughout the Internet. The database is constantly being updated and must be replicated on many major name servers throughout the Internet.

Transmission Control Protocol (TCP)

While IP takes care of basic end-to-end delivery of datagrams on the Internet, it does not do anything to ensure correct delivery. TCP is one of the network protocols that ensures that all the datagrams are received intact and in the correct order. Especially in complex networks, it is possible for packets to follow different routes and arrive in a different order than transmitted. TCP uses a convention called "sockets," where each network application communicates on an assigned socket number. TCP performs error checking to ensure that the data arrives without error and resequences the packets into the order in which they were originally transmitted. If packets are missing or contain errors, TCP requests a retransmission.

User Datagram Protocol (UDP)

UDP, like TCP, operates on the transport layer, ensuring that packets are received without error and in sequence. It also uses a system of sockets. UDP uses less error checking than TCP but operates considerably faster. UDP does not guarantee error-free delivery. Applications that need fast and efficient transport can be written on top of UDP instead of TCP, but the application must take responsibility for error checking and correction.

Users do not have to worry about whether to use UDP or TCP. Software developers decide which one best fits their application. Programs such as Telnet, File Transfer Protocol (FTP), and mail rely on TCP, while Network File System (NFS) and DNS use UDP.

TCP/IP Network Applications

While protocols such as IP, TCP, and UDP operate behind the scenes on all TCP/IP networks, there are also a number of other protocols and applications that relate to specific network programs. These applications use the underlying TCP/IP protocols. Some have been associated with TCP/IP from its UNIX heritage, and others have evolved more recently to become part of the Internet Protocol Suite.

Telnet

Telnet is a program that allows you to log in to a remote computer. Once you are connected through Telnet, the commands you enter are executed on the processor of the remote system. To establish a Telnet session, you might have to have an account and password on the remote system, but many systems, like library catalogs, are available for open Telneting. Telnet uses TCP as its transport protocol and is associated with socket 23.

FTP

FTP, for "File Transfer Protocol," functions as a utility for moving files from one computer to another on a TCP/IP network. Establishing an FTP session looks much the same as that for Telnet—the remote system prompts for a user name and password. But once the connection is established, you can only issue commands that relate to moving files and listing directories. You cannot run programs on the remote computer. The original FTP utilities followed a UNIX-style command interface, requiring you to know quite a bit about UNIX commands and syntax. Most current FTP utilities use a graphical interface, allowing you to point-and-click or drag-and-drop to manipulate files. FTP runs over TCP using port 21 for the command session and port 20 for the data transfer.

TN3270

While most other systems follow the standard VT100 terminal emulation for a Telnet session, IBM mainframes often require 3270 emulation. TN3270 is a variant of Telnet that implements IBM 3270 emulation instead of VT100. In the library world, if you want to connect to an online catalog that runs NOTIS, it is likely that you will need to use TN3270.

Simple Mail Transport Protocol (SMTP)

One of the most prevalent uses of the Internet involves electronic mail. SMTP is the protocol that is used for exchanging mail between computers. The delivery of mail on the Internet is a fairly complex operation, using many different protocols and applications. While SMTP takes care of the server-to-server delivery of mail, other protocols come into play for moving mail to individual client systems and for attaching files. Post Office Protocol (POP), for example, is a commonly used protocol for retrieving mail from a central mail server to individual mail users. Another mail protocol has become popular recently, called "Internet Message Access Protocol" (IMAP). (For more information on IMAP, see Carnegie Mellon University, 1995.) This protocol provides more of a client/server architecture than POP, and offers more flexibility for remote mail users. IMAP offers the possibility for keeping mail folders on the server so that they can be read from multiple remote locations. Increasingly, mail users want to send programs, data files, graphics, and sound clips along with the text of mail messages. Multipurpose Internet Mail Extensions (MIME) is the protocol that enables other files to be sent as mail.

Network File System (NFS)

While FTP allows you to move files from one computer to another, NFS provides access to file systems on a remote computer. NFS, although originally developed by Sun Microsystems, has been implemented on many other computer systems and is widely used for sharing disk devices in TCP/IP networks. NFS allows you to establish a drive letter as the remote file system, so you don't have to move files one-by-one to your computer. The administrator of an NFS server will define mount points that allow other users to access selected subsets of the complete file system. You then perform a mount command that associates the server's mount point with a drive letter. From that point, you use the same commands to access the remote file system that you would apply to a local disk.

Internet Gopher

Although nearly passé now, the Internet Gopher was once a very popular system for the dissemination of information on the Internet. It was used for many campuswide and corporate information systems. Gopher, originally developed at the University of Minnesota, follows a hierarchical menu system and provides access to many different types of files.

Web Browsers

An indispensable part of a TCP/IP application suite is the software used to access the World Wide Web, called a Web browser. HyperText Transfer Protocol (HTTP) defines the way that browsers communicate with Web servers. Information placed on a Web server is organized by a set of rules called HyperText Markup Language (HTML).

Connection Models

Options abound for ways to connect to the Internet. Are you going to connect a single computer or a network? Are you part of a campus or corporate network that already has Internet access, or do you need to work with an ISP to establish a connection? In this section, we will consider some of the connectivity models that are commonly used for Internet access, the hardware components. Later, we will take a look at the software that you'll need.

Network Connectivity Model

If you have a whole group of computers for which you want to provide Internet access, you will probably want to use a network connection rather than providing dial-up connections for each computer. This method involves first connecting all the individual computers to form a local area network (LAN) and then connecting this LAN to the Internet.

The network model for connecting to the Internet includes a number of hardware and software components.

Each of the computers on the network needs to have a network interface card and TCP/IP network software. The network interface card will either be an Ethernet or a Token Ring card, depending on your environment.

A cabling scheme will connect all the computers to the network. Again, the type of cable used depends on your network.

For most network environments, you will need a device called a "hub" that connects each of the cables from your computers into the central network.

Your network will need devices to control the flow of data. Minimally, you will need a router (a device that directs data packets on the network) to connect your local area network to the Internet.

Depending on the size of your network, you may have other network control devices, including bridges, repeaters, or switching devices. Several specialized computers will be needed to provide important network services, such as a name server and a mail server. Many sites will have other servers for Web- and Gopher-based information.

The goal of this type of network connectivity is to allow each of the computers on the network to be a node on the Internet. It may be that not all computers are given this capability for security or other concerns, but the potential is there. Figure 1 illustrates the overall structure of the network connectivity model.

The Link to the Internet. To connect a network to the Internet, you will need several components, including a contract with an Internet Service Provider (ISP), a telecommunications circuit leased from the telephone company, a Channel Service Unit/Digital Service Unit (CSU/DSU) or equivalent device for connecting equipment to this data circuit, and a router. Figure 2 illustrates a common method for implementing a link to the Internet.

Telecommunications Link. Your first step in implementing access to the Internet will involve determining the type of connection required and selecting an Internet Service Provider. The options offered by ISPs vary, as does the prices charged for their services. Some of the options available for telecommunications links to the Internet include

- T3 line to transmit a Level 3 formatted digital signal at 44.746 megabits per second (Mbps)
- T1 line to transmit a Level 1 formatted digital signal at 1.544 Mbps
- 256 kilobits per second (Kbps) leased line
- 56 Kbps leased line
- Basic-Rate Integrated Services Digital Network (ISDN) up to 128 Kbps

In most cases, your ISP will make arrangements with one of the telephone companies to install the data circuit to your site. The phone company will install the line and provide a wall jack.

Interface Equipment. The next device needed is the appropriate interface to the telephone line. In most cases a CSU/DSU will be provided by the Internet Service Provider. This device has one cable that connects to the telephone jack and has a serial cable. The type of serial cable normally used is a V.35 cable, not the RS-232 type used by personal computers.

Internet Gateway Router. The intelligence for connecting your network to the Internet is the gateway router. In most cases the ISP installs and configures this router, but some larger organizations provide and configure their own Internet gateway router. A router consists of a box with multiple network interfaces and software to control how data pass from one network to another. A typical router has one serial channel for connecting to an external network such as the Internet and one or more Ethernet ports that

FIGURE 1   Model for Connecting a Network to the Internet

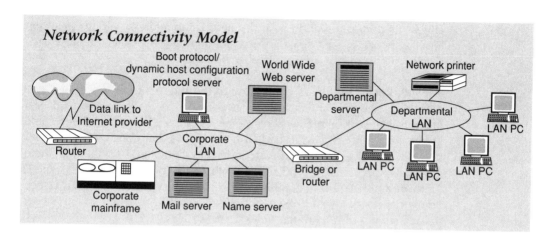

Network Connectivity Model

FIGURE 2   Components Required for Connecting a Network to the Internet

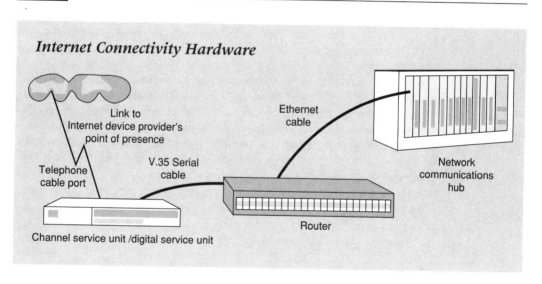

Internet Connectivity Hardware

connect to your central network. The V.35 cable from the DSU/CSU attaches to a serial port on the router. The Ethernet port on the router can connect in any number of ways to your local network. In many cases it will connect to an intelligent Ethernet hub, but there are lots of other options, depending on the configuration of your network environment.

The primary function of the router is to make sure that traffic for the local network stays local and that the packets destined for other networks are passed to the external network. Routers must be aware of the network protocol used by each data packet. Different network protocols can exist on a network at the same time, and different rules or pathways may exist for routing them. Remember that the protocol used by the Internet is TCP/IP, so that only TCP/IP packets are eligible for being passed across your Internet gateway router. A router looks at each packet that it receives and checks its destination address. If the destination address belongs to an external network, it is passed across to the Internet. The router validates each packet to ensure that it hasn't been corrupted.

Network Cards. If you are connecting to the Internet from a network, you will use a network interface card on each of the computers instead of a modem. Network interface cards come in two main types, Ethernet and Token Ring, and you will need to use the one that corresponds to your network type. Even within the categories of Ethernet and Token Ring, there are many variations. For Ethernet, some of the options include 10BaseT, Thinwire (10Base2), and 100BaseT. (For more information on Ethernet, see Spurgeon, 1996.) Token Ring networks generally operate at 16 Mbps, though some still require the older 4 Mbps cards.

For desktop computers, almost all network interface cards are inserted into the system bus. Make sure that you get the type that corresponds to your computer. For PCs you will need to select from Industry Standard Architecture (ISA), Extended Industry Standard Architecture (EISA), MicroChannel, or Peripheral Component Interconnect (PCI). For Macintosh computers, you will need a NuBus, PCI or any of the proprietary Apple bus types, again making sure that the card you buy matches what your computer requires.

Once you have the network interface card installed in your PC, you will need to make sure that you have the software that makes it work. Network software follows a layered approach that isolates all the hardware-specific parts to a single section. This allows the same software to run with all the different hardware options. The manufacturer of the hardware will provide software drivers that allow it to operate with all the standard network environments.

There are a number of different approaches to implementing this layered network architecture. For DOS, Windows, and OS/2 there are two competing versions, Novell's Open Datalink Interface (ODI) and Network Device Interface Specification (NDIS), which originated from 3Com and Microsoft. This layered design evolved not only to more easily accommodate different types of hardware but also to allow computers to operate with multiple network protocols. This approach allows a computer to use TCP/IP networking for access to the Internet but also to use others such as Novell's IPX (Internetwork Pocket Exchange) network protocols for communicating on a LAN.

ODI implements network access in layers. One layer, the Multiple Link Interface Driver (MLID), consists of a hardware-specific device driver. This driver almost always comes packaged with the network hardware, be it an Ethernet, a Token Ring, or an ISDN card. The Link Support Layer (LSL) of ODI creates a generic interface between the MLID and any other network software. The next layer of ODI implements specific network protocols, such as IPX or TCP/IP. In practical terms, a computer that uses ODI will execute a program called LSL.COM and its MLID driver, which usually reflects the name of the network device. ODI uses a file called NET.CFG that specifies the particular hardware devices, protocols, and configuration parameters involved.

Network Security. Connecting networks to the Internet generally involves two-way communications. Not only can you access resources out on the Internet but users on the Internet can potentially access computers on your internal network. One of the main concerns with connecting to the Internet involves the possibility of making the computers on your local network vulnerable to attack from unwanted intruders.

Many organizations will segment their networks so that all the critical systems are well isolated from the Internet. Only selected systems, such as the organization's public Web server or mail gateway are on the part of the network accessible by the Internet. You can choose to make only some of your computers available to users that come into your network from the Internet.

Routers can help to provide security to your network by selectively routing information. The use of a router to provide security is often called a "firewall." You can buy security products that include firewall routers and other applications to further decrease your network's vulnerability to intruders from the Internet.

Other approaches to providing Internet security involve application servers or proxy servers. These systems use software that serves as an intelligent intermediary, allowing access to information on internal servers but without providing a direct connection. (See "The American Public, the Public Library, and the Internet" and "Security and Authentication" for discussion and pointers to more information.)

The Dial-Up Connection

Connecting an entire network of computers to the Internet can be an expensive and complex ordeal. In the absence of a direct network connection, you can also gain access to the Internet through a modem and a regular telephone line. This method is widely used by home computer users and by organizations that lack internal computer networks or that have chosen not to connect their networks to the Internet.

What You Need to Get Started. To connect to the Internet with a modem, you will need an account with an Internet Service Provider (or with your local network), a personal computer, a modem, and TCP/IP networking software that supports Serial Line Internet Protocol (SLIP) or Point-to-Point Protocol (PPP). (See "Internet Access Options for Libraries" for more information about getting started with an ISP.)

Telephone Line. If you have a single computer that you want to use to access the Internet, you will need to use some sort of telephone line. Most people will be able to share this use with the telephone line installed for voice conversations, but you might want to consider getting a second line if you plan to spend a lot of time online.

Computer. To connect to the Internet, you will need some sort of computer. All varieties of computers can be connected, whether you have an Intel-based PC running any of the varieties of Windows, a Macintosh, or a UNIX system.

Modems. You will also need a modem. Modems (MOdulator/DEModulators) translate the digital information native to your computer to the analog signals required by the telephone system. Modems also include features for placing and receiving calls and negotiating connections with other computers and circuitry that performs error checking and correction to ensure that all data are transmitted and received correctly. The latest models of modems can compress signals to allow for faster effective communications speeds. Most current modems also include the ability to send and receive facsimile transmissions.

A consideration in buying a modem is its communication speeds. The performance capabilities of modems have increased dramatically in the last fifteen years. The first modems that I used operated at a rate of 300 bits per second (bps). About every two years, the standard for modem speeds has increased. The next jump was to 1,200 bps, then to 2,400 bps, and then to 9,600 bps. A couple of years ago, V.32bis modems that communicate at 14.4 Kbps became popular. More recently V.34 modems that operate at 28.8 Kbps have become available. Throughout the evolution of modems, the most current technology sells at about $350, while the price of last year's model drops to around $100. (See also Jonker, 1995.)

Modems come in both internal and external versions. An internal modem is a card that plugs into the system bus of your computer. It has two RJ-11 telephone jacks, one that connects to the telephone line and another that connects to a telephone. Internal modems get their electrical power from the computer itself. To install an internal modem, you open the case of the computer, remove one of the blank-slot covers, and press the modem card into the slot connector in your computer.

You will then have to configure your computer appropriately. Internal modems will use a logical serial communications port, COM1, COM2, COM3, or COM4. The most common port for an internal modem is COM2. Though some modems are self-configuring, most require that you set a jumper to select a COM port. The setting that you choose on the modem must not already be used for another device in your computer. You may have to run the configuration program that comes with your computer when you install an internal modem. Once the modem is installed, be sure to remember what COM port you selected. You will need this information later when you install your communications software.

External modems reside in their own separate enclosure. They have the same two telephone jacks as internal modems. External modems connect to the serial port of your computer through a data cable. Since external modems are not installed directly inside the computer, they must have a separate source for electrical power. Most will have a transformer that plugs into an electrical outlet; the transformer has a low-voltage DC power cord that plugs into the modem. External modems do not provide their own logical COM port but use an existing physical serial port. Most computers have one or more serial ports with connectors to access them on the back of the computer. Older computers may have 25-pin serial connectors, but most modern models use 9-pin connectors. Make sure that you get the right kind of serial cable for your computer. Again, remember which serial port you used to connect your modem. You'll need to know when you install your software.

Communications Software

For your computer to become part of the Internet, you must have software that implements TCP/IP network protocols. There are a number of software packages that fill this need: some available as freeware or shareware and others available commercially.

If you intend to connect to the Internet, you need to have the right type of communications software. There are at least two major types of communications software for microcomputers. One type allows your computer to connect with other computers or online systems using asynchronous serial communications. This type of software can be used to establish a session with a mainframe or minicomputer, emulate a terminal, and perform file transfers. Examples of this software genre include the popular shareware program Procomm as well as commercial programs such as Hayes Corporation's SmartCom, Delrina's WinCom Pro, and many others. This software will allow you to connect to the Internet in a text-based mode, but if you have yet to connect your computer to the Internet, you will probably want to plan on using the components described below. This will allow you to use the World Wide Web in a graphical mode.

To connect to the Internet in graphical mode, you will need communications software that implements TCP/IP networking protocols. This software is not just one program but involves a suite of components and programs. Which of these components you need depends on how you connect to the Internet and the type of activities you need to perform once connected. The three main components of a TCP/IP communications package include the hardware interface, the TCP/IP kernel, and network applications.

Hardware Interface

There are many different hardware devices and methods that can be used for Internet access. Developers design network software in layers so that most of the programs are completely independent of the communications hardware used. Only one layer is hardware-specific. This layer accommodates different communications methods as well as the specific hardware devices they use. The hardware interface will include support for SLIP or PPP if you use a modem, a device driver for an Ethernet or a Token Ring card, or the support software needed for other access methods such as ISDN.

Modems: SLIP or PPP

If you use a modem to connect to the Internet, you will need your TCP/IP communications package to include the appropriate support software. There are two main variants of the communications protocol used for connecting modems to the Internet, SLIP or PPP. While many Internet Service Providers now use PPP, some still rely on SLIP. Both of these protocols allow TCP/IP network protocols to operate over asynchronous serial line communications like those used by modems. SLIP works only with TCP/IP networks and requires that the IP address be configured as a separate process. PPP works with other network protocols such as IPX and includes an automatic process for assigning an IP address. In most cases, your ISP will specify which of these protocols you should use.

There are several steps involved in getting a SLIP or PPP session connected. During the installation of the software, you will specify the brand and model of modem, the telephone number of your ISP, and other communications parameters. In most cases, you will be assigned an account name and password. These can be programmed into your software to automate the connection process. When you are ready, you will run a program that establishes the connection. This program will initialize your modem and dial the telephone number. When the remote system answers, your software will process a script of commands necessary to begin the session. The script will usually include commands to pass on your user name and password and initiate the SLIP or PPP session. Once the session has been initialized, other applications can communicate with the Internet.

If you are used to modem software like Procomm, SLIP or PPP software will seem quite different. With Procomm, the modem commands, log-in sequence, and the communications session itself are all seen from the same program. But with SLIP and PPP software, the modem commands and log-in sequence are performed from one program, and the applications that use the network connection run separately. The log-in utility may show the status of the connection, but usually it does not show the information being sent to and received from the Internet. With most SLIP or PPP communications software, you use a program called a "dialer" that initializes the modem, dials your Internet Service Provider, and executes a log-in script. The log-in script will enter your account name, password, and the command to activate the communications session. Once the dialer has finished its work, you can launch programs such as Netscape that operate over your active communications session. Some SLIP/PPP applications offer a feature called "dial-on-demand." With these, you simply run the applications that access the Internet and the software automatically initiates or drops the communications session as needed. As soon as the application attempts to transmit or receive from the Internet, the SLIP/PPP software automatically dials the ISP and initiates a communication session. After a set interval of inactivity, the connection is allowed to close.

Network Applications

A number of companies produce TCP/IP communications software. These commercial applications include not only the dialer application and the

TCP/IP communications software but usually include a suite of network applications. Most will provide a Web browser, a Telnet and FTP client, a mail application, and other utilities. For Windows 3.1, some of the products include Chameleon from NetManage Corporation, SuperTCP from Frontier Technologies, LAN Workplace from Novell Corporation, OnNet from FTP Software, PC-TCP from Sun Microsystems, and others. A popular shareware version, called Trumpet Winsock, is available from Trumpet Software International. (See also Kriz, 1995.)

With Windows 3.1, you had to get TCP/IP software from another vendor to connect your computer to the Internet. Microsoft offered a free version of TCP/IP for Windows for Workgroups. This software initially did not come as part of Windows for Workgroups but could be obtained from Microsoft's FTP server on the Internet. Windows NT and Windows 95 come with TCP/IP software integrated into the operating system. Now, for almost any computer you buy, it will come with built-in capability to connect to the Internet. Whether you are buying a PC running Windows 95 or Windows NT Workstation, a Macintosh, or a UNIX Workstation, it will come with built-in TCP/IP software and a SLIP/PPP dialer. You may need to obtain a Web Browser or other network utilities, but the basic connectivity software comes pre-installed.

Getting connected to the Internet is getting easier and easier all the time. Not that long ago, the process of getting the necessary hardware and software installed on your computer was a technical and involved process. Now, most computers already come with a modem and provide the software necessary to get connected. With the information in this chapter, you should be acquainted with the components necessary to access the Internet regardless of whether you are connecting a single computer or a network of computers. Go forth and get connected!

References

Breeding, Marshall. (1995). *TCP/IP for the Internet: The Complete Buyer's Guide for Micro-based Products.* Westport, CT: Mecklermedia.

Carnegie Mellon University. (1995). *IMAP Protocol Resources.* [Online]. Available: *http://andrew2.andrew.cmu.edu/cyrus/email/standards-IMAP.html*

Hecker, Frank. (1994). *Personal Internet Access Using SLIP or PPP: How You Use It, How It Works.* [Online]. Available: *file://ftp.digex.net/pub/access/hecker/internet/slip-ppp.txt*

Jonker, Niels. (1995). *Practical Guide to Modems.* [Online]. Available: *http://www.myhome.org/modems.html*

Kriz, Harry M. (1995). *Windows and TCP/IP for Internet Access.* [Online]. Available: *http://learning.lib.vt.edu/wintcpip/wintcpip.html*

Souvatzis, Ignatios. (1995). *Comp.Protocols.PPP Frequently Wanted Information.* [Online]. Available: *http://cs.uni-bonn.de/ppp/faq.html*

Spurgeon, Charles. (1996). *The Ethernet Page.* [Online]. Available: *http://wwwhost.ots.utexas.edu/ethernet/ethernet-home.html*

It's Time Once Again to Ask [Alternate] Dr. Internet!

A number of readers have written to ask how I find the ideas for Alternate Dr. Internet columns. Most of them seem to believe that they come to me in the middle of the night, and they usually suggest that I stop eating spicy foods before bedtime.

In fact, like many library operations, I have a detailed plan to solicit user input, ensuring that my service meets their needs. Also like many library operations, I inevitably find that it's too difficult to find actual users, and when I do they always tell me the wrong things. So then I make it all up myself.

1. Where did the major networking technologies come from?

We owe much of our current networking landscape to engineers in the British Isles. In the early 1970s, for example, the Dutch computer scientist Anders ten Beys, who was teaching at Cambridge, brought together some of Britain's most creative networking specialists in a series of afternoon social gatherings. The ten Beys Teas generated ideas about physical connectivity at around the same time as the messaging work carried out by members of an Oxford literary club, the Tolkien Ring.

Eamonn de Innes, an Irish undergraduate who belonged briefly to both of these groups, became intrigued with the mechanics of identifying one specific computer on a very large network. The de Innes name server, while not perfect, routinely locates remote hosts with an apparent magical ability that one might—but shouldn't—call legerdomain.

2. I've been assigned to coordinate our library's new Internet services. Do I need to know a programming language?

There is no greater misconception today than the idea that you can manage network services without a strong grasp of a programming language. In fact, to run your network efficiently, you will probably need to know several languages.

Of course, when I say that you need to know a language, I don't for a minute mean that you should burden yourself with the niggling little details that generate gibberish like:

```
foreach $key (sort keys(%in)) {
if (($out = $in{$key}) =~ s/\n/<BR>/g)
    {$output .= "<DL
    COMPACT><DT><B>$key</B> is
    <DD><I>$out</I></DL>";}
else {$output .= "<B>$key</B> is
    <I>$out</I><BR>";
}
}
```

No, what you need to know is the sociology of any particular language in the techie community and how to use that to your advantage. A common example these days is the development of scripts to process Web forms; these scripts are commonly written in PERL [Practical Extraction and Report Language] and most techies feel that writing anything other than C++ is beneath them, making it hard to convince them to write your script. (Your programmers are all writing distributed operating systems in C++ in much the same way that all advertising copy writers have the Great American Novel half-finished at home.)

The simple solution to this problem is to send them e-mail saying "Don't worry about it—I can put together something with a Korn shell script. Can you loan me your Sed and Awk book?" In most cases, this will get you a well-honed PERL script by midnight. This works because of your insight into the following languages:

C++   The one true language for real programs (with the little problem that it doesn't always work and you might have to go back to C).

PERL   An acceptable substitute for little jobs beneath your notice, like those dumb scripts the library is always asking for.

Ksh   The wrong tool for the job.
Sed, Awk   The wrong tool for *any* job.

Note that you probably do not want your technical folks to start thinking you really do know a lot about programming languages. That can lead to embarrassments; they might, for example, suggest that you handle any future changes to the script by editing the code yourself. If you sense this is happening, ask them if they ever write in Pascal.

3. What is Java?

A few years ago, Singapore suddenly developed a reputation as a developing country that embraced high technology. Other nations in Southeast Asia, seeing investment dollars going to Singapore, have tried to follow suit.

The most successful of these attempts is a programming language developed in Indonesia. "Java" (early test versions were called "Bali" and "Sumatra") is a platform-independent language, meaning that it is equally buggy on Macs, PCs, and UNIX work stations. So far, the only practical applications written in Java are an animated advertisement from the Djakarta Chamber of Commerce and the Krakatoa virus, which causes your PC to explode violently if it detects a copy of Microsoft Internet Explorer. Microsoft has protested this behavior, claiming it copies its look and feel from the way the Microsoft Network seeks out and destroys competing WIN-SOCK.DLL files.

4. Our computing center has expressed some concern about users spoofing e-mail addresses in Netscape. What does that mean?

Various reports have indicated that Netscape can be set up to suggest that the user is anyone on the Net. Dr. Internet Labs tested this by getting a copy of the latest beta version of Netscape, complete with Java support, and installing it on three different computers. On one, we used our own address. On the other two, we used the addresses BILLC@LACKOF.ORG and NEWTG@GOPAC.COM. The first machine crashed with a GPF message, the second machine simply froze, and the third machine flashed a toll-free number onscreen and then froze. This proves that Netscape works equally well no matter what e-mail address you enter in the configuration files.

Why are such fake e-mail addresses called spoofs? Well, hackers being what they are, they usually fall back on the classics: They spoof Roman names from Monty Python's "Life of Brian."

Tune in next time for Ask Dr. Internet—"I have a master's degree . . . in Internet!"

Dr. Internet, Master of All Knowledge
Benedictine On the Rocks With a Twist
No official connection to Dr. Science

Editor's note: [Alternate] Dr. Internet is channeled by Thomas Dowling, who holds copyright on these effusions. You can find his contact information in his chapter on "Multimedia File Formats," which is more serious. At least, I think it is.

Anyway, you can find more wisdom of [Alternate] Dr. Internet at http://chehalis.lib.washington.edu/dri

WIRELESS AND UBIQUITOUS COMPUTING

Steve Cavrak

Steve Cavrak *(STEVE.CAVRAK@UVM.EDU)* is with academic computing services in computing and information technologies at the University of Vermont. His interests lie in teaching in the online age; find out more at *http://www.uvm.edu/~sjc/.*

Fifty years ago, scientists were busy constructing the first gigantic, room-filling electronic brains called Univacs. At almost the same time, a square-jawed, dime store detective named Dick Tracy was busy chasing criminals, foiling plots, and entertaining readers with his wristwatch radio telephone. It scarcely occurred to most of us following the news and cartoons that the two technologies were on a collision course.

Mobile computing and wireless communications are introducing changes as large if not larger than those brought about by computers or radio themselves. Corporations plan for telecommuting employees working in virtual organizations. Schools imagine distance learning being integrated into an electronic classroom. Hollywood and Madison Avenue dream about a TV set in every notebook and an advertisement on every page. Technology watchers expect a flood of new activities and products, some frivolous and entertaining, others profound and disturbing.

Technology does not evolve in a vacuum but in response to real and perceived needs. Companies are constructing "work at anytime, anyplace" business plans as ways of improving customer support and cutting costs as well as ways of attracting and developing a dynamic work force. Schools see technology as a way of supporting individual needs as well as a way of preparing students for the changing world of work. All of these work together to create an atmosphere where the need for learning, planning, information, and imagination is ever increasing.

These changes naturally affect the the whole of a community and its social life as well as the technological infrastructure that supports them. Mark Weiser, formerly of the Xerox Palo Alto Research Center (PARC), has called this emerging computing and communication environment "ubiquitous computing." Ubiquitous computing refers less to particular technologies than to a technological climate packed with easy-to-use devices that are smart, cheap, useful, and practically invisible. Some of these devices are small and portable; others might be as large as rooms and might even be the rooms themselves.

The Radio Spectrum

The wireless world is a world we take for granted—TV remote controls, cordless telephones, Walkmen, Watchmen, boom boxes, pocket pagers, satellite TVs, cellular phones, radar speed traps, remote microphones, microwave ovens, garage door openers, air traffic navigation, Doppler radar weather maps, electronic fences for our pets—enough to make our heads spin. F. B. Morse's 1844 telegraphic "What hath God wrought" seems more appropriate today than he imagined.

All of these devices use electromagnetic radiation, waves of linked electrical and magnetic "fields" that traverse an ethereal vacuum at the speed of light. Sometimes these waves travel in wires; other times in the air; and still other times through the nearly perfect vacuum of space.

These waves include visible light as well as the wide array of radio signals, which range from AM, shortwave, FM, TV, microwave, and eventually to infrared, visible, ultraviolet, X-rays, and gamma rays. Radio waves may be labeled by their wavelength, commonly measured in metric units (meters) but more often by their characteristic frequency, specified in hertz (a per-second measurement, abbreviated as Hz or hz). What are some of these frequencies? Based on the "orders of magnitude" (multiples of ten), the most familiar frequencies are shown in table 1.

Are these the same megahertz that are used in your personal computer? Unfortunately, yes! All active electronic devices emit radio waves. Just as we call flowers growing out of place "weeds," electromagnetic radiation emitted out of place is called "noise" or "static." If you have any doubt, you can verify this by placing a small FM radio close to your computer, tuning it to a place where you have nice static, and then start doing typical computer things—typing, moving and clicking the mouse, reading and writing to disk, rebooting the system, etc. All the while your radio will beep and squawk and whistle and hiss; soon you will recognize the squawk of a mouse click and the hiss of a disk drive in action.

What makes the megahertz in a computer different from those used for radio, TV, etc.? One of the important differences is power—the strength of the signal. Radio power is measured in watts. The power radiated by your PC is tiny, measured in milliwatts or even microwatts; if you move your test radio across the room, the noise from the PC vanishes. A hand-held cellular

	Frequency	Wavelength	Application
TABLE 1 The Electromagnetic Spectrum	1 Megahertz (Mhz)	300 meters	AM radio
	10 Mhz	30 meters	Shortwave radio
	100 Mhz	3 meters	FM radio
	1,000 Mhz	0.3 meter	Microwave
	1 Gigahertz (Ghz)	300 millimeters (mm)	Microwave
	10 Ghz	30 mm	Police/weather radar
	100 Ghz	3 mm	Satellite radar
	1,000 Ghz	0.3 mm	Remote sensing
	1 Terahertz (Thz)	300 micrometers (μm)	Remote sensing
	10 Thz	30 μm	Thermal infrared
	100 Thz	3 μm	Thermal infrared
	1,000 Thz	0.3 μm	Visible

phone has a power rating on the level of 1/2 watt (500 milliwatts). Commercial stations, however, operate transmitters that broadcast signals measured in kilowatts or even megawatts. The more powerful a signal, the farther it travels.

A second important difference is the way the radio is used to encode signals. The signals coming out of your computer are pretty much raw—nothing is really being done to them except perhaps turning them on and off in gross ways. The signals coming from devices designed for communication are modulated in very strict ways so that the encoding at the transmitting end can be correctly decoded at the receiver. For example, the *AM* in AM radio refers to signal amplitude modulation, the *FM* refers to frequency (shift) modulation.

The regulation of signaling method is usually a technical matter left to the users of the spectrum. These users work together, generally following the procedures of national and international standards organizations. In the United States, the Institute of Electrical and Electronic Engineers (IEEE) plays the preeminent role in radio standards. Globally, the International Organization for Standardization (ISO) fulfills this role.

There is a similarity between your computer's megahertz and those of communications media. The higher the frequency, the more information (and information processing) that can be done. This means that the higher frequencies in the spectrum are not only the most useful, they are also the ones with the most capacity. One of the biggest competitors of wireless communications is another form of "wire" lessness—fiber optics, or plastic wires for light.

Keeping the radio signal separated from the chaff is the task of civil authorities. In the United States this is assigned to the Federal Communications Commission (FCC). In Europe the national bodies are coordinated by the Conférence Européenne des Administrations Postes et des Télécommunications (CEPT). Global coordination is provided by the International Frequency Regulatory Board.

TABLE 2

Assigned Radio
Spectrum

Application	Frequency (in Mhz)
Cordless telephone	46/49
Mobile cellular telephone	824–849
Site cellular telephone	870–894
Unlicensed radio devices	902–928
Common-carrier paging	959
National Information Infrastructure Supernet	5,250
Police X band radar	10,525
Police k band radar	24,150
Police Ka band radar	34,200

Sprinkled throughout the spectrum are special bands, parts of the spectrum assigned to a particular class of users by the FCC. For example, table 2 lists the bands for certain applications.

Common Wireless Networks

Wireless technology has been a part of computer networking essentially from day one. Today's most common form of wired networking—Ethernet—owes its origin to a radio-based ALOHAnet created by Norman Abrahamson at the University of Hawaii. ALOHAnet used radio transmission between the islands to provide terminal connections to a mainframe computer; satellite-based connections were used to link the islands to the mainland-based ARPANET (Advanced Projects Research Agency Network, the predecessor of today's Internet).

ALOHAnet also nicely illustrates the basic design criteria for a network—the network has to carry data to a specific geographical area. Knowing what to network and where allows experts to examine and combine various technologies to provide the biggest bang for the buck. This means that any specific network will be a mixture of technologies—some wireless and some wire-based. The slogan should be "different networks for different folks."

Infrared

One of the simplest wireless technologies is infrared light, sometimes abbreviated as IR. The underlying technology is compact, low cost, low power, and quite safe. Infrared devices are generally based on the same light-emitting diode technology found on most electrical devices that have an on/off indicator. It is also completely unregulated. All of this leads to a wide variety of possible networking niches.

The most popular use of infrared technology is the universal remote control. Click here to change a channel on your TV, click there to zap a commercial, click, click again to pause or rewind the VCR, click again and your TV is silenced and your stereo kicks in with the evening jazz program. The remote control is not a particularly earth-shaking invention, yet it is one of the more user-friendly technologies developed—so easy to use that it is almost indistinguishable from a toy. This is a harbinger of the qualities that characterize ubiquitous computing.

One of the earliest uses of infrared signaling in a computer setting was the IBM PCjr "remote" keyboard. The PCjr was designed for home rather than office use. The developers assumed that many of its users would not have a desk to keep the computer on, and if they did, it was probably not a very big one. Sometimes the desk would be the kitchen table, sometimes a countertop, sometimes the floor. The cordless keyboard provided an easy way to set up a unit without an ensuing cabling mess. Wireless keyboards are often envisioned as part of the "set top" generation of home computers—computers the size of a VCR or a CD player that sit on the top of a TV set and allow a viewer to interact with the TV in computer-like ways: perhaps voting along with the audience for the "funniest video," or "virtual cheering" at a hockey game, or "cruising the Web" when "nothing else is on," or pressing a "buy now, pay later" offer on a cubic zirconium ring.

Several steps up in a level of sophistication are the communication tools built into the Apple Newton Message Pad, an early member of the class of personal digital assistants. The message pad comes with a built-in infrared channel that allows Newtonians to beam messages, notes, and phone numbers back and forth across conference tables. The message pad has a special feature that allows the exchange of "virtual business cards"—a "look ma, no hands" way to build a personal telephone book. Similar infrared capabilities are included in higher end business, engineering, and scientific calculators that allow the exchange of data, formulas, and programs.

Infrared networking is also built into the Apple PowerPC generation of notebook computers. In this case, IR provides full Macintosh-style Appletalk networking—file, document, and printer sharing. Everything works in a point-and-click fashion automatically; no network engineer is needed to assign network numbers or install drivers or add special software. The main limitation of this style of networking is that it is direct notebook-to-notebook signaling.

More-traditional computer networking services are provided by other vendors. IBM, for example, offers an infrared network that behaves just like Ethernet. The IBM technology uses diffuse infrared radiation, bouncing signals off ceilings and walls to connect computers that might otherwise be blocked from direct view of each other. Technologies like this have been tested in conference, seminar, and classroom settings and, because they are self-organizing, have met with a good measure of success.

Radio

Infrared is unregulated because it is so easily controlled and managed; infrared networking is "just another lighting" application. Radio, because it so easily penetrates walls and invades space, is treated a bit differently. The very low powered applications are treated as unlicensed personal communication services (PCS); these are applications that affect a room or perhaps a backyard. Up the power a bit, and you begin to generate radio signals that can affect a whole building or even a close neighborhood of buildings. These private networks operate in what is commonly referred to as the industry, science, and medicine (ISM) arena. Finally there are popular subscriber services that operate regulated businesses as Radio Common Carriers (RCC).

The devices available in this market are evolving very rapidly. Most of these operate in the 900 Mhz region; the older specialized service niches are slowly being abandoned—partly because of cost and partly because of capacity. Most are also migrating to newer digital technology, making each device more and more of a computer, less and less a unique piece of hardware.

Cordless Telephone

The cordless telephone is another household device that illustrates wireless networking. Besides helping to avoid unsightly cable mess, the cordless phone allows people to chat on the phone while walking around the kitchen or perhaps walking out to the patio and sitting down and relaxing. The original cordless telephones had several channels—not because a person might be talking to several people at once but because several cordless phones might be operating at once, creating an unintentional "party line" effect. Accordingly, newer phones have more channels, cutting down on the chance of "cross talk" but not guaranteeing that a particularly nosy neighbor might not eavesdrop. The next generation of digital cordless phones includes scrambling (encrypting) technology to help provide the degree of privacy that people expect. They have also triggered anxieties in government that there might be a generation of untappable telephones in the future.

Cordless phone technology can also be used in cordless computer networks; here the party-line effect is the intent rather than an accident. Several computers want to share information, share printing, and maybe even converse in real time. Since radio signals can penetrate doors and walls, there is some concern that the party might get out of hand; a bridge party in one room might not coexist with a polka party next door.

Now, however, since we are talking more about "parties" rather than just conversations, the excitement level is a bit higher. Cordless networks can be imagined for small- and medium-sized businesses, for school classrooms, for library reading and reference rooms, for warehouses and factories, in fact, for a very large number of environments. This area of networking is in its infancy; in the United States, for example, a petition to the FCC by Apple Computer, supported by the WINForum, is in early stages of approval. The petition calls for setting aside a part of the 5 Ghz band for unlicensed data networks, envisioning a vibrant niche for low-cost, high-performance self-managing networks.

Ethernet Radio

Outside that future direction, however, there are quite a number of more traditional local area computer networking solutions available—it is very easy to build a complete Ethernet-compatible local area network without much more than a few feet of cable. Users of these networks wouldn't notice anything weird, except that they didn't have to "plug in" to become "hardwired."

In designing most networks, there is a nice balance between the cost of the network hardware that gets put into a computer and the cost of wiring that ties the computers together. Sometimes, however, the cost of wiring is quite high—the building belongs to someone else who is not willing to remodel to suit the tenant, the offices span properties owned by different individuals who have a high charge for "right of way," the building may have hazards preventing remodeling, or the use of the space may be so variable that hardwire is not viable. Wireless Ethernet solves the problem.

Airlan is one company that offers a variety of devices that allow the construction of a completely wireless local area network. There are wireless cards for individual PCs, wireless hubs for sections of buildings, and wireless bridges for linking different buildings together. And since all of these follow existing Ethernet standards, different parts of a network may use different technologies, and no one else on the network is the wiser.

Cellular Radio

Cordless technology works easily in an environment where there is really "one" telephone number—in a home, in an office, in a building, or perhaps on a campus. It also assumes that, for the most part, the communication taking place on the network is local—that's why one telephone number works.

On a campus, however, we know there is really not one telephone number; it is more like an exchange, and in fact, a private branch exchange (PBX). The computer equivalent of the PBX is the campus "Intranet"—a network that allows for 256 or 16,000 or 64,000 internal connections under one manager.

All of these environments, but especially the campus one, point out a difficulty with the "one"-number approach. A faculty member may have one phone number on campus, a different phone number at home, and maybe even a third phone number when going between the two. With students, it's even more confusing. Sometimes they are in an apartment off campus, sometimes in a classroom or study room on campus, sometimes at a workplace, sometimes studying at a friend's place, sometimes at home on vacation or break, and sometimes somewhere else altogether. Both populations want to use e-mail and the World Wide Web for their work. In industry, it's really not much different.

When networks begin to ooze out of the bounds of a particular organization, things get interesting. All of a sudden, the private networking model begins to break apart, and some form of third-party networking organization has to step in. The wireless model of these commercial networking "common carriers" are the cellular telephone companies (who are more and more often just a different branch of the plain old telephone companies).

The cellular model is interesting because it offers excellent coverage over a metropolitan area—hitting most of the places where most of the people are going to be most of the time. It also provides roaming capabilities for those times when people are elsewhere.

At the personal end of the application spectrum are the personal communication services—beepers, pagers, reminders, and messengers. These credit-card-sized devices allow a one-way series of messages, from the form "You have a call," to "You have a call from 987-6521," to "Mr. Watson, Come here. I want you. Alex." Messages may be stored, deleted, or transferred to computer and recalled later. Each generation in the pager marketplace adds more features, more message power, and more capacity. The pager marketplace advantage is its low cost, with basic service in the $15-a-month range and sophisticated services at $30 a month.

The cellular telephone model begins with a two-way, interactive model of communication. Both parties in the conversation are expected to talk about the same amount of time. This leads to a slightly larger package, a heftier monthly rate, and a fairly expensive per-minute usage charge. The cellular market leads by its interactivity, with each iteration of technology lowering the cost. One of the driving factors in the cellular market is expected to be the Telecommunications Act of 1996 that is opening the local telephone service market to competition. Wireless technology may be one of the tools that will enable newcomers to compete with the people who already own the wires.

Just as each iteration of pager technology adds more two-way interactivity to the device, so each generation of cellular telephone adds more paging and information capabilities to the telephone. We may see the two markets converge, or we may see the emergence of a new one altogether. E-mail conferencing and World Wide Web browsing may generate a third stream.

Several universities on the west coast have experimented with extending their campuses into metropolitan networking models, for example, those based on Metricom. Students use the same internetworking technology at home as they do in class, and they can send e-mail and voice mail to their parents at no additional cost. "Look ma, no telephone!"

Wireless technology is also being developed in community networking contexts. The Telluride (Colorado) InfoZone has created seven wireless test sites connecting remote computers to its Internet service. Wireless terminals provide access at the Bank of Telluride and the Steaming Bean Cafe to a community of tourists, transient workers, and hard-core locals. In South Africa, the Community Information Delivery System (CiDS) is being tested in a Metropolitan Area Network (MAN) that covers fairly large geographical areas, typically 15 kilometers in diameter. Wireless connections like these allow information service to be delivered to sites where wiring is impractical, difficult, or simply unavailable.

Yet another twist on metropolitan networking is packaged under the interesting name of "wireless cable." Cable TV began when rural areas found that they were being left out of the television era; the expensive antennas needed to receive very weak signals could be "shared" under the sponsorship of a small company. As more and more of the TV networks began to deliver their materials via satellite broadcast, the cable companies found that they could receive better signals and more channels by installing big dishes. Soon cable companies began to install cables almost right under the town's TV broadcasting station. Eventually, cable companies found that they could make more money rewiring cities than wiring farms, and rural communities found themselves again being left out. This time, however, microwave technology had come down in price and a small entrepreneur could use it to rebroadcast TV without having to lay cable. Since the new signals are in the microwave area and not in the standard TV channels, wireless cable was able to secure a new niche.

Direct Radio

In today's world, people move and the technology stays fixed. That is the model for desktop wiring, for the cellular telephone system, and for our geostationary satellite broadcasts. Need this be the case?

The low Earth-orbiting satellite approach says no. Satellite communications systems often form the backbone of networks—TV networks are satellite based, international telephony is still satellite based, and even the most popular paging service by far, SkyTel, is satellite based. The network of uplinks and downlinks as well as the launching cost of the satellite itself forms a substantial cost component of ordinary communications.

It's possible to build a communication system in which a large number of small, nearby, and low-powered satellites pick up and route signals sent by hand-held transceivers. The satellites themselves would be cheaper to manufacture and launch, and a significant part of the ground-based support system would be eliminated (perhaps the only part to be left on Earth would be the billing system).

Two low Earth-orbiting satellite systems have been proposed. The first is Iridium, a project headed up by Motorola. Originally, Iridium was to consist of 77 satellites, thus deriving its name from the element that had 77 electrons orbiting the nucleus. Scheduled to begin operating in 1998, Iridium will support a variety of personal communications services—voice, data, facsimile and paging messages—to anyone from anywhere on Earth via hand-held wireless telephones and pagers. Three years later, the Teledesic system will become available. Teledesic, headed by Bill Gates from Microsoft and Craig McCaw (McCaw Cellular Communications), will be a similar system consisting of 840 orbiting satellites. Both proposals would work by grabbing signals from Earth, passing them between satellites, and then beaming them back to the intended recipient, signaling an interesting challenge to the wired, wired, world.

What Next?

Where is all of this going? What is the networking environment going to look like in ten years?

It's hard to say. Consider the case in the mid-'80s. There were a variety of network wiring technologies around. There was Arcnet that ran over community antenna (CA) TV cable, there was broadband networking that ran over coaxial cable, there was Corvusnet that ran over telephone wire, there was Ethernet that ran over special Ethernet cables that were as thick as a thumb, there was Token Ring that had its special cable, and there was a brand new technology called Thinnet—Ethernet that ran over a different form of cable.

All of these technologies more or less bounced against each other until the early '90s. Then, almost out of nowhere, came a new technology. "Twisted pair" looked like telephone wire, ran as fast as Ethernet (identically, in fact), and was very easy to work with. Voila! A nonstandard that became standard.

In the meantime, the technology that everyone expected to be the future sine qua non, fiber optics, has not quite done it—at least not the way people expected it to be done. Fiber has succeeded and has almost totally replaced the telephone infrastructure in the U.S. without much more than a peep. (Or the sound of a dropping pin.)

Flipping the years around and looking into the next decade is daunting. George Gilder (see the bibliography) grows excited about the mind-boggling technological possibilities. Nicholas Negroponte has a somewhat more-sobering approach—the essence of all of our efforts is intelligence. If we proceed with digital technologies, then the digital part is more important than the technologies part. Once we have digital information, then we can build digital intelligence. Otherwise, we just have to wait until we get it.

Wireless Glossary

GSM   Global Standard for Mobility forms the basis of several second-generation international cellular systems.

CDMA   Code Division Multiple Access is a system for managing the spectrum among a large number of users by digitally encoding information so that the sender and receiver can operate as if they had a clear channel; incorrectly coded signals are ignored.

CDPD   Cellular Digit Packet Data is designed to send computer data over a cellular network and is especially suitable for short bursts of data such as pager messages, e-mail, and some database applications.

ISM   Industry, Science, and Medicine applications operate in specially allocated regions of the radio spectrum. These applications generally operate at low power without license.

PCS   Personal Communications Service is a generic term used to include voice, data, facsimile, and paging messages.

TDMA   Time Division Multiple Access divides a communication channel into time slots, with individual users getting one of several available slots.

Bibliography

Davis, Peter T., and McGuffin, Craig R. (1994). *Wireless Local Area Networks Technology, Issues, and Strategies*. New York: McGraw-Hill.

Gates, Bill. (1995). *The Road Ahead*. New York: Viking.

Gilder, George. *Telecosm*. (forthcoming).
Seventeen chapters have been serialized as part of the *Forbes Magazine* ASAP series and are also available at the Official George Gilder Web Site at *http://www.discovery.org/ggindex.html*

Muller, Nathan J. (1994). *Wireless Data Networking*. Boston: Artech House.

Negroponte, Nicholas. (1995). *Being Digital*. New York: Knopf.

Nemzow, Martin. (1995). *Implementing Wireless Networks*. New York: McGraw-Hill.

Weiser, Mark. (1991, September). "The Computer for the 21st Century." *Scientific American,* 94–110. Available: *http://www.ubiq.com/hypertext/weiser/SciAmDraft3.html*

Additional Resources

The World Wide Web teems with sites related to wireless networking projects, taking on the characteristics of an infoswamp.

alt.2600
The alt.2600 FAQ (Frequently Asked Questions) is a fine starting point for understanding the nitty-gritty of computing and communication. The FAQ was recently found at *http://www.pe.net/~rthomas/hack/2600faq.html;* the newsgroup itself is at alt.2600.

Communications Week Interactive
The online version of a weekly trade newspaper is available: *http://techweb.cmp.com/techweb/cwk/current/*

Federal Communication Commission. Available: *http://www.fcc.gov/*

Metricom, a manufacturer of wireless LAN and MAN (Metropolitan Area Network) components. Available: *http://www.metricom.com/*

Mobilis: The Mobile Computing Lifestyle Magazine. Available: *http://www.volksware.com/mobilis/*

Motorola, a manufacture of pocket pagers and cellular telephones. Available: *http://www.mot.com/*

Solectek, a manufacturer of Airlan wireless LAN components. Available: *http://www.solectek.com/*

TAL, a manufacturer of wireless LAN and MAN components. Available: *http://www.tetherless.com/*

Wireless Policy Net. Available: *http://www.policy.net/wireless*

3

Read Your Mail!

COLLEAGUES IN CYBERSPACE

A GUIDE TO USING MAILING LISTS

Ann Thornton

Ann Thornton is electronic training coordinator of the Science, Industry and Business Library of the New York Public Library. She is co-maintainer of *Library-Oriented Lists and Electronic Serials*. She can be reached as *ATHORNTON@NYPL.ORG*.

Ever had a reference question you just couldn't answer?

> What is the average number of police officers per thousand population in U.S. metropolitan areas?
> What's Singapore's national fruit?

Try posting such difficult reference queries to STUMPERS-L, one of the electronic mailing lists of interest to librarians. Reference librarians from all over the world post numerous questions to the STUMPERS-L list each day and help other online colleagues with their challenging questions. This list is just one example of the many thousands of mailing lists available on the Internet.

Of all the different types of resources the Internet has to offer, electronic mailing lists are one of the most popular and easiest to use. In simplest terms, they allow a group of people who share an interest to exchange messages with each other. Mailing lists were developed to give e-mail users the ability to send mail to a single address and have it forwarded to everyone else on the list. There are lists for virtually every subject you could imagine, from professional topics to personal interests. Best of all, anyone with an Internet mailing address can participate in lists.

While participating in lists can be rewarding and even fun, it can be confusing for the beginner. This chapter will give you a basic introduction to the different types of lists, tell you how to find them, and explore the different problems you may encounter in your use of them.

Types of Lists

Lists are either open for general subscription or closed, available to a select group of members. Private organizations often restrict list membership to approved persons within the organization. Lists that are open for general subscription are available to anyone with an e-mail address. There are two major types of lists: discussion and distribution.

Discussion Lists

E-mail discussion groups are a popular type of list. The basic purpose of discussion groups is to bring together people with common interests to share ideas and opinions, ask questions, and offer solutions. Discussion lists can be either moderated or unmoderated.

Moderated Lists. A volunteer for a moderated list reviews each posting submitted to the list and decides whether or not it is relevant to the subject of the list. If the posting is relevant, it will be sent to every list member. If a posting is determined to be inappropriate for the list, it may simply be discarded, or the person who sent the message may receive a message from a moderator that explains that the posting was not relevant and was not included.

Unmoderated Lists. Most lists fit into the unmoderated category. Messages are automatically sent to all the members of the list. Unmoderated discussion lists rely upon peer pressure to keep postings on topic and in line.

While moderated lists require much more effort on the part of the list owner and volunteers, they are generally much more useful than unmoderated lists. When messages are automatically forwarded to everyone on an unmoderated list, it is possible for list subscribers to receive many useless messages, including subscription requests and replies mistakenly directed to the list rather than to an individual.

Distribution Lists

An e-mail distribution list is a moderated list that distributes information or broadcasts announcements to its members. Discussion is not permitted on distribution lists.

Digests

A list in digest form involves a computer process that collects all submissions into a single message and sends it out periodically. This can be quite useful for lists that have many postings. The types of discussion and distribution lists mentioned above can be available in regular and digest format.

How to Find Mailing Lists

There are many "lists of lists" on the Internet that you can peruse. Following are some compilations of mailing lists that are of interest to librarians and information professionals.

The Directory of Electronic Journals, Newsletters, and Academic Discussion Lists is compiled by Drew Mogge and the Association of Research Libraries directory staff and Diane K. Kovacs and the directory team. It is available in print as an annual serial from ARL. Contact *pubs@cni.org* for information. Currently in its sixth edition, the directory contains a listing of discussion lists related to library and information science.

Diane Kovacs of Kovacs Consulting and the directory team have made the *Directory of Scholarly and Professional Electronic Conferences* available on the Internet for six years. The ARL print edition includes this directory. The official 1996/97 edition is available at *http://www.n2h2.com/KOVACS*. The site is searchable by keywords and phrases. To obtain a copy of the file, send the following message to *listserv@kent.edu: get acadlist library*.

Library-Oriented Lists and Electronic Serials is a publication of the University of Houston Libraries compiled by Steve Bonario and Ann Thornton. It provides brief information for more than 250 lists and electronic serials that are open for general subscription. Readers can use the subject index, which includes subsections such as library administration and management, interlibrary loan, and library automation and technology. The document is available at *http://info.lib.uh.edu/liblists/home.htm*.

How to Subscribe

When you find a mailing list to which you would like to subscribe, read the address carefully. Most mailing lists have separate addresses to distinguish between submissions to the list and administrative requests to the list. This is so that members of the list are not burdened with an endless stream of "subscribe" messages and so that the subscription process can be automated. In fact, the receipt of administrative request messages is often offensive to list members who sometimes have little tolerance for *newbies,* the nickname for new list members.

The convention is that the submission address actually begins with the list name; in contrast, the administrative address usually begins with the name of the software used to run and manage the list. For example, the popular PACS-L list at the University of Houston has a submission address that is *PACS-L@uhupvm1.uh.edu*. Its administrative address, to which all requests are sent, is *LISTSERV@uhupvm1.uh.edu*. The PACS-L list uses the listserv software, and it is to its listserv address that all subscription and other requests should be sent.

If the administrative address for a list contains the word *LISTSERV, LIST-PROC, MAILSERV, MAILBASE,* or *MAJORDOMO,* the list is most likely automated. With most such programs, the convention for subscribing to the list is to send a message to *software@host,* where "software" is the software type for that list (e.g., *LISTSERV)* and "host" is the Internet address for the machine on which the software resides.

Leave the subject of the message blank, and do not send a copy of the message to yourself or to anyone else. Also, if you normally use a signature file when sending e-mail, turn off that feature or simply do not include the signature file.

In the body of the message type the following:

subscribe mailinglistname YourFirstName YourLastName

For example, to subscribe to the PACS-L list, address the message to

LISTSERV@UHUPVM1.UH.EDU

In the body of the message type

subscribe PACS-L Ann Thornton

For more information on the commands used for the various kinds of list software, check Jim Milles' comprehensive guide to essential mailing list commands. It can be browsed on the World Wide Web at *http://lawlib.slu.edu/training/mailser.htm.* The most recently updated, plain-text version of his publication is available via e-mail. Send the following message to LISTSERV@UBVM.CC.BUFFALO.EDU: GET MAILSER CMD NETTRAIN F=MAIL.

Most mailing lists are automated, but some are managed manually without special software to handle commands. Your subscription message to such a list is read by a human being who updates the list's files to place people on and take them off the list. For such a list, you may be required to send a subscription request to a person's e-mail address. Provide the person with the name of the list to which you would like to be added as a member and give your full name. While you will receive personal service, the person who maintains the list may not be able to service your request for a while (often because of the demands of a real job). Be patient.

When you subscribe to a list, manual or automated, you will usually receive some sort of confirmation and welcome message. Often, this message will contain useful information regarding the list's subject and instructions for posting, unsubscribing, and other functions. It may also provide contact information in case of technical problems. Save this message! You will need to refer to it periodically.

So Many Messages!

If you subscribe to a very busy list or to several lists and do not regularly clear out your e-mail box, the number of mail messages you receive could exceed your system's limitations and could result in lost mail messages.

When you know that you will be unable to check your mail for a few days in a row, find out if your list can be set to "no mail" while you are out. Check the welcome message you received when you subscribed. Many automated lists can employ this handy feature. It allows list members to temporarily stop mail without having to unsubscribe from the list. If you do not have this option or do not use it when it is available to you, you may be surprised at the large number of messages that will quickly fill your e-mail box while you are unable to check them.

If you will be unable to access your e-mail for an extended period of time, consider temporarily unsubscribing from your mailing lists. You would probably not be able to read all of the numerous messages you would get while you are away, so the messages would just tie up your e-mail resources and would be an annoyance upon your return.

If you are concerned about the number and frequency of messages from a single list, you may want to find out if the list is available in digest format. Again, check your welcome message for this information.

Posting to Lists: A Brief Lesson in Netiquette

Before you begin posting messages to lists, you need to understand the basic principles of *netiquette,* the unwritten laws of ethics and etiquette for cyberspace. Netiquette is basically a matter of using common sense and knowing how to avoid conflict with other Internet users. With regard to mailing lists, you need to be considerate of other subscribers. Here are a few tips.

Remember that the address you use to send subscription and other requests to a list is different from the address you use to post messages to the list itself. List members may become angry if you send subscription, unsubscription, or other such requests to the submission or posting address.

Lurking on the list before posting for a while is a good idea. In this context, *lurking* means simply reading many posted messages prior to actually participating. Everyone is a newbie when they first join, and while there is no such thing as a dumb question, you will probably want to get a better grasp of the current topics before posting a query. Check the welcome message you received when you first subscribed to the list to find out if there is a Frequently Asked Questions (FAQ) listing that you can browse. This will prevent you from the embarrassment of posting a question that has been asked and answered numerous times on the list.

Always look at the header of a message before replying to it. Determine whether it is appropriate to reply to the whole list or just to the person who posted the message to which you are replying. Be careful to note the "Reply-To:" line in the header of the original post if there is one, and check the "To:" line in the header of your reply before sending it.

When responding to a message posted by another member, if you include a copy of the original message, trim it down to the most relevant portions.

Always include a subject for your posting so that list members will have some idea of what your message is about before they decide whether or not to read it. When responding to someone else's original posting, use the existing subject.

Say what you mean and proofread your posting before you send it.

Consider whether or not your posting could be misinterpreted. It is important to keep in mind that sarcasm and other subtleties of communication that are easy to translate in face-to-face discussions do not translate as well in ASCII text.

Take care if you choose to participate in debates over the most obviously controversial topics.

Many have found out the advantage of advertising and announcing events, services, programs, and other items of interest on mailing lists. It is easy to do and virtually free of cost. While this has become a somewhat accepted and popular practice, be careful when selecting lists on which to post your advertisements or announcements. Make sure that the lists you choose have subjects that relate to your posting. Also be careful not to post to a large number of lists, a practice known as "spamming." Many Internet users are sensitive about the ever-growing commerciality of the Internet and become angry when seeing numerous advertisements on lists. If you do send your announcement to more than one list, be sure to include something similar to the following statement at the beginning of your announcement: "This message has been cross-posted; please forgive any duplication."

If you fail to follow these suggestions, you may be *flamed,* the term for being the subject of harsh e-mail. Such a personal attack could occur either to your personal e-mail account only or to the discussion list for all other list members to see.

Tips for Being a Conscientious List Subscriber

Warning: lists can be time wasters. Do not subscribe to more lists than you can handle realistically; start out with one or two lists and see how well you manage their flow of mail messages. Remember why you subscribed in the first place? You were looking for a list that would give you ideas and possible solutions to help you in your work. Do not get so distracted reading and posting to a list that you fail to follow through on job responsibilities.

While corresponding with colleagues via discussion lists can be professionally rewarding and can enhance reference service, patron confidentiality needs to be considered. Employing other specialists' knowledge is valuable in answering patron queries, but when questions are posted to a list, even if patron names are not mentioned, the slightest hints can indicate to insiders who is asking the questions. A good tip is to make the queries as anonymous as possible. Remove as many clues as you can before posting, and never include a patron's name or mention his or her organization.

Use your best judgment. Above all, enjoy the rewards of being a responsible list member: having virtual colleagues all over the world with whom you can share ideas, problems, and possible solutions.

So You'd Like to Start a List? A Few Suggestions

If you are thinking about starting a list on a particular topic, first check as many "lists of lists" as you can to make sure that a list with your topic does not already exist. Make a note of any lists that are close to your topic, and then send postings to those lists to ask their members if they are aware if a list with your topic exists. Also, post the question to the NEW-LIST list at NEW-LIST@VM1.NODAK.EDU. If you find out that there is already a list on your topic, you will not want to duplicate it by starting one of your own. You can also use the postings to the lists with similar topics to poll interest for your topic and potential list. Save your responses from interested persons; they are your potential subscribers.

If your search and postings do not uncover an existing list on your topic, you will need to consider the time commitment involved in becoming a list manager. To manage a list you will need to find a networked computer that can host your discussion group. You will want to contact your organization's systems or computer services division administrator to find out if one of your organization's servers can host your list.

You may want to begin your list by handling all subscription requests yourself. Your system administrator will need to set up two new mailboxes. One will be an alias for the list of your subscribers' e-mail addresses. All messages sent to this mail account, which should contain the name of the list in the address, will automatically be distributed to all subscribers on the list. The other will be for administrative requests (to subscribe and unsubscribe) and will point to your e-mail address. You will need to take care of the administrative requests when you receive them. If you do not want to handle messages and subscriptions, your system administrator may be able to provide you with recommendations of software that you may use to automate your list.

If you want to moderate your list, you will need to review all posted messages before they are distributed to subscribers. In this case, the first new mailbox will need to be aliased only to your personal e-mail address rather than to a list of all your subscribers' addresses. You will need to maintain a separate list of all your subscribers' addresses that will be aliased to a third e-mail address. Then you can send the messages you approve for distribution to this e-mail address.

Once you have worked out the details of how your subscriptions and message distributions will be handled, you will want to announce that your list exists. Send a message to the NEW-LIST list at

NEW-LIST@VM1.NODAK.EDU and to other lists with similar subjects. Also, contact the maintainers of the different "lists of lists" so that your list will be added to their compilations.

For More Information on Using Mailing Lists

Crumlish, Christian. (1995). *A Guided Tour of the Internet*. San Francisco: SYBEX.

Milles, James. (1996). *Discussion Lists: Mail List Manager Commands*. [Online]. Available: *http://lawlib.slu.edu/training/mailser.htm*

O'Donnell, James R., Jr. (1995). "Using Internet Mailing Lists." In Mary Ann Pike (Ed.), *Using the Internet* (2nd ed., 359–81). Indianapolis: Que.

Paxton, Phillip. (1994). "Joining In on Discussions: Using Listservs and Mailing Lists." In Phillip Baczewski (Ed.), *The Internet Unleashed* (319–41). Indianapolis: Sams.

Shirky, Clay. (1994). *The Internet by E-Mail*. Emeryville, CA: Ziff-Davis.

For More Information on Starting a Mailing List

Kovacs, Diane, and Kovacs, Michael. (1994). "Creating and Maintaining Listserv Mailing Lists and Electronic Journals." In *The Internet Unleashed* (343–66). Indianapolis: Sams.

Robison, David F. W. (1994). *The Internet Passport: NorthWestNet's Guide to Our World Online* (5th ed.). Englewood Cliffs, NJ: Prentice-Hall.

References

Crumlish, Christian. (1995). *A Guided Tour of the Internet*. San Francisco: SYBEX.

Tennant, Roy. (1994). *Crossing the Internet Threshold* (2nd ed.). Berkeley, CA: Library Solutions.

USENET AND THE LIBRARY

Larry Gainor and Erin Foster

Larry Gainor can be reached as *LGAINOR@TEXAS.NET.* He is the assistant branch librarian at the Carver branch of the San Antonio Public Library. Erin Foster *(ERIN_FOSTER@BBDO.COM)* is office manager of the Information Resource Center at BBDO New York Advertising.

Originally appeared in (1993, Fall) *RSR: Reference Services Review,* 7–22. Copyright held by Larry Gainor and Erin Foster.

Editor's note: Some illustrations and references to them are not included. One statement and footnote was updated to include current references.

Network resources have become widely used by libraries in recent years. More than ever before, librarians are expected to become familiar with such tools as electronic mail, file transfer protocol (FTP), and Internet-accessible online catalogs. Many online professionals consider Usenet to be the world's largest computer network and an essential resource to academics, yet it has received little attention from the library community. This article will provide a brief description of Usenet and discuss how it may be applied to library settings.

What Is Usenet?

Usenet is a computer-mediated conferencing system. It began in 1979 as a network for users of UNIX systems at Duke University and the University of North Carolina at Chapel Hill.[1] In the beginning, Usenet was propagated through UUCP (UNIX-to-UNIX Copy [Program]) computers over long distance telephone lines and thus was available only on UNIX machines.[2]

More recently, however, Usenet has been transmitted over a number of different networks and to non-UNIX as well as UNIX machines. Originally intended as a forum for discussion of technical issues, today social and recreational messages or articles constitute the bulk of Usenet traffic. By 1991, Usenet had an estimated one and a half million readers in 37,000 organizations, both public and private. The number of participants continues to grow.[3] Reflecting this trend, the number of news groups (discussion groups) has multiplied from an initial three to a 1992 figure of over two thousand.[4,5]

Usenet has no administrative structure. In order to become a Usenet site, an institution must find someone who is already on Usenet who is willing to provide the news feed (i.e., the continuing stream of articles). In addition, a full news feed requires a computer with sufficient disk space to store the news programs and articles (approximately 400Mb per month). Each site pays its own telecommunication charges.[6]

The articles on Usenet are posted to a "news group" selected by the author according to the article's topic. News group topics range from daytime television gossip to data-compression algorithms and Turkish culture. The news groups are divided into broad subject classifications such as "comp," which is limited to topics concerning computing, and "talk," which includes groups that discuss such controversial issues as abortion and gun control. Site administrators (the individuals in charge of the mainframe computers at particular institutions) select which groups will be available at their particular locations.[7] Thus, an administrator at a corporate site may not wish to allot disk space to groups in the "talk" hierarchy but may prefer to limit the news feed to scientific and technical news groups. This local autonomy is typical of Usenet's decentralized structure.

Major News Group Categories

alt	"alternative" group
bit	listserv gatewayed to Usenet
comp	computer-related topic
misc	group that does not fit into one of the other major categories
news	group for discussion of Usenet and its administration
rec	recreation-related group
sci	science-related group
soc	group for socializing and discussion of social issues
talk	controversial topics producing vociferous argument and strong feeling

Becoming a Usenet User

Many academic and corporate librarians will find that Usenet is available through their employers. If an organization is not connected to Usenet, organization members may be able to gain access through a public access system such as the WELL in San Francisco.[8]

Systems and access points vary; specific instructions may be obtained from the institution's computer center. Once an account with Usenet access is created, the user needs to become oriented to his or her system's news-reading program. In general, it is a good idea to work with someone who is familiar with the system at first, since many news readers are confusing to novices and documentation may be hard to find.[9]

Many Usenet beginners find it helpful to read some of the introductory articles in the group *news.announce.newusers*. Particularly useful articles are "A Primer on How to Work with the Usenet Community," "Emily Post-news Answers Your Questions on Netiquette," "Hints on Writing Style for Usenet," "Rules for Posting to Usenet," and "Answers to Frequently Asked Questions." These articles provide background information to help beginners understand how Usenet operates.

Librarians and Usenet

Librarians can take advantage of Usenet for both social and technical purposes.[10] Indeed, use of Usenet has been associated with "relationships, marriages, conventions, lost friendships, software packages, papers, and books."[11] Specific news groups recommended for their value to librarians include listserv lists such as *bit.listserv.libref-l* and *bit.listserv.govdocs-l*, which discuss library reference and government documents librarianship, as well as *soc.libraries.talk*, which provides an avenue for socializing and discussion of issues that do not neatly fit into the scope of other library-oriented groups. Also helpful are computer-related groups that are relevant to librarians, such as *alt.cd-rom* and *bit.listserv.cd-romlan*.[12]

Usenet Groups of Interest to Librarians

alt.books.reviews—An unmoderated news group to which participants may post book reviews. Requests for reviews of new books are also encouraged.

alt.online-service—Covers commercial Internet access providers and commercial network services such as CompuServe and Prodigy.

alt.zines—Sample issues of small, noncommercial magazines are posted.

comp.infosystems.gopher, comp.infosystems.wais, and *comp.infosystems. www*—These groups provide discussion and support for the Gopher, WAIS [Wide Area Information Server], and WWW [World Wide Web] information servers.

comp.internet.library—A moderated news group that discusses Internet-accessible libraries. Used by many nonlibrarians to inquire about availability of various library resources on the Internet. The first library-oriented Usenet group.

comp.society—Moderated discussion of the effects of computer technology on society.

rec.arts.books—High-volume (50,000+ readers) group that discusses books and book-related topics (e.g., bookstores). This group is useful for tracking down titles of books when the bibliographic information is lacking and all that is known is the plot or a character's name. Frequently used to solicit recommendations of books with a particular theme or feature.

soc.libraries.talk—The only unmoderated library-oriented forum. Addresses all issues relevant to libraries and librarianship including those that do not easily fit into the scope of more narrowly focused library related listservs and news groups.

In addition to its use as a forum for discussion of librarianship and library technology, Usenet may also be used to access information in other fields that may be difficult to find. For example, a colleague was looking for negative reviews or criticism of Sylvia Plath's work. Apart from *Magazine Index* (which includes few scholarly journals), most DIALOG databases do not allow the searcher to retrieve material according to the critic's attitude toward the text. A simple request to the *rec.arts.books* news group elicited six relevant citations (over a period of a few days) that would have otherwise been very difficult to retrieve.

Usenet can also be used for collection development, particularly if it involves a topic that has a strong following on the Net. In response to an article posted requesting book suggestions in cognitive science (a relatively new field, for which there are few reference sources), an unpublished fifty-page bibliography was sent. The author was still working on it but had circulated a few copies to interested parties.

Librarians may also wish to promote libraries on Usenet. For example, an article appeared in *rec.arts.books* in which the author (in response to another article mentioning the American Library Association's "Your Right To Know" campaign) expressed surprise that libraries received federal support and suggested that such support might not be in the public interest. Respondents from the library community can counter this perception.

Usenet may also be used as a medium for recruiting new members to the profession. Occasionally, requests for information about library and information science graduate programs are seen on the *soc.college* and *soc.college.grad* groups. Schools of Library and Information Science would do well to make themselves more visible to the popularity of Usenet with college students. Happily, some schools have already begun to take advantage of this opportunity. The University of Pittsburgh's Information Science program has been promoted on the *soc.college.gradinfo* group, as have several others.

On a more speculative note, the possibility of collecting Usenet threads as material for a "vertical file" may prove useful. For example, during the 1991 coup in the Soviet Union, Usenet news was one of the most-current sources of information on Soviet conditions. In another example, an incident occurred later that year in Iowa in which a graduate physics student from China shot some of his professors and a fellow student. The discussion of this situation in the *soc.culture.china* group was in many ways more illuminating than the coverage in the mass media. It included articles written by people who knew the participants as well as a different perspective on the Chinese educational system. Faculty and students in such areas as sociology, political science, and communications might be interested in this type of material.

Integrating Usenet and Other Electronic Conferences

In addition to the thousands of Usenet news groups, there are an even larger number of electronic mailing lists (listservs). Coping with this abundance of information can be daunting without some guidelines as to the nature and purpose of these different types of conferences. Moderation status, scope, and number of subscribers are three factors with regard to which listservs and news groups differ.

Most listservs are moderated, whereas Usenet news groups are generally unmoderated. As a result, listservs tend to have a higher signal-to-noise ratio but at the cost of a slower response time. Thus, a question posted to a Usenet group may receive an answer before the moderator of a listserv to which the same question has been sent has had an opportunity to see the question—much less send it to the listserv's subscribers.

Listservs tend to have a narrower scope than Usenet groups; indeed moderators spend much of their time ensuring that the discussion remains properly focused. Long discussions on a particular topic (known as *threads*) have a tendency to drift off into peripheral areas if the moderator is not careful to ask the participants to "take it to private e-mail" when the articles are no longer relevant to the listserv's focus. Thus, a discussion about government information policy may turn into an argument over the merits of different political parties. Although this type of restriction is generally welcomed by the listserv's subscribers, it can be frustrating to the reader who is interested in the new topic. In Usenet groups, on the other hand, a discussion that drifts into an area included in the group's scope is generally tolerated as long as people continue to respond positively.

A final difference between listservs and Usenet news groups is the number of participants. In general, a Usenet group will have a much larger number of readers than a listserv. Reasons for this disparity include the narrower scope of listservs that will usually appeal to fewer people, as well as the fact that most Internet accounts have a limited amount of space available for receiving listserv messages, thus limiting the number of listservs an individual is likely to join. Finally, it should be mentioned that there are exceptions to the distinctions that have been made here. There are a few unmoderated listservs with broad scopes and a large number of subscribers as well as moderated, narrowly focused Usenet groups that have a relatively small number of readers.

In determining how to use electronic conferences, the differences between conferencing systems should be kept in mind. As a recent Internet handbook points out: "Just within librarianship there are dozens of discussions that range from discussing the automated system of a particular vendor to all computer systems to which patrons have access and beyond. It is easy—perhaps all too easy—to oversubscribe and become inundated with messages that may or may not be germane to the work at hand. Cultivate a keen sense of when a list is productive professionally and when it is not."[13] Because subscription to a listserv entails storage of e-mail messages in a limited amount of disk space, it is important to select a few groups that closely match one's interests for regular perusal. Usenet groups, on the other hand, will prove useful when information is needed on a topic that is outside one's usual area of interest. Thus, a reference librarian may subscribe to LIBREF-L for information peculiar to reference librarianship, but if one needs a list of humorous war novels one may find that *rec.arts.books* will provide responses that are both more timely and more plentiful.

Some sites include gatewayed listservs in their Usenet feed. In addition to saving space in the user's electronic mailbox, this type of access has other advantages: "By initiating a 'readnews' session, you can select the bulletin board of discussion that you wish to read and use the increased functionality that the readnews software affords you. For example, if you read a message that did not interest you, you could delete (or mark as 'read') all messages that subsequently replied to that message. This way you can delete entire discussion 'threads' quickly and easily."[14]

Conclusion

As Libes and Foster observe, the information on Usenet is in many ways different from that found in books and magazines:

> It has many of the characteristics of electronic mail. For example, it is typically informal and opinionated. Much of it is also timely and transient as befits its mode of delivery. Nonetheless, it contains much useful material.[15]

Indeed, many of these differences are likely to prove vexing to librarians. The fact that Usenet articles generally expire after two weeks (unless posted to an archived news group) may not be comforting to the librarian accustomed to working with permanent media. Moreover, new users of Usenet should prepare themselves for the vituperation that often accompanies discussion on certain news groups.

Despite the impermanence, the invective, and the generally chaotic nature of Usenet, it is also a source of information that can be found nowhere else. Whether looking for information on the synthesis of fluoresceinesters that have not been indexed by Beilstein yet or a list of rock and roll lyrics with science fiction themes, librarians will find that Usenet provides a source of expertise that is unequaled elsewhere.

Notes

1. John S. Quarterman, *The Matrix* (New York: Digital Press, 1990), 243.

2. Brendan P. Kehoe, *Zen and the Art of the Internet*. Revised FTP edition (February 1992), 16.

3. Lee Sproull and Sara Kiesler, "Computers, Networks and Work," *Scientific American* 265, no. 3 (September 1991): 116–24.

4. Quarterman, 248.

5. Gord Nickerson, "Networked Resources," *Computers in Libraries* 12, no. 4 (April 1992): 31.

6. Jonathan I. Kamens (*JIK@ATHENA.MIT.EDU*), "How to Become a USENET Site," Usenet article (*news.announce.newusers*) (21 April 1992).

7. Quarterman, 246.

8. *Editor's note:* The following site lists Usenet news groups and provides a thorough introduction to Usenet—*Phoenix DataNet—Explore—Newsgroups*. [Online]. Available: *http://www.phoenix.net/pdn/explore/newsgroups.html*

   The following sites give links to public access Usenet feeds.

   Positron—USENET News Readers. [Online]. Available: *http://positron.qc.ca/html/USENET.html*

   UseNet News (Information and Public Access). [Online]. Available: *http://pegasus.uthct.edu/OtherUsefulSites/UseNet.html*

9. Several news readers are discussed in Grace Todino and Dale Dougherty, *Using UUCP and Usenet* (Sebastopol, CA: O'Reilly and Associates, 1991); Anatole Olczak, *The Netnews Reference Manual,* 2nd ed. (San Jose, CA: ASP, 1989); and "Usenet," in *Directory of Computer Conferencing in Libraries,* ed. by Brian Williams (Westport, CT: Meckler, 1992).

10. Quarterman, 242.

11. Quarterman, 243.

12. Gord Nickerson, "Networked Resources," *Computers in Libraries* 12, no. 5 (May 1992): 39. See also Gord Nickerson, "Networked Resources," *Computers in Libraries* 12, no. 6 (June 1992): 51–4 for a guide to retrieval of software from Usenet.

13. Roy Tennant, John Ober, and Anne G. Lipow, *Crossing the Internet Threshold: An Instructional Handbook* (San Carlos, CA: Library Solutions Press, 1993), 52.

14. Tennant, et al., 53.

15. Don Libes and Sandy Foster, *Life with UNIX: A Guide for Everyone* (Englewood Cliffs, NJ: Prentice-Hall, 1989).

URBAN LEGENDS AND HOAXES ON THE INTERNET

There are a number of references that recur in discussion lists whenever some poor sucker encounters them somewhere for the first time. They can give you a lesson in not passing something on that you have not checked out, but if you want to avoid learning that lesson painfully, avoid the topics listed below. What will happen if you don't? You will waste bandwidth, waste people's time, and probably call down a firestorm of vituperation on yourself.

Some of them are actually Internet related. One of the major ones is the "Good Times" virus hoax, where you are warned to look out for e-mail messages with the subject line "Good Times" since this will spread a virus that wipes your hard drive. This is completely false. Another persistent story is that the Federal Communications Commission (FCC) is trying to pass a modem tax; this attempt was actually apparently made almost ten years ago, but it is not happening now!

An annoying perennial hoax is the one about Craig Shergold, who has been dying for years now and purportedly needs postcards from you. This bore some resemblance to truth at one time, *but is no longer anything you should act on.* Another story I've seen recur countless times is one about a cookie recipe from Mrs. Fields or Nieman Marcus; the nature of the story is such that it asks you to pass this recipe on—don't do it!

One of the more recent gags perpetrated on the Net was the request to shut down the Internet on February 29, so it could be cleaned *(http:// www.lib.berkeley.edu/Web4Lib/archive/9602/0269.html).* Perhaps whoever started this thought it could not possibly be taken seriously, but it's a big, wide Internet world out there, folks, with a large variety of people. Some of them took it seriously enough to forward it to lists, asking if it was true. At least this one should not show up again for four years!

Sources of More Information

Crispen, Patrick. (1994). *Spamming and Urban Legends.* [Online]. Available: *http://www.users.interport.net/~ednorman/map09.html*
   Talks in depth about spamming, the "make money fast" message, and the Craig Shergold situation.

Bern, Jochen. (1995, May). *About the "Good Times" Hoax.* [Online]. Available: *http://www.informatik.uni-trier.de/~bern/GoodTimes-Hoax/*
    Includes a list of frequently asked questions about the Good Times hoax, with a lot of background.

The Brain Tumor Boy, the Modem Tax, and the Chain Letter. [Online]. (1994, March). Available: *http://www.jyu.fi/~kallio/atk/verkko/BDGI/4.4.txt*
    The title says it all.

Burr, Simon. *What Are Some Other Hoaxes and Urban Legends on the Internet?* [Online]. Available: *http://www.tcp.co.uk/tcp/good-times/otherhoax.html*
    Discusses the Craig Shergold story, the Good Times hoax, and the FCC modem-tax alert. Includes link to a list of frequently asked questions on urban legends.

Hammer, Mike. *Mike's List of Urban Legends.* [Online]. Available: *http://hammer.arts.cornell.edu/urbanleg.html*
    Brief, but contains a description of the cookie hoax.

Hymes, Charles. *Don't Spread that Hoax!* [Online]. Available: *http://www.crew.umich.edu/~chymes/newusers/Think.html*
    Very useful in that it gives you guidelines for avoiding spreading false messages. Mentions a few of the more prominent hoaxes and includes some links to information about Good Times.

Rosenberger, Robert. (1996, May). *Computer Virus Myths Home Page.* [Online]. Available: *http://ourworld.compuserve.com/homepages/virus_myths/*
    Very good page, with information about several computer-related urban legends. Also debunks many myths about viruses, and links to many other sites. Discusses "false authority" syndrome, and warns you to check him out!

Wave Reviews—Urban Legends. [Online]. Available: *http://maui.netwave.net/wave_reviews/feature10.html*
    This is a great collection of annotated links about urban legends. Goes beyond just Internet urban legends.

To keep up with new sites and find other current ones, look on Yahoo at *http://www.yahoo.com/Society_and_Culture/Folklore/Urban_Legends/.*

Know Your Rights

Access to Electronic Information, Services, and Networks

An Interpretation of the Library Bill of Rights

Editor's note:
The following document was adopted by ALA Council on January 24, 1996.

Introduction

The world is in the midst of an electronic communications revolution. Based on its constitutional, ethical, and historical heritage, American librarianship is uniquely positioned to address the broad range of information issues being raised in this revolution. In particular, librarians address intellectual freedom from a strong ethical base and an abiding commitment to the preservation of the individual's rights.

Freedom of expression is an inalienable human right and the foundation for self-government. Freedom of expression encompasses the freedom of speech and the corollary right to receive information. These rights extend to minors as well as adults. Libraries and librarians exist to facilitate the exercise of these rights by selecting, producing, providing access to, identifying, retrieving, organizing, providing instruction in the use of, and preserving recorded expression regardless of the format or technology.

The American Library Association expresses these basic principles of librarianship in its *Code of Ethics* and in the *Library Bill of Rights* and its Interpretations. These serve to guide librarians and library governing bodies in addressing issues of intellectual freedom that arise when the library provides access to electronic information, services, and networks.

Issues arising from the still-developing technology of computer-mediated information generation, distribution, and retrieval need to be approached and regularly reviewed from a context of constitutional principles and ALA policies so that fundamental and traditional tenets of librarianship are not swept away.

Electronic information flows across boundaries and barriers despite attempts by individuals, governments, and private entities to channel or control it. Even so, many people, for reasons of technology, infrastructure, or socio-economic status do not have access to electronic information.

In making decisions about how to offer access to electronic information, each library should consider its mission, goals, objectives, cooperative agreements, and the needs of the entire community it serves.

The Rights of Users

All library system and network policies, procedures, or regulations relating to electronic resources and services should be scrutinized for potential violation of user rights.

User policies should be developed according to the policies and guidelines established by the American Library Association, including *Guidelines for the Development and Implementation of Policies, Regulations and Procedures Affecting Access to Library Materials, Services and Facilities.*

Users should not be restricted or denied access for expressing or receiving constitutionally protected speech. Users' access should not be changed without due process, including, but not limited to, formal notice and a means of appeal.

Although electronic systems may include distinct property rights and security concerns, such elements may not be employed as a subterfuge to deny users' access to information. Users have the right to be free of unreasonable limitations or conditions set by libraries, librarians, system administrators, vendors, network service providers, or others. Contracts, agreements, and licenses entered into by libraries on behalf of their users should not violate this right. Users also have a right to information, training, and assistance necessary to operate the hardware and software provided by the library.

Users have both the right of confidentiality and the right of privacy. The library should uphold these rights by policy, procedure, and practice. Users should be advised, however, that because security is technically difficult to achieve, electronic transactions and files could become public.

The rights of users who are minors shall in no way be abridged.[1]

Equity of Access

Electronic information, services, and networks provided directly or indirectly by the library should be equally, readily, and equitably accessible to all library users. American Library Association policies oppose the charging of user fees for the provision of information services by all libraries and information services that receive their major support from public funds (50.3; 53.1.14; 60.1; 61.1). It should be the goal of all libraries to develop policies concerning access to electronic resources in light of *Economic Barriers to Information Access: An Interpretation of the Library Bill of Rights and Guidelines for the Development and Implementation of Policies, Regulations and Procedures Affecting Access to Library Materials, Services and Facilities.*

Information Resources and Access

Providing connections to global information, services, and networks is not the same as selecting and purchasing material for a library collection. Determining the accuracy or authenticity of electronic information may present special problems. Some information accessed electronically may not meet a library's selection or collection development policy. It is, therefore, left to each user to determine what is appropriate. Parents and legal guardians who are concerned about their children's use of electronic resources should provide guidance to their own children.

Libraries and librarians should not deny or limit access to information available via electronic resources because of its allegedly controversial content or because of the librarian's personal beliefs or fear of confrontation. Information retrieved or utilized electronically should be considered constitutionally protected unless determined otherwise by a court with appropriate jurisdiction.

Libraries, acting within their mission and objectives, must support access to information on all subjects that serve the needs or interests of each user, regardless of the user's age or the content of the material. Libraries have an obligation to provide access to government information available in electronic format. Libraries and librarians should not deny access to information solely on the grounds that it is perceived to lack value.

In order to prevent the loss of information, and to preserve the cultural record, libraries may need to expand their selection or collection development policies to ensure preservation, in appropriate formats, of information obtained electronically.

Electronic resources provide unprecedented opportunities to expand the scope of information available to users. Libraries and librarians should provide access to information presenting all points of view. The provision of access does not imply sponsorship or endorsement. These principles pertain to electronic resources no less than they do to the more traditional sources of information in libraries.[2]

Adopted by the ALA Council, January 24, 1996
[ISBN: 8389-7830-4]

Notes

1. See: *Free Access to Libraries for Minors: An Interpretation of the Library Bill of Rights; Access to Resources* and *Services in the School Library Media Program;* and *Access for Children and Young People to Videotapes and Other Nonprint Formats.*

2. See: *Diversity in Collection Development: An Interpretation of the Library Bill of Rights.*

CRIME AND PUNISHMENT IN CYBERSPACE

Sonia Orin Lyris

Sonia Orin Lyris has had published numerous science fiction and fantasy stories as well as nonfiction articles about cyberspace and other topics. She has been a Net denizen for many years and can be found at *http://www.teleport.com/~cos/sol.html*.

Originally appeared in (1992) *Thinking Robots, an Aware Internet and Cyberpunk Librarians*. Copyright held by Sonia Orin Lyris.

Cyberspace is a computer-mediated place where people (or "inhabitants") can meet to exchange information. So any place that people communicate with each other with the aid of computers is a cyberspace. There are plenty of embellishments possible, of course: equipment that adds sensory experience and enhances realism (virtual reality) or that makes it seem that an inhabitant is in another location entirely (telepresence). Today's cyberspaces are primarily text based. Inhabitants "post" to electronic bulletin boards (bbs) or conference groups, send electronic mail to each other (e-mail), and have real-time exchanges via computer chat-lines (e-chat or e-talk).

To outsiders, this sort of computer-based communication may seem little more than a quicker way to send written mail. But it is more than that. In cyberspace, information is the medium of exchange, and an inhabitant's actual physical location is unimportant. So communication actually defines a given cyberspace community. Cyberspace communities have different problems than physical world communities and, as a result, adopt different rules.

Many of these rules are nonetheless based on the physical world's rules and are still under construction. Cyberspace communities are constantly trying to figure out the best ways to support their needs in a world of changing technology and diverse users. System administrators evaluate the practicality of enforcing appropriate guidelines for cyberspace behavior while lawmakers try to determine appropriate laws to protect against crime in the computer age.

But what is a crime in cyberspace? "Crime" covers a multitude of meanings, from the complex laws of our legal system to the complex rules of social interaction. Cyberspace is a world with new rules and old rules and sometimes no rules. It can be a confusing place for a newcomer.

For example, we all know that it is a crime to steal someone else's physical property. But is it a crime to steal someone else's information in cyberspace? The answer depends on the location and type of information. For example, if the information is in a cyberspace inhabitant's private storage area, it may require system-breaking to read, which in most circumstances is a prosecutable crime. But it is not a crime to steal ideas, in or out of cyberspace. Since information in cyberspace is still largely textual, it is protected by existing copyright laws. But copyrights can only protect the presentation of an idea—in this case the actual text—and not the ideas themselves. Inventions can be protected with patents, but patents protect implementations and processes, not general ideas. Besides, a patent must usually be filed before an idea is made public.

So there is a great deal of information that is simply not protectable. In cyberspace, where information is easily and publicly available, taking, using, and even claiming to have created someone else's ideas is simply not a crime.

But most cyberspace inhabitants will not stand for it. In a world where every item of exchange is information or information-based, inhabitants have a healthy respect for those who give information. People in cyberspace share and present information more freely and widely than in any other culture that has ever existed before and usually at little or no benefit to themselves. Cyberspace inhabitants share knowledge and information because it is an essential part of the cyberspace culture to do so.

So while there may be no laws to prevent someone in cyberspace from stealing someone else's ideas, when the theft comes to light, other inhabitants are likely to be unhappy about it. The offender's credibility will suffer significantly. This is likely to limit the offender's ability to get and give information. A good reputation in a cyberspace community can buy the generous effort of thousands of people at a moment's notice. Losing that can be costly.

Even so, there are many cyberspaces, and anonymity and name changes are often easy to come by. Strict monitoring of a cyberspace is impractical or impossible. At the heart of cyberspace "crimes" is misrepresentation. An inhabitant can claim another's idea as their own or can claim to be someone they are not. Scams, chain letters, and pyramid schemes are trivial efforts to launch and mass distribute in cyberspace.

What's an Honest Cyberspace Inhabitant to Do?

Rule 1: Know your neighbors.

Cyberspace is a large community, in which neighborhoods are built—not along lines of location, as they are in the physical world—but along lines of interest. For example, a conference group that discusses software engineering is a neighborhood of inhabitants who are interested in (and probably knowledgeable about) the topic of software engineering. In that neighborhood, over time, inhabitants will come to know each other not only by name but also by the style and content of information that they present to each other. When someone who is well-known and respected says something to their neighbors, their neighbors will listen carefully.

Rule 2: Read critically and cross-reference whenever possible.

Cyberspace is very much like a living library. Books, essays, poems, and fiction are easily available, and the authors are often around if an inhabitant wants to discuss their works with them. But putting words in print does not make them fact, and much of the information available in cyberspace is based primarily on opinion. As with paper libraries, readers must read with care.

Rule 3: Verify the personal identity or reputation of your source when the validity of information is important.

In systems where inhabitants must use their real names or a traceable account number, forcing them to account for their actions is much easier. Those who break rules can be identified, and others can be warned about their behavior. But since many cyberspaces allow some or total anonymity, inhabitants can often present themselves as someone else. Even the Internet, the largest world-wide cyberspace, cannot enforce individual identification. Anyone on the Internet who has appropriate privileges or knowledge can create a new account or forge another name and account on messages. When the content of information is important, inhabitants need to make sure the source is reliable.

Rule 4: Verify the personal identity of your cyberspace neighbors before becoming personally involved with them.

While online, reading up on the latest technical writing conferences, Fred happens across Julia, another technical writer. They exchange e-mail about technical writing and eventually include other personal information about themselves. Over time Fred becomes quite fond of Julia. One day another inhabitant tells Fred that Julia is really Max, and Max has been telling everyone except Fred details of how Fred was taken in. Fred discovers that Max considers the whole thing a hilarious joke. Fred feels humiliated, betrayed, and angry.

This happens repeatedly in many cyberspaces. Far too often, cyberspace inhabitants are credulous, believing everyone to be as honest as they are.

There are a number of approaches to verifying the identity of another cyberspace inhabitant, such as in-person meetings, phone calls, personal references, and so on. Since it is impractical to take the time to try to verify the identify of everyone in a cyberspace, it is a matter of assessing the risk if the other person is not telling the truth—whether the risk is flawed technical information or personal discomfort. Friendship and information exchange are often closely linked in cyberspace neighborhoods, so inhabitants often establish significant personal ties as well as information-based ones.

Rule 5:   *Don't be afraid to apologize publicly if you make a mistake, whether the mistake is technical or personal, big or small.*

After Fred gets over his embarrassment, he posts a recounting of the events for his cyberspace neighbors, including information on the fake Julia and the real Max. Some fellow inhabitants are amused, saying that Fred got what he deserved for taking what Max said at face value, but most inhabitants are irritated. Some send angry letters to Max, and some refuse to talk to him at all. Max didn't realize his actions would cause so many people to be upset. After he sees the reactions of his fellow inhabitants, he begins to regret the whole thing and even considers leaving the system entirely, or finding a way to get a new account and start over under a new name.

Everyone makes mistakes, and cyberspace inhabitants place great store by a willingness to admit them. Public apologies are fairly common in cyberspace, where personal cues are often easy to misinterpret. If Max were to make a public apology to Fred, most people would probably forgive Max.

Rule 6:   *Consider the possible risks and benefits of sharing information, but remember that in all but a few circumstances the benefits outweigh the risks.*

Alice has a great idea for a new kind of cyberspace, but she isn't sure if her idea is really new. She considers posting a summary of the idea to the cyberspace conference to see if anyone else has heard of it before or can offer her advice for what to do next, but she's afraid someone will steal the idea.

It is good that Alice is seriously evaluating the risks of posting her idea to a public cyberspace, but she is probably worrying too much. If she posts publicly, other inhabitants will see that it was her idea, and if someone else should claim the idea later on, she'll have evidence of a prior claim. Unless, of course, the idea isn't original after all, in which case, asking her cyberspace neighbors about it could save her a lot of time and work. In any case, most ideas presented in cyberspace are not stolen. While ideas can indeed change the world, most ideas simply don't. Some of the best ideas the world has seen were ignored for long periods of time.

Impersonation and intellectual property theft are among the most serious of the cyberspace crimes, but they are relatively rare. Most people are not in cyberspace to engage in such activities; they are there because they want the exchange that cyberspace best supports: communication with people who have similar interests in an environment where physical distance is not an obstacle.

Rule 7: *Expect to make mistakes if you are new to a cyberspace, but don't be afraid to ask for help or references from older inhabitants, who are usually glad to be of assistance.*

Susan is new to the cyberspace conference group. She asks the group what their definitions of "cyberspace" are. Twenty people in the group immediately respond, telling her that this is an inappropriate question. They explain that this particular question gets asked every month by some newcomer, and while it is a worthwhile question, it has already been talked to death, and it takes the discussion away from other important topics.

It is easy for the new cyberspace inhabitant to be unaware of the serious problem of information overload. In cyberspace, more information is available than any one person can possibly assimilate. When information exchanges are free and spontaneous, some issues arise often, starting up discussions that repeatedly follow similar paths. In an established cyberspace with many inhabitants, some issues come up so often that older inhabitants become understandably tired of them. In some cyberspace groups, archives or regular postings discuss reoccurring issues for the benefit of the newcomer. On the Internet, this list is posted monthly and is called an "FAQ," which contains answers to "Frequently Asked Questions."

Rule 8: *Remember how easy it is to misinterpret someone's intent in cyberspace. Stay cool, even if you're sure you've been insulted. If you must say something, say it privately.*

In Joe's PC conference group, someone asks for advice on purchasing a computer. Joe posts a reply. Someone else posts a message saying that Joe doesn't know what he's talking about. Joe is irritated and replies to the posting. Before long the discussion has moved from technical discussions to name calling.

Cyberspace makes immediate replies easy, so misunderstandings can quickly blossom into arguments. Because tone of voice cannot easily be conveyed with text, many arguments start up because someone attributes to malice what is adequately explained by poor expression or miscommunication. Substantive and relevant discussion usually becomes impossible when these exchanges are public. These fiery interactions usually start with little misunderstandings and are often preventable.

Cyberspace crimes are similar to crimes in the physical world, with the essential difference being the ease of obtaining and distributing information. Whether the information contains new ideas, poetry, opinions, hoaxes, or outright lies, the dissemination of information—or misinformation—in cyberspace is easy. This is what makes cyberspace such an unusual environment, with great potential for both sharing information and taking advantage of the unwary.

It is difficult to formalize and enforce rules in cyberspace, so cyberspace communities tend to construct and enforce rules that suit their needs as specific problems arise. Many of these rules are based on the in-person social conduct rules we are all familiar with. As in the physical world, it is considered improper to badger, slander, or reveal personal information about someone without their consent. Impersonating someone, or "blowing someone's cover" on anonymous systems (giving out names, phone numbers, and so on) is also highly unacceptable. Some systems have rules governing behavior, but such rules are hard to formalize and enforce. On one system, the rule is both simple and vague: "be polite." Surprisingly, it works most of the time.

Administrators who try to enforce rules often end up having to read a prohibitively extensive amount of text, and they are often forced to invade an inhabitant's privacy in order to be thorough. A number of law suits dealing with the privacy rights of cyberspace inhabitants have been brought to the courts. The bottom line, however, is that it is impossible to monitor all the communications between cyberspace inhabitants in cyberspace. Between sheer volume and unbreakable cryptography algorithms, there is no sure way to know what information a group of cyberspace inhabitants are exchanging.

Thus, in practice it is the cyberspace community itself that enforces the rules, with the tried and true methods of the schoolyard: peer review, disapproval, and—if necessary—ostracism.

Since most cyberspace administrators are limited in their ability to hold inhabitants accountable for their actions, today's cyberspaces are largely run by educated anarchy. The biggest disadvantage of cyberspace anarchy is confusion; questions of proper behavior arise constantly and must be worked out among the inhabitants every time a problem surfaces. The advantage is that a more mature citizenship arises out of these efforts, one where inhabitants adopt rules because they work well and not simply because they are handed down from a higher authority.

When children play in a schoolyard they decide for themselves what the rules for various games will be, and they enforce the rules themselves. There are always bullies who badger or harass, but for the most part, children manage to interact with each other in ways that support the rules they have created. Children learn in a schoolyard what behavior works in a social environment and what behavior doesn't. If a child wants to be a part of a social community or an inhabitant wants to be part of a cyberspace community, each must learn from that community what behavior is appropriate in order to remain part of the community.

Editor's note: To read further on this topic, locate the following article, which has a bibliography.

Raeder, Aggi. (1995, January). "Beyond Netiquette." *Searcher,* 26, 28–30.

THE COMMUNICATIONS DECENCY ACT

The Communications Decency Act (CDA) was signed into law as part of a major telecommunications bill on February 8, 1996. At the time of the writing of this book, it cannot be said with certainty whether it will be an absurd footnote to Internet history or something that drastically changes the way libraries in the United States offer Internet access to the public since the constitutionality of the Act is still being considered in the courts.

However, unless the Act is completely overturned, it seems likely that libraries will have to become familiar with the provisions of whatever parts of the Act still continue in force. Libraries have tended so far to assume that somehow the provisions of the Act will not apply to them or to think that having an access policy in place is complete protection. If parts of the Act are upheld, every library will almost certainly need to consult legal counsel to determine what needs to be done. Whatever is left will be the law of the land, sad as that may be, with criminal penalties in force. Even if the Act is found unconstitutional, libraries must follow further developments in this area.

No matter what happens in regard to the Communications Decency Act, censorship is affecting the Internet on a worldwide basis. Much of the rest of the world does not have even the presumption of freedom of speech that the United States has, and other governments have not hesitated to censor the Net. Companies that want to have a place in the global Internet are likely to fall in with the strictures of whatever market they want to enter. All of this affects what we all see, or more likely, don't see, on the Internet.

Here are a few sites for more information. As usual, Yahoo is a good place for ongoing information. Go to *http://www.yahoo.com/Society_and _Culture/Civil_Rights/Censorship/Censorship_and_the_Net/* to keep up; the Communications Decency Act has an entry on this page.

Bruce, Marty. (1996). *Censorship on the Internet.* [Online]. Available: *http://pegasus.cc.ucf.edu/~mab17431/ip.htm*
> A fairly complete page about the Communications Decency Act. Includes the history of the Act, information about the court challenge, and links to the text of the Act, the text of the complaint, and more.

Electronic Frontier Foundation. (1996). *EFF "Censorship—Exon Comm. Decency Act & Other Net Censorship Bills" Archive*. [Online]. Available: *http://www.eff.org/pub/Censorship/Exon_bill/*

> This is an extensive, rambling archive of texts related to the CDA and other Internet censorship bills. Includes some links to related sites, including a site dealing with filtering and rating attempts.

Electronic Privacy Information Center. (1996, May). *Legal Challenge to Internet Censorship*. [Online]. Available: *http://www.epic.org/free_speech/censorship/lawsuit/*

> By the time you read this, the point may be moot, but let's hope this page remains in place because it provides an excellent set of connections to information about the legal cases filed against the CDA.

Human Rights Watch. (1996, May). *Silencing the Net: The Threat to Freedom of Expression Online*. [Online]. Available: *http://www.cwrl.utexas.edu/~monitors/1.1/hrw/index.html*

> This goes far beyond the United States to give a global view of governmental attempts to regulate the content and use of the Internet. Gives a summary, overviews major global areas, and makes recommendations.

It's Time Once Again to Ask [Alternate] Dr. Internet!

1. There have been many news stories about the Internet providing access to pornography. This is a serious problem, and it raises an obvious question: How can I see these images?

Typically, a picture on the Internet will look like this.

```
begin 644 smut.gif//
M1TE&.#======AE /$@ $!! !!!! !!!! !!!!!

00000000000000000
M1TE&.#==AE /$g AR@!\ /$ /_ _ _ S P,+]@4#'
0KRP R@!\ "_ H2/J@<0M#2.
<MM-,-+]z\^P@&XDB6YHFFZLJV0\DDO&^09\DDZ
HWG^L[M_@\,'H?$$H&(3''J7S^;SM''8M4

II2J8K-:K?:<KO<+#H0'Y++YC$zku^RV
^PV/R^? TNOV.S^OW_+[_#QA(M(T!82,
A@6+ B0*(!@B*@(P#@9"4CYF# "IH"F
N1EYR ?D7ZFD@@VGLGH6D2EK:M]Q@@@
*YNHFBAK:X@K6;B;NSL;H!L\ZS=,++
PZZ<M[&V#:^@*''#@[3&P<C8P-M3=V+*!!,
+3WA6x0 ?!V</2Z-P*W[W2T>3AYM7H_/
;%F[L-X <3EXS>K0*3<MWM<!\_2@
WBG 1MHT. O=^ 0''NH6*J$N_h$[3V
<J(^B(%JD)GZ+%0%>Oi$<609''MQA CR7
#.\ID*;&BPI';^K5$.2[E1YTX55Y,T%/>,*#UA
%HD&O+H*W0VRS&RMIC+GS:@7?:YL'';
''=4X5:P4I]Y>R954,#VKI]^Y;06U10B\*]''_?
W 5[R;C2M!C817KQRW0IV:W<P7KUN
&?3U6W*=4\5P''[>]W#8QY;Z/$70>,S/
6O\F&M1&+MJZBNR&NJD0%0K0!VF6
VTWQ6C&JU[=R(@\E&>KJWZ]^,, [L$L_NV;
6:R=-VM30P ,N?%HK_NK68;@W]
4J<< 6WAR[@G_6KQ0_?EY0^>(#?**U/4-
[Z>SV;V\WM+_Y!_/KY] 'Q0^_.?
#RQ5]Z@?QGP&\''M@#?>_7MQ=UV''
C8H&,5FM?>-@O>M(>$z%!KHP'
[&37=AA.!I]V&&$8B8(8D@_C%?BA#''
=Z%\)>X18WX;LJC0AG;DM:.''.-5;H8QU
JLA@?32^F''22GMU(''Y0I4K:DDT\R620
=1^*GY)56#ECEC'QPMUP''9''1GIIG+':
?F'VT''MP^:RN%VW)ESKGF4G6+2''2>:
?99YIW2!YDEHH88>MBFBBBB[*:*../
@III)).2FFEEEZ*::::;LIIIYY^''FJHHHY*:
JFFGHIJJJJN<RFJKKKX*:ZRRSDIKK;;
>BFNNNN[*:Z\6% .YY^

end
```

This is one of those "Magic Eye" 3-D images. To appreciate the artist's use of lighting and composition, you should print this out, hold it at arm's length, and try to concentrate on a point about eight inches behind the paper. Relax and let your eyes go out of focus, and you will then see a three-dimensional image of smut and filth.

2. What is "Spam"? What kind of advertising is allowed on the Internet?

Spam is Spiced Ham, which is to say it is a form of amateur radio with electronic components designed using the SPICE circuit design modeler. This was very popular during World War II ("Spam, Spam, the Serviceman's Ham" was a frequent motto). During the battle of Iwo Jima, three Marines used Spam to transmit advertisements to U.S. forces; this was immortalized in a photograph of them raising their antenna, along with a flag, on a mountain top, and so we remember them today by calling such widely broadcast advertisements Spam.

It is a misconception that advertising is prohibited on the Internet. Permits for Internet advertising are available from a law firm run by a pair of skilled Internet experts. These permits, or green cards, allow any Internet user to send an advertisement to thousands of news groups, even if the group has no relevance to the product being advertised. This is a very successful marketing technique and will generate many e-mail responses.

3. What are FAQ lists?

On many news groups, the same questions come up again and again and again. Inevitably, two or more factions insist that theirs is the one canonical answer; the resulting flame wars elevate these issues to the rank of Furiously Argued Questions. At some point, moderates on the group—not to be confused with moderators—exert some centrist control. As a way to prevent these arguments from flaring up again, the FAQs are compiled in a list. New users should read the list to determine which questions they must never ask, as that will just plunge the entire group back into this circular debate.

Needless to say, the most common FAQ in any group is "Where can I find the FAQ list?"

4. Is there really an online Coke machine? How do I use it?

Yes, there are actually several Coke machines hooked up to the Internet. Unfortunately, you can't really use them unless your Internet connection runs over an ISDN (Integrated Soft Drink Network) line. Even that won't solve all your problems. To pay for your drink, you'll have to use one of two competing plans to allow security of monetary transactions over the Net. Coca-Cola is endorsing Soda HTTP (HTTP-S) while Pepsi-Cola is backing the Soda Security Layer (SSL).

Given the existence of Coke machines on the Net, it was predictable that companies like Pizza Hut would start taking pizza delivery orders via the Net. Unfortunately, this system isn't completely working yet; orders for double anchovies seem to cause 100 percent packet loss.

5. How do I ensure no one else is reading my e-mail?

Many antique stores sell old tripod cameras, the kind where the photographer held a pan of flash powder aloft and then ducked under a heavy black hood. I recommend buying one of these and attaching it to your monitor. When you duck under the hood, no one will be able to look over your shoulder; if they do, you can always blind them temporarily with the flash powder.

Some people are so concerned about their online privacy that they use e-mail encryption. Unfortunately, most of these people were pretty cryptic to begin with, leaving us with no way to understand their messages.

6. I am afraid that I'm becoming a network nerd. How can I tell for sure?

How many syllables do you think there are in the word *coax*?

> Tune in next time for Ask Dr. Internet— "I have a master's degree . . . in Internet!"

> Dr. Internet, Master of All Knowledge Benedictine On the Rocks With a Twist No official connection to Dr. Science

Editor's note: [Alternate] Dr. Internet is channeled by Thomas Dowling, who holds copyright on these effusions. You can find his contact information in his chapter on "Multimedia File Formats," which is more serious. At least, I think it is.

Anyway, you can find more wisdom of [Alternate] Dr. Internet at http://chehalis.lib.washington.edu/dri

A Declaration of the Independence of Cyberspace

John Perry Barlow

John Perry Barlow has been called a subculture icon. He is a retired Wyoming cattle rancher, is cofounder of the Electronic Frontier Foundation, and was lyricist for the Grateful Dead. He is also a member of The WELL Board of Directors. His home page is at *http://www.eff.org/~barlow/*.

Appears at *http://www.eff.org/pub/Publications/John_Perry_Barlow/barlow_0296.declaration* with an explanation of how it came to be written. Copyright held by John Perry Barlow.

Governments of the Industrial World, you weary giants of flesh and steel, I come from Cyberspace, the new home of Mind. On behalf of the future, I ask you of the past to leave us alone. You are not welcome among us. You have no sovereignty where we gather.

We have no elected government, nor are we likely to have one, so I address you with no greater authority than that with which liberty itself always speaks. I declare the global social space we are building to be naturally independent of the tyrannies you seek to impose on us. You have no moral right to rule us nor do you possess any methods of enforcement we have true reason to fear.

Governments derive their just powers from the consent of the governed. You have neither solicited nor received ours. We did not invite you. You do not know us, nor do you know our world. Cyberspace does not lie within your borders. Do not think that you can build it, as though it were a public construction project. You cannot. It is an act of nature and it grows itself through our collective actions.

You have not engaged in our great and gathering conversation, nor did you create the wealth of our marketplaces. You do not know our culture, our ethics, or the unwritten codes that already provide our society more order than could be obtained by any of your impositions.

You claim there are problems among us that you need to solve. You use this claim as an excuse to invade our precincts. Many of these problems don't exist. Where there are real conflicts, where there are wrongs, we will identify them and address them by our means. We are forming our own Social Contract. This governance will arise according to the conditions of our world, not yours. Our world is different.

Cyberspace consists of transactions, relationships, and thought itself, arrayed like a standing wave in the web of our communications. Ours is a world that is both everywhere and nowhere, but it is not where bodies live.

We are creating a world that all may enter without privilege or prejudice accorded by race, economic power, military force, or station of birth.

We are creating a world where anyone, anywhere may express his or her beliefs, no matter how singular, without fear of being coerced into silence or conformity.

Your legal concepts of property, expression, identity, movement, and context do not apply to us. They are based on matter. There is no matter here.

Our identities have no bodies, so, unlike you, we cannot obtain order by physical coercion. We believe that from ethics, enlightened self-interest, and the commonweal, our governance will emerge. Our identities may be distributed across many of your jurisdictions. The only law that all our constituent cultures would generally recognize is the Golden Rule. We hope we will be able to build our particular solutions on that basis. But we cannot accept the solutions you are attempting to impose.

In the United States, you have today created a law, the Telecommunications Reform Act, which repudiates your own Constitution and insults the dreams of Jefferson, Washington, Mill, Madison, de Tocqueville, and Brandeis. These dreams must now be born anew in us.

You are terrified of your own children, since they are natives in a world where you will always be immigrants. Because you fear them, you entrust your bureaucracies with the parental responsibilities you are too cowardly to confront yourselves. In our world, all the sentiments and expressions of humanity, from the debasing to the angelic, are parts of a seamless whole, the global conversation of bits. We cannot separate the air that chokes from the air upon which wings beat.

In China, Germany, France, Russia, Singapore, Italy and the United States, you are trying to ward off the virus of liberty by erecting guard posts at the frontiers of Cyberspace. These may keep out the contagion for a small time, but they will not work in a world that will soon be blanketed in bit-bearing media.

Your increasingly obsolete information industries would perpetuate themselves by proposing laws, in America and elsewhere, that claim to own speech itself throughout the world. These laws would declare ideas to be another industrial product, no more noble than pig iron. In our world, whatever the human mind may create can be reproduced and distributed infinitely at no cost. The global conveyance of thought no longer requires your factories to accomplish.

These increasingly hostile and colonial measures place us in the same position as those previous lovers of freedom and self-determination who had to reject the authorities of distant, uninformed powers. We must declare our virtual selves immune to your sovereignty, even as we continue to consent to your rule over our bodies. We will spread ourselves across the Planet so that no one can arrest our thoughts.

We will create a civilization of the Mind in Cyberspace. May it be more humane and fair than the world your governments have made before.

Davos, Switzerland
February 8, 1996

SECURITY AND AUTHENTICATION

Librarians frequently show a lamentable, and even dangerous, lack of knowledge and concern about issues of computer security and data authentication. Traditionally, our trust factor has been high, and we have not had assets anyone was trying to acquire or destroy. Well, it's time to wake up and smell the coffee—there are a lot of untrustworthy people out there tapping on keyboards, and we have a lot of valuable electronic information to protect. Here are some pointers to resources available on the Web. For an ongoing source of information about this subject, look on Yahoo at *http://www.yahoo.com/Computers_and_Internet/Security_and_Encryption/*.

Graham, Peter S. (1995, July). *Long-Term Intellectual Preservation.* [Online]. Available: *http://aultnis.rutgers.edu/texts/dps.html*
> Excellent overview of the issues involved with preserving electronic information; much of the paper concerns electronic authenticity. Links to a very good bibliography and some other related papers by the same author.

Kenyeres, Christian A. (1996, April). *Authentication of Users and Access Control On the Internet.* [Online]. Available: *http://www.cs.uml.edu/~ckenyere/term2.html*
> Seems to be a student paper; however, it does a good job of giving an overview of the issues involved with encryption, protection, and authentication of data. Includes a bibliography.

Rutgers University. (1995, December). *World Wide Web Security.* [Online]. Available: *http://www-ns.rutgers.edu/www-security/index.html*
> "This document indexes information on security for the World Wide Web, HTTP [HyperText Transfer Protocol], HTML [HyperText Markup Language], and related software/protocols." The most useful information is under the heading References—links are included to information on HTML and HTTP security and all Internet drafts and Request for Comments document series (RFCs) concerning security.

Stein, Lincoln. (1996, April). *WWW Security FAQ.* [Online]. Available: *http://www-genome.wi.mit.edu/WWW/faqs/www-security-faq.html*

> A thorough, outstanding site with more than 70 "questions" about WWW security including doing secure PERL (Practical Extraction and Report Language) scripts, a whole section on CGI (Common Gateway Interface), confidential documents, and more. Extensive bibliography of print and electronic materials. The organizer of this site is the author of *How to Set Up and Maintain a World Wide Web Site: The Guide for Information Providers* published by Addison Wesley.

World Wide Web Consortium. (1996, May). *W3C Security Resources.* [Online]. Available: *http://www.w3.org/hypertext/WWW/Security/*

> Excellent collection of links about security in all of its ramifications. Includes links to useful organizations, information on privacy, cryptography, digital cash, and more.

5

I'll Have My Agent Call Your Agent

Intelligent Agents

Software Servants for an Electronic Information World (and More!)

Marina Roesler and Donald T. Hawkins

Marina Roesler is a member of the technical staff at AT&T Bell Laboratories, where she is affiliated with the information services and computer platforms group in the architecture area. Since 1992, she has also been a member of the AT&T PersonaLink Information Services team. Marina has M.Sc. and Ph.D. degrees in computer science from the University of California, San Diego. Her doctoral work was in the area of object technology and distributed computing systems. Prior to joining AT&T, she was an associate professor of computer science at the Universidade Federal de Pernambuco, Brazil.

Donald T. Hawkins is a distinguished member of the technical staff in AT&T's business communications services (BCS) unit, where he is a product manager for the information publishing activities of the newly announced AT&T Network Notes product. Immediately before joining BCS, he was with the AT&T architecture area at AT&T Bell Laboratories. Don is the AT&T representative to the Association of Information and Dissemination Centers (ASIDIC) and serves as editor of the ASIDIC Newsletter. He has been with AT&T since 1971 and has a Ph.D. from the University of California, Berkeley.

Communications to the authors may be sent to Marina Roesler, AT&T Bell Laboratories, Room 1M-321, 101 Crawfords Corner Road, Holmdel, NJ 07733; (908)949-1049; fax (908)949-8569; Internet: *marina.roesler@ att.com* and/or to Donald T. Hawkins, AT&T Business Communications Services, Room 34B03, 55 Corporate Drive, Bridgewater, NJ 08807; (908)658-2450; fax: (908)658-2248; Internet: *dthk@mantic.ho.att.com*.

Originally appeared in (1994, July) *Online*, 18–32. Copyright held by Online, Inc.

Editor's note: Some sidebars omitted. See end of article for URLs of some of the products highlighted.

The term *agent* often suggests the shadowy world of espionage, betrayal, and divided loyalties. In the software area, however, smart agents or intelligent agents not only have a different purpose, but they also have the potential to be extremely useful to their users, especially as the technology becomes further developed. This article is the first appearing in *Online* on the topic of intelligent agents. We will therefore introduce the concept, discuss some of the properties of agents, the need for agent technology in a number of areas, and then focus on information retrieval, discussing several interesting software systems that exhibit agent functionality.

Intelligent agents are autonomous and adaptive computer programs operating within software environments such as operating systems, databases, or computer networks. Intelligent agents help their users with routine computer tasks, while still accommodating individual habits. This technology combines artificial intelligence (reasoning, planning, natural language processing, etc.) and system development techniques (object-oriented programming, scripting languages, human-machine interface, distributed processing, etc.) to produce a new generation of software that can, based on user preferences, perform tasks for users. (For a tutorial on artificial intelligence and a discussion of its application to information retrieval, see Hawkins' 1987 and 1988 articles in *Online*.[1,2]) Nicholas Negroponte, director of MIT's Media Lab, is often credited with initially identifying the agent concept and likening it to an English butler.[3]

Typical tasks performed by intelligent agents could include filtering electronic mail, scheduling appointments, locating information, alerting to investment opportunities, and making travel arrangements. Individuals are capable of handling these routine tasks and have been doing so for years, of course, but intelligent agent technology holds the promise of easing the burdens on users by automating such tasks.

Why Agents?

The modern and increasingly competitive global business environment and the growing complexity of personal lives create high demands to perform many (often simultaneous) tasks efficiently and promptly. To help accommodate these far-reaching lifestyle changes, new tools are needed to support the imperatives of this rapidly changing environment. Intelligent agent technology has a significant potential to affect peoples' lives in many areas. Here are some typical examples:

Users can be easily overwhelmed by the huge amount of information available and the effort required to find specific information they need (assuming they can locate an appropriate source in the first place). Support is needed to automatically sort and filter an incoming data stream into a manageable amount of high-value information that can be customized for each individual user.

In an increasingly mobile business environment, messages must be filtered and routed intelligently to recipients on the move.

There is a strategic need for increased support for tasks performed by "knowledge workers" (such as managers, technical professionals, and marketing personnel), especially in the decision-making area. Timely and knowledgeable decisions made by these professionals greatly affect their personal success and the success of their businesses in the marketplace.

There is a pressing need to automate tasks performed by administrative and clerical personnel in functions such as sales support or customer care to reduce labor costs and increase office productivity. Today, labor costs are estimated to be as much as 60 percent of the total information delivery cost of sales, service, and support organizations.[4]

In a fast-paced society, time-strapped individuals need new ways to minimize time spent on routine personal tasks so they can devote their leisure time to more gratifying activities.

Developments in computing, information management, miniaturization, and human-machine interface (e.g., pen- and voice-based interfaces) are at the center of a trend toward production of new kinds of computers and software that are more natural to use and exhibit smarter and more personalized behavior. While demands on people's professional and personal lives have made the creation of intelligent software agents necessary, these technological developments have made their creation possible. The goal and challenge is to offer a computing environment that truly supports and helps people perform their tasks exceptionally well.

General Characteristics of Intelligent Agents

Intelligent agent technology is relatively new on the computing scene, so no firm consensus on what constitutes an intelligent agent has been clearly established. However, the following capabilities are often associated with the notion of an intelligent agent:

Autonomous agency is the ability to handle user-defined tasks independent of the user and often without the user's guidance or presence. The user does not become directly involved in executing the task. Once he or she specifies how and when a task should be performed, the software agent is delegated to perform it when the right conditions are met. Note that the agent can execute the task immediately while the user waits for a response ("tell me the best route to get to my hotel from the airport") or at a time when the user is not present ("place any incoming e-mailed requests for meetings on my calendar").

Adaptive behavior is the ability to mimic the user's steps when normally performing a task. For example, learning agents would learn the user's habits and preferences over time and either respond to requests or act on the user's behalf—based on what they learned.

The learning usually occurs through observation, user feedback, or training.

One of the techniques used when learning by observing is to track the user's actions and memorize the situations that prompted those actions (these are called "situation-action pairs"). When a new situation occurs, the system computes the correlation between the new situation and previous situation-action pairs to decide the course of action. The agent may suggest the action to the user or act directly without further intervention.

In the user-feedback learning method, users can instruct the agent how to act directly ("never perform that action again") or indirectly by, for example, ignoring a suggestion given by the agent. The system stores the feedback actions.

In user-training learning, the user inputs hypothetical situations and actions to the system, building a database of scenarios (situation-action pairs) for the agent to use when deciding future actions.

Mobility capability is the ability to traverse computer networks, carrying actions for remote execution.

Autonomous agents are usually created via scripting languages (for example, AppleScript, Telescript, or NewtonScript). Creating agents using interpretable scripts helps their movement across computing platforms with multiple architectures, which is a major factor in the popularity of scripting languages for agents. Additionally, communications-oriented scripting languages like Telescript may facilitate construction of agents that communicate with other agents residing on different processors.

Cooperative behavior is the ability to engage in complex patterns of two-way communications with users and other agents. Agents are usually developed to provide expertise in a specific area and can, through cooperative work, jointly accomplish larger and more-complex tasks. For example, in a messaging environment, an agent carrying a message from Peter to Jane marked "urgent" interacts with Jane's mailbox agent to find out how Jane wants urgent messages to be handled. The mailbox agent, knowing that Jane is on vacation, instructs Peter's agent to deliver the message by fax to Jane's secretary. Here both agents, in executing the task, take into account the desires of the user they represent.

Cooperative behavior of computing entities has been studied by researchers in the area of "distributed artificial intelligence." This field of research studies how agents, each with partial knowledge of a situation, can jointly communicate and cooperate to perform nontrivial tasks.

Reasoning capability is the ability to operate in a decision-making capacity in complex, changing conditions. This property is usually associated with making inferences, having the competence to choose among different strategies or the capability to plan a task. Below are three different approaches to building agents with reasoning capabilities.

1. The rule-based approach uses user-scripted controls for information handling. Users must recognize where an agent would be useful, program the agent with rules or their profile of preferences, and update the rules or profiles as preferences change.
2. In the knowledge-based approach, a human expert compiles a large amount of information, which is then passed to an agent and used to deduce proper behavior. This method requires a substantial amount of work from the expert and is not applicable to all types of tasks.
3. In the artificial-evolution model, agents are implemented as "genetic" algorithms. They can spawn new generations of agents that take their parents' place and, as they are used, acquire statistical history and new knowledge that will guide their future behavior.

Anthropomorphic interface is the ability to exhibit human-like traits. The notion of a software agent that can effectively help humans perform daily tasks is even more powerful when users think of the agents as some sort of humanoids. Some researchers believe that computer users will be more likely to trust and feel comfortable with a system that presents a human-like interface. Apple's *Knowledge Navigator* [a video that appeared in 1988] is an example of this type of interface. Natural language (requests entered by the user in plain English) and voice interfaces are natural candidates also, as is a pictorial representation of the agent as a human face. Some systems go as far as having the face express feelings. Expressions of confusion, satisfaction, surprise, etc., can be used by a learning agent to denote its reaction to actions taken by the user.

Software does not necessarily need to have all these qualities to be classified as an intelligent agent. On the other hand, it is probably reasonable to say that the intelligence level of agents can be correlated to the degree to which they implement these properties. Thus, it is better to think of agents as providing a range, or different levels, of intelligence. On one end of the spectrum are agents that simply record the sequence of actions taken by a user and try to mimic it when invoked. On the other end are agents with the ability to learn from user behavior, adapt to new situations, plan tasks, make decisions, infer what behavior is expected based on past history or information context, and so on.

Using Intelligent Agents for Information Retrieval

The problem with online information today is not that too little of it is available. On the contrary, an increasing amount of information is being converted to electronic form. The number of publicly available online databases has now passed 5,000[5] and shows no sign of abating. Information users are in a difficult position. They need information to help them make intelligent decisions and do not want to miss relevant information. However, the information may not only be scattered in several different data-bases, but it may reside on different systems, each with a different user interface and a different database structure. In addition, not all users have access to all the information systems they need.

Given these problems, simple, convenient, cost-effective and user-friendly access to electronic information has been a long-standing (but elusive) dream of information seekers and providers. For example, in 1984 Cleverdon[6] observed that the information retrieval systems of the day were, ". . . inefficient and over-expensive products, packaged in the shiny wrapping of modern technology, and hostile to end users."

Important strides have been made in the last decade, but readily available methods to help users extract meaningful information from the sea of electronic data are still only in their infancy. Many attempts have been made to solve this problem, but only a few have been reasonably successful.

The Internet is a good example of a potentially rich source of useful information, but it has not yet been made easily accessible to the faint-of-heart. Traditionally, fishing information from the Internet was a privilege reserved for relatively savvy users with a working knowledge of UNIX and a general idea of where the information resided. The recent appearance of navigation tools and search interfaces for the Internet such as Gopher, WAIS [Wide Area Information Server], Mosaic, and the World-Wide Web (WWW) has provided better access to Internet information, but these tools are not yet the ultimate solution. They show users the way through the maze of information, but they do not actually do the navigation for them. Even with more friendly systems such as Mosaic, links to the information must be built and maintained and, at best, they provide only pointers to the actual information. Users, however, want answers to their questions, not merely pointers to possible sources for those answers. And they do not want to invest a lot of time learning how to use or find systems that might contain the answers.

As Alan Kay has pointed out so eloquently,[7] intelligent agents have a significant potential to solve these problems:

> In ten years, we will be hooked up to more than a trillion objects of useful knowledge, and no direct manipulation interface can handle that. People are not going to sit down with a super SQL application and start fishing around the entire world for things that might be of use to them. Instead, the interfaces are going to be 24-hour retrievers that are constantly firing away doing things.

In 1988, Hawkins, Levy, and Montgomery[8] envisioned a "knowledge gateway" to help meet some of the difficulties discussed by Cleverdon. They proposed a system that would go beyond simply retrieving the desired information for the user. The knowledge gateway would, among other things, also offer optional information processing capabilities (for example, the compilation, correlation, and analyses of data). Although they did not use the term "agent" in their article, their description of the knowledge gateway could be viewed as an early description of an information retrieval intelligent agent.

Only very recently, some progress has been made toward resolving many of the problems identified by Cleverdon and the realization of information retrieval intelligent agents. In the following section we describe some of these advances.

Status of Intelligent Agent Technology

So far, no software has been developed that includes the full range of intelligent agent properties as described at the beginning of this article. However, several products displaying one or more intelligent agent features have appeared in the marketplace in the last two years.

We will briefly describe some of these key products plus projects in progress in academic institutions and research laboratories. This list is not intended to be comprehensive and is limited to those products having significant potential in the information retrieval area.

Other products displaying intelligent agent capabilities in the areas of smart messaging, message filtering, workflow automation, financial services, help desks, file management, and so on are available but will not be covered here.

Information Retrieval Agents

Several search engines that provide varying levels of search and retrieval capabilities exist in the marketplace (Oracle's ConText, Fulcrum's FullText, Personal Library Software's Personal Librarian, ConQuest Software's semantic network, etc.). Often these engines are licensed to original equipment manufacturers (OEMs) that then develop and incorporate information retrieval agent capabilities into the original search engine. Some of the services and products described below are examples of this kind of development.

Applesearch. Apple's AppleSearch software enables creation of personal search agents called "Reporters" to search incoming mail messages and documents obtained from online feeds or residing on servers or CD-ROM discs. The user can schedule Reporters to run at preset intervals, or on demand.

AppleSearch uses Apple's proprietary technology to automatically translate page layout, word processing and spreadsheet documents into searchable text-only documents. It uses Reporters to scan the available content, employs a relevance-ranking algorithm to select the information of most value to the user, then allows the user to view the text of the selected documents without invoking the application (word processor, spreadsheet, etc.) that originally created them. The system supports plain-English and Boolean queries. AppleSearch's search engine is built on the Personal Library Software's Callable Personal Librarian (CPL) search engine. (See Ed Valauskas' review of AppleSearch for more detailed information.[9])

Pagekeeper. Caere Corporation's PageKeeper software provides roughly the same functionality on Windows platforms that AppleSearch offers on the Macintosh. PageKeeper creates compressed images of both text and image documents (originally obtained by scanning, faxing, etc.), indexes and stores them, and then allows users to execute searches of stored documents from anywhere on a network.

PageKeeper uses a weighted relevance scheme to rank the retrieved documents. It can also transform retrieved documents into "document agents" that locate other documents with similar content. Its features include automatic indexing, support for scanned and fax images, OCR [Optical Character Recognition], document annotation, support for electronic-mail delivery and work-group document sharing.

Homework Helper. Infonautics Corporation is using the ConQuest search engine as the core engine for its forthcoming Homework Helper service. Homework Helper is an educational online information retrieval system addressing the needs of the K–12 education market, expected to be launched on the Prodigy service in the summer of 1994. Students will be able to pose questions such as "What is the height of the Empire State building?" to which the system may respond (depending on the content to which it has access) with a snippet from an encyclopedia, a travel brochure for New York, etc., containing the answer to the question. [Homework Helper is currently available through Prodigy and as a stand-alone service.]

(ConQuest Software's concept-based text retrieval engine provides document search and retrieval capabilities, linguistically enhanced through a semantic network of 335,000 dictionary terms and acronyms that expands to three million related terms or linkages. ConQuest has combined many significant searching techniques developed by linguists and information specialists into its search engine. Among the components used are a natural language query interface, statistical processing using vector methods, a semantic network of words and word relationships, relevance ranking, query by example, linguistic rules and analyses, and Boolean logic.)

ConText. Oracle's ConText software uses a client/server architecture to understand the structure and analyze the content of English text and queries. The server processes a document and identifies thematic, semantic and structural information about it. Different client tools then interpret this information and give the user capabilities such as speed/scan reading (highlights the most important segments of text to allow the reader to skim it), text summarization (paraphrases the document and reduces the content of the original by one-half to one-quarter), generation of abstracts (creates a new document approximately one-tenth as long as the original and covering all its themes), and information extraction (allows the creation of information retrieval agents to extract specific information from textual databases, such as expected trends in the stock market based on quoted analyst predictions, or information about mergers and acquisitions).

Advanced Information Agent. Users of J&T Associates' Advanced Information Agent can instruct it to watch for items of interest in e-mail in-boxes, online news services, electronic discussion forums, etc. The Advanced Information Agent will pull the relevant information and put it in the user's personalized newspaper at predetermined intervals. This agent runs on the Lotus Notes platform.

Hoover. SandPoint Corporation's Hoover system can be viewed as a collection of information filtering agents that search, retrieve, and integrate data from several electronic information sources, including online databases, CD-ROMs, and broadcast feeds such as newswires. Hoover delivers its output via the Lotus Notes platform. SandPoint predefines scripts for several of the most widely used online information services. If a user wants to access an information service for which a script is not available, SandPoint will write the script for a fee or will sell the tools to create the script. Once the script is in place, customizing the information is simply a matter of changing search terms.

SandPoint also offers a series of pre-defined filtered products such as company profiles, news alerts, and the full text of the *Wall Street Journal*. Users indicate the topics for which they are searching by filling out a simple template that then becomes an agent that conducts the search across several online databases or databanks. (More information about the Hoover system appears in Hunter McCleary's article.[10])

News Filtering Agents

NewsEDGE. Desktop Data's NewsEDGE service delivers real-time online news. Users can indicate topics of interest, and NewsEDGE will alert them to news stories on those topics as they appear on the newswire. Users can also create personalized news-clipping reports by selecting from approximately 130 news services including the Associated Press, Dow Jones, Reuters, Federal Filings, etc. NewsEDGE customers can receive their news stories through the delivery channel of their choice, one of which is the Lotus Notes platform.

PowerNews. NewtonMail subscribers can use Pentekk Technologies' PowerNews software to create a user agent that, based on the user's selection of categories, will daily download news clips on the computer, business, financial, or medical industries to the subscriber's Newton device.

First! and HeadsUp. Individual, Inc. offers two similar news filtering services primarily targeted to executives who need to keep current concerning their areas of interest. The HeadsUp service delivers a daily customized newspaper consisting of news synopses via several delivery channels, including pagers and hand-held devices using Motorola's EMBARC System. The First! service delivers custom news daily by fax, electronic mail, or as a Lotus Notes database. The primary distinction between the First! and HeadsUp services is that HeadsUp is available only for a series of topics preselected by Individual, Inc., whereas First! newspapers can be created for any topic the subscriber chooses.

Individual [Inc.] uses the SMART text retrieval and filtering technology developed by Professor Gerard Salton at Cornell University to select material for subscribers' personal newspapers. Sources of information include general business news feeds (e.g., Reuters, Financial Times) as well as sources specific to clients' markets (e.g., Network World). (For further details about both NewsEDGE and Individual, Inc. see McCleary's article.[10])

Research Work at Academic Institutions

The concept of intelligent agents has stimulated a growing body of research, mostly in the area of artificial intelligence. We will very briefly highlight a few of these projects.

In 1988, Robert Kahn and Vinton Cerf[11] proposed an architecture for a set of information retrieval agents, called "knowbots." Knowbots are agents that search a variety of information sources to find an answer to a query. For example, a knowbot trying to satisfy a user's query, "Why is the sky blue?" can return a poem, a physics article, a snippet from an encyclopedia, etc. The goal is to let the knowbot do the navigation, instead of having the user navigate the web of cyberspace.

Pattie Maes at MIT[12,13] is using artificial-evolution techniques to create user agents that can learn to perform "administrative" activities that distract people from their primary activities, such as scheduling meetings or scanning databases for information. The MIT project's emphasis is on the agent's learning capability. These agents develop different confidence levels as they monitor a user's activity. The user can set thresholds that specify whether or not the agent needs to notify him or her before it takes a particular action.

Oren Etzioni at the University of Washington[14] thinks of agents as "robots" operating in a software environment instead of the physical world. He calls them "softbots," shorthand for "software robots." As an example, some softbots (implemented as shell scripts) are meant to help a user in his or her daily work on a UNIX system. Etzioni's softbots incorporate modern artificial intelligence planning techniques. A softbot is viewed as an agent that needs to find a way (a "plan") to satisfy its user's goal. The user tells the softbot what to do, not how to do it. For example, to satisfy a user's request, "find out where Marina Roesler is logged on," a shell script would be produced to search for this information on many different machines, possibly using the Internet.

Tom Mitchell and his colleagues at Carnegie Mellon University[15] have developed an agent that helps schedule meetings. The agent tries to adapt to the user. For example, the program will not schedule meetings early in the morning, once it has noticed that the user never schedules early meetings. The objective of this work is to demonstrate that it is feasible to design a learning agent capable of capturing useful training data and generalizing from such data in ways competitive with hand-coded knowledge.

Yoav Shoham at Stanford University[16] is developing a general programming model and programming language for designing and building agents.

Shoham's agents have mental states, such as beliefs, capabilities, choices, commitments, etc. Agent capabilities include inter-agent communication primitives, e.g., inform, request, offer, and promise. This paradigm can be viewed as a specialization of object-oriented programming.

Philip Cohen, et al., at SRI International[17] is developing an open agent architecture and user interface to support transparent (users don't need to know where or how their requests are being executed) distributed execution of users' requests. To facilitate delegating tasks to agents, the architecture is served by a multimodal interface, including pen input, voice input, and direct manipulation.

Conclusion

Although they are still in their infancy, the promise of intelligent agents is an appealing one. The intelligent agents of tomorrow will relieve users of the burden of time-consuming and tedious searches through a massive, intricate and globally dispersed web of electronic information. Agents will find, assemble, and analyze information that users need to solve problems, become better informed, and make intelligent decisions.

Intelligent agents could play the roles of a highly competent secretary, reference librarian, personal and relentless world-events watcher, news-clip agency, office and personal "Gopher," personal shopper, personal investment advisor, or decision-making counselor. These capabilities, of indisputable value, will bring about a welcomed service-model shift that we can expect will touch and shape all of our lives significantly.

References

1. Hawkins, Donald T. "Artificial Intelligence (AI) and Expert Systems for Information Professionals: Basic AI Technology." *Online* 11, No. 5 (1987): 91–8.

2. Hawkins, Donald T. "Applications of Artificial Intelligence (AI) and Expert Systems for On-line Searching." *Online* 12, No. 1 (1988): pp. 31–43.

3. Negroponte, Nicholas. *The Architecture Machine: Towards a More Human Environment.* MIT Press, 1970.

4. *Intelligent Agents: Making Sense of the Data Swamp.* LINK Resources Corporation, August 1992.

5. "Online Databases." *Gale Directory of Databases,* Vol. 1. Detroit: Gale Research, January 1994.

6. Cleverdon, Cyril R. "Optimizing Convenient Online Access to Bibliographic Databases." *Information Services and Use* 4, Nos. 1–2 (1984): 37–47.

7. Kay, Alan. "On the Next Revolution." *BYTE,* No. 241 (September 1990).

8. Hawkins, Donald T., Louise R. Levy, and K. Leon Montgomery. "Knowledge Gateways: The Building Blocks." *Information. Processing & Management* 24, No. 4 (1988): 459–68.

9. Valauskas, Edward J. "AppleSearch: How Smart Is Apple's Intelligent Agent?" *Online,* No. 4, Vol. 18 (July 1994): 52–64.

10. McCleary, Hunter. "Filtered Information: Revolutionary New Product or a New Marketing Strategy." *Online,* No. 4, Vol. 18 (July 1994): 33–42.

11. Kahn, Robert E., and Vinton G. Cerf. *An Open Architecture for a Digital Library System and a Plan for Its Development.* Corporation for National Research Initiatives Technical Report, March 1988.

12. Maes, Pattie, and Robyn Kozierok. "Learning Interface Agents." *Proceedings of the Eleventh National Conference on Artificial Intelligence.* AAAI Press/The MIT Press, 1993: 459–64.

13. Maes, Pattie. *Social Interface Agents: Acquiring Competence by Learning from Users and Other Agents.* Presented at 1994 AAAI Spring Symposium on Software Agents.

14. Etzioni, Oren, Neal Lesh, and Richard Segal. *Building Softbots for Unix.* Technical Report, University of Washington, 1992.

15. Dent, Lisa, Jesus Boticario, John McDermott, Tom Mitchell, and David Zabowski. "A Personal Learning Apprentice." *Proceedings of the Tenth National Conference on Artificial Intelligence.* AAAI Press/The MIT Press, 1992: 96–103.

16. Shoham, Yoav. "Agent-Oriented Programming." *Artificial Intelligence,* No. 60 (1993): 51–92.

17. Cohen, Philip R., Adam Cheyer, Michelle Wang, and Soon Cheol Baeg. *An Open Agent Architecture.* Presented at 1994 AAAI Spring Symposium on Software Agents.

For Further Reading

Editor's note: The following sources will provide updated information on the products mentioned in this article.

Advanced Information Agent: *http://www.lotus.com/partcat/c50a_462.htm*

ConText: *http://www.uk.oracle.com/europe/emea/info/products/context/*

First! and HeadsUp: *http://www.newspage.com/NEWSPAGE/nptb-individual.html*

Homework Helper: *http://www.infonautics.com/products.htm*

Hoover: *http://www.iacnet.com/~corp/sandpoint/hoover.html*

NewsEDGE: *http://ftc.bus.utexas.edu/corp/newsedge.html*

PageKeeper: *http://www.provantage.com/DE_06821.HTM*

Editor's note: For more information on some academic projects, see

MIT: *http://agents.www.media.mit.edu/groups/agents/*

Stanford: *http://robotics.stanford.edu/groups/nobotics/home.html*

University of Washington: *http://www.cs.washington.edu/research/projects/softbots/www/softbots.html*

Editor's note: Two recent articles on this topic are

Etzioni, Oren, and Weld, Daniel S. (1995, August). "Intelligent Agents on the Internet: Fact, Fiction, and Forecast." *IEEE Expert,* 44–9.

Hedberg, Sara Reese. (1995, August). "The First Harvest of Softbots Looks Promising." *IEEE Expert,* 6–9.

Clarence Meets Alcuin

or, Expert Systems Are Still an Option in Reference Work

Eric Lease Morgan

Eric Lease Morgan *(ERIC_MORGAN@NCSU.EDU)* is a systems librarian at the North Carolina State University Libraries. He considers himself a librarian first and a computer user second. His professional goal is to discover new ways to use computers to improve library service while providing as much information to as many people as possible for the lowest possible cost. To that end, he has been the chief architect of the NCSU Libraries File Transfer Protocol (FTP), Wide Area Information Server (WAIS), ListProcessor, Gopher, and World Wide Web (WWW) servers as well as the author of numerous support applications written in HyperTalk, AppleScript, Practical Extraction and Report Language (PERL), VisualBasic, and Digital Command Language (DCL). He has also published and spoken widely in his professional areas.

Editor's note: A version of this essay can also be found at *http://www.lib.ncsu.edu/staff/morgan/clarence-meets-alcuin.html,* and you can see the very beginnings of Ask Alcuin at *http://www.lib.ncsu.edu/staff/morgan/alcuin/.*

This essay outlines the definition of expert systems, describes how this definition has been applied to reference librarianship, and suggests future directions of study.

Sometimes the functions computers perform seem like magic. They can add faster than any person can. They can remember the smallest of details for the longest periods of time. They can consume, propagate, and regurgitate vast amounts of information in an instant. Many times these features of digital computers have been compared with human knowledge, and this has given rise to the field of computer science called artificial intelligence.

Clarence

Clarence Reid entered the library for the purposes of beginning his art history class essay. A sophomore at State University, Clarence was studying design and hoped to be an interior decorator someday. He, unlike some of his classmates, understood the value of his library's collection of traditional resources. Even though the global Network hosted vast amounts of information, available at anyone's fingertips, much of the information was not necessarily academic in nature. The available information that was academic or scholarly was not necessarily accessed for free. Consequently, people had to have their Personal Debit Cards handy to fund any purchases. In short, visiting the library was a bit inconvenient but much less expensive than the commercialized network, especially for a starving student like himself.

As Clarence entered the library he saw a sign: "Try out our 'Portable Library Assistants.' Inquire at the Reference Desk." Feeling a bit overwhelmed by the size of the university's library and having his curiosity piqued by the sign, Clarence made his way to the reference desk.

"Hi. I would like to know more about the 'Library Assistants,' " said Clarence to one of the reference librarians behind the desk.

"No problem," said the librarian. As he brought out a small, handheld computing device from under the counter, the librarian continued, "If you give me your student identification card as collateral, then I will lend you one of our 'Library Assistants.' The software saved on these devices is designed to help you use the library more effectively. Would you like to try it?"

"Sure," said Clarence, giving his card to the librarian.

"Simply turn it on here," pointing to a switch on the device's side, "and use this special pen to supply your input," said the librarian. "If you have any questions, then just tap the Explain button. Okay?"

"Cool! Thanks."

A Short History of Expert Systems

Expert systems (sometimes known as knowledge-based systems) are a branch of the study of artificial intelligence. Alex Goodall has defined an expert system as "a computer system that uses a representation of human expertise in a specialist domain in order to perform functions similar to those normally performed by a human expert in that domain." Similarly, Donald Waterman defined an expert system as "a computer program using expert knowledge to attain high levels of performance in a narrow problem domain." Put less formally, expert systems are computer programs mimicking the decision-based processes of humans in a limited area of expertise. The concept of expert systems has been applied to a wide variety of tasks ranging from the configuration of computers to playing chess to locating natural-resource deposits.

Surveys of expert systems work applied to librarianship turns up a range of applications from classification to indexing to database selection. One of the earliest expert systems to be applied to the field of librarianship was a system done in 1967 by a University of Chicago master's student, Cherie Weil, who was studying reference work. The system was designed to answer basic biographical questions. The method used by Weil seems to be the method employed by many of the implementations following her work. Namely, a database of reference materials is created. Each item in the database is described, sometimes using an extended subject/quality classification system. Then, through some sort of question and answer process or a series of menus, the expert system queries its patron, searches its databases for matches, and presents the end-user an answer, usually in the form of a title to a reference work. REFSEARCH by Joseph Meredith, the Hepatitis Knowledge Base by L. M. Bernstien, Plexus by B. C. Vickery, AquaRef by Deborah Hanfman, and POINTER by Karen F. Smith all exemplify this technique.

While there have been quite a number of expert systems attempting to model reference services, none of them ever seem to have lasted very long. Why don't we hear about successful, long-standing systems that have been put into place over a long period of time? According to Richardson, all of the reference service expert systems to date have fallen short because they have not taken into account all aspects of reference service. By reviewing the Kuhnian paradigms of teaching reference work, Richardson identified three schools of thought: structuralist, proceduralist, and "psychologicalist." The structuralist reference method stresses reference materials. The proceduralist favors standardized methods for accomplishing successful reference services. The psychologicalist believes the analysis of the mental traits of the librarian and patron are paramount for quality services. Based on this analysis, Richardson posits that only when reference is taught emphasizing each of these perspectives will libraries be providing the best possible service. By extension, if expert systems in reference service do not incorporate these same principles, then they are doomed to be incomplete and lacking.

Alcuin

Clarence went over to a nearby chair and tapped the Explain button. The machine responded with a cheerful beep and presented Clarence with the following message: "Greetings! My name is Alcuin, your personal library assistant. My goal is to help you get the most out of the library by providing you with information about the library's collections and services. More importantly, I am designed to help you find the information you seek through a simple question-and-answer process. At the end of this process you will be presented with a strategy for fulfilling your information needs. To use me, read the questions carefully and answer them to the best of your ability. If at any time you don't understand something, then tap the Explain button. If worst comes to worst, ask a real live human for assistance. Tab to the Begin button to start the process."

As Clarence tapped the Begin button, Alcuin responded, "Welcome! My name is Alcuin." What is your name?" Naturally, Clarence tapped the Explain button.

The machine responded, " 'What is your name?' The purpose of this question is to make your interaction with me a bit more human friendly. It also gives me the opportunity to remember you the next time you visit the library. Answer the question and tap the Next Question button. Incidentally, my name is Alcuin. I died in 804 after a career as a librarian and advisor to Charlemagne."

Clarence thought the entire concept more than just a bit strange, but he continued anyway by entering his name and tapping the Next Question button.

The question-and-answer process continued. Alcuin proceeded to query Clarence about his educational background and expertise. Alcuin asked him for the subject of his information need and, in a Socratic sort of way, helped Clarence clarify and better define the subject. Alcuin asked Clarence what sort of work he had already done in this area and whether or not Clarence knew of any authors or works of significance. Alcuin queried Clarence for his preference of information media types such as books, journals, slides, Internet resources, etc. Alcuin asked Clarence how much time he had to spend on his work today and asked him how much money he was willing to spend if required. Throughout the process, Alcuin presented Clarence with intermediate results. These results were incomplete in that they were not based on the full exploration of Alcuin's questions. On the other hand, they gave Clarence the opportunity to verify Alcuin's progress.

Unlike "library assistants" before Alcuin, the Alcuin Library Assistant offers absolutely no answers to any of the end-user's questions. Instead, through the question-and-answer process (a nontraditional reference interview) Alcuin's primary objective is to create search strategies that can be applied to various databases. The reason for this is simple. There is no way any one library assistant (expert system) can keep track of the myriad individual information resources. But, if the information resources are systematically organized and consistently classified in databases, then searches can be applied to the databases throughout time and draw on new information the databases may contain. In short, Alcuin grounds its usefulness in its ability to ask questions and not necessarily in knowing specific answers. Specific answers change as quickly as publishers, but the questions remain the same. While databases may come and go, and while their structure may change over time, databases change at a much slower rate than the data they represent.

The interview was over. It only took about ten minutes. At the end, Alcuin knew that Clarence was an undergraduate student studying art history, specifically rococo. Clarence knew that Versailles was a good example of the rococo style and that the style grew out of baroque period. Through the process, Alcuin determined Clarence wanted to locate pictures of rococo architecture, but Clarence was not willing to pay for anything. Lastly, Clarence had about another hour and a half to spend on the project today before his next class.

Advances in Service

Despite the lack of any long-term, sustained successes in the area of reference expert systems, I still believe, like Richardson, that the profession can develop an expert system for the purposes of enhancing or supplementing reference services. I believe this for two reasons.

First, the majority of reference expert systems are doomed to failure because they try to suggest particular reference works. As the number of reference works increases, so does the difficulty in implementing and maintaining the expert system. As reference librarians interact with their clientele, they assemble qualities describing the client's information need. Then, rather intuitively, the librarian matches the set of qualities with a known reference work. In other words, librarians construct queries in their minds and identify one or more works from their experience embodying one or more of the qualities in question.

The same technique can be employed by computers to supplement reference service. The computer could be used to interact with patrons. This interaction would be in the form of a question-and-answer session. The questions would address issues surrounding the patron themselves such as

- age
- education level
- subject expertise
- time and money willing to spend on information gathering
- purpose of the information gathering

Additionally, the questions would address the information need itself, querying patrons about, but not limited to, the

- subject
- format of materials sought
- preferred location of the materials
- date ranges of acceptable materials
- names of authors or titles of known items on their subject
- the depth of detail in which patrons want the information

After (and during) this question-and-answer process, the system constructs search strategies that can be applied to databases of information. These search strategies could be applied to online public access catalogs of traditional library materials and bibliographic databases such as the databases hosted by DIALOG or MEDLARS. There is no reason these same search strategies cannot be applied to databases of Internet resources as well. Once the strategies are constructed, they are given to the end-user for execution. At that time end-users can evaluate the results for themselves, or, as described later, the system can assist the end-user in evaluating the search results.

The keys to success in this method are, first, to know the structure of each of the databases intimately and, second, to construct very finely tuned search strategies individually based on the strengths and weaknesses of each database. The fortitude of this approach lies in its ability to always identify valid resources without knowing particular items. Its weaknesses, on the other hand, are directly proportional to the completeness and integrity of the databases.

The second reason it will be important to build a successful expert system supplementing reference service is the need to advance and raise the level of services libraries can provide. Traditional library services have involved the issues of identifying, collecting, organizing, and disseminating data and information. Rarely have librarians formally asserted their abilities to evaluate information.

In today's world, technology is empowering individuals to identify, collect, and organize their own sets of data and information more easily. There is less need for the traditional set of library services. On the other hand, the profession harbors an ability to evaluate information. This is something new we can share with our clientele, and since our clientele is increasingly reluctant to visit libraries, we can provide this new service through electronic means such as expert systems. It may be quite possible for these expert systems to determine the importance of particular resources based on things such as the

number of times a resource has been used or checked out of the library
number of times the resource or resource's author has been cited
number of footnotes contained in the resource
length of the resource
number of times search terms appear in the resource (ranked relevance)
reviews of the resource
number of editions of the resource

Librarians could even take the leap and assign value judgments to resources in databases, such as educational level or thoroughness, and then expert systems could search for resources based on those judgments.

How Alcuin Helps

Based on this information, Alcuin generated a number of search strategies. First, it recommended that Clarence browse a number of art-related dictionaries and encyclopedias to gather more-specific terms such as the names of artists. Second, Alcuin generated a search of the library's catalog including the term "plates," "illus.," and "pictorial works," trying to generate lists of books containing photographs. This was enough to get Clarence started, but before the last search strategy was presented, Alcuin said, "Clarence, once you have looked over these initial resources, be sure to go through the question-and-answer process again. I'm sure we can uncover more relevant materials!"

Clarence proceeded to look over the dictionaries and encyclopedias. Sure enough, he came across terms he remembered his professor mentioning. After looking at a few of the books located through another of Alcuin's searches, Clarence discovered a number of similar books in the same area. Delighted with his success, Clarence started up Alcuin again to see what could possibly happen next.

"Do you know of any books that are of particular significance about rococo?" asked Alcuin.

Clarence promptly answered "Yes" and proceeded to supply the names of two of the new books he found on the shelf.

"Based on the subject entries for the books you entered, you may be interested in the following books," responded Alcuin.

Selecting one of the resulting titles, Clarence asked Alcuin for the location of the material. Alcuin responded with a map of the library with a blinking cursor pointing to the book's location.

Clarence was getting a bit tired and decided to call it a day. He checked out a few of the books and returned Alcuin to the reference librarian as directed. He was sure he would visit the library and Alcuin again soon.

Conclusion

It has been said that understanding is like a four-rung ladder. The first rung on the ladder represents data and facts. As the data and facts are collected and organized they become information, the second rung on the ladder. The third rung is knowledge, where information is internalized and put to use. The last rung of the ladder is wisdom, knowledge of a timeless nature. Technology has enabled more people to climb from the first to the second rung of the ladder with greater ease. Similarly, technology may enable libraries and librarians to climb higher on the ladder as well and provide knowledge services instead of simply information services. Expert systems in reference may be one manifestation of such a climb.

Bibliography

Alberico, Ralph, and Micco, Mary. (1990). *Expert Systems for Reference and Information Retrieval.* Westport, CT: Meckler.

Goodall, Alex. (1985). *The Guide to Expert Systems.* Oxford, England: Learned Information.

Richardson, John V. (1995). *Knowledge-based Systems for General Reference Work: Applications, Problems, and Progress.* San Diego: Academic Press.

Waterman, Donald A. (1985). *A Guide to Expert Systems.* Reading, MA: Addison-Wesley.

Suggested Readings

Alberico, Ralph, and Micco, Mary. (1990). *Expert Systems for Reference and Information Retrieval.* Westport, CT: Meckler.

> This book "attempts to address the development of expert systems for reference and information retrieval." It contains recommended readings and a large bibliography.

Aluri, Rao, and Riggs, Donald E., eds. (1990). *Expert Systems in Libraries.* Norwood, NJ: Ablex.

> This collection of essays describes numerous expert systems for reference work. It contains many references and a large selected bibliography.

Richardson, John V. (1995). *Knowledge-based Systems for General Reference Work: Applications, Problems, and Progress.* San Diego: Academic Press.

> This relatively new book is the most scholarly of the readings listed here. It outlines definitions of reference work as well as of knowledge-based (expert) systems. It then suggests ways to incorporate the two disciplines into a cohesive whole. Included are many references. If you are only going to read one of the suggested readings, this is the one to choose.

Roysdon, Christine, and White, Howard D., eds. (1989). *Expert Systems in Reference Services.* New York: Haworth.

> This is another collection of essays describing expert systems, but, unfortunately, some of the examples are not really "expert systems." This is a good book for understanding the principles of expert systems and methods for constructing them.

Power Tools for
Cyberspace

THE CYBRARIAN'S TOOL KIT

Bill Britten

Bill Britten is the systems librarian at the University of Tennessee Libraries. He has authored numerous articles about the Internet, especially focusing on collection development. His Web page is at *http://zuma.lib.utk.edu/bill.html*.

The purpose of this chapter is to provide an overview of the broad categories of network tools and how they are used. Descriptions of the tools will be followed by a general discussion on how to obtain them and keep your tool kit current in this rapidly changing area.

Just a few years ago, a librarian who was newly connected to the Internet would become indoctrinated into the world of Telnet and File Transfer Protocol (FTP). The use of these "raw" protocols was nongraphical and, for the most part, involved making a connection to a large computer and learning the arcane command language of the protocol. I can remember installing an Ethernet card in my PC in 1989 and quickly accumulating an unwieldy collection of Telnet and FTP address lists. The extra "tools" required then were typically limited to a utility program for uncompressing FTP files and a viewer to look at image files.

Those early days of Internet access seem quaintly simple now. In 1992 the University of Minnesota launched the Internet client-server revolution with the first Gopher client. Today, a librarian introduced to the Internet encounters a plethora of browsers, clients, viewers, plug-ins, and other assorted essential utilities and accessories. There is a synergy among these tools that engenders a type of ecology in the creation, organization, retrieval, and use of Internet documents. Many of the tools have evolved not as stand-alone applications but as niche players in the ecology of Internet information, so that knowledge of one tool often requires knowledge of how to use it with other tools. For example, Adobe's Acrobat Reader is a "helper application" for Internet browsers that enables them to display files with the popular .pdf (portable document format) extension.

Several essential components of a tool kit are discussed in the sections that follow, beginning with the all-important Internet browsers (which are becoming so rich in features that some predict they will develop into "operating systems for the Internet," eclipsing the many special-purpose network clients).

The browser is your navigator and your window on the Internet world. It is the most important network application in your tool kit.

If the browser is thought of as an "operating system," the terminal clients and multimedia applications discussed next are the software that runs on that operating system. Many documents can be handled by the browser alone, while for others the browser needs assistance. Your browser receives information from the server about each file encountered, and teaching your browser to know what to do with this information will pay great dividends as you access Internet documents. You might use this analogy to understand the process: when a book or magazine is placed in your hands, you can read it immediately, but when a videocassette or roll of microfilm is placed in your hands, you must have other tools at hand and the knowledge of how to use them.

Following the browser and its helper applications, several other network tools are discussed that can be used as stand-alone applications for special purposes. The last section will give more information on locating all of the software packages discussed.

Internet Browsers

The original Internet browser was created at the National Center for Supercomputer Applications (NCSA) at the University of Illinois in 1993. Called Mosaic because of its ability to weave a multimedia display from the main Internet protocols, this amazing software captured world-wide interest and propelled the Internet beyond its academic/government origins. Mosaic's chief architect, a graduate student named Marc Andreesen, went on to co-found Netscape Communications Corporation. Netscape has become the preeminent Internet browser, but there are several others, including the original Mosaic and Microsoft's Internet Explorer.

Browsers have continued to evolve as the centerpiece of Internet information delivery software. They allow the user to access World Wide Web (WWW) documents, initiate Telnet sessions, download documents via FTP, read news groups, and even transmit and receive e-mail. Auxiliary and "plug-in" software extend the browser's capabilities to include viewing of proprietary document formats, listening to real-time audio, viewing video clips, and much more.

Each browser will have a pull-down help menu on the right side of the menu bar, and this is a good place to explore. Also, all browsers have a configuration area that is the key to their ability to navigate the myriad of file types and connections found on the Internet. For Netscape, look under the "options" menu, and especially the "helpers" area under "general preferences." (In Microsoft's Internet Explorer, look under View/Options/File Types.) This screen looks quite daunting at first, but it is simply a list of file types that the browser might encounter and instructions on what to do with them. The browser will come preconfigured for many common file types, such as .gif (graphics interchange format) and .jpg (Joint Photographic Experts Group) image files. For other file types, such as Adobe's .pdf format or RealAudio's .ram format, you will need to download a copy of the appropriate software. Once this software is installed on your computer, add a configuration line in the "helpers" section to have the browser call upon the application. The help button of the browser will have detailed instructions on how to do this.

For many librarians, maintaining the browser and its essential auxiliary software will be sufficient for staying current with the Internet, while others will want to build a complete tool kit with all the tools discussed in the following sections. Browsers change rapidly however, with new versions announced several times a year, so librarians new to the Internet may want to focus on the browser first.

Terminal Clients and Multimedia Accessories

The basic Telnet connection to a remote computer is gradually being replaced by graphical client-server applications. However, many legacy computer services, including the majority of online catalogs, still rely on Telnet. A Telnet connection is one in which your powerful, graphical desktop computer emulates a terminal with few capabilities beyond taking keyboard input and displaying text. Typically, the emulation is one of two types: a Digital Equipment VT terminal or an IBM 3270 terminal. These two brands represent the dominant mainframe computers in use during the 1980s.

Although Telnet is a fading link to our computing past, it is essential that your tool kit include both Telnet and TN3270 clients. They can be used as stand alones for direct connection to a remote computer, but your browser should also be configured to call upon these clients whenever it encounters a Telnet or TN3270 link on the Internet. Use the configuration hints in the previous section to do this. In my library many first-time Netscape users will call the computer help desk to ask if the online catalog is down when in fact the problem is that Netscape has not been configured to make a Telnet connection.

There is a growing profusion of multimedia widgets known as "file viewers" that can be used as stand alones, but they are typically configured as "plug-in" or "helper applications" for the Internet browser. These include graphics viewers for the many image file formats, audio and video players, virtual reality (VRML for virtual reality modeling language) browsers, and specialized document viewers such as the RealAudio audio file player. The best place to learn about these helper applications is to visit one of the software archives listed at the end of the chapter. If you encounter a file that your browser is not configured to use, it will prompt you for information. This is a hint for you to go out and find the software that your browser needs.

E-Mail Clients

Sending and receiving e-mail is an essential network activity, and today's e-mail clients have evolved far beyond a simple terminal connection to a host mail system. Central to their functionality is the ability to download mail from a mail server, with "mail" including the traditional pages of text as well as binary files such as software, word-processing and spreadsheet files, and image and sound files—virtually any computer file can be sent as mail. Sending binary files as mail involves some type of encoding, and e-mail clients will automatically decipher popular methods such as MIME (Multipurpose Internet Mail Extensions), UUencode (UNIX to UNIX Encoding), and BinHex. Other features can include spell checking, automatic query of the mail server, filtering of incoming mail, and the creation of nickname and distribution lists.

Internet browsers such as Netscape incorporate the features of a basic e-mail client. You may want to become familiar with the e-mail abilities of your browser before deciding to investigate the many stand-alone packages. In either case, the first step in configuring an e-mail client is to enter the address of the mail server. You may have an e-mail account on a host computer that you log onto via a Telnet session. But that computer may also be running a mail server that would allow an e-mail client to download your mail. Once mail is downloaded to your desktop computer, it can be read and processed by your e-mail client. How do you know if there is a mail server running? You could ask the administrator of the host computer, or you could enter the name of the computer into your e-mail client, along with your user name and password, and see if the e-mail client can "fetch" your mail.

In my experience, one of the most frustrating aspects of e-mail clients is the sending and receiving of binary attachments such as word-processor files. Users seem to quickly learn how to attach documents and send them to a colleague, and the receiver usually has no problem in learning to detach a file from an e-mail message. Where the process often breaks down is not in the functioning of the e-mail client at all, but most typically is related to the *type* of file sent. It's no different than handing a person a file on diskette—that person must have software to read the file! While most software can import a file from the competition's product, there is often a gap when it comes to the version of the software. Since most software can also save files in various versions of the competition's product, it is best to agree ahead of time on a file format that can be read successfully by all persons receiving the e-mail attachment. For example, committee members might agree that all e-mail attachments will be in Microsoft Word for DOS version 6.0 because that is the lowest common denominator among them.

FTP Clients

Along with Telnet, FTP is among the original suite of Internet protocols. Like Telnet, the use of FTP as a stand-alone process is declining as Internet browsers incorporate FTP capability. Unlike the Telnet clients, however, you do not need to configure a separate FTP client to be called by your browser. If your file transfer activities are confined to downloading WWW software and documents, you may not need a separate FTP client. But if you plan to transfer your own files from one computer to another over the network (for example, if you create HyperText Markup Language [HTML] files on your desktop computer for transfer to a WWW server), you will need to obtain an FTP client application.

FTP clients are usually straightforward to use. Most will maintain a list of remote computer addresses with log-in requirements such as user name and password. After making the connection to an address, you see a graphical "file manager" view of the remote computer and your computer. Files are then transferred from one computer to the other simply by pointing to them and clicking a transfer button.

News Readers

The Internet is populated with thousands of discussion lists, or news groups. You can subscribe directly to these groups and have dozens (hundreds!) of e-mail postings sent to you each day, or you can employ a news reader to read selected postings at your leisure without having them actually sent to you. The first news readers did little more than allow posting, reading, or replying to news-group mail discussions. Modern news clients have many advanced features such as sorting capabilities for following the threads of discussion topics, automatic decoding of binary file attachments, and "kill files" to filter unwanted discussion postings.

Internet browsers such as Netscape have built-in news-reading capability that may not be as feature-rich as a stand-alone client but will suffice for many users. Many other news readers can be found in the archives listed at the end of this chapter.

Miscellaneous Tools

There are many other software programs that might be put in a cybrarian's tool kit. HTML editors are helpful for composing WWW documents. Compression utilities, decoders, and virus scanners can be invaluable for dealing with files coming off the network. Clients for Internet "phone" and "chat" offer entry into a fascinating area of network-based group communication.

For the advanced cybrarian, server software allows you to set up your own WWW or FTP site. Again, several key archives for this software are listed at the end of this essay.

Getting and Staying Current

By now you know that the Internet and all of its related software are constantly changing. In fact, they have doubtless changed greatly since this was written! How can you hope to catch up and then stay current? A first step would be to get an Internet browser such as Netscape and become familiar with it. After that, there are several sites on the Internet that specialize in keeping abreast of the latest network developments. It's a good idea to check in at these sites often to see if a new version of your browser has been released, to get auxiliary software, or to find out about important new software applications and the Internet file types that require them. The most important of these to maintain your cybrarian's tool kit follow.

Archives

Internet Resources by Tool or Type
http://lcweb.loc.gov/global/internet/bytool.html
> The Library of Congress Internet Resource Page is a comprehensive encyclopedia of Internet tools, and it has many links to other general resources similar to John December's, listed below.

John December's Internet Tools Summary
http://www.rpi.edu/Internet/Guides/decemj/itools/internet-tools.html
> This is an exhaustively comprehensive taxonomy of all Internet tools, great and small. It is not a software archive per se, but it does provide links to software from the definitions of the tools. It is an excellent site for the serious student.

Macintosh Internet Archives
http://www.macatawa.org/~mthomas/   or   *http://fly.hiwaay.net/~cwbol/macarc.html*
> Both of these addresses will lead you to comparable Macintosh sites for Internet-related software.

Stroud's Consummate Winsock Apps List
http://cws.wilmington.net/ or *http://cwsapps.fibr.net/*
> Stroud's CWSApps list is currently the best site for locating PC network software. This site is continuously updated and contains hundreds of software applications in all of the categories discussed in this chapter.

Ultimate Collection of Winsock Software
http://www.tucows.com or *http://gfn1.genesee.freenet.org/tucows/*
> The "ultimate collection" is a site with the same mission as Stroud's: to give you access to all current PC software related to the Internet.

Windows95.com
http://windows95.com

A very good site for Windows 95 shareware (network and non-network) applications, although not as comprehensive as *Stroud's* and *Ultimate Collection* for Internet-related software.

Yahoo:Computers and Internet:Operating Systems
http://www.yahoo.com/Computers_and_Internet/Operating_Systems/

This address will lead you to a menu for all operating systems (Mac, PC, UNIX, OS/2, etc.). From there you can find many archives for Internet-related software. This is a good place to look if the other sites listed do not meet your needs.

Browsers, Extensions, and the Kitchen Junk Drawer

Judi Copler

Judi Copler is editor of *Database* magazine and the former director of the Computing Technology Assistance Center in Bloomington, Indiana. She has more than twenty years' experience in computing in both academe and the private sector and is a columnist for both *Online* and *Database* magazines. She has spoken nationally and internationally on a wide range of computing topics.

For the first nine and one-half years of my professional life, I was a medical librarian. When I made a transition to software training and sales, my mom never quite got it straight. When her friends would inquire about me, she'd tell them I was doing something in the field of "software cartilage." That's why it made perfect sense to retreat to her house to write this chapter, right? No undue influence on my thinking. No one with a Mac bias hanging around. Of course she was curious, so I told her I was writing on browsers and extensions. "Well, if we have any, they're in the bottom kitchen junk drawer," she said, taking refuge in the TV room. As information professionals, we are at a crossroads. Just like a junk drawer, we have many options. Can we reach in and find anything that will be useful?

A *Very* Short History

We know that the early tools for information services delivery were controlled by nonsleeping techies who drank massive amounts of caffeine and lived in a world called UNIX, and by stock brokers who couldn't get into library school. The techies created ways to allow their friends around the world to use valuable information resources paid for by large corporations and public university tax dollars. Eventually, these tools came to be generically called browsers and developed quaint/cool names like Gopher (no relation to the Love Boat role), Cello, Mosaic, and Lynx (links—get it?). These tools got more and more sophisticated, allowing greater amounts of information to be made accessible.

At about the same time, the average person mastered the e-mail component of all this, and the Internet as we know it today was born. Clinton/Gore got elected and everybody started calling the Internet the "Information Highway." Then Marc Andreessen's Netscape Navigator Web browser caught the attention of stock brokers and journalists. To many people, the multimedia-laced World Wide Web became the Internet. Netscape Navigator quickly became the standard tool, or browser, for surfing the Internet. Now, while my mom is pondering how you surf a highway, the rest of us are wondering what happened to the days when our biggest decision was whether to order this year's almanac in paper or hardcover.

Browsers—The Ultimate Graphical User Interface

It is the browser that makes the World Wide Web accessible and allows the cybrarian to jump from computer site to computer site around the world instantaneously, retrieving information in text, graphic, audio, and video formats. The World Wide Web uses the concept of hypertext to present information that resides on many different computer systems connected to the Web. Browsers "read" World Wide Web documents written in a computer language called HyperText Markup Language (HTML). HTML formats documents by describing their appearance, the text delivered, links to other documents, and other media images. The Web is easy to navigate because the "addresses" for finding other information or Uniform Resource Locators (URLs) can be embedded in the document being reviewed.

I've already mentioned some of the older browsers, but for now, out of 50 plus on the market, there are only three that are the major players in terms of sophistication and user acceptance: Netscape Navigator, HotJava, and Microsoft's Internet Explorer. These three, particularly Netscape Navigator and HotJava, are where cybrarians should be focusing their efforts. The savvy cybrarian needs to have access to the latest Internet browsers in their most recent incarnation. That means using to our advantage any extensions and developments in the software to present our unique collections to the cyberworld. For information on browsers, visit the following site.

http://www.browserwatch.com/
Everything you want to know about finding available browsers, servers, Common Gateway Interfaces (CGIs), and HTML editors and changes being made in them can be found at this BrowserWatch Web site.

Information on HTML

For a librarian wanting to make information available on the World Wide Web, the first step is learning HTML. HTML is a watered-down version of Standard Generalized Markup Language (SGML), and it is not difficult to learn. Practically every week a new HTML editor, a tool that can help automate the coding process, is introduced. The following resources are guides for the beginner.

http://www.ncsa.uiuc.edu/General/Internet/WWW/HTMLPrimer.html
    This site provides help for the beginning beginner.

http://melmac.harris-atd.com/about_html.html
    This is a lot like the one before it, but some people like the format better.

Lemay, L. (1995). *Teach Yourself Web Publishing with HTML in 14 Days*. Indianapolis: Sams.net.
    Updated version of Lemay's earlier books with a different title. The books are getting better all the time, so go with the latest version you can find.

The following resources may be of interest for more advanced users.

http://info.med.yale.edu/caim/StyleManual_Top.HTML
    A serious site for serious HTML people.

December, J., and Ginsburg, M. (1995). *HTML & CGI Unleashed*. Indianapolis: Sams.net.
    The classic and definitive work. A "must buy" for the serious HTML developer.

The Netscape Phenomenon

Some of you may know me as the "Hardcopy" columnist for *Online* and *Database* magazines. In my ten years of doing the column, I've never seen a technology catch fire faster than Netscape Navigator. In a mere three months, Mosaic was gone and Netscape Navigator ruled.

Information on Netscape Navigator

The following site offers basic stuff.

http://home.netscape.com
    Here you'll find Netscape's very own home page. You can download the browser and catch all the latest news on Navigator.

For really advanced or experimental stuff, see

http://home.netscape.com/commun/netscape_user_groups.html
    This site will lead you to the news groups where really cool people post things. Plan to spend some time digging.

Netscape Extensions

HTML as a language has been limited. To allow developers to be more creative, Netscape HTML extensions were introduced by Netscape Communications Corporation to make up for the shortcomings. Fortunately or unfortunately, depending on your point of view, Netscape didn't bother to get approval from the people who are supposed to approve these things. I won't go into tedious detail, but these extensions are really pretty simple. In a generic sense, extensions are little add-on programs or features that allow you to do things above and beyond what you can do with the standardized version of HTML. It takes care of those frustrating things you'd like to be able to accomplish but HTML is too limited to do. For example, some HTML extensions allow you to do cool things with your document like centering text, adjusting font sizes, adding rule lines, etc. How it works is that everybody fights for awhile and then gradually, most extensions end up being approved and become accepted standards.

When it comes to extensions and whether or not to use them, there are two camps, and valid arguments can be made for both viewpoints. There are people like me who think we should push the envelope and use every tool and technique available to produce attractive and usable Web sites, and there are people who believe that Netscape is out of control and shouldn't be off implementing its own tags that are not part of a standard. To be fair, we'd have a mess on our hands if every browser developer had a Netscape attitude. So here is where we are at the moment. First you've got your regular old HTML tags commonly called HTML 2. Then there are the Netscape HTML extensions supported by Netscape and a few other browsers to some extent. Lastly, there are HTML 3 tags that are those under consideration. Some browsers, but not all, support these. As I said, it is a big fight, and Microsoft has started making up its own extensions, too, so my recommendation is to watch the Web sites I've recommended.

There is a secondary argument related to extensions and even to the use of graphical user interface (GUI) browsers that cybrarians will want to consider. That is, many of our users and patrons do not have access to state-of-the-art computing technology. If we do the fun thing and develop for the high-end, we may be cutting off the people who need us the most.

Beginning with Netscape Navigator version 2.0, the browser can run programs downloaded from the Web that were created in Sun Microsystems' Java programming language. And to complicate things further, new browsers like HotJava are adding new functionality to Web searching.

For information on HTML extensions, visit the following site.

http://home.netscape.com/assist/net_sites/html_extensions.html
This is the definitive list of HTML extensions.

HotJava

Java is a programming language based on the C++ language, but it is even better. It was developed by Sun Microsystems and it is used to create content. The cool thing about Java and its companion scripting language JavaScript is that Java allows for executable content. That is what makes Java pages different from HTML Web pages and that means real-time, dynamic interactions between users and databases or other applications. You can't see Java content unless your browser is Java enabled. HotJava is the special browser created to be used with the Java language. HotJava is free. It includes all the standard features of Netscape Navigator, and it can use some of Navigator's more popular extensions. The most recent version of Netscape Navigator is also Java enabled.

For cybrarians, Java is exceedingly interesting from the database perspective. With true object databases, where procedural information is stored along with more-traditional data types, having a universal language that is compact and secure is of tremendous value. Java's new Database Connectivity (JDBC) is designed to allow Java applets (mini applications) to directly access back-end databases. We need to pay attention to this because so much of what we do has a database context or component to it.

Sun is committed to making Java a standard and is building browsers for Windows 95, Windows NT, Mac OS 7.5+, and Solaris. There has been considerable buy-in from companies such as IBM and Oracle.

In addition, Java is toying with a non-UNIX based operating system appropriately called Java OS. It is too soon to tell whether this will ever get off the ground, but it has potential, especially in those gutless, cheap computers that people have started to talk about. I think Java OS is less likely to succeed than some of the company's other ventures. But, hey, I could be wrong.

Java, only officially released in the spring of 1996, is still in flux. Pay attention to the sources that follow for the latest information.

Information on Java/HotJava

http://java.sun.com/doc/programmer.html
Just what it sounds like, Java programmer documentation.

newsgroup: *comp.lang.java*
The most popular Java news group. You can describe, share, or dissent, and no one cares.

December, J. (1995). *Presenting Java: An Introduction to Java and HotJava.* Indianapolis: Sams.net.
Updates to this book can be found at: *http://www.rpi.edu/~decemj/works/java.html*

http://java.sun.com/Mail/usrgrp.html
A listing of all known Java/HotJava user groups, both domestic and international.

Microsoft's Internet Explorer

I learned a long time ago to never underestimate Bill Gates. Many scoff at Microsoft's Internet Explorer—its icons are confusing, it's intertwined with MSN (Microsoft Network) online service, and it is difficult to use with other online services. Rumor has it, though, that the next version of Windows 95 will eliminate the need for a separate browser program. It will have the ability to display any document written in HTML. Originally, the Microsoft Network Service planned on offering information by proprietary content providers. That strategy has changed, and it opens the door for more content from libraries and other traditional content providers. Also, since Internet Explorer is free, it is cheaper to deploy in large organizations.

Information on Microsoft's Internet Explorer

http://www.microsoft.com/windows/ie/ie.htm
> This is the site where Microsoft tells you what it officially wants you to know about Internet Explorer. You can download it from here.

http://www.microsoft.com/ie/author/htmlspec/ie20html.htm
> This is Microsoft's extensions for Internet Explorer.

Sagman, S. (1995). *Traveling the Microsoft Network*. Redmond, WA: Microsoft. The "official" book about MSN tells you about Internet Explorer. It's a hard sell, but informative.

The Future—What Is in the Works?

Real-Time and VRML

One area that could have important implications is in real-time interfacing. Netscape Communications Corporation has plans to make Netscape Navigator compatible with real-time audio, video, and data conferencing applications. What this means is that sometime in the future, cybrarians may be working face to face with their remote patrons in a teleconferencing mode.

By the end of the 1990s, we'll start to see Virtual Reality Modeling Language (VRML), or something close to it, coming into mainstream use. VR poses a particular problem for site designers because even most techies aren't trained to think and work in three dimensions. Paper, Inc., of Woodstock, New York, is working on a VR product called GlobalScope. It is calling it an information display model, and it will let users access news, weather, or even visit their hometown library by "zooming in on the county and city of their choice."

Microsoft and everybody else are having regular fights over VR standards. As of today, Microsoft is trying to come up with its own and do it its way, but I wouldn't be at all surprised to read in tomorrow's *Wall Street Journal* that it has gone off and partnered with someone else. Whatever happens, expect to see VR components in future releases of Internet Explorer and other popular browsers. Currently, there are several VRML browsers. None has emerged as a standard.

Information on VRML

http://vrml.wired.com/
   The VRML Forum is at this site. It has lots of links to other sites.

http://www.csl.sony.co.jp/project/VS/evrml1.htm
   This site gives Sony's extensions to VRML 1.0 standards.

http://www.lightside.com/~dani/cgi/virtual-reality-index.html
   Neat site! It serves as an index to other VRML sites.

Pesce, M. (1995). *VRML: Browsing & Building Cyberspace*. Indianapolis: New Riders.
   A great little book with a CD-ROM in the back that has VRML browsers, file converters, and other neat things. The author is the co-creator of VRML.

What It Means to the Professional

The last time I checked, there were several thousand library sites on the World Wide Web. They range from the simply awful (those that list their hours, the names of the staff, and outdated information on new bookmobile books) to some truly excellent ones that make use of multimedia. We're seeing new partnerships between telecommunications companies, cable television companies, and entertainment media giants. I'm currently working on a project with a distance learning company in which we're looking at franchising super-professors and offering degree programs around the world. Franchised library services might not be far behind.

For the cybrarian, this will be a whole new world. Few of the library science programs in the country are offering course content on HTML, much less C++ or Java. To remain active players, we're going to have to educate ourselves and become more technical or form partnerships and learn to work cooperatively with technical professionals outside our field.

What You Should Read Regularly

InfoWorld
   InfoWorld Publishing Company
   155 Bovet Road, Suite 800
   San Mateo, CA 94402
   $130/yr. Published weekly except for Christmas and New Years.

InternetWork
   Cardinal Business Media, Inc.
   1300 Virginia Drive
   Ft. Washington, PA 19034
   Complimentary subscriptions available for those who qualify.

WEBWEEK
  Mecklermedia Corp.
  20 Ketchum Street, Westport, CT 06880
  $50 for 12 issues.

Web Developer
  Mecklermedia Corp.
  20 Ketchum Street
  Westport, CT 06880
  $21 for 4 issues.

Bibliography

Bank, D. (1995, December). "The Java Saga." *Wired,* 166–9, 238–46.

Booker, E. (1996, February). "Where is VRML?" *WebWeek,* 40.

Clark, D. (1996, February 5). "Microsoft Ends Plans for Tool Designed for Online Service as It Shifts Focus." *Wall Street Journal,* B3.

LaMonica, M. (1996, February 12). "Sun Standard Creates Tight Java-Link." *InfoWorld,* 1.

Singleton, A. (1996, January). "Wired on the Web." *Byte,* 77–80.

Watt, P. (1995, December 4). "Java Tool from Netscape and Sun No Average Joe." *NetworkWorld,* 1.

Wingfield, N. (1996, February 5). "Netscape Web Tools to Gain Conferencing." *InfoWorld,* 8.

It's Time Once Again to Ask [Alternate] Dr. Internet!

1. How fast do the new CPU chips go?

Too damn fast, if you ask me. When I was getting started on the net, I had an XT and a 1200 baud modem, and was happy to have that much, I can tell you.

2. My coworkers tell me I'm becoming a Web geek. How can I be sure?

The fact that you still recognize who your coworkers are suggests that you still have a way to go, but here is some general advice about Web geekdom.

The mere surfers tend to get a little suspicious of those who have completely immersed themselves in the Web. There are questions you can ask yourself to determine if you have joined this elite (if you ask—and answer—these question aloud, your coworkers will be sure you're headed in the right direction). First, how many browsers do you have on your work station? If you use browsers on multiple computers, count those, too. You should aim for at least four or five—anything over half a dozen is a very good sign. Second, how many of your browsers have a *b* in their version number? How many have an *a*? Being able to talk in depth, or even at length, about current beta and alpha versions is another good sign. Finally, how many of your browsers do you actually like? Since a true Web aficionado is always looking down the road, you should affect a sneering disdain for the weaknesses of all browsers you currently use. But recommend one of the more obscure ones to your friends as "the best available today." UdiWWW is a good choice for this sort of showing off.

As a special extra, learn to say something snappy about Web terminals running off of cable modems. Don't worry about what to say, exactly, as no one can possibly contradict anything in this cloud of vaporware; pick something pithy like "This is the Newton of the late '90s." Try to avoid gaffes like "Didn't Larry Ellison write *The Invisible Man?* You're thinking of Harlan Ellison.

3. What is Java?

Java (or the version being developed in Dr. Internet Labs, "Single Tall Skinny Hazelnut Latte With A Little Foam" or STASHLEWALF) is a programming language designed to extend the length of Web pages. Extensive user surveys have determined that users believe the most valuable Web pages are the ones they have to wait longest to download. The brilliance of Java is that it can triple or quadruple the amount of code transmitted for one document without affecting its content at all.

Java was developed by a handful of Webmasters who realized everyone else in the systems office had the word "programming" in their job descriptions and therefore had substantially higher salaries.

3a. Wait a minute. In a previous column, didn't you say Java was developed to woo high tech investment to Indonesia away from Singapore?

Yes, but I occasionally throw in something silly just to keep you on your toes.

4. What's the deal with these "Top 5% of the Web" logos I see on different sites?

Approximately 80% of all sites on the Web are now included in one or another service that lists the Top 5% of the Web. Some sites have created their own Top 5% lists just to include their own pages.

The reasons behind the 5% listing are rooted in cultural anthropology. Confronted by confusing new technology, we take refuge in primitive numerology, and 5 is a powerful magic number. It's the number of fingers on one hand, the number of planets visible to the naked eye (at night, of course), the number of platonic solids in geometry, and the number of URLs most people can remember without using bookmarks. There are some indications that Pythagoras maintained the first "Top 5% of the Web" list. Given that, it's natural that some people should flock to this 5%. These are the same people who build tetrahedra around their monitors to store up pyramid power.

5. My systems administrator wants to put up a firewall. What is that, and why would we want one?

Many organizations whose internal networks connect to the Internet are being forced to make difficult choices about access, security, and the openness of their networks. It is only natural that some of these choices will irritate or even anger network users.

Because of this, many systems administrators are installing firewalls, which are security devices intended to protect them from their more vocal users. They are large asbestos-filled barriers that can be quickly dropped over the door of the systems office in case users turn to arson as a means of discussing their feelings about access restrictions. Other systems departments are using metal detectors or guard dogs.

6. What do you think is the best way to respond to the Communications Decency Act?

The best response to the CDA cannot be described on a list that might be open to minors.

The second best thing is to write strenuously vociferous messages to mailing lists where everyone already opposes the CDA.

An alternate approach (recommended, of course, by the Alternate Dr. Internet staff) is to make a point of accessing indecent material every day. And do it at work because most of the really good sites get busy at night, and you don't want to download those graphics over your dial-up connection anyway. Just tell your coworkers that you're researching civil libertarian issues on the Net, and to make sure they knock before opening your office door.

Tune in next time for Ask Dr. Internet—"I have a master's degree . . . in Internet!"

Dr. Internet, Master of All Knowledge
Benedictine On the Rocks With a Twist
No official connection to Dr. Science

Editor's note: [Alternate] Dr. Internet is channeled by Thomas Dowling, who holds copyright on these effusions. You can find his contact information in his chapter on "Multimedia File Formats," which is more serious. At least, I think it is.

Anyway, you can find more wisdom of [Alternate] Dr. Internet at http://chehalis.lib.washington.edu/dri

Searching Cyberspace

Bob Craigmile and Andrew Wohrley

Bob Craigmile *(LIBRLC@EMORY.EDU)* is currently doing reference and computer support for the Pitts Theology Library, Emory University, and has been an avid Internet user since 1991. He has written for several computer-related library publications. Andrew Wohrley (*WOHRLAJ@ LIB.AUBURN.EDU*) is currently working in the library at Auburn University; he previously worked in Caterpillar, Inc.'s Technical Information Center. His library degree is from Indiana University.

Currently, Web search systems can be divided into two categories, automatically generated and people-generated. Automatically generated search systems, or indexes, tend to be more comprehensive than people-generated indexes, while people-generated indexes tend to provide more cross references. In fact some automatically generated Web indexes use people to fine-tune their systems.

A brief note about methodology: since this paper was begun, at least one system, Alta Vista, has been introduced. The velocity of change on the Internet ensures that results from any particular Internet search system become obsolete immediately. Better, then, to just judge these systems by interface features and by how their results for the same question differ. To compare these systems we used three terms familiar to librarians: "Blaise Cronin" (Dean of Indiana University's School of Library and Information Science), "Dublin, Ohio," and "bar codes." We hoped that by searching for a person, place, or thing, we would provide a reasonable test of each system. While not scientific, this anecdotal approach gives a "quick and dirty" indication of the relative merits of each.

One point cannot be emphasized enough: *The same search terms will obtain different results on each system.* Therefore, comprehensiveness in a search must be sought by searching several systems.

Searching the Internet puts a premium on relevance. Unlike the controlled vocabulary databases librarians are familiar with, there is no controlled vocabulary on the Internet in any meaningful sense. The best Internet search systems will try to assign relevance to each hit and then sort those hits in descending order.

The speed of the search system is perhaps the least quantifiable aspect of Internet searching, and your mileage will vary. A popular system might be slow due to demands on its processors, or a system might simply have a slow Internet connection, or it might be located a continent (or an ocean) away. However, the speed of the system in retrieving results is a factor that affects user friendliness. When it seems appropriate, slow links are noted.

Ease of use and search features are interrelated. Most systems offer a basic interface that is easy to use but without advanced features such as Boolean searches, limits on results, limits on the time range searched, or sorting for relevancy. A cybrarian should learn all the advanced features for each system to use them effectively.

A word of caution about our results in that, while relevancy ranking tends to concentrate the best hits at the top of the list of hits, it does not mean that all the hits at the top will be germane to the question. Also, although the index may say that there are X number of hits, actually one-third X is a likelier result for the items that precisely answer this question. Usually these cases reflect a lack of context or are only partial matches.

The focus in this review of Internet search systems was simply identifying systems of use to cybrarians and not on specifically identifying all the features of those systems. The reason for not emphasizing the features was simply because these systems change from day to day, and details that are important today can be obsolete tomorrow.

Alcuin   *http://library.ncsu.edu/drabin/alcuin*

"In the format of USMARC records, Alcuin is a database of Internet resources. It is a part of an informal experiment at the North Carolina State University (NCSU) Libraries to determine how easily traditional practices of librarianship can be applied to the collection, organization, classification, and dissemination of Internet resources." Alcuin searches the same government data as does its companion Alex system and includes full e-texts from Project Gutenberg, which converts public domain materials into e-texts. At the time of this writing, Alcuin is nearly a year old and represents an early attempt to make non-MARC data available in an Online Public Access Catalog (OPAC). Read all about it at: *http://www.lib.ncsu.edu/staff/morgan/alcuin/alex-meets-alcuin.html*. In essence, Alcuin is a kludge of different programs working together. Since Alcuin was created, many library automation vendors have jumped into the fray, using the 856 field, Web interfaces, etc. to display links to electronic texts. Our results were

Blaise Cronin: 0 hits
Dublin, Ohio: 0 hits
bar codes: 0 hits

Though it struck out on our searches, Alcuin's interface is simplicity itself, with only a search box, choice between full and tagged records, and a choice box for the number of hits you want returned. In fact, in comparison with the other Internet search engines available, and given its limitation of data searched, Alcuin is too simple.

When Alcuin can't find what you're looking for, it doesn't tell you, but merely redisplays the search screen. Although you are warned of this in the scope notes for the system, it is nevertheless annoying when it happens. Given our results, you're no doubt thinking it would be tough to evaluate the search interface; you're right. So, we performed a search that would garner results (the term "alice") and got the result:

Title: Illustrations for Alice in Wonderland
- Author: Tenniel, John, Sir 1820–1914
- URL: *ftp://etext.archive.umich.edu/pub/Gutenberg/etext94/algif10.zip*
- Electronic Access: *gopher.lib.ncsu.edu*

Chances are that Alcuin will either be left behind or metamorphose into something new. If it doesn't evolve, it will be like one of the displays of early rocketry at the Smithsonian: a great experiment that taught us something new.

Aliweb   *http://web.nexor.co.uk/public/aliweb/aliweb.html* and *http://www.cs.indiana.edu:800/aliweb/form.html* (mirror)

Aliweb is a registration-based service. Since the Web is so huge and dynamic, Aliweb doesn't want to try to search it all. Instead, users can register their site with Aliweb, which will perform the retrieval and indexing of the registered page(s). That's right, only those sites that are registered are available. Worse, Aliweb depends upon a specific format for the registration. So Aliweb relies on those who have data and are willing to go through their process of making it searchable. We assume the line there is not long. Our results:

Blaise Cronin: 0 hits
Dublin, Ohio: 19 hits
bar codes: 1 hit

The interface is a little intimidating. There are many choices you must make, but they seem fairly self-explanatory. The form is fairly tight. One feature is the ability to limit searches by domain (e.g., "edu" or "uk"). This is a feature more search engines should build in, although Aliweb cheats by getting the domains from the registration process.

Alta Vista   *http://www.altavista.digital.com*

Alta Vista claims to be the largest Web index and provides a powerful and comprehensive search system. It operates in three modes: basic, advanced query syntax, and results ranking criteria. Basic search mode is on the home page and is the first system new users see (and could be the only system that they need). Advanced query syntax allows you to search using "and," "or," "not," or "near" to have finer control of the search parameters. Results ranking criteria sorts the results so that the best match to the search criteria is listed first and the less-well-matched items are listed in descending order of relevancy. Alta Vista provides better control of the items that you search for than most other systems. Not only does Alta Vista search the Internet but it also searches Usenet groups the same way.

The index is generated automatically by an Internet Spider called Scooter. Alta Vista benefits considerably from its corporate patron (Digital Equipment Corporation) in terms of resources devoted to this project. Currently, Alta Vista offers quick response time, but whether this will last as Internetters discover what a valuable resource it is remains to be seen.

Alta Vista scored the best by far of all of the Internet search systems that we reviewed.

> Blaise Cronin: 48 hits
> Dublin, Ohio: 800+ hits
> bar codes: 1,000+ hits

The results were uniformly more comprehensive and relevant to the search terms than any of the other systems. It seems clear that a computer should be able to tell Dublin, Ohio, from Dublin, Ireland, but only Alta Vista managed this feat. If only Digital would apply the same effort that it puts into its Internet Index system into creating a browseable subject directory for the Internet, Alta Vista would be complete.

CUI (Centre Universitaire d'Informatique) W3 Catalog   *http://cuiwww.unige.ch/w3catalog*

CUI is based in Geneva, Switzerland, and has mirror sites around the world. Always choose the mirror site closest to your site to improve your response time and to keep from avoidably clogging long-distance connections. Although based in Switzerland, the text (as we found it) was in English. CUI provides both subject organization and keyword access to Internet sites. To be included on the list, the site must be registered by its creators with CUI. While this hurts comprehensiveness, it tends to promote inclusion of high-quality Internet sites. Because CUI is so selective, there were no hits, even on bar codes, a term that found hits on almost every other system we tested.

> Blaise Cronin: 0 hits
> Dublin, Ohio: 0 hits
> bar codes: 0 hits

However, technology subjects are generally covered very well, so CUI might be worthwhile if you wish to run a search in a well-established discipline.

CUSI from Nexor   *http://www.nexor.co.uk/public/cusi/doc/list.html*

Configurable Unified Search Engine (CUSI) is the Swiss Army knife of Internet search systems; on one interface, a cybrarian can access systems such as Yahoo, Lycos, Netfind, etc. It has lots of sites around the world. CUSI is more an interface to Internet search systems than a system in itself. All of the Internet indexes are loosely organized either by how the system is indexed, whether manually or automatically as in CUI or Yahoo for example, or by the information searched by the system, like Netfind. You just click on the radio button to the system that would most effectively run the search and enter the search terms.

Because many of the Internet search systems are provided in one convenient place with CUSI, searches can be done with greater speed and assurance of comprehensiveness. The CUSI address given is to the list of CUSI sites worldwide, so choose the one closest to you since the connection to the United Kingdom is very slow from North America.

DejaNews   *http://www.dejanews.com*

DejaNews is unique in that it searches only Usenet archives. DejaNews has a very nice index to Usenet postings that is updated every two days. The operators of DejaNews intend to charge for at least some of their services in the future; however, right now the service is free. Searching the four gigabytes of Usenet posts by both keywords and user names requires a bit of interpretation of the results because the precision of the search is fairly low for obscure topics. Response time is good, and DejaNews has a very easy interface.

DejaNews allows you to set the maximum number of hits to be viewed, to specify the format of the results, to get a ranking of the relevance of the results, and to specify if the search terms are to be linked by a Boolean "and" or "or." Our results were

Blaise Cronin: 3 hits (all from current cites)
Dublin, Ohio: 326 hits
bar codes: 395 hits

Excite   *http://www00.excite.com*

Excite comes from a hot young company in the Internet industry: Architext. Excite has all of the good things that people should expect from an Internet search system: Boolean search capability, relevancy ranks, and a subject organization option. Search results for Dublin, Ohio, were uniformly trivial. The results from the bar-code search were good. Some trivia was included, but the results were what one would expect. The Blaise Cronin search was the best. All of the results were specific to the right man.

One unique point about Excite is that Architext is marketing its system from the start to database owners so they can organize and provide access to their own information.

Blaise Cronin: 85 hits
Dublin, Ohio: 164 hits
bar codes: 1,088,466 hits

Four11   *http://www.Four11.com/*

You're probably sitting there thinking that with one quick mouse click you can find anyone else on the Internet. Well you're wrong. It's better than it used to be, but things are still pretty tough. Why? Consider that many services that sell Internet time offer no finger or phone book services. Many institutions that are "wired" don't want you to be able to figure out who's there, period, especially if you don't work there. And network security is always high on any company's priority list.

Four11 is a Web-based search service that claims more than 3 million e-mail listings. It is both a search engine and a registry, meaning that it will let you add your e-mail address (or Uniform Resource Locator [URL]) to its database.

The search engine is straightforward. You use a forms-capable Web browser to input first and last names and domain information, if known. It will accept last-name-only queries, but *caveat netor*. Our test search for "Blaise Cronin" yielded no matches, even though I specified the domain "indiana.edu" and still didn't find him when I omitted the first name and domain!

To get some idea of how Four11 works when successful, I did a search on the last name "craigmile." This strategy yields nine hits, two of which are me, with one of those addresses now defunct, so updating is a problem. More disturbing is that none of them are my wife! Luckily the registry allows users to correct such omissions.

GILS, Government Information Locator System   *http://info.er.usgs.gov/gils/index.html*

GILS promises to be an exciting new resource for accessing government Internet information. However, GILS currently consists of a rather disjointed collection of disparate government databases from the U.S. Geological Survey, Library of Congress, Lawrence Berkeley Labs, and the Defense Technical Information Center, with the user receiving no information as to why some sites are not accessible through GILS while others are. The organization of the site provides access through headings such as U.S. Federal, International, and U.S. States and through specific headings such as Global Change Data Clearinghouse. GILS receives the benefit of the doubt, since although the current system is less than impressive, the federal government has made a commitment to have its information accessible through GILS in the future. The Internet surfer should put this site on a home page and then monitor it closely for changes and the addition of sites of interest.

Harvest   *http://harvest.cs.colorado.edu/*

The Harvest Information Discovery and Access System is a relative loser when it comes to Internet searching. This is a bit unfair, in that it appears to be more of a technology than a service. That is, unlike Opentext, which provides a search engine and the data for as much of the Net as possible, Harvest provides the engine and very little in the way of data to be searched. Part of the reason for this is that it is meant to be used for "local" databases, and the search software is downloadable for those UNIX users who want to try it. It was unable to find any of the search terms we tried.

Searches using more than one term require Boolean operators, which slows down those of you (and you know who you are) who like "quick and dirty" searching. Thankfully, searches with bad syntax generate a help screen. I'm guessing you'll see this screen a lot. Unfortunately, searches with a hit rate of zero produce only the less than helpful "0 Returned Object(s). Return to the Broker Home Page" message. You'll probably see this too much as well.

Harvest's initial screen gives the searcher too many options, none of which are really explained. Harvest's limited data set is the big drawback and makes it of little use to most folks who simply need to search the Web.

Inktomi   *http://inktomi.berkeley.edu*

Inktomi has an impressive pedigree—created at the computer science department at the University of California at Berkeley; sponsored by the folks who brought you the Internet itself, the Advanced Research Projects Agency; and operating on Sun work stations. However, the execution leaves much to be desired. While the interface is easy to use, and the results are displayed in decreasing order of relevance, more work must be done on this system. Boolean searching is not currently explicitly permitted, although you can search more than one word at a time, and there is no subject organization. While Alta Vista shows that subject organization is not a requirement for a satisfactory system, Inktomi suffers without one. Inktomi provided precise results on both the question on Blaise Cronin and on bar codes. (As pointed out earlier, nearly all of the search systems got good results searching the term "bar codes.") However, it inexplicably could not provide satisfactory results searching for Dublin, Ohio. Though Inktomi provides a feature that uses the plus (+) sign to tell the computer that both terms must be in the results, Dublin, Ohio, was still confused with Dublin, Ireland.

> Blaise Cronin: 8 hits
> Dublin, Ohio: 1,087 hits
> bar codes: 1,486 hits

Inktomi may eventually become a valuable Internet search system for librarians, but its lack of Boolean searching and a subject index must be rectified.

InterNIC   *http://www.internic.net*

InterNIC is the central repository of American Internet hosts. Although the listings can be accessed by all the major Internet systems (Gopher, Telnet, File Transfer Protocol [FTP], World Wide Web [WWW], etc.), the information is currently displayed in a Gopher format. Although InterNIC is narrowly focused on the Internet itself and does not have much information about non-Internet sources, much of the information contained here is simply not available anywhere else. Response times are fairly slow.

InterNIC has three systems of particular interest to cybrarians: "White Pages," "Yellow Pages," and the Internet Scout. The White Pages allow searching for people with Internet accounts, the Yellow Pages for organizations, companies, and registered network addresses, and Net Scout is a weekly newsletter detailing new Internet sites. One word of caution: The White Pages system is not particularly user-friendly, so it pays to read the documentation before using the system.

Lycos   *http://www.lycos.com*

Lycos has a fast, easy-to-use system that supports searches by both subjects and keywords. Unlike some other sites, Lycos will rank-order the findings of a search and move the item with the most hits to the top of the list of possibilities that answer your search.

The searches in Lycos delivered acceptable results with a fair degree of precision on all terms, although Lycos still ranked some sites on Dublin, Ireland, as more relevant than other sites about Dublin, Ohio. You can improve search precision by setting the search options ahead of time.

While Lycos has a well-earned reputation for being the largest index of Internet information, we were still able to find information elsewhere that it missed. We found the best results setting Lycos to the "fair match" setting, which provided the best compromise between the comprehensiveness of the "weak match" and the precision of the "strong match."

Blaise Cronin: 7 hits
Dublin, Ohio: 46 hits
bar codes: 415 hits

Netfind   *Telnet://bruno.cs.colorado.edu*

Like the town of Lake Wobegon, Netfind is a service that time cannot forget and the decades cannot improve. You don't need a Web browser to use it, but it does require at least Telnet capabilities. Once you log in to a Netfind server (using the user name "netfind," oddly enough) you are given a simple menu. The help option is a last resort or worse. It's a basic nightmare. What you need to do here is enter a last name and whatever other information you have about the person in question, such as the institution and its type. For instance:

==>jones mit edu

Be careful not to insert the usual dots (.) in the search. A big problem with Netfind is its inability to know what you mean regarding the target machine. For instance, a search like the one for Jones will swamp you with a list of possible machines at MIT. You can choose any three from the possible hundreds of servers. With help like this, who needs hindrance?

Opentext   *http://www.opentext.com*

Opentext is a Canadian company that provides a variety of Internet products, including a powerful search engine. That Yahoo (see final discussion) has chosen this technology for its own service speaks well of this company's future. By searching the Web directly from the Opentext page, you can get a sense of why Yahoo favors this engine.

The default, "simple search," starts with exact term/phrase searching with one text entry box but allows Boolean "or" and "and" searches as well. The "power search" feature permits up to five boxes for data entry, and each has its own limiting and Boolean operators. The "weighted search" option also has these features, but it lets the user determine rankings and weights of search results. Unlike other search engines, Opentext doesn't restrict its searching to any single element of Web pages.

We've always liked this search service and have found the results to be very fast and thorough. Opentext boasts not only hit lists but Keyword in Context (KWIC) views, too, which are especially nice when doing power searching since the relevance can be low. Our results were

Blaise Cronin: 4 hits in exact simple search; 22 hits with power search
Dublin, Ohio: 184 hits in exact simple search; 1,330 hits with power search
bar codes: 256 hits in both exact simple search and power search

The power to do complex searching in a decent interface should make this a favorite of every cybrarian.

Web Crawler   *http://webcrawler.com*

Owned by America Online (AOL), Web Crawler is a fast system that delivers results in a convenient rank-ordered title format. The title format allows you to review a number of sites and quickly identify and link to the one that most completely answers your question.

However, we found Web Crawler to be lacking in comprehensiveness. The question on Blaise Cronin came up with only two hits, and while both were relevant, they weren't the best sites. The features are also limited with no obvious provision for Boolean searching or for controlling the search settings. It appears that AOL designed Web Crawler more for the amusement of AOL users and not to provide them with a tool that would satisfy their information-seeking needs. The list of top 25 sites and "Random Links" to Internet sites tend to confirm this view.

Blaise Cronin: 2 hits
Dublin, Ohio: 148 hits
bar codes: 198 hits

World Wide Web Worm (WWWW)   *http://guano.cs.colorado.edu/wwww/*

The WWW Worm boasts that "WWWW allows you to locate almost any WWW hypertext (text seen underlined in a Web Browser) or WWW information resource (URL), simply by specifying some keywords." In other words, it is not full text. It goes on to warn that "WWWW provides four types of search databases: citation hypertext, citation addresses (URL), HTML [HyperText Markup Language] titles and HTML addresses." Given its lack of comprehensiveness and search limits, the Worm has been pretty famous on the Web for a few years. Our results were

Blaise Cronin: 1 hit
Dublin, Ohio: 0 hits
bar codes: 14 hits

The worm's interface is very simple, offering the four databases as choices with the choice of Boolean "and" and "or." Searches don't take long either. To its credit, it does allow for up to 5,000 hits to be retrieved. On the down side, it displays the results as URLs in a simple list, which may not be helpful in certain circumstances (i.e., 5,000 hits).

Yahoo   *http://www.yahoo.com*

Yahoo has the best, most-detailed and specific subject divisions of any of these sites on the Web. If you just wish to browse, Yahoo identifies cool sites in its links. However, the keyword searching feature isn't quite as good as its browseable subject-division features. On the first two terms the precision of the results ranged from poor for Blaise Cronin to only fair for Dublin, Ohio.

> Blaise Cronin: 22 hits
> Dublin, Ohio: 3 hits
> bar codes: 11 hits

Boolean searching with "and" and "or" is supported, but more features for limiting search results would be nice.

Yahoo is currently an independent entity, although closely affiliated with Netscape. Yahoo claims as its mission, "To be the world's best guide for information and online discovery." If it starts to devote more time to improving its search features, it just might live up to its boast.

Editor's note: Other recent articles on this topic include the following:

Eagan, Ann, and Bender, Laura. (1996). "Spiders and Worms and Crawlers, Oh My: Searching on the World Wide Web." [Online]. Available: *http://www.library. ucsb.edu/untangle/eagan.html*

Lager, Mark. (1996). "Spinning a Web Search." [Online]. Available: *http://www. library.ucsb.edu/untangle/lager.html*

Webster, Kathleen, and Paul, Kathryn. (1996, January). "Beyond Surfing: Tools and Techniques for Searching the Web." [Online]. *Information Technology.* Available: *http://magi.com/mmelick/it96jan.htm*

More comparisons can be found at the following sites:

Campbell, Karen. (1995). "Comparing Search Engines." [Online]. Available: *http: //www.hamline.edu/library/links/comparisons.html*

Koch, Traugott. (1996, April). "Literature about Search Services." [Online]. Available: *http://www.ub2.lu.se//desire/radar/lit-about-search-services.html*. This is the most complete site I've found on this topic.

Welcome
to the Hololib

James Powell

James Powell is programmer/analyst of scholarly communications and library automation at Virginia Polytechnic Institute and State University. He is the creator of HTML-Editor for Nextstep and the author of *HTML Plus!* His Web page is *http://scholar.lib.vt.edu:80/jpowell/jpowell-person.html.*

A library is a place. It is even a place on the Web. Sure, its electronic resources are scattered about the Net, but there is a Uniform Resource Locator (URL) that defines a place on the Web that can still be called a library. Instead of going to the physical library, users sometimes choose to go to the library home page. But what would happen if the library were not just a Web site but a virtual building with walls, study carrels, work stations, electronic collections, and even virtual assistants with a three-dimensional presence. What would be gained? Would there be any advantages over a home page on the Web?

No speculation about the potential impact of virtual reality in the mid 1990s could be complete without an examination of television's most famous virtual reality device—*Star Trek's* Holodeck. For those of you who've been under a rock reading books instead of watching TV, the second incarnation of *Star Trek* and all its successors feature a place constructed of a host of twenty-fourth-century technologies indistinguishable from magic that comprise the Holodeck. This device allows people to explore strange new worlds without traveling a single parsec, and all in a space the size of a racquetball court. It simulates three-dimensional objects using apparently exhaustive descriptions of everything known to humankind stored in *The Computer.* These simulations can include inanimate objects such as tables, walls, snow, trees, and rocks. They can also include interactive simulations of animate objects, including people. The items are referred to as holographic projections, but they can be touched, tasted, and, presumably, smelled. They can hurt you if you forget to specify that deadly weapons should act like butter knives instead of butcher knives. Even more amazing is the fact that within this confined space people ski, kayak, and battle simulated aliens in what appears to them to be the great outdoors instead of a computerized rumpus room. Such trickery involves real people without headgear or bodysuits and without apparent concern for the amount of power and computing resources being consumed for mostly frivolous next-generation entertainment.

Indeed, this mythical Holodeck is mostly wasted on sappy plots that often involve placing aliens in medieval Earth settings. But there have been a few instances where the potential applications of such a device have been explored. In one episode where the *Enterprise* had fallen into some kind of trap (a recurring story line), someone had the good sense to use a Holodeck simulation to work out solutions to that weeks *heure de drame*. An engineer reconstructed the birthplace of the *Enterprise's* warp drives (the things that make it go) to squeeze a few more drops of performance from them. He also reconstructed the inventor, and aside from the fact that she turned out to be beautiful and he instantly fell in love, etc., etc., he was able to repeatedly simulate potential resolutions to the crisis until he hit upon a solution. The ability to interact with the collective intellect of the engine inventor in a simulated engineering laboratory with all the required tools and materials made all the difference to this imaginary ship and crew.

Issues

Virtual reality is all about tools. It isn't enough to provide blocky simulations of places where people silently drift as if touring a museum or searching for the exit to a cybermaze. People need an overwhelming reason to devote time and energy to supporting and developing virtual spaces. Users must be convinced that there is a good reason for them to immerse themselves in databases and information resources instead of peering into them through indexes and search engines. Today we are pretty much in the silent, blocky touring phase. In the future, systems will immerse us in three-dimensional sound effects, track eye movements rather than require manipulation with keyboard or mouse, and create three-dimensional 360-degree visual presentations with visual and tactile feedback just like the real world.

Desktop systems are only now capable of supporting even crude virtual reality simulations. We are years away from immersive interfaces both in terms of hardware to support them and in developing such interfaces. And for the foreseeable future we will be developing these interfaces rather than having them magically appear as the computer sifts through unimaginable amounts of data to auto-magically reproduce places both real and imaginary that act as metaphors for data collections or as simulations of the item described by the data.

VRML Browsers

Thanks in part to the Web, there have been recent advances in virtual reality that make it possible for virtual worlds to take up residence on the Internet. While overshadowed by Java, the development of a cross-platform standard for representing 3-D objects known as the Virtual Reality Modeling Language (VRML) was a huge leap forward in the development of cyberspaces. Along with a standard language for representing spaces and shapes came the twentieth-century equivalent of a Holodeck: VRML browsers. VRML browsers are three-dimensional rendering and navigation tools that run on a variety of computer platforms. They work similarly to Web browsers in many ways. The VRML data file is a text file that describes a virtual world. VRML files are usually published with Web servers. A VRML browser requests the contents of the URL through a Web client such as Netscape Navigator or requests and retrieves the file itself if it is a stand-alone Internet client. Once it retrieves the file, all similarities to Web browsers end.

VRML browsers interpret the contents of VRML files to create objects and spaces (called *worlds*). These objects are rendered in pixels on a computer screen. (See figure 1.) The pixels form objects and spaces in which users

FIGURE 1   A VRML Browser

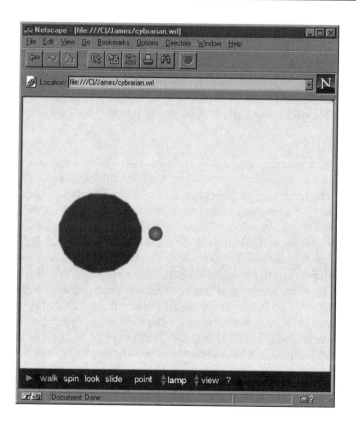

can navigate. In addition to rendering a space, VRML browsers present the user with navigational and object-manipulation controls. Users can travel forward, backward, left, right, up, or down in a virtual space either by simply selecting a direction from a matrix of buttons or by using a simulated joy stick to steer themselves. When users encounter an object, they can rotate the object along three axes.

Some browsers treat rendered objects as solids while others let you glide right through objects as if they did not exist. Each time a user manipulates an object or moves in any direction, the browser redraws the space. Thus VRML browsers use and require much more processor time and system memory than Web browsers. VRML browsers must also be able to present and retrieve the contents of data targeted by hypertext links. Objects in a VRML world can act as links to other objects or regions of the current space or to other VRML worlds stored on the Internet.

The Virtual Reality Modeling Language

VRML is a language for describing objects and the environment in which they reside. It has a set of basic shape elements that can be used as is or combined to form more-complex shapes. Other elements let you specify various colors and lighting effects for objects and regions of space. You can apply textures and graphics to objects and configure objects to act as hypertext links. VRML links use URLs to specify their targets just like HyperText Markup Language (HTML) anchor tags.

VRML files usually use the .wrl extension, which is short for *world*. Each VRML file is in fact a self-contained world that the user downloads and navigates on his or her local computer. Every VRML file starts with a header that identifies it as a VRML file, specifies the version, and tells how the VRML node information is stored in the file, for example:

#VRML V1.0 ascii.

The contents of the file are human-readable VRML code. VRML files can be created manually just like HTML files. But because of the complex nature of the language and because it explicitly describes graphical objects, it can easily be generated from three-dimensional design software. VRML authors often use design tools to create worlds and sometimes use a text editor to add refinements such as hypertext links or additional lighting sources.

Each object in a VRML world is called a *node*. A node can be a point, sphere, or other shape. A VRML file contains nodes and information used to describe the nodes' characteristics. Each node specifies what type of object it is, what its name is, and what, if any, descriptive fields it has that control the appearance of the object. Nodes can have child nodes that are drawn in relation to other nodes. For example, you might create VRML code to draw a large blue sphere to represent the Earth and then give it a child node that describes a smaller white sphere representing the moon to be drawn in relation to the first. The two objects will act as one when rotated by the user. Figure 2 shows the VRML code for these two objects.

FIGURE 2   VRML Code for a Node and Child Node

```
#VRML V1.0 ascii.
DEF earth Separator {
    Material {
        diffuseColor 0 .3 .7
        shininess 1
    }
    Sphere { radius 5 }
    DEF moon Separator {
    # Moon is a child node of earth
        Transform { translation 7 0 0 }
        Material {
            diffuseColor .9 .9 .9
            shininess 1
        }
        Sphere { radius 1 }
}
```

As you can see, VRML doesn't look a lot like HTML, but it is readable. Let's examine the file line by line so we can see what is going on. The first line is the content declaration, which is required in every VRML file. The second line defines a separator node named "earth." The left curly bracket surrounds all the nodes that are related to this one. The remaining code defines this object and a child object. The next four lines starting with Material describe a set of characteristics that should be applied to objects defined in this node. The diffuseColor field uses RGB (red-green-blue) intensity values to declare a color for the object. Color values can be from 0 (no color) to 1 (maximum intensity) for each of the three primary colors. The next field, shininess, is set to 1, which means the object is highly reflective. Finally, the first Sphere node defines the shape and size of this object, a sphere with a simulated radius of 5 meters in the example.

The line that starts with a pound sign is a comment. Comments have no function other than to remind the author of the purpose of a node or to annotate a specific field or node for future reference. The Transform node declares a triplet of offset values from the center of the first object. The second object is to be drawn simulated 7 meters from the first object on the x axis, otherwise aligned with it on the y and z axes. The Material node sets the color and shininess values for the next object. The second object is almost white (.9 .9 .9) and as shiny as the first sphere. Finally, the object itself is defined as a small simulated 1-meter sphere.

Designing a complex space would be a very tedious task if you hand coded each Material, Transform, and object node in a text editor. And you would likely end up with many errors, such as objects not appearing where you had intended or being the wrong color. That's why there are tools for creating VRML worlds graphically. Objects can be placed, resized, colored and textured with a few mouse clicks. (See figure 3, for an example of the

FIGURE 3   Virtus VRML Editor

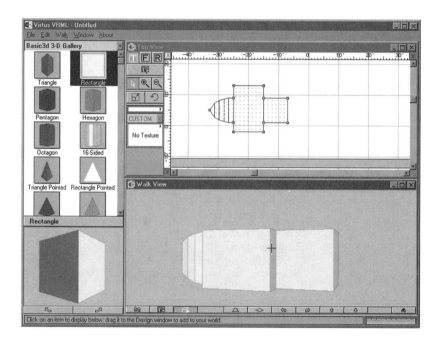

screen for creating an object.) VRML design tools usually provide several simultaneous views of a world. There is usually a floor-plan style view for placing objects, an inspector for selecting Material field values, and a browser-like window that lets you view and navigate your world. It is not as slick as simply telling a computer that you want to simulate a smoke-filled jazz bar in New Orleans and having it almost instantly appear, but it is more fun than coding piece by piece a virtual world using a text editor!

Conclusion

VRML still has a long way to go to satisfy today's Doom and Myst video game veterans, not to mention the crew of the *Enterprise*. At present the system has many limitations. For example, every space is composed of polygons. Many of these polygons have to be drawn and redrawn each time the user moves (although some clever browsers draw only what is in the field of view). Complex worlds can quickly become unnavigable. Multiple users cannot be present in the same space at the same time because each user has his or her own instance of a world rather than actually entering a single place stored on a remote system. Objects can be viewed but they cannot be moved or altered in any way. Efforts are under way to use technology such as Java to allow these types of interaction in virtual worlds. Java-capable VRML browsers should be able to communicate across the

Internet to update users sharing a space, provide the user with a virtual presence in a virtual world, or keep track of alterations to objects by a user.

There is no reason, however, that VRML could not be used to develop a Virtual Library. Even in its current state, it presents some interesting possibilities for developing (Common Gateway Interface) CGI/VRML interfaces to indexes of data. The user might be presented with a basic input device not much different from an HTML form. There's nothing earth-shattering about that, but then consider how the result sets might be presented. Clusters of similar results might be represented as different sized and shaped objects, with nearness and color representing still other characteristics of a result set. With a little training, users could sift through huge result sets with just a few glances around the result set space. And with further advances, such as Java applet-driven worlds, users could (literally) toss results sets together and hand them back to a virtual search agent that would resubmit the refined search and present new results sets for browsing and manipulation.

It is up to us to decide how to apply this technology to the massive amount of data that libraries are amassing and presenting to increasingly bewildered users without bombarding them into apathy. VRML is an incomplete tool set to be sure, but it is the first and only virtual reality standard for the Internet. It certainly holds great promise for providing new interfaces between computers and people. It isn't the twenty-fourth century yet, but it is starting to look more like the twenty-first. Welcome to the Hololib.

To Learn More

Check out the Silicon Graphics, Incorporated's (SGI) Webspace VRML Repository at *http://webspace.sgi.com/Repository/*. SGI was heavily involved with the development of VRML. Here you will find many lists of software and many sites using VRML in fields such as architecture and chemistry.

Another great site is San Diego Supercomputing Center's VRML Repository at *http://rosebud.sdsc.edu/vrml/*. This site has links to browsers and to the VRML specification.

Inquiring Minds Want to Know . . . UNIX

Kate Wakefield

Kate Wakefield is the Western Library Network (WLN) network services manager. She is a director-at-large on the Executive Board of the Library and Information Technology Association of the American Library Association and has been a member of the Internet Room Steering Committee. She may be reached at *WAKE@WLN.COM.*

Some people may wonder why there's a chapter on UNIX in this book when most people who use the Internet seem to be moving toward Windows or Macintosh graphical user interfaces (GUIs) as their preferred means of access. Basic UNIX commands are still useful in the age of GUIs and are likely to remain useful for the near future. Some reasons you may use UNIX include troubleshooting a File Transfer Protocol (FTP) site that doesn't respond properly to your GUI tool; working with World Wide Web (WWW) files and directories; and managing some aspects of your Internet account, such as changing passwords, monitoring the amount of space your files are using, and working with the full range of Internet utilities.

There are many flavors of UNIX, each with specialized commands or options available, but a core set of commands will work on most systems. Those commands will be covered in this chapter. Some of the most common varieties of UNIX include AIX for IBM mainframes, HPUX for Hewlett-Packard hosts, ULTRIX for Digital Equipment Corporation (DEC) machines, and the original BSD (Berkeley Systems Development) flavor of UNIX.

Your command prompt will vary depending on the operating system used on your host, and may be "tweaked" by your local system administrator. In most cases it will be a dollar sign ($) or pound sign (#) or percent sign (%), although it may also show your user ID or other locally designated information such as userid> (where user ID is replaced by your own log-in name). In most cases, you will not be shown the current working direc-

172

tory as part of the prompt as you are in most MS-DOS computers. (However, there is a command to request this information, if needed.) Be aware that some public-access sites may be set up so that you cannot get to the UNIX command prompt. Check with your system administrator if there is not a clearly designated command prompt option at your home Internet site.

MS-DOS Versus UNIX

Microsoft's Disk Operating System (MS-DOS or just DOS) is widely used in IBM-compatible personal computers (PCs). If you are familiar with entering DOS commands and the organization of files in a PC that uses DOS, you will find that UNIX is very similar. Macintosh users or those who use Windows File Manager exclusively to work with their files will need to reacquaint themselves with how to issue commands to a computer.

The most important rule to remember is that the computer won't begin processing your command until you hit the <Return> or <Enter> key. Although this bit of advice may seem ludicrous, many novices find themselves staring at the screen waiting for a command to finish processing that hasn't even been sent yet! This also means that you can "take back" or make corrections to any command that hasn't yet been entered simply by using the backspace key. (Note: on some systems or in some terminal emulation packages, the backspace key will produce garbage on your screen. If this happens to you, try Ctrl-backspace, or Ctrl-H instead.)

There are three major differences between UNIX and DOS:

1. UNIX is case-sensitive: whether you type uppercase or lowercase letters matters. Always enter UNIX commands in lowercase, unless specifically directed to do otherwise.

2. UNIX uses forward slashes instead of backslashes to designate directories.
   for example: /usr/local/bin/filename
   instead of: \windows\system\filename
   This will be especially important as you issue commands to change directories.

3. UNIX file names can be long and may have more than one dot in them. DOS files (prior to Windows 95) can be only eight characters with a three-character extension. For example: Copyright-Info.txt.new is a valid UNIX file name, but it could not be used in DOS. When you refer to specific file names, use the same mixture of upper- and lowercase as the file name displays.

Those unused to entering commands need to be aware of UNIX command syntax. If you begin reading UNIX documentation (called man pages where "man" is short for "manual"), you will find that many commands introduced in this chapter have several more-advanced options available. Commands are typically entered in this format:

command option argument

Arguments are what you want the command to operate on. For example, some commands such as "copy" or "move" require file names or directories—these are the "arguments" for that command. Typically you can either use a full path to the file name or simply specify the file name itself if it is in the current working directory. Options are typically entered as hyphens preceding certain letters. They may also be referred to as "flags."

To cancel processing of a particular command or break out of a particular process, use Ctrl-C (hold down the Control key while pressing the letter *C*). In most cases, this break key will stop the command in progress. In some cases, it may only temporarily suspend processes. Check with your system administrator to determine how to check what jobs are running on your system and how to kill those jobs. This may be very useful information, but it is often system specific.

File Structure

UNIX files are arranged hierarchically in a tree. Typically the top level of the tree is designated with a / and is called the root directory. This is analogous to being at the c:\> prompt in a DOS computer. In most cases, only system administrators will be able to work with files in the top directory level of a UNIX system. Other common file systems, or main directory groups, include /etc, /home, /usr, /var, and /tmp. Your system administrator may have created other file systems to group together related files or types of users, such as /staff or /patron or /branch1, and so forth. For example:

/cust/vraptor/software/winsock.zip
/cust/vraptor/public_html/index.html

Macintosh users can think of directories as being folders within folders. In the previous example, the main cust folder includes separate folders for each individual user's files (under their log-in name or user ID). The folder for "vraptor" may include additional folders that the user has decided to create, such as "software" and "public_html" in the example. Individual files are typically recognized by their extensions. For instance, .txt or .html are common extensions for ASCII text files or HyperText Markup Language files. (See a list of common file extensions at the end of the section Multimedia File Formats by Thomas Dowling in Part 8.)

Do you know how your UNIX system is organized? Try this: Go to the UNIX command prompt of your system and type pwd (present working directory). This command will show you where your home directory is in relation to the root file system or explain what is meant by the full path to your files.

Listing Your Files

While you are logged in, try this: To see a list of the files in the current directory, use the "list files" command: ls -l

The hyphen-L option requests the long format for output of the command results, which presents much of the same information you see when you type a "dir" or directory command in a DOS system. If you simply type "ls" for list, you will receive only a listing of the names of the files and directories (and won't be able to tell one from the other). When you type the ls -l command, you will see output similar to this:

```
-rw-r--r--    1 vraptor   cust  235    Aug 21 12:15  1995-report.txt
drwx--x--x  2 vraptor   cust  512    Mar 2 1994    News
drwx--x--x  2 vraptor   cust  512    Mar 2 1994    mail
-rwxr--r--   1 vraptor   cust  2345   May 5 17:43   soap-digest.n235.txt
```

The first character at the far left is *very* important. If it is a *d,* the name at the far right is a directory; if it is a hyphen, the name at the far right is a file. Less frequently, you may see an *l,* which indicates a link. Note that you will see uppercase files or directories listed before lowercase files or directories. You may even have two directories with similar names, such as Mail and mail—to your UNIX system, these are completely separate entities. On a DOS system, you would not be able to create two directories like this because uppercase and lowercase letters are equated with each other.

The first group of letters and hyphens indicate file permissions. In a UNIX system, files are owned by particular individuals or user IDs that belong to various groups. Permissions allow you to specify who else is able to view or read your file, who can make changes to or write to your file, and who can execute the file (if it is a working program). The permissions come in groups of three *r*s, *w*s, and *x*s, which indicate individual, group, and world permissions.

The output of the "list files" command also shows who owns the file (in this example, "vraptor" represents the user ID) and what group that user ID belongs to (in this example, "cust" for customer). The next column of numbers is the file size (for directories, this will usually be 512, unless a large number of files reside within it) and the date the file was created or last modified. Finally at the far right is the name of the file or directory. If the file name is too long to be displayed, it may wrap to the next line, or it may simply not show up. Use the "ls" command without the long option if you receive an error warning that a file name does not exist when you're certain that it does.

Invisible Files

UNIX makes use of some special files to record information such as individual user configurations, address books, news group subscription lists, and so forth. These files are known as dot files, because they begin with periods. For instance, the .forward file (or dot forward) is a file that contains an e-mail address identifying where you want all your mail to be forwarded. To display these files, you must use a special flag with your "list" command for list files, long format, all files:

```
ls -la
```

Using the "all" files option displays all of your dot files, then all of your files beginning with numbers, then capital letters, then lowercase letters. Dot files can be displayed or deleted just like other files, but be sure to include the dot and no spaces in the file name within the command. Be careful when editing or deleting dot files, as some are required to run various UNIX programs. Ask your system administrator if you are not sure of a particular file's function.

Moving around UNIX Systems

When you do a manual FTP, you need to be able to browse or move among the directories and files available. Or, within your home directory, you may choose to create directories and later need to work with those files. To change directories, type:

    cd dirname

where dirname is the name of the directory you wish to enter. If the directory is not immediately below your present working directory, you can designate the full path to the directory from root, such as:

    cd /usr/local/www

If you would like to move up a level in the directory tree, use this command:

    cd ..

Note that there is a space before the two periods in this command. In DOS you can use cd.. without a space to move up a level, but UNIX requires that you place a space between the command and the argument. If you'd like to get fancy with your directory changes, most UNIX systems also support commands such as:

    cd ../dirname

where you can both move up a level in the tree, and then down into the directory called dirname—this allows you to move into another directory at exactly the same level of the hierarchy all in one step.

Copying, Moving, and Deleting Files

Three commonly used commands when working with files are "copy," "move," and "delete." Good computer housekeeping requires that you delete files when you no longer need them. It is helpful if you go through your files at least once each month and discard useless files. If you do this frequently, you won't end up asking yourself, "What does that file name mean, anyway?" as you go through the list.

Copying

To make a copy of a file, type:

cp oldfile newfile

where oldfile is the current file name and newfile is the new file name. Copy creates a second duplicate file. Your original file remains untouched.

Moving

To move or rename a file, type:

mv oldfile newfile

In this example, the original file "oldfile" will have its name changed to "newfile." This is the equivalent of the DOS "rename" command. Your original file will no longer exist. "Move" is also used to take a file from one directory and move it into a new directory. The generic form of this command is:

mv filename dirname

For instance, if you are in one directory and have the subdirectory "public_html" where all of your World Wide Web files are stored, you can move a graphic image file called blue-ribbon.gif from your main directory to the WWW directory by typing:

mv blue-ribbon.gif public_html

Note that since the public_html directory is immediately below my present working directory, all that needs to be typed is the directory name. If you wish to move the file to another file system, simply include the full pathway to the directory you want to move the file to, such as:

mv blue-ribbon.gif /usr/local/www/images

Deleting

One of the most important commands is the "remove" command, which is used to delete files. To permanently delete a file that is no longer needed, type:

rm filename

Note that in most UNIX systems there is no "undelete" command to restore a file that is accidentally deleted. Your system administrator may back files up to tape, but most system administrators are not willing to restore individual users' files from tape. (Commercial Internet systems may do so for a fee and after a long wait.) So be careful when you delete files.

If you want to delete all of the files in a particular directory, you can use the "recursive" option to this command. The recursive option will delete all of the files in a particular subdirectory as well as all subdirectories contained within that directory. To be safe, I recommend only using the "recursive" option with the "interactive" option, which will list each file name for confirmation before deleting it. For example:

rm -ri software

would allow me to discard all of the files in my directory called "software," but it would list each file for a "y" or "n" confirmation before moving on to the next file. ***Warning: be careful when you use the recursive option!***

Wild Cards. To save typing time when deleting files, you can make use of wild cards to truncate file names. In most UNIX systems, the asterisk (*) is a wild card that substitutes for any number of characters, and the question mark (?) is a wild card that substitutes for a single character. For instance, if you have two files called CNI-file1.txt and CNI-file2.txt you could remove them both with a single command:

rm CN*.txt

The trick is not to remove any files that you want to keep, so be certain to specify enough letters to uniquely identify the files you wish to remove. Using the single character wild card is the safest way to remove these two files:

rm CNI-file?.txt

This command could still remove something called CNI-file3.txt that you meant to keep. If that's the case, you will need to delete the files individually or use the interactive option mentioned previously, for example:

rm -ri CNI-file?.txt

This would allow you to approve the deletion of each file that matches the search string.

Housekeeping Tips

If you are going to keep many files on your UNIX system, I recommend creating directories to store related information in. For instance, in my UNIX account I keep copies of Macintosh Serial Line Internet Protocol/Point-to-Point Protocol (SLIP/PPP) shareware and Windows SLIP/PPP shareware ready to download. To keep one group separated from the other and to reduce clutter in my main directory, I have a subdirectory called "sw-mac" and one called "sw-win" as well as a miscellaneous "software" group for other utilities.

To create a new directory, simply type the "make directory" command:

mkdir dirname

Once the directory has been created, use the "copy" or "move" commands to transfer the files into it. When you no longer need a particular directory, remove it using the "remove directory" command:

rmdir dirname

Note that on most systems the directory must be empty before this command will work.

Working with Text Files

When you need to make a simple change to your WWW home page, or if you have some other file that needs to be edited or viewed, you will need to make use of a text editor. Each UNIX system has several editors available. Some of the most common editors are linked to popular e-mail programs; for example, "pico" is distributed with the Pine e-mail package from the University of Washington. The Gnu's Not UNIX (GNU) software project distributes a popular editor called Emacs, while hardcore UNIX types love "vi" (pronounced vee eye). Your system administrator should be able to point you to one of several editors and provide a simple cheat sheet for using the editors that are available.

You can also view your text files online by typing this command:

cat filename

If the file is more than one screen long, you will see it scroll by in a blur and only be able to read the end of the file. To see the whole file again, screen by screen, type:

cat filename |more

or

more filename

This command shows the first screen of text and waits for you to press the space bar to display the next page of the file. (If you have used a text-based Gopher client, you have seen "more" at work.) If the "more" command doesn't work with your system, try "page" instead. The space bar should move you to the next screen, and a Crl-C will break you out of a long file.

Tip: The "more" command can be used with most other UNIX commands if you want to view the output of the command screen by screen. The vertical bar is known as a pipe. UNIX allows you to take one command and redirect the output through another command—one way of doing this is with the "pipe" command. There are also redirect symbols such as < > and >> that are covered in basic UNIX books.

Additional Useful Commands

As an Internet user who interacts with other sites primarily through a UNIX host, you may wish to try several other useful commands.

Who and What

To see who else is logged into your host system at any given time, simply type "who" at the command prompt. The output of the command will list the other users, the time they logged in, and the program or process they are currently running.

A similar command available on some systems is the "what" command, which is simply a "w" at the prompt. This command again returns a list of the users currently logged in, but the far right-hand column lists the originating Internet Protocol (IP) address or domain name from which the user is coming to your host.

Talk

Using either the "who" or "what" command allows you to know who else is logged into your system. You can start up a conversation with any of these users by entering the "talk" command. The format for this command is:

talk userid (or talk userid@hostname.domain.name)

When you type this command, a request to talk to you is displayed to that user. If they also respond "talk userid," then both of you will be placed into a split-screen mode that allows you to type messages to each other.

Note that some systems disable "talk" or may use a variation such as "ntalk" or "ytalk." Ask your system administrator for help if "talk" doesn't work at your site. If you don't want to be disturbed by talk requests, type "mesg n" to turn off receipt of "talk" commands. Toggle this feature back on with a "mesg y" command.

Finger

If you want to identify the real name associated with a particular user ID, use the "finger" command. The format of this command is:

finger userid

The output typically returned includes the user ID, the full name of the person represented by that user ID, the home directory, and other useful information. Users can create .plan or .project files that display to users who finger them. Finger is also used to search for the user ID of a person on a host. This is useful if you can't recall someone's e-mail address. In this case, type:

finger lastname

to get a list of all users with the same surname as the person you want to locate. Send e-mail to them at their user ID or user@host.domain.name if they are on another site. Note that you can try to finger users on another host machine using the format:

finger lastname@host.domain.name

However, many system administrators disable "finger" for users outside their own system to protect their users' privacy.

Passwords

Finally, most users will want to know how to change their password. On many systems, users are required to change their password periodically. If you are a system administrator, a configuration file on your system allows you to specify the number of days between password changes. As a user, you will want to change your password any time that you believe it may have been compromised, and probably at least once every three months. To change your password on most UNIX systems, type:

    passwd

Typically, you will be prompted to type in your old password, then to type in a new password twice. This is to be sure that you type exactly the same new password twice, without line noise or errors that might prevent you from accessing your account with the new password.

Warning: Be smart about your password choices. Most people whose accounts are hacked into are compromised due to poor password selection. Never use your user ID plus a number, or the name of a pet, child, or spouse. Most UNIX books recommend not even using common words but instead coming up with a phrase that means something to you and using the letters that start each word as the password. Your chances of being hacked are reduced if you use a mixture of upper- and lowercase letters, and if you include a special symbol or number in the password, especially if it is somewhere besides the very end. There are even random-password-generator software packages available for downloading from the Internet, if you want to pick really obscure passwords.

Online Resources

To learn more about UNIX, check out the following online resources. All UNIX sites should support online manual (man) pages. To access the man pages for a particular topic, type

    man subject

where *subject* is a particular command or function you wish to explore. The man pages typically list all options available and give examples of how to use the command to accomplish specific tasks. Be aware that man pages are written in "geek-speak," which is a particularly obtuse form of computerese. If you have difficulty interpreting the man pages, check out a UNIX book written for real humans. (Some favorites of mine follow.) If the man command doesn't work on your home system, ask your system administrator for the equivalent or for alternative syntax.

The following URLs are for some World Wide Web pages that provide more information about UNIX. Although several of these documents include information that is only relevant to a specific site, the general concepts are valuable.

Baylor College of Medicine Genome Center. *UNIX Survival.* [Online]. Available: *http://gc.bcm.tmc.edu:8088/gc_help/unix.html*
    The best overall introduction.

Carleton University. (1996, January). *Beginner's Guide to UNIX.* [Online]. Available: *http://www.carleton.ca/~jmiller/doc/unix_ToC.html*

Covault, Corbin. (1993). *Corbin's UNIX Help for Beginners*. [Online]. Available: *http://hep.uchicago.edu/%7Ecovault/Unix_help/unix_help.html*
This is actually *not* for beginners, but it is useful nonetheless.

Smith, John. *UNIXhelp for Users*. [Online]. Available: *http://www.shu.edu/projects/unixhelp/TOP_.html*
A good in-depth overview of UNIX, including a searchable index.

There are also several Usenet news groups that may be valuable for specific questions. Look in the area *comp.unix*, for example, *comp.unix.aix* for IBM AIX users.

Print Resources

Abrahams, Paul W., and Larson, Bruce R. (1992). *UNIX for the Impatient*. Menlo Park, CA: Addison-Wesley.

Hahn, Harley. (1993). *A Student's Guide to UNIX*. New York: McGraw-Hill.

Libes, Don, and Ressler, Sandy. (1990). *Life with UNIX: A Guide for Everyone*. Englewood Cliffs, NJ: Prentice-Hall.

Waite, Mitchell (et al.). (1992). *The Waite Group's UNIX System V Primer* (2nd ed.) Carmel, IN: Sams.

Information Retrieval

The Client/Server Model and Libraries

Anthony Toyofuku

Anthony Toyofuku *(TOYOFUKU@UCI.EDU)* is electronic services librarian and Spanish and Portuguese bibliographer at the University of California, Irvine. He is a reviewer for *Telecommunications Electronic Reviews.*

Anyone who has been within ten feet of a newsstand in the past few years has undoubtedly heard the term "client/server." Headlines tout the "client/server revolution," the "hot growth area of client/server," "client/server architectures increase productivity" . . . the hyperbole goes on and on. In 1995 alone, the computer newspaper *ComputerWorld* had no less than 169 articles with the words "client" and "server" in the title. But beyond the marketing shibboleths, what is the "client/server model"? And what does it mean for libraries?

The term *client/server* is so frequently used, and used in such varying contexts, that seemingly anything dealing with a network and a database can now be described in terms of "client/server." If you speak with ten different computing professionals, you will likely get ten wildly different definitions for what the "client/server model" actually means. Although there is a plethora of definitions, for our purposes, we'll stick to a simple definition that broadly splits the client/server architecture into three parts.

1. A desktop "client" work station, usually with a graphical user interface (GUI).
2. A "server," which is a minicomputer or a mainframe. This computer houses a database, or databases, that can be accessed by multiple simultaneous users.
3. A network that connects the client and the server.

Note, however, that there are exceptions to every rule. In the *X* Windows environment, the server is the desktop work station and the client is the remote computer.

Of Dumb Terminals and Command Lines

Before we view the client/server model more closely, we must first take the requisite quick look toward the past, a time when dumb terminals populated the library world. During the age of the dumb terminal, accessing your favorite Online Public Access Catalog (OPAC) meant sitting down at a terminal and typing in a sequence of arcane commands at the "command line." After typing in the commands, you hit the "enter" key and waited expectantly for the mainframe to spit back the results.

Later, along came the microcomputer. This meant that you could use "terminal emulation" to connect to your favorite OPAC, but except for being able to print a little more easily and view the screen in sixteen different colors and maybe download your search results, it really wasn't much different from the old dumb terminal.

Alas for most of us, those dumb terminal days aren't too hard to remember, because for many of us, dumb terminals are still the primary way to access our favorite OPAC. Take for instance the University of California's MELVYL System. MELVYL is actually a collection of databases, from the book holdings of the entire UC system to journal indexes on a wide range of subjects. MELVYL is exceptionally powerful, both in the wealth of its databases and in the speed at which it executes searches. But while MELVYL is a lot of nice things, it's anything but user friendly. Consider the typical search:

f tw of time and the river

After you look at this for a while, you can probably figure out that this search is for a work with the title words "of time and the river."

Taking that information, what then would be the most efficient way to search for the weekly magazine *Time*? See if you can select the correct answer:

1. f tw time
2. f pe time
3. f xpe time
4. f xpe "time"

If you chose number four, you win the prize. But why, you ask, answer four? Since *Time* is a periodical, you must specifically use the syntax "f pe" (for *find periodical*), not "f tw" (for *find textword*). And since "time" is such a common word, doing an exact periodical search, "f xpe time" (for *find exact periodical*) greatly decreases the number of false hits, but even that still retrieves more than 150 records from the database. The best way to do the search is to enter "f xpe "time"; that searches for the one-word periodical title *Time* and cuts the results down to 11 titles. MELVYL has some of the best online documentation I've ever seen, but it would take some time to figure out the proper search phrase by yourself.

Not only is a blinking cursor interface nonintuitive, but a search will be executed at the same speed, whether you're sitting at a VT100 dumb terminal or at a PC (personal computer) with the latest and fastest processor that Intel makes. With all of the idle computing cycles on these high horse-power PCs going to waste, someone came up with the idea to harness this power on the desktop. After all, why not share the computing load between the mainframe and the PC? And thus was born the "client/server revolution."

This revolution has been going on for a few years now in the business world, but it's just now taking hold in libraries. Although there are many examples of client/server technology in use, such as the growing presence of World Wide Web (WWW) browsers in libraries or POPmail e-mail systems, I will stick to what's near and dear to librarians' hearts: the nascent world of client/server-based information retrieval systems.

What does a client/server-based information retrieval system offer? Once again, you will get wildly different opinions, depending upon with whom you speak, but generally it offers three features:

1. GUI interface
2. Distributed processing
3. Customized clients

GUI Interface

The first order of business for almost any client/server system is to have a GUI interface loaded on the client. This interface, also called the "presentation layer" in client/server lingo, replaces the old command line with a more intuitive collection of pull down menus and dialog boxes. Instead of having to read 100 pages of documentation and memorize such incantations as "f tw . . . ," you can click the mouse over a button with the word "title," click on another button with the words "search book titles," then enter the title words. At the click of the "send" button, the request is on its merry way.

If all we do is add a Microsoft Windows user interface to an OPAC, we've certainly gone a long way toward aiding the user, but we still have a very skinny client. In the language of client/server computing, the "skinny client syndrome" occurs when all of the processing (or as client/server folks say, "business logic") is handled on the server. This is really nothing more than a spiffed up dumb terminal, for the client just gets input from the user, sends it along the network to the server, and then displays the results on the screen.

Distributed Processing

The graphical user interface is only one piece of the client/server-based OPAC. Another component of the puzzle is the ability to share the computing load between the client and the server computers. In the traditional dumb terminal, "master/slave" online system, if you request a list of all of the books that the library owns written by the author Wolfe with the word *home* in the title, the mainframe searches for authors with the name *Wolfe,* then takes those intermediate results and sorts them looking for the word *home* in the title. After finding the work *You Can't Go Home Again* by Thomas Wolfe, that record is displayed on your dumb terminal.

Now let's consider the same example, but this time the search is being executed on an OPAC designed in the client/server model. Since this is a distributed system, the client PC sends the request to the server. First, the server finds all of the works with the author *Wolfe.* Then instead of the server sorting the records to find works with the word *home* in the title, the server returns all of the records to the client terminal. The client computer then takes over and sorts the records. The results are exactly the same; the book *You Can't Go Home Again* is displayed, but the way the tasks are divided between the mainframe and the PC is different.

What's the benefit of sharing the work load? Originally one of the selling points for client/server systems was cost. In hardware terms, it's cheaper to have PCs connected to a relatively inexpensive minicomputer than it is to have terminals connected to an expensive mainframe. The minicomputer can share the burden of processing with the PCs and not have to be nearly as powerful as the mainframe. It's cheaper still when you consider that PCs can serve multiple purposes besides searching OPACs.

Customized Clients

Since the computing load can be partitioned between the client and the server, it's possible to build clients that are tailored to the needs of users. Imagine that your users want to download their records formatted in accordance with the Modern Language Association's (MLA) style sheet. With a smart client interface, there could be a little button that says "save results in MLA format." In just one step, the client software parses the records, formats them in MLA style, and saves them all to disk.

Another nice option might be to have a customized user profile. Perhaps you always want to limit your searches to books written in English. You could set up a personalized user profile stored on your client that, upon retrieving records from the server, scans the MARC fixed field language tag for the code "eng."

The Z39.50 Standard and Client/Server Computing in Libraries

Such talk of custom-tailored interfaces leads directly into the subject of the current zenith of library client/server technology: the Z39.50 standard. In a very small nutshell, Z39.50 provides a standard computer-to-computer search protocol between diverse OPACs; this frees the user from having to know search commands for various online systems. Instead of having to know that MELVYL uses "f tw," OCLC uses "s ti:," and Nexis uses "headline(..)" for a title search, the Z39.50 client can issue a known set of commands to obtain the information the user requests.

Among the many benefits of the Z39.50 standard, there's one that stands out: it is an open standard that enables any programmer to write a Z39.50 client; you need not be employed by OCLC, the Research Library Group, or any other Z39.50 database vendor to write a client to access those systems. This does not imply that you don't need to pay for access to these systems, only that you can use one user interface, with the correct authorization to use all of these products. Someone can create a client that will "talk" to any publicly available Z39.50 server. Since many such servers are accessible via the Internet, instead of having one program for SilverPlatter's ERL, one for OCLC, one for RLG, and another for MELVYL, a user can have one interface for access to all of these systems.

With one interface to all those systems, it's now possible to design a client that connects to multiple databases simultaneously. A user wanting information on Peruvian history could search for journal articles in the *Hispanic American Periodical Index,* the *Handbook of Latin American Studies,* and the monographic holdings of the University of California, all at the same time. The client would retrieve all of the records from the various databases, sort out the duplicate records, then do a search against the local circulation records to see if the material is available for checkout, all at the click of a button.

An open standard such as Z39.50 also gives programmers the ability to create client software to fit the needs of their local users. Who knows, perhaps English professors around the world will lobby MLA to create a value-added client that can create MLA bibliographies from Z39.50 accessible databases.

Client/Server Considerations

Of course, before you think that client/server systems will give us lasting world peace, as with everything, there are some hidden "gotcha's."

Bandwidth

It's enticing to make the client software as "fat" as possible, but keep in mind that the fatter you make the client, the more data you have to send over the network. Using the analogy of the network as a series of large pipes, if you're not careful you could end up with a network that seems like it's constructed out of a series of small straws.

Consider a small public library that uses an OPAC with a client/server architecture; in this library, the server is located in a librarian's office in the back of the library. A user makes a request for all of the books written in Spanish on the subject "Jorge Luis Borges." The client sends the request to the server, and the server then returns all of the records on the subject "Jorge Luis Borges." As this is a small library, two records are returned to the client. The client then sorts the two records and finds that one of them is in Spanish. Within less than a second of the user's transmitting the request, the GUI client displays the one book on screen, stating that the book is available for checkout.

Now consider the same online catalog system, but instead of being used in a small local library, it's installed in a large library consortium spread throughout the state of California. Access to this database is via phone lines. If we do the search described above, we first get 2,000 records on the subject "Jorge Luis Borges." Before the client can even begin to sort the records, all 2,000 records then must get sent to the client via a slow phone line. After twenty minutes of staring at an hourglass, the user gives up and goes home.

Cost

Initially, cost was the motivating factor for moving to a client/server architecture. The rationale was that you could unchain yourself from the costly mainframe and move to a mix of relatively inexpensive minicomputers and desktop computers. While the idea sounds appealing, it turns out that client/server is a lot more expensive than it first appeared. It's true that the total hardware costs are lessened, but because client/server systems require a lot of administration, there are hidden labor costs. It seems to be turning out that client/server systems might actually be more expensive than their master/slave cousins.

In a parallel vein, moving to a client/server architecture requires a rethinking of resource allocation. In the days when the mainframe ruled the universe, it was easier to allocate your money because you could pour most of it into a central computing facility. Now, clients are located across departments and even in different geographic locations. Trying to redo the entire information system's budget to reflect this new reality can be difficult.

Future

The future holds great promise for client/server systems in libraries. Although they may be expensive to implement and maintain, users are going to demand that we provide better, faster, and more custom-tailored products. And perhaps because the Z39.50 standard enables any programmer to write a Z39.50 client, we will see more decoupling of the interface from the database. This in turn might lead to competition between interface vendors, ultimately leading to better products.

Undoubtedly the "client/server revolution" will cease to be big news—not because it's going to disappear, but because it becomes so commonplace that it moves from the realm of the trendy to the realm of the mundane.

Bibliography

Atre, S. (1995, June). "The Hidden Costs of Client/Server." *DBMS,* 71–4.

Kennedy, M. D., and Gurbaxani, A. R. (1994, November). "Can the Mainframe Compete with Client/server Systems on Cost?" *Telecommunications,* 28–31.
    This article finds that client/server appears to be a little cheaper overall.

Levy, S. (1984). *Hackers: Heroes of the Computer Revolution.* Garden City, NY: Anchor Press.
    Levy's work presents interesting characters from the earlier days of computing. It's good reading.

Library of Congress. (1996, February). *Articles and Papers about Z39.50.* [Online]. Available: *http://lcweb.loc.gov/z3950/agency/articles.html*
    Look at this for technical articles related to the Z39.50 standard.

Orfali, R., Harkey, D., Edwards, J. (1994). *Essential Client/Server Survival Guide.* New York: Van Nostrand Reinhold.
    This is a readable, humorous book on client/server architecture.

Quinn, B., Shute, D. (1996). *Windows Sockets Network Programming.* Reading, MA: Addison-Wesley.
    If you are interested in writing MS-Windows client applications, this book is a nice place to start.

7

We All Need a Happy Home (Page)

WEBMASTER BEWARE

CORPORATIONS KNOW THEY NEED A WEB SITE . . . BUT DO THEY KNOW WHY?

Lou Rosenfeld

Lou Rosenfeld *(http://argus-inc.com/staff/rosenfeld.html)* is president of Argus Associates, Inc., a firm that specializes in consulting on the conceptual design of large-scale Web sites. He is the founder of the Argus/University of Michigan Clearinghouse, a popular Internet reference resource.

This article first appeared in (1996, January) *Web Review, http://webreview.com/* (It can be located at *http://webreview.com/96/02/09/tech/webarch/index.html.*) Copyright held by Lou Rosenfeld.

Editor's note: Yes, this is about corporations, but the principles in it need to be applied by more libraries! It might also help explain some of those corporate Web sites we see out on the Net. Besides, it's funny.

So you just graduated from college, are new in town, and are un- or underemployed. You buy the local rag to go with your cafe latte and begin to thumb through the classifieds in search of an interesting job. You glance over McDonald's grillmaster, office faxmaster, city busmaster . . . but what's this: corporate Webmaster? Sounds interesting . . . you read further:

> *Webmaster:* Use cutting-edge technologies to design and implement our World Wide Web home page. Spend much of your time playing and become famous in the process as people all over the world access our page. Should know a little bit about writing code, graphic design, information design, and maybe some other things; at least be more computer literate than we are. No particular degree required; it's such a new area, and we know so little about it, that we want you to tell us what's needed to make our home page a rollicking success! Webmaster salaries typically run from $40K–$60K, so that's what we guess we'll pay you. If interested, contact . . .

"Yee-Hah!" you blithely think to yourself, circling the ad in highlighter. You've got a bit of computer experience—you're intimate with the entire suite of Microsoft office products! And you certainly know all about the Internet—you've been using America Online for months! Webmastering sounds more interesting than the alternatives, and it sure pays better. So you drain the rest of your latte and head off to the personnel office. Moments later, you're a Webmaster. Congratulations! Now get to work.

Welcome to Dilbertworld

You're probably thinking to yourself, "Lou, you are a grumpy, cynical bastard, aren't you? What happened: did you spill latte on your laptop or something? How about writing about Web design instead of kvetching for once?"

Well, you caught me. I am indeed grinding a huge ax. I realize that not everyone designing Web sites is a naive sprout making $60K just out of college. Many Webmasters are extremely talented, savvy individuals who have years of experience implementing information systems.

In fact, my negativity has nothing to do with the person in the position of Webmaster. No, what really bugs me is the position itself.

Consider the sorts of things that *didn't* make it into the job description:

- We don't know why we want a Web site. But everyone else, especially our competitors, is doing it, and someone at the top wants it done. We have to respond hurriedly to media hype. It just seems cool. We don't know!
- We haven't heard of anyone making money on the Web yet, but we're sure you'll help us become the first firm to have a profitable Internet presence.
- The budget for this project is huge. It will even cover the cost of your desk, your cubicle, your computer, and as many whiteboard markers as you'll need.
- Our staff is involved. They'll be glad to promise you as much as you need and will interfere and scuttle the process no less than three days before launch.
- We understand that designing a Web site is a long, involved process, and we want you to do it right. But we have to complete next year's budget in five weeks, so you'd better have it finished by then.

Not every organization is run by Dilbert's boss, of course. But whether you're a consulting or an in-house Webmaster, you'll have to confront many of these issues on the job.

Dogbert's Six Maxims for Webmasters

So should you work at McDonald's instead? Nah, you don't look good in a hair net anyway. There are a few things, however, that might make your life as a Webmaster easier. I haven't seen him comment on Web design yet, but I imagine that the great philosopher and fount of all wisdom, Dogbert, would advise you to ask your employer the following questions.

- *Motivations/expectations:* Why is the company investing in a Web site? Are they just testing the waters? Do they know that the site may never make them any money? Perhaps they have no better reason beyond the fact that their competitors have sites—but hey, that's a strong reason nonetheless.

- *Chain of command:* Who will you report to, the president or CEO? If not, why? The lower the level, the more you will encounter these two danger signs: (1) the site isn't that important to the company's overall strategy; and (2) the site doesn't have the broad-based support that it needs within the company.

- *Buy-in and participation:* Are other departments prepared to participate in the design of the site? If the company envisions a quality site emerging from your cubicle and your cubicle alone, they've got another think coming. You need to know about the company's markets, its technical infrastructure, its promotional look and feel. You even need to know the person at the switchboard who fields frequently asked questions.

- *Budget:* Ask them right away: What is the budget for this project? The number of digits in the answer will help you determine how serious the company is about a Web site.

- *Schedule:* Does the company understand that most large Web sites take at least three to six months to develop? You'll need time for research, for understanding the organization, for generating and testing ideas. And at the end of that time, the site really won't be complete. Web sites never are.

- *Tools and resources:* Is a technical infrastructure for hosting the site in place? If not, is the company expecting you to find or build one? Are there people capable of administering the network, or will that be your job too?

Flipping Burgers Can't Be All That Bad

You think you can cover all this stuff once the project has begun, huh? Don't look a gift horse in the mouth, you say? Well, think twice. If you don't get satisfactory answers to these questions, red flags should fly through the air—the company probably isn't serious about a Web site in the first place. It's better to burst (your and their) bubbles now rather than spend some valuable resources and frustrating time developing a site that goes nowhere. Besides, in the time it would have taken to realize that the situation is hopeless, you could have worked your way up to manager at McDonald's!

SPINNING THE WORLD-WIDE WEB

AN HTML PRIMER

James Powell

James Powell is programmer/analyst of scholarly communications and library automation at Virginia Polytechnic Institute and State University. He is the creator of HTML-Editor for Nextstep and the author of *HTML Plus!* His Web page is *http://scholar.lib.vt.edu:80/jpowell/ jpowell-person.html.*

Originally appeared in (1995, February/March) *Database,* 54–9. Copyright held by Online, Inc.

The World-Wide Web is doing for publishing what the word processor promised over a decade ago—making it possible for everyone to become a publisher. With the enormous popularity of World Wide Web client software, such as Mosaic, Winweb and Cello, it is no wonder that more and more people and organizations are interested in publishing on the Web. Unlike the word processor, which ultimately relied on paper for document distribution, the Web includes its own electronic document delivery mechanism. But many people find it hard to get started since it does not use any popular document format but instead relies on a markup language invented specifically for the Web. The HyperText Markup Language (HTML) is actually a rather small set of commands or tags that an author uses to create a Web document. In addition to being easy to learn, additional tools exist to simplify further the task of Web authoring.

The wonder of the Web is the ease with which you can follow a thought. The World Wide Web presents information as a train of thought, often spinning off many threads but seldom dull. HTML is but one of several components of the Web (Tim Berners-Lee provides an excellent history and system overview[1])—a World Wide Web client, a Web server, and a markup language for documents. HTML is the centerpiece of this networked publishing system. It can be used to publish articles, journals, books, or just pointer documents (known as a home page) to documents and data in other formats. HTML enables you to place related documents and multimedia data within easy reach of readers.

To Hypertext or Not . . .

Hypertext has many applications for learning and communicating ideas or facts and is commonly used for computer manuals, encyclopedias, dictionaries, and tutorials. Hypertext documents tend to be short, often no longer than one or two screens of text (50 to 80 lines) and restricted to a single topic. The interrelation of documents specified by links provides more control to the readers but allows you to encourage them to read your document a certain way if the material is unfamiliar.[2]

There are some instances where hypertext is less applicable than others:[3] reports, articles and books can become unwieldy mazes if a great deal of time is not spent building good links and dividing topics into hypertextable sections. There is nothing wrong with selecting a linear format to publish a document on the Net and simply building a summary, review, or abstract that is hypertext with links to the ASCII, PostScript, or other format.

When planning to publish on the Web, consider whether or not hypertext is an appropriate mode of communicating your document and whether you are willing to surrender navigation and appearance to World Wide Web browsers before you commit to a large project. HTML provides little in the way of formatting control, but Web browsers can display ASCII text files and other non-HTML formats directly or by using another program on the users' computers.

Getting Started with HTML

To use HTML effectively, you must first understand and master the concept of markup. Markup consists of inserting special characters or sequences of characters to indicate structure, formatting, or other often hidden aspects of a text. HTML tags allow you to capture the basic structure and format of a document. An HTML tag consists of one or more letters, such as *P* for paragraph, enclosed by angled brackets: <P>. Most tags are placed around the items to be marked up or tagged, so there is also an end tag: <H1>Big text</H1> where a forward slash is added to the tag to create an end tag. Some tags, such as the paragraph tag, imply termination when a new instance of the same tag is encountered; i.e., no </P> is necessary since a new <P> serves both purposes.

This may sound like a lot of work, but there are many helper applications available on the Internet (see the sidebar [at the end of this article] "HTML Helpers: Converters, Editors and Tools"). One type of application invaluable for performing HTML markup is an HTML editor. This is an application similar to a word processor with quick access to HTML tags. They can often perform some markup tasks automatically, such as tagging paragraphs or lists. Another type of work saver is a converter application. These can [consist of] word processor macros or full-featured converters that transform various document formats to HTML. One of the best is rtftohtml, which can take a document exported from a word processor in Rich Text Format (RTF) and do most of the HTML markup required to make an attractive Web document. Converters can rarely determine anything about the content of a document, so some cleanup is usually required.

If you choose or need to enter tags manually, enter them in uppercase letters. They may be mixed-case or even lowercase but are easier to spot when entered in uppercase. Unless a tag deals with a small segment of text, such as a word or phrase, separate end tags from new text with a carriage return. This should make HTML documents easier to "debug" if a problem arises.

Structure

While there are a variety of ways to structure a document, HTML only supports basic structure. Items such as paragraphs, lists, header, and body may be tagged in HTML. The <HTML> tag encloses the entire document. The <HEAD> tag is used to contain information about the document, such as a title and HTML document values. The <BODY> tag is used to indicate the textual body of the document. Of course each of these tags is paired with an end tag, which signals the end of a document structure. There is no way to denote structures such as sections, chapters, or other items found in print publications, such as books and magazines. For such items, heading tags may often be used as acceptable substitutes, although they merely imply divisions rather than actually encompass them.

Headings (not to be confused with the document header) divide and describe sections of an HTML document. There are six levels of headings (<H1> to <H6>) that are displayed by most browsers at smaller font sizes as the level increases, but at a larger font size than the document text. World Wide Web browsers, such as NCSA's Mosaic, put the bulk of display control in the hands of the client program, so a user might specify any font size for any level heading. Therefore, it is better to worry more about structure and less about the appearance of your document when viewed with any particular browser. This is what gives the World Wide Web a certain familiarity to users and makes it so easy to learn.

Document Head Elements

Every HTML document has a header section at the beginning of the document marked with the <HEAD> tag. The <HEAD> tag can include only the following tags, which may not appear outside the header section of the document: <TITLE>, <BASE>, <ISINDEX>, <NEXTID>, and <LINK>. The title should be unique and descriptive for the document. While it is not displayed with the document, many browsers display the title elsewhere and use it when constructing hotlist entries. <BASE> sets the URL [Uniform Resource Locator] of relative links within the current document (relative links are connections to related documents stored on the same computer). This tag is not required but can be useful when a document includes many local hypertext links. It requires a Hypertext REFerence (HREF) attribute. Some tags, such as <BASE>, are actually compound tags made up of the tag and one or more attribute/value pairs: <BASE HREF="http://scholar.lib.vt.edu/ejournals/">. [The tag] <ISINDEX> indicates a document is keyword searchable, though this is usually an unnecessary tag, as documents are considered searchable by default. <NEXTID> is usually generated by automated markup systems as a portion of anchors within this particular document. There is no need to insert this tag manually. <LINK> is used to indicate relationships between documents, glossaries, related indexes, and document author. Multiple <LINK> tags can be used:

<LINK="mailto:jpowell(at)vt.edu">

<LINK="glossary.html">

All remaining HTML tags are elements of the body of an HTML document. They may not occur before or past the <BODY> tag.

Information Type Elements

Information type elements are directly related to document content. Some of these tags are not displayed differently than the surrounding text by Web browsers, but they should be used, as they provide access to text elements that might be accessible by the browser.[4] There are two logical style tags for emphasis: <EM> and <STRONG>. [The tag] <STRONG> indicates stronger emphasis than <EM>. There is a definition tag <DFN>, a citation tag <CITATION>, and several tags tailored to displaying computer/human interactions: <CODE> to display computer source code, <SAMPLE> to display sample computer output such as a status message, <KBD> to display the data a user should enter at the keyboard when interacting with a computer program, and <VAR> to display a variable. The latter tags are probably some of the least used, but tags such as <EM>, <STRONG>, <DFN>, and <CITATION> should be used wherever applicable.

Physical Style Elements

HTML has limited support for controlling how text will look. As you might expect, there are Bold <B> and Italics <I> tags. The Typewriter Text <TT> tag will display enclosed text in a fixed, typewriter-style text. There are also tags for controlling line breaks in text. By default, HTML allows the browser to decide when to start a new line with displaying text. The <BR> tag forces a line break in text. The browser will end the current line and display the text that follows on a new line. [The tag] <HR> displays a horizontal rule line between portions of text. The <NOBSP> tag is inserted around text that should not be allowed to include line breaks.
 and <HR> are inserted as needed without a corresponding end tag, since they do not encompass any text.

Text Elements

There are several tags for encoding portions of text in HTML. The <P> tag indicates a paragraph. The <PRE> tag is used to mark a section of text that has been formatted, such as a table or passage from another work. Normally, tabs and extra spaces are ignored by Web browsers, such as Mosaic, but these are displayed when they occur within <PRE></PRE>. Tags, such as anchors for hypertext links, may also occur in preformatted tag segments. <BLOCKQUOTE> is used to include a section of text included from another source.

Lists

Lists of items can be tagged using several different tags depending on the type of list. An unordered list <UL> is used when the list items can occur in any particular order. Each list item is indicated by the list item tag <LI>. It has an accompanying </LI> tag, but like the paragraph tag, the end list item tag is implied by the next list item and thus is rarely used.

There are several other list structures in HTML. A numbered or ordered list <OL> contains items in a specific sequence, and each item, again denoted by <LI>, is numbered in incremental order. A definition list <DL> is a list of terms <DT> and their associated definition <DD>. A list of any type can be nested within another list and is usually indented or otherwise offset to clarify the relationship of the two lists. Just be sure to include end tags for each list. Other list types include menu lists <MENU> and directory listings <DIR>. These lists have <LI> elements like unordered and ordered lists.

Anchors

Anchors are what make HTML a hypertext language.[5] They also allow it to function as a multimedia authoring tool. Anchors are tags that designate an item to be a target of a link or linked to another item in the same document, another document on the same computer, or some document located elsewhere in the world. The anchor tag is a compound tag consisting of the following parts: an open anchor tag followed by link information or anchor name, followed by a close tag character, followed by the text constituting the link, followed by a close anchor tag:

<A HREF="somelink">Some Text</A>

Compound tags define certain attributes for a tag. The anchor name attribute assigns a name to an anchor so that it can be used as the target of a link: <A name="References">References</A> creates an anchor that can be the destination of another anchor. To create a link to this anchor, use the HREF attribute to specify the link target: <A HREF="#References">See references</A>. A pound sign is prefixed to anchor names when they are referenced. The text, "See references" will appear as underlined or otherwise highlighted text, selectable by the user. When this text is selected, the Web client will move to the indicated section of the current document.

Hypertext links to other files can simply link to documents or target anchors within other documents. Here is a link to a second document:

<A HREF="http://scholar.lib.vt.edu/references.html"> See references</A>

Here, a Uniform Resource Locator (URL) is used in place of an anchor name. URLs take the form:

resource://server.net.edu/filename

where a resource can be an HTML document (http), a Gopher, Usenet news group, FTP [File Transfer Protocol] site or other resource. Here is a link to a Gopher:

<A HREF="gopher://vatech.lib.vt.edu/00/references.txt">See references</A>

This link accesses a linear file in ASCII stored on a Gopher. The easiest way to construct URLs is to use a Web client, such as Mosaic, to access the resource to be the target and copy this document's URL from the client URL window. Named remote targets are formatted so that the anchor name occurs after the document URL:

<A HREF="http://scholar.lib.vt.edu/addendum.html# references">See references</A>

Here, the anchor named "references" in the document "addendum.html" on the Web server at *scholar.lib.vt.edu* is the target of this link.

Multimedia data can be included with anchors. Simply construct an anchor that points to video, audio, or other data. It is also a good idea to include a graphic, such as a film or speaker icon, to indicate that the data is nontextual (see the sidebar HTML Anchor Dos and Don'ts [at the end of this article]).

Images

To include a graphic, photograph, or special icon in an HTML document, you can use the <IMG> tag. Images can be local files or retrieved from a remote server using a URL:

<IMG SRC="photo.gif">

<IMG SRC="http://scholar.lib.vt.edu/photo.gif">

Images must be in either the Graphics Interchange Format (GIF) or the monochrome X bitmap (XBM) format. Several useful attributes for the <IMG> tag are optional. The ALT attribute specifies text that can be displayed by a browser incapable of an image when the browser cannot display graphics. The ALIGN attribute indicates how the text following an image should be displayed in relation to the image. Align values are top (to align text with the top of the image), middle, and bottom. Here are examples of the ALT and ALIGN attributes in use:

<IMG ALIGN="TOP" SRC="photo.gif">

<IMG SRC="photo.gif" ALT="Photo displayed here">

Images can become interactive weather maps or anatomical tutorials using the image map function. A graphic, such as a map, can have selectable zones that retrieve other documents or data from the Web. Zones can be round, rectangular or various polygon shapes. Each zone is indicated by sets of coordinates and a URL is associated with each zone. The ISMAP attribute for the <IMG> tag tells the browser to send the coordinates of a users' mouse click to the server and the appropriate URL is returned. Here is an example:

<A HREF="http.//server.lib.vt. edu/cgibin/imagemap/pie-chart-map"> <IMG SRC="pie-chart.gif" ISMAP></A>

The anchor attribute refers to a collection of URL/coordinate pairs, and the ISMAP attribute with the <IMG> tag indicates this image should be an image map. There are several tools available[6] to make image maps, such as WebMap for the Macintosh, and MapEdit for Microsoft Windows.

Miscellaneous Tags

HTML includes tags for comments. These are not displayed by the browser. Here is a comment:

<!--This is version three of this document-->

Comments usually occur in the document head section but may occur anywhere in the document. An author can include his or her name, an electronic mail address, or other contact information at the end of a document using the <ADDRESS> tag.

Forms

All the tags covered so far are level 0 or level 1 conformant HTML tags.[7] Level 0 tags are rendered very consistently by Mosaic, Cello, and all other Web browsers. Level 0 tags include most HTML tags in use today. Level 1 tags include information type elements, the image and anchor tags, and the LINK element of the <HEAD> tag. Level 1 tags can be rendered differently depending on the browser. They are disconnected from document appearance, and there is no one right way to display them. For example, Mosaic underlines anchors while Cello displays them in rectangles.

Level 2 HTML tags are form tags that are supported in version 2 releases of Mosaic and some other recent Web browsers. Forms can be built using five basic tags:[8]

<FORM>, which functions as a body tag for HTML forms
<SELECT>, which can be used to build selection boxes
<OPTION>, which is an element of <SELECT> used to indicate a
    selectable option
<TEXTAREA>, for entering multiple lines of text
<INPUT>, to accept user input, such as radio buttons <INPUT
    TYPE=radio>, checkboxes <INPUT TYPE=checkbox>, brief text
    input or submission buttons <INPUT TYPE=submit>

Each tag has one or more attributes. The contents of a form are then delivered to a program for processing (e.g., they might be mailed to someone or serve as a search query). Building a form is but half the battle, as programming skills are needed to build the processing hooks for a form. There are several excellent online tutorials that cover all aspects of forms. A good starting point is *Mosaic for X Version 2.0 Fill-Out Form Support* at: *http://www.ncsa.uiuc.edu/SDG/Software/Mosaic/Docs/fill-out-forms/ overview.html*

Character Entities

Some characters are considered special characters by HTML, and in order for these characters to be represented in a document, an alternate encoding strategy called character entities is used. For example, left and right brackets, <>, already serve a purpose as tag enclosures. If you wish to include a bracket in the text of your document, you need to insert the entity: < for <, > for >, and & for &. Other commonly used entities include &quot for double quotes, and   for a nonbreaking space. Character entities are also used to represent the complete ISO Latin 1 character set. For example, a ç is represented with &ccidilla;. A complete list is available at *http://info.cern.ch/hypertext/WWW/MarkUp/ISOlat1.html*. [*Editor's note:* this connection no longer works. The kind of list specified seems to be available at *http://www.uni-passau.de/~ramsch/iso8859-1.html*. CERN is no longer supporting such documents; they have moved to *http://www.w3.org/pub/WWW/.*]

Some editors, such as HTML Assistant, include a panel for inserting such characters; others include automatic conversion mechanisms.

Conclusion

HTML changes gradually, and these changes usually appear when a popular Web browser, such as Mosaic, is updated to support new tags. One of the first commercial Mosaic clients, Netscape, supports several documented extensions to HTML, such as attributes to control character size, image position and, of course, a copyright character entity (©). Also, a formal set of changes is proposed as a new version of HTML is in the works. [See the following article.] HTML+, now referred to as HTML level 3, is already supported by one browser for X windows called Arena. It includes support of mathematical symbols using a <MATH> tag and a syntax similar to TeX, resizable tables, flowing text around graphics, and many new content-specific tags. HTML editors often lag behind browsers in updating their support for new tags, so when using HTML, keep an eye out for new browser releases. Multiple browser support for HTML extensions is a good indicator that new tags or a new HTML level is gaining acceptance.

Just as the Internet is becoming a global nervous system, the World Wide Web may very well become its brain. Web browsers, such as Mosaic, are currently the hottest software on the Internet and may become as common as e-mail in a year or two. Mastering HTML is essential to participating in this great new revolution in global publishing.

HTML Helpers: Converters, Editors, and Tools

HTML Converters translate formatting information in a word processor or page layout document to HTML tags. HTML Editors provide quick access to one or more levels of HTML tags. They function as a sort of HTML "word processor." HTML Tools check documents for valid tags and simplify tasks such as creating image mapping. [*Editor's Note:* the original list or URLs with this article was out of date. You can locate HTML helpers by using Yahoo and looking under Computers, then WWW, then HTML converters or HTML editors. You can also look at *http://www.w3.org/pub/WWW/Tools/.*]

HTML Anchor Dos and Don'ts

1. Avoid the urge to make "click here . . ." links. Make titles or descriptive words anchors.
2. Add icons to indicate multimedia data.
3. Be sure to use the ALT attribute with images that function as links.
4. Try to avoid making every occurrence of a word an anchor. The first occurrence is usually sufficient.
5. Avoid making anchors of headings.
6. Don't dismiss menu-style anchor lists. They still work for Gopher and can in WWW.
7. Include file size with anchors if the link will retrieve a large document, file, or image.
8. Make anchors a word or phrase, not whole sentences.
9. Use directional arrows with slide shows or tours. Use left/right, or up/down pairs—as long as you are consistent.
10. Include a "way back"—a link back to the home page or starting-point document.

References

1. Berners-Lee, Tim, et al. "The World-Wide Web." *Communications of the ACM* 37, No. 8 (August 1994): 76–82.

2. Berners-Lee, Tim. *Style Guide*. URL=*http://www.w3.org/hypertext/WWW/Provider/Style/*

3. Crawford, Walt. "A Hypertext Story." *DATABASE 14,* No. 4 (August 1991): 6–7.

4. *A Beginner's Guide to HTML*. URL=*http://www.ncsa.uiuc.edu/demoweb/html-primer.html*

5. *A Beginner's Guide*.

6. Levitt, Jason. "Image Mapping: Almost Child's Play with New Web Tools." *Open Systems Today* (October 10, 1994): 48.

7. Connolly, Daniel W. *HTML Specification*. URL=*http://www.w3.org:80/hypertext/WWW/MarkUp/html-spec/*

8. Grobe, Michael. *HTML Quick Reference*. URL=*http://www.cc.ukans.edu/info/HTML_quick.html*

HTML—Which Version?

Jon Knight

Jon Knight is a member of the department of computer studies at the Loughborough University of Technology in the United Kingdom.

Originally appeared in (1996, January) *The Ariadne Newsletter* [Online]. Available: *http://ukoln.bath.ac.uk/ariadne/.* Copyright held by Jon Knight.

Most people concerned with Electronic Libraries have by now marked up a document in the HyperText Markup Language (HTML), even if it's only their home page. HTML provides an easy means of adding functionality such as distributed hyperlinking and insertion of multimedia objects into documents. Done well, HTML provides access to information over a wide variety of platforms using many different browsers accessing servers via all manners of network connections. However, it is also possible to do HTML badly. Badly done HTML may tie a document down to a particular browser or hardware platform. It may make documents useless over slow network connections. As the Electronic Libraries programme is concerned with empowering people by giving them easy access to information via the Net, deciding what is and is not bad HTML and then avoiding using it is obviously something many librarians and library systems staff will currently be grappling with. This article aims to provide an informal overview of some of the issues surrounding good HTML markup and hopefully highlights some resources that may be of use in helping to improve the markup used in Electronic Library services.

The Versions Available

Before looking at what may constitute good and bad HTML markup, let us first review the wide variety of HTML versions available. There are currently only two versions of HTML that are on the Internet standards track: HTML 2.0[1] and HTML 3.0.[2] All other versions are bastardised, vendor-specific extensions to one of these open, nonproprietary versions. There is a version of HTML prior to HTML 2.0 known, unsurprisingly, as HTML 1.0. It provides the basic hyperlinking and anchors that make HTML a *hypertext* markup language and some elements for highlighting text in a variety of ways. HTML 1.0 provides us with a lowest common denominator of all the different versions. If you mark a document up to the HTML 1.0 specification, then the chances are that more or less every browser will do something vaguely sensible with it and so the information will be conveyed to the user intact. However HTML 1.0 was an informal specification that was never entered as part of the Internet standards process, and its use is somewhat depreciated today.

One problem with HTML 1.0 is that it only offers a way to present basic textual information to a user; the means of getting feedback from the user are very limited. HTML 2.0 helps to overcome this problem by providing the document author with the FORMs capability. The markup tags allow you to embed forms with text-input boxes, check boxes, radio buttons, and many of the other features that are common in user interfaces. These forms can be interspersed with tags from HTML 1.0 to provide additional functionality to a FORMs document and also to provide some form of access to the available data to non-HTML 2.0 compliant browsers. However, such browsers are few and far between these days. HTML 2.0 is thus regarded by many as the base level of HTML to code to if you wish to reach the largest population of browsers and still have reasonable document presentation.

The latest version of HTML, HTML 3.0, is still really under development. HTML 3.0 addresses the lack of detailed presentation control in the previous two versions with the introduction of style sheets and tables. The specification for HTML 3.0 also includes a mathematics markup that was very reminiscent of that provided with LaTeX. As HTML 3.0 is still under development, no browsers can claim to be fully compliant with the standard, although many of the more recent browsers have added some of the core HTML 3.0 elements to their own HTML 2.0 base.

Vendors also add their own proprietary tags to the core, standard HTML specifications. These tags are often presentation oriented or make some use of a feature peculiar to that vendor's browser. The most well-known commercial browser is currently the Netscape Navigator,[3] versions of which estimates have placed at anywhere between 50 percent and 90 percent of the total browser population. It adds many presentational tags that are widely used in many documents purporting to be HTML. Reading one of these "Netscaped" documents on another browser can result in anything from a slight loss of visual attractiveness to a completely unreadable (and therefore unusable) document. Some document authors are so intent on trying to use these "Netscapisms" that they even place a link to the Netscape distribution site on the Net so that those not blessed with Netscape can download it to view the author's documents. Things are only set to get worse with the entry of Microsoft[4] and IBM[5] into the fray.

It is in part the fact that browser authors add extra tags from one version of the HTML standard to a core from an earlier version and make up their own proprietary elements that causes some of the problems experienced by users. This is compounded by the fact that as the markup gets more complicated the opportunity for bugs to creep into different browsers increases. The result is that we have browsers and documents that all claim to be HTML when in fact many of them are not. To make matters even worse, many people don't specify which version of HTML a document is marked up in or even validate their documents to check that they match one of the specifications (known as a Document Type Definition or DTD).

Many browsers are *very* tolerant of the markup that they receive, which in some ways is a good thing as it means that the end user is likely to see something even if the document's author has made a complete mess out of marking up the document. This has probably helped contribute to the Web's rapid growth as people perceive it to be relatively easy to add markup to documents and get working results. Unfortunately, the flip side is that we are left with a Web full of poorly marked up documents not conforming to any of the standards, even the vendor-specific extensions.

Notes

1. *ftp://ds.internic.net/rfc/rfc1866.txt*

2. *http://www.w3.org/hypertext/WWW/MarkUp/html3/CoverPage.html*

3. *http://www.netscape.com/*

4. *http://www.microsoft.com/*

5. *http://www.ibm.com/*

Editor's note: The HTML 3.2 draft was released by the World Wide Web Consortium in May 1996. This draft would validate most of the tags currently in use. For more information, see *http://www.w3.org/pub/www/markup/wilbur.*

UW–Madison Campus Libraries' Web Page Standards and Guidelines

Electronic Library Access Committee
User Documentation Working Group

Members are Cheryl Becker, Patricia Herrling, Dennis Hill, Don Johnson, Nancy McClements. Nancy McClements may be reached as *MCCLEMEN@ DOIT.WISC.EDU.*

Originally appeared at (1995, December) *http://www.library.wisc.edu/help/tech/ Web_standards.html.* Copyright held by University of Wisconsin System Board of Regents.

Content

Required

1. On every home page: name, address, and e-mail address of responsible person or entity, for example, *webadmin@libraryname.wisc.edu*
2. Date of last update for pages with substantive content
3. Full name of unit (in title heading, document text, address, and/or graphical link) and/or URL in order that the source can be recoverable

Recommended

1. Copyright statement (if and when appropriate)
2. Statement of document status if in progress (for example, "prototype," "under construction")
3. Indication of restricted access where appropriate
4. Warning statement if link will lead to large document or image
5. "What's New" section on home page
6. No browser-specific terminology (for example, "pull down the File menu and select Save")

7. Link text should make sense even if link isn't present, as with a paper copy. For example, "To ask a reference question: *askmemorial @doit.wisc.edu,*" instead of "To ask a reference question, click here."
8. Use of a general style guideline (for example, *Strunk & White's Elements of Style*)
9. Always think of your users—test with primary user groups

Design

Required

1. A link to the UW–Madison Electronic Library, including the .gif icon, accessible by two or three direct jumps (clicks) from each document
2. A link to return to the parent home page ("Return to xxx Home Page") on all supporting local documents

Recommended

1. Style sheet (or template) to provide visual consistency across related documents
2. Small graphic that identifies all of the documents of a Web site
3. Short and simple home page
4. No "monster" graphics; avoid many little graphics
5. Navigational aids useful to your users ("Return to Top," Table of Contents, Next/Previous Page for documents in a series, etc.)
6. Active links to mentioned documents
7. "Hot buttons" for shortcuts to most important links
8. Minimum text in lists or menus
9. Logical tags used as intended instead of forcing them to serve as a graphical device (for example, use headings <H1> as true headings, not just to achieve bold text)
10. Sparing use of bold, italics, blinking, etc.
11. Always think of your users—test with primary user groups

Procedural/Technical

Required

1. A plan on how revisions will take place (schedule for updating, who will do, etc.); GLS Automation Services will e-mail a standard reminder notice to library home page developers (via HTML-FOLKS) before each semester (fall, spring, and summer) to review and revise pages and to update links.
2. Test of links before mounting as well as a schedule for checking links and removing dead links

3. Spell-check and proofreading of documents
4. Conformance to HTML 2.0 or 3.0 DTDs (Document Type Definition) —avoid use of browser-specific tags
5. ALT attribute for images <IMG>—for benefit of browsers without graphics capabilities

Recommended

1. Markup language that is readable by future (human) maintainers (for example, liberal use of line breaks and white space in the source documents)
2. Check finished document with variety of browsers, both text (Lynx) and graphical (Netscape, Mosaic, etc.)
3. High-level elements in every document (<HTML> <HEAD> <BODY>)
4. Low-resolution thumbnail images in text, pointing to full-resolution external images
5. Development in nonpublic directories only
6. Test with primary user groups

You've Got a Web Page—What Next?

A vast amount has been written in several literatures about how to develop a home page, but what about once you've already gotten it going? How do you maintain it, and how do you expand it further? There seems to be a consensus in more than just the library world that developing things is glamorous, but maintenance is boring. No matter how flashy and great it is at the start, though, your Web page will quickly lose any respect it has gained if you don't keep it up-to-date and develop it further.

Maintenance involves checking facts and checking links to make sure data has not become inaccurate. A large site should be rechecked at least twice a month—you've heard how things change constantly; believe me, this is not too often. Increasingly, programs are available that automate this checking process, although some human intervention is needed to check sites that have been reported as changing. Also remember that these programs usually just check to see if a link is still active; they cannot tell you if it's one of those pages that say "Housewives Anonymous has moved to a new site; please update your links."

Developing your site can go in a couple of directions: new capabilities may be added, and new topic areas may be covered. Broad sites like those of most libraries should continue to be developed so that people know they're worth checking periodically to see what has changed, and, anyway, you'll never be able to honestly say you've covered all the subjects you need to! New capabilities may include the use of forms, which involves use of CGI (Common Gateway Interface), and scripting in a language like PERL (Practical Extraction and Report Language). You might also start generating some pages through use of database management programs. Your library might also want to get into using something like Java to perform new Web page functions. (See "Browsers, Extensions, and the Kitchen Junk Drawer" for references to Java sites.)

Here are some sites with links to resources helpful to Webmasters. For more sites and to stay up-to-date on what's out there, check Yahoo at *http://www.yahoo.com/Computers_and_Internet/Internet/World_Wide_Web/Programming/.*

Allison, Bob. (1996, May). *The Web Master's Page*. [Online]. Available: *http://gagme.wwa.com/~boba/masters1.html*

This is a pretty good-sized collection of links to help you to create and maintain your Web page. Extensive sections on browsers, CGI, PERL, SGML (Standardized General Markup Language), and more. Only a few annotations.

Athenia Associates. (1996, May). *Webreference.com*. [Online]. Available: *http://www.webreference.com/*

Be sure to go to the table of contents for this site; that's where you'll find references for Webmasters to programming, interactivity, Frequently Asked Questions (FAQs), and more. There are tutorials and articles on optimizing for various browsers, programming forms, various versions of HyperText Markup Language (HTML) and Netscape, and much more.

Kelly, Brian. (1995, September). *Running a WWW Service*. [Online]. Available: *http://www.leeds.ac.uk/ucs/WWW/handbook/handbook.html*

This is done in the style of a handbook. It includes a chapter on "Libraries and the WWW."

Richmond, Alan. *Web Developer's Virtual Library*. [Online]. Available: *http://www.stars.com/*

This is a fantastic site! Go here first, before you go anywhere else, and look under "Library." You'll find the most useful information under "Server Side." There are sections on icons and images, forms, CGI (over 60 links!), validation (HTML and links), and databases, plus much more. And the links are even annotated.

Schnell, Eric H. (1996, April). *Writing for the Web: A Primer for Librarians*. [Online]. Available: *http://bones.med.ohio-state.edu/eric/papers/primer/webdocs.html*

This is formatted more like a handbook and is aimed at librarians. It focuses on what is involved with creating documents for the Web. Links to useful sites are also included.

Strom, David. "Webmaster Sites." [Online]. Available: *http://www.strom.com/places/webmaster.html*

This is not a lengthy list of items, but it is annotated and has sections on where you should publicize your Web page, style guides, and server-related information.

Tennant, Roy. (1996). *The Art and Science of Web Management*. [Online]. Available: *http://www.library.ucsb.edu/untangle/tennant.html*

This is a paper by someone managing a Web server in a library setting that addresses many of the maintenance issues.

CONSIDERING COMPUTER-MEDIATED COMMUNICATION

THE FUTURE IS NOW!

Craig A. Summerhill

Craig Summerhill is the systems coordinator and program officer for the Coalition for Networked Information. He has spoken and written extensively about the Internet, including coauthoring *Internet Primer for Information Professionals: A Basic Guide to Internet Networking Technology*. He may be reached as *CRAIG@CNI.ORG*.

Defining Computer-Mediated Communication

As one might surmise from the name, computer-mediated communication (CMC) is simply the application of computing machinery to the process of communication, with all of its defined elements.* The computer serves a role in mediating or regulating the process between the people involved in communicating, and it facilitates the transferral of information and the preservation of knowledge. By far, the most common type of CMC currently employed is electronic mail. However, many other applications of CMC exist in the Internet and other networked environments, including bulletin boards, conferencing systems, discussion lists, news groups, and hypertext publishing. Hypertext publishing, as a form of CMC, will be the focus here.

---

*A working knowledge of the process of communication is useful in assessing the role CMC plays in the exchange of ideas and the transference of knowledge within a society. A more-detailed version of this work, including a definition of communication as a process, an examination of several forms of human communication, a more-detailed consideration of literacy, a more-detailed examination of likely future directions of CMC, and suggested actions on the part of the library community, is available at *http://www.cni.org/~craig/cmc.html*.

In 1945 Vannevar Bush's now famous article, "As We May Think," in *The Atlantic Monthly,* was published. Reprints of this article have appeared many times since its original publication (see Suggested Readings). Bush, the first director of the U.S. Office of Scientific Research and Development, was the chief science advisor to President Franklin D. Roosevelt during World War II. In his article, Bush notes how technology has been employed to extend humankind's physical powers and theorizes that similar technological breakthroughs could be used to augment the intellectual powers of humanity. He predicted the widespread use of a number of objects in the article, including the Cyclops Camera—a device that is not terribly unlike a hand-held video camera, except that Bush believed the device would be mounted on the head. Of particular interest to the librarian would be his predictions concerning the use of microfilm for the storage and retrieval of pages of printed documentation. He also proposed the development of an intelligent machine, named *memex,* that would file information by association—a method he believed the human brain employs.

Three decades later, advances in computing machinery made hypertext at least a theoretical possibility if not an inevitability. And half a century after Bush wrote this article, the World Wide Web (WWW) has demonstrated a workable, if somewhat imperfect, model for a global hypertext system. While there are notable differences between Bush's proposed memex and the WWW (primarily, the WWW employs thousands of computers to accomplish a function similar to that of the proposed single machine, memex), the similarities in function are striking. One of the chief characteristics of the theoretical memex system was the ability of the computer's operator to build associative trails of concepts throughout documents/files on the system.

> The owner of the Memex, let us say, is interested in the origin and properties of the bow and arrow. Specifically, he is studying why the short Turkish bow was apparently superior to the English long bow in the skirmishes of the Crusades. He has dozens of possibly pertinent books and articles in his memex. First he runs through an encyclopedia, finds an interesting but sketchy article, leaves it projected. Next, in a history, he finds another pertinent item, and ties the two together. Thus he goes, building a trail of many items. Occasionally he inserts a comment of his own, either linking it into the main trail or joining it by a side trail to a particular item.

The concept Bush refers to as "trailblazing" is, in the modern parlance, referred to as a *hyperlink.* Multiple documents from multiple sources are linked, intellectually and physically, through the use of these links, thus creating trails throughout the document(s) that are indicative of human associative thought. It should be noted that Bush writes about what has been characterized as full-hypertext, while the WWW employs semi-hypertext. The chief distinction between the two is that full-hypertext supports bidirectional linking, meaning that the person navigating the system can move either direction across the link. The HyperText Markup Language (HTML), which serves as the basis of the WWW, really only supports unidirectional linking. Although several Web browser interfaces support a reverse navigational function through another facility (e.g., the "left arrow—back" button in Netscape Navigator), this is not the same as full-hypertext. For further consideration of the theoretical elements of hypertext systems as opposed to the WWW practice, consult Drexler and Kappe et al. (listed in Suggested Readings).

A metaphor commonly applied to the Web and the underlying technologies is that of the traditional publication process. While there are some differences between these processes, the ability to write and disseminate HTML documents in the WWW is more similar to publication than it is different from it.

Hypertext as Publication

Knowledgeable library patrons typically expect high-quality written communication from the libraries they frequent. As a result, concerns about the poor quality and perceived biases of some Web sites is of great concern to many. One of the chief criticisms of the Web, as commonly espoused by librarians among others, is that while materials in the traditional publication process undergo detailed editorial scrutiny prior to release in print, the materials that appear in the World Wide Web have undergone no similar scrutiny. Therefore, the informational value of much of this Web-published material has been drawn into question by those familiar with both the inner workings of the Internet technologies and the traditional print publishing industry. On the surface, this seems a valid criticism.

However, a closer examination of WWW-publishing reveals this criticism may not be entirely valid:

Motivation and skill of authors can be drawn into question in both environments.

While there are currently few, if any, publishing houses (in the traditional sense) operating within the networked environment to which authors formally submit their works for consideration of publication, in an abstract manner a network server can be thought of as serving a hybrid function that is somewhat a cross between a publishing house and a print shop.

Further to the point, it is really unfair to say that documents in the WWW go forth with no editorial scrutiny. In fact, a very strong argument can be made that a hypertext document will undergo far more scrutiny within its lifetime than the vast majority of traditionally printed documents ever will. In fact, it is the nature of this continuous scrutiny (and subsequent revision) that makes many of the WWW-published works such a moving target for libraries. The practice of peer review (both prepublication and post-publication) in the World Wide Web may be made considerably more easy by the ubiquitous nature of the network, for example. Also, it is much more likely that a hypertext document in the WWW will receive consideration from interdisciplinary researchers outside the domain of knowledge of any particular author due to the network's ubiquitous nature.

The clustering of like items (both by collocation upon a single server and through author-generated associative trails, or hyperlinks) serves a similar intellectual function to that of specialty publishing—the practice of a publishing house to focus on literature within a specific domain of knowledge (library and information science, for example). WWW-published documents may have considerably more value than the relatively static paper-based publications when viewed in this context.

Additionally, the creation of associative trails augments the traditional process of collection development within libraries by creating predefined natural linkages between related concepts. When a library decides to make access to a particular WWW-published document prominently available, associated links are provided similarly high-profile treatment.

Libraries, as the final link in the publication process, provide context to documents by actively collecting and organizing them. Librarians (most notably in academic environments) have begun to systematically explore methods and strategies for lending their organizational skills to the collection, storage, and dissemination of Internet resources (see Dillon et al. article in Selected Readings). Although the evolutionary nature of these resources, as previously noted, makes this a daunting task, it is something that clearly is recognized by some to be within the boundaries of library expertise.

To be fair, there are shortcomings to the WWW publishing environment. Most notably, what is sorely lacking in the Internet and the World Wide Web is the extensive secondary publishing market (reviews, literary criticisms, bibliographies, catalogs, and other critical publications) that analyze and rate electronic documents. These practices, in the traditional print marketplace, serve an important function by adding context and authority (or lack thereof) to a publication, and they are employed by both librarians and researchers to assist in the location of authoritative information. It would be inaccurate to say that no secondary publication market exists in the Web, but it is accurate to note the number of documents being "self-published" on the WWW vastly outnumbers critical and analytical publications at this time.

Another significant shortcoming of the WWW publishing environment is the lack of ability for authors and publishers to control the dissemination of the intellectual content of their publications. So long as the network environment lacks user authentication, encryption, and copyright-control systems, many of society's most qualified authors and publishing agencies will be reluctant to enter the WWW publishing market. After all, most authors expect a fair return on their works, and rightly so. Despite this observation, it is unclear to many that the WWW as a publication system can be wholly dismissed as a source of legitimate and useful information. Throughout the history of humankind, many important intellectual contributions have been considered marginalia at one time. Such is true in the electronic frontier.

Literacy and Acculturation of Information Technology

During the preparation and writing of this paper, I consulted several dictionaries seeking a definition of literacy. In all, as has been the tendency within Western civilization, literacy is narrowly defined in terms of an ability to read and write alphabetic languages. This is, of course, the form of literacy that has long been the traditional concern of educators and librarians within our society. I propose, however, that literacy can be viewed as a convention or a measurement tool to determine the effectiveness of any particular communication process. If the person receiving the communication has comprehended and retained the transmitted data as knowledge, she or he can be said to be literate on the topic at hand.

As topics of communication become more complex, requiring more requisite knowledge to properly receive and interpret the message, the nature of self-sufficient learning becomes an important consideration. The structuring and organization of the collective memory (knowledge) of humankind—a task generations of librarians have already undertaken as theirs—is of critical importance in building environments for self-sufficient learning. One must understand how to locate and assimilate pieces of information in the existing knowledge base to synthesize new knowledge. In such a manner, much knowledge is evolutionary in nature—each subsequent generation of people building on the learning of past generations. Drexler (see Suggested Reading) provides an interesting insight into the potential role of hypertext in the evolution of knowledge.

Do not be readily misled by the praises for telecommunication technologies that are currently emanating from Madison Avenue and Wall Street. Achieving societal literacy in this new electronic frontier will take time. Currently, too many people lack the equipment to connect to networks such as the Internet, or they lack the personal skills and knowledge to employ technologies such as the World Wide Web to their fullest degree, or the communications infrastructure in their corner of the world simply lacks the capacity to handle the volume of users mandated to achieve societal levels of literacy in information technology. So long as 80 percent or more of our society is locked out of the environment variously referred to as the Internet, the Matrix, the World Wide Web, or simply the Net, it is reasonable to assume the real potential for using hypertext and associated technologies to augment the intellectual development of humankind, as outlined by Vannevar Bush some fifty years ago, will not be realized.

In 1993 a new subject—social intelligence—was given treatment in the *Annual Review of Information Science and Technology* (see Cronin and Davenport, in Suggested Readings). While the term currently has disparate meanings to many different scholars in a wide range of disciplines, there is a growing interest in defining a single theory for the definition of intelligence and the measurement of knowledge. A large part of social intelligence in the Internet must be, by definition, a literacy in using information technology tools. Modern communication technologies are useful tools that do provide an opportunity to make significant and positive changes to society in an extremely rapid manner. They can positively affect the collective memory of humankind, providing context and definition to self-sufficient learning. Highly advanced computing machinery and software costs a fraction of the price it did just two years ago. And so goes the industry.

As a result of these trends, we might reasonably expect the coming fifty years following the first real deployment of a memex-like system—namely the World Wide Web—will provide many more opportunities for societal change than the fifty years preceding that deployment. Consider, for example, how far we have already come in the ten short years since the National Science Foundation built a backbone network to serve as the core of the ARPANET (Advanced Research Projects Agency Network) in terms of understanding the social context of these technologies. The spirits we have unleashed will not go back into the box willingly, but unlike the ills unleashed by Pandora, this technology holds great promise for the intellectual growth of humankind. Vannevar Bush saw this a half century ago. We are unlikely ever to have less computer-mediated communication capacity in the future than we currently have now. It is up to all of us to determine how to manage this technology in a socially beneficial manner, and cybrarians have a large role to play in this process.

Concerning computer-mediated communications, the future is now!

Suggested Readings

Bush, Vannevar. (1986). "As We May Think." In Steve Lambert and Suzanne Ropiquet, Eds., *CD-ROM: The New Papyrus.* Redmond, WA: Microsoft Press. (Original work published in *The Atlantic Monthly,* 1945)

Bush, Vannevar. (1991). "As We May Think." In James Nyce and Paul Kahn, Eds., *From Memex to Hypertext: Vannevar Bush and the Mind's Machine.* San Diego, CA: Academic Press. (Original work published in *The Atlantic Monthly,* 1945)

Cronin, Blaise, and Davenport, Elisabeth. (1993). "Social Intelligence." In *Annual Review of Information Science and Technology, 28,* 3–44.

Dillon, Martin, Jul, Erik, Burge, Mark, and Hickey, Carol. (1993). "Assessing Information on the Internet: Toward Providing Library Services for Computer-Mediated Communication. Results of an OCLC Research Project." *Internet Research, 3,* 54–69.

Drexler, K. Eric. (1995). *Hypertext Publishing and the Evolution of Knowledge.* [Online]. Available: *http://reality.sgi.com/employees/whitaker/ Hypertext/HypertextPublishingKED.html*

Kappe, Frank, Pani, Gerald, and Schnabel, Florian. (1993). "The Architecture of a Massively Distributed Hypermedia System." *Internet Research, 3,* 10–24.

Matrix Information & Directory Services. (1996). *Matrix Information & Directory Services Home Page*. [Online]. Available: *http://www.mids.org/*

Summerhill, Craig A. (1996). *Computer-Mediated Communication as Publication: Considering the World Wide Web in the Broader Sociological Context of Communication*. [Online]. Available: *http://www.cni.org/~craig/cmc.html*

8

Beyond Text

Using Multimedia File Formats

Thomas Dowling

Thomas Dowling *(TDowling@ohiolink.ohiolink.edu)* is assistant director of systems, client-server applications at OhioLINK. He is a member of the editorial board and a reviewer for *Telecommunications Electronic Reviews*. He sometimes goes under the alias of "[Alternate] Dr. Internet."

The past several years have seen explosive growth in libraries' use of online information, particularly information on the Internet, and especially documents on the World Wide Web. While coping with the sheer amount of information on the Net is a daunting task by itself, it is increasingly exacerbated by the many formats and media available. This chapter is provided as a field guide to identifying, understanding, and making use of the file types commonly found on the Net.

The need to understand different file formats is symptomatic of the way we have come to communicate electronically. A single librarian can scan and retouch a photograph of his reference room to include in a brochure, which was drafted in Windows Notepad and then brought into Word for Windows, and print the final document on a high-quality printer without needing to know about the Tagged Image File Format (TIFF) image, American Standard Code for Information Interchange (ASCII) text, formatted text, or PostScript document that were created along the way. But once he needs to provide a copy for a colleague using a Macintosh computer, or send it by e-mail, or create an online version for the library's Web server, he not only needs to know what those formats are but what formats his colleagues and users can handle and how to get his document from one to the other.

In this chapter we will look at the commonly used formats in several different media, focusing on their relative strengths and weaknesses and providing guidelines about when to use what. The five media I will examine are text, document presentation, images, audio and video, and compression and archiving formats.

Several factors are constant across all these media. First, because multimedia documents get very large very quickly, many file formats either provide options for compression or are automatically compressed. Others are commonly used with one or more external compression programs. In many ways this is a great service to the network community; the larger a file is, the longer it takes to transfer or download (making it more expensive for many of us to download) and the more space it takes on a hard drive. However, a compressed file must be uncompressed before it can be used; if it was compressed with a program you don't own, you may be unable to use it even if you have the necessary program to handle the uncompressed file. A problem that has cropped up with several file formats is that some compression methods rely on patented computational algorithms; it may not always be clear if the patent owners have granted permission for programs to use their method, leaving software developers uncertain if they can support files compressed that way.

A second factor that appears in all media is the give and take involved in defining file formats. In some cases, a format is defined by a specification from one company. This may lead to a very concrete definition with few ambiguities, but it means that a single company controls both the definition and its future developments. In other cases, the definition may be a product of a formal standards body. This usually means the future development of the standard will be open and inclusive, but sometimes it also means that

---

FIGURE 1   A Field Guide to File Extensions

File Extensions	File Type
.txt	ASCII files
.html, .htm	HTML hypertext files
.ps	PostScript documents
.pdf	Adobe Acrobat Portable Documents
.tex, .dvi	TeX document files
.gif	Graphics Interchange Format images
.jpg, .jpeg, .jfif	JPEG images
.tiff, .tif	Tagged Image File Format images
.png	Portable Network Graphic images
.avi	Video for Windows (Audio/Video Interleave) video files
.wav	WAVE audio files
.mov	QuickTime movie files
.mpeg, .mpg	MPEG video files
.au, .snd	AU sound files
.zip	PKZIP archives
.tar.Z, .tar.gz	Compressed UNIX tar archives (using compress or gzip)
.sit, .sea	StuffIt archive or self-extracting archive

a format has been defined very broadly to incorporate the work of many developers. In such cases, the standard may provide numerous options not supported by all programs that claim to handle that file type.

Finally, for any given medium, there are several file formats, sometimes competing and sometimes complementing each other. Selecting which to use requires an understanding of several factors, including each format's intended purpose and limitations, the user's needs, and constraints imposed by network bandwidth. Figure 1 summarizes the common file formats and their extensions.

Text-Related File Formats

Multimedia is hard to define, but for many of us it suggests something more than just text. However, it is important to realize that "just text," in several forms, accounts for an overwhelming percentage of what gets carried around the Net. In fact, for some applications, the need to be carried around the Net includes the requirement that a file be in a text format.

Many users have an intuitive sense of what text is; the letter *A*, for example, separate from any information about its appearance, font, or location on a page, is text. With a high degree of reliability, you can type an *A* on your keyboard and e-mail it to me, and then I can view it onscreen, download it to a file, print it, and still get an *A*. The fact that this works—regardless of who made your keyboard, my printer, and either of our computers or e-mail programs—is a tribute to one of the oldest telecommunications standards around: ASCII.

ASCII, as used today, involves three standards. In the United States, ASCII is defined by the American National Standards Institute as ANSI X3.4-1986 (R1992). Internationally, a slightly more generalized form of ASCII is defined in the International Organization for Standardization's ISO 646. ISO 8859 uses ASCII as a subset around which ten Latin alphabet character sets are created. The set of characters currently supported on the World Wide Web is ISO 8859-1, or ISO Latin 1. ASCII uses seven bits to define each character, allowing for 128 (2^7) characters. The character sets in ISO 8859 add an eighth bit, providing space for another 128 characters.

Our intuitive notion of text extends to the 56 upper- and lowercase letters of the Roman alphabet and the numerals 0 through 9, but other characters are more ambiguous. Periods, commas, exclamation marks, and question marks are probably included, but what about the dollar sign, or the symbol for the British pound? A *U* with an umlaut, or an *N* with a tilde, or an *A* with a tilde? Few of these are covered by unadorned ASCII, yet these are all from comparatively similar Western European alphabets. ASCII does not extend support to Cyrillic alphabets; Chinese, Japanese, and Korean characters; or to other alphabets used outside the Western world.

Major Text Formats

Format:	Internet (ARPANET) Mail Format
Definition:	RFC (Request for Comments) 822: Standard for the format of Advanced Research Projects Agency (ARPA) Internet text messages
Availability:	*http://ds.internic.net/rfc/rfc822.txt*

Format:	Multipurpose Internet Mail Extensions (MIME)
Definition:	RFC 1521 and 1522: MIME
Availability:	*http://ds.internic.net/rfc/rfc1521.txt* and *rfc1522.txt*

Internet e-mail is not typically viewed as a file format. I am including it here, however, because it represents an amazing amount of information, and its specification requires that all messages be composed of ASCII text. To some extent, this is self-evident, but it also means that sending anything other than text requires a mechanism to convert non-ASCII data into text and reliably convert it back to its original format. In fact, many e-mail programs now include this facility in the form of MIME support.

Format:	Unicode
Definition:	The Unicode Standard, Worldwide Character Encoding
Availability:	Not available online

The Unicode project *(http://www.unicode.org/)*, which has been in development since 1988, is creating a standard to replace 7-bit ASCII and 8-bit ASCII extensions with 32-bit character definitions that provide space for more than 4 billion characters. Unicode, which is already supported by the Microsoft Windows 95 and Windows NT operating systems, will eventually create a single, standard system for describing alphabetic characters from around the world.

Document Presentation Formats

One of the longest-standing purposes of the Internet is to share access to documents. While ASCII documents are certainly capable of conveying textual information, document authors frequently require more control over appearance than ASCII provides. This is increasingly true as the Web becomes a greater tool of commerce and publishing.

The basic challenge that these presentation systems try to address is to carry formatting and layout created on one system to another system that may have different software, different system resources such as fonts, and different output capabilities such as printer quality than the original system.

Major Document Presentation Formats

Format:	HyperText Markup Language (HTML)
Definition:	HTML—2.0
Availability:	*http://www.w3.org/pub/WWW/MarkUp/html-spec/ html-spec_toc.html*

HTML, the file format used by the World Wide Web, is now ubiquitous. However, it is used by many people who do not know its origins, and librarians in particular should understand HTML in the context of information standards.

HTML, as originally conceived, is one iteration of the Standard Generalized Markup Language (SGML), a formal method for describing the functional aspects of any given kind of document. SGML explicitly separates the server-oriented function of identifying parts of a document—title, section headers, or author address, for example—from the client-oriented task of deciding how each of those elements should look and where on a page or onscreen they should appear. While this is an efficient way to handle highly structured documents, it gives SGML (and HTML) authors much less control over their documents' appearance than they would have using almost any other document presentation system.

Several outcomes stem from this. First, recent extensions to HTML have added many functions related to document appearance, from font size controls originated by Netscape to the ability to specify typefaces in Microsoft's Internet Explorer. A second, and related, development is that for some purposes Web authors are sidestepping HTML entirely in favor of an actual page description language such as Adobe Acrobat's Portable Document Format (PDF).

Third, the real world usage of HTML has changed so much and so quickly that the deliberate pace of the standards process has been unable to keep up. At the moment, the only actual HTML standard in place is HTML 2.0; a draft version of HTML 3.0 put forth in March 1995 has formally expired without being replaced; parts of the 3.0 proposal will be broken out and added in pieces to a new "modular" standard, perhaps to be called HTML 2.1. Finally, most current Web browsers understand formatting tags that were created by browser manufacturers rather than any standard and that are not always thoroughly documented. (See "HTML—Which Version" earlier in this book for an update.)

Format: PostScript
Definition: PostScript Language Reference Manual
Availability: Not available online

By Internet standards, PostScript is ancient. It is not specifically a file format but is instead a complete programming language. While it can be used for general-purpose programming, it was designed to excel at describing the placement of text and graphics on a page, independent of any specific printer's capabilities. A PostScript printer contains sufficient computing power to interpret programs written in PostScript, and a PostScript document is, in fact, an ASCII file containing the programming code necessary to describe pages in PostScript.

PostScript has been very important on the Internet for several reasons. First, it is the preferred laser printer format for the Macintosh and most UNIX computers, operating platforms that were highly visible on the Net before the PC. Second, PostScript successfully accomplishes its goal of platform independence; the same document can be printed on virtually any UNIX or Macintosh computer or on any PC whose printer interprets PostScript with virtually identical results. Third, PostScript is comparatively difficult to turn back into editable text; while this means that a reader can do little with a file other than print it (there are also programs to display PostScript files onscreen), it means that authors can distribute their documents with some level of assurance that they will be read with the formatting intended and will not be copied wholesale into anyone else's writing.

> *Format:*   Adobe Acrobat Portable Document Format (PDF)
> *Definition:*   Portable Document Format Reference Manual
> *Availability:* *ftp://ftp.adobe.com/pub/adobe/Applications/Acrobat/*
>   *SDK/TECHDOC/PDFSPEC.PDF*

Even before the Web became such a popular phenomenon, companies were coming to grips with network distribution of documents from one computer with one set of software and fonts to another computer that could not be guaranteed to have the same capabilities. In the past, such distribution would have used PostScript files in the expectation that the documents would simply be printed out. Increasingly, however, users expect to view—or at least preview—such documents on screen.

Adobe Acrobat is a system related to Adobe's PostScript language that allows users to view a document with their own computer's best approximation of the original formatting. PDF is becoming increasingly common on the Internet as both authors and readers come to expect Web document access, and especially as both come to grips with the limitations of the Web's native HTML format. Version 2.0 of Netscape Navigator comes with Adobe's Acrobat file viewer.

Image Formats

Still images have become a major part of working on the Internet, largely because of their prevalence in World Wide Web pages. Several different formats are widely used, and each has distinct advantages in certain contexts.

Before exploring the specific image formats, it is necessary to discuss some of the factors that define image quality. Usually, two measurements affect quality: the image's resolution, or its relative width and height on-screen, and its color depth, measured in bits.

The first measurement, resolution, is measured in pixels. Computer monitors display images as arrangements of pixels ("Picture Elements"), essentially the smallest region of the screen for which color and brightness can be individually controlled. Because different settings on different monitors allow for different pixel sizes, it is impossible to know how large an image will be on different computers. Therefore, resolution must always be a relative measurement.

The second measurement, image depth, indicates how many bits determine each color. This number controls the total number of separate colors the image can contain; if the image depth is X pixels, the total number of colors attainable is 2^x.

For example, the format used by fax messages has an image depth of one bit; since a bit can take either of two values, this means faxes have two colors, usually rendered as black and white. Color images more typically have image depths of 8 bits (2^8, or 256 colors) or 24 bits (2^{24}, or approximately 16 million colors).

The size of an uncompressed image file, excluding a little overhead for identifying the format type or providing comments, is largely a matter of arithmetic: the number of pixels times the number of bits for each pixel. A photograph rendered as an 8-bit color image at a resolution of 640 × 480 will be roughly 640 × 480 × 8 = 2,457,000 bits in size, or about 300 kilobytes. The image may look substantially more realistic with 24-bit color at a 1,024 × 768 resolution, but the same math informs us that the resulting file will be about 2.25 megabytes in size.

Compression

Given sizes like the ones just mentioned, it is easy to see why most of the image formats used on the Internet include compression. Compression techniques employ computational algorithms to describe regions of an image more succinctly than a pixel-by-pixel listing. For example, if an image includes 97 pixels in a row, all the same shade of blue, it is much briefer to say, "The next 97 pixels are blue" than it is to say, "The first pixel is blue. The second pixel is blue. . . ." (Image compression is actually much more involved than this example, looking for such compressible sequences all around each pixel rather than just in a pixel-by-pixel sequence.)

The two main types of compression are compression that can be reversed, or uncompressed, without losing any data from the original image (*lossless* compression) and compression that loses some data when uncompressed (*lossy* compression). At first glance, it may not be clear why someone would ever want to use a technique that was designed to lose information from an original document, but in fact most photographic images contain barely perceptible details that will not be missed and may not even be wanted in the first place. A photograph of a white wall, for instance, may actually detect thousands of shades of "white" according to slight lighting differences, the texture of the wall, and blemishes in the paint. If this level of detail is not needed in the image, it can make sense to use a compression technique that reduces this level of detail to attain a smaller file.

Even when a format using lossy compression makes sense, document creators will usually be careful to save an image in such a format only after making all necessary changes to it. If you scan a photograph and save it to a file, then open the file to crop the image and save it again, then re-open the file to retouch the colors and save it again, you lose details in the image each time you save the file. Doing this repeatedly will lose enough detail to detract from the perceived image quality.

Transparency

The rapid growth of the World Wide Web has made many users familiar with images that contain a degree of transparency. Usually this means that one color within an image is ignored when the image is rendered on top of another image or solid color. Many home pages use this technique to float a logo or other small image above the document without needing to encase it in a rectangular field.

This single transparent color is often insufficient, however. Suppose that the logo on this home page is not a simple drawing but a photograph of a wine glass. The region beyond the outline of the glass will be completely transparent, but the glass itself will range from nearly complete transparency in the middle to a dark outline at either edge. If the glass actually contains some wine, it will also have varying degrees of opacity, as will any shadows cast by the glass.

To handle cases like this, some image formats use what is called an "alpha" channel to specify a level of transparency for each pixel. This allows a more natural look when one image is superimposed on another. While this ability is included in many image editing programs, as of this writing no such format is commonly seen on the Net.

Major Image Formats

Format:	Graphics Interchange Format (GIF)
Definition:	Graphics Interchange Format, version 89a
Availability:	*ftp://ftp.ncsa.uiuc.edu/misc/file.formats/ graphics.formats/gif89a.doc*

The GIF (pronounced "jif") format is one of the oldest and most stable image formats available, but it has also become one of the most controversial. GIF is a product of CompuServe, which created it in 1987 to provide a standard format for subscribers who were exchanging graphics across different computer platforms. A revised specification appeared in 1989 that added a small number of refinements, most notably support for transparency. From its inception through 1994, CompuServe actively encouraged developers to support the GIF format in graphics programs.

Like most major image formats, GIF incorporates compression automatically; it uses the lossless LZW compression technique named for its two inventors, Abraham Lempel and Jacob Ziv, and Terry Welch, who refined it into a faster algorithm. Since some implementations of LZW are in the public domain, CompuServe apparently believed that it was available for use in GIF; in fact, the core algorithm is protected by a patent now owned by Unisys. Following a court settlement in late 1994, Unisys has begun to charge fees to software developers working with the GIF format. It should be stressed that Unisys is not collecting fees from people who simply view GIF files or use preexisting software to create GIFs.

When GIF was developed, personal computers had less support for graphics than they do now. At the time, it was reasonable to assume that 8-bit color graphics represented the high end of users' capabilities, so GIF supports a maximum of 256 colors, which are specified in a palette of requested colors. Since each image can define its own palette, different GIFs can display different sets of 256 colors. Most graphics programs that can create GIFs provide the option of specifying fewer colors; since many small images like logos require only a handful of colors, and since most programs that display GIFs reserve as many palette entries as possible (reducing the number of colors available for other images), it is often advantageous to specify smaller palettes in creating GIF images.

GIF's strengths lie in its broad support in all operating environments, its control over palette size and number of colors used, and its use of lossless compression. In online environments, it has another advantage in that it can be displayed as it is being downloaded. Images can either fill in from top to bottom as the image is received, or if the file has been formatted as an "interlaced" image, it can gradually fill in detail for the entire picture. Interlaced files divide the image into groups of eight lines and load the first line of every group, then the fourth line, then the second and sixth lines, and finally the first, third, fifth, and seventh lines.

GIF's most restricting weakness is its limitation of 256 colors per image. This makes it a less useful format for photographic quality images than *truecolor* formats that support 16 million or more colors in an image.

Format:	Joint Photographic Experts Group (JPEG)
Definition:	ISO/IEC 10918-1:1994
Availability:	Not available online

JPEG provides a useful complement to GIF in many respects. Where GIF is owned by CompuServe, JPEG was created by two international standards bodies. GIF uses lossless compression while JPEG uses lossy compression; GIF is restricted to 8-bit colors while JPEG uses 24-bit colors; and GIF uses a proprietary compression scheme while JPEG's compression scheme is an open standard.

The JPEG group was established by the ISO (International Organization for Standards) and the CCITT (now renamed the ITU or International Telecommunications Union) to examine methods for compressing photographic-quality images. This original goal was important in the group's eventual decision to use a lossy compression method. The background level in most photographs is so detailed that it can lose a lot of data without compromising perceived content.

The JPEG standard actually describes only a compression method, not a file format. Most JPEG-compressed images are actually distributed in the JPEG File Interchange Format (JFIF). For most purposes, the distinction between the two is unimportant, but occasional references on the Net to JFIF files make it helpful to be aware of both names.

Format:	Portable Network Graphics (PNG)
Definition:	PNG Specification, version 0.93
Availability:	*http://www.w3.org/pub/WWW/TR/WD-png*

PNG (pronounced "ping") is a format still in development that is intended to fill in some of the gaps between GIF and JPEG. Specifically, it addresses GIF's color limitation and legal encumbrance by allowing up to 48-bit colors and a public domain compression scheme; it complements JPEG's lossy compression by providing lossless compression. In addition, it includes an alpha channel to provide more-thorough information on transparency than is provided in the GIF89a specification.

PNG development is being steered by a group of volunteers, who worked out the main details of the format within a few months after CompuServe and Unisys announced their resolution to the GIF patent lawsuit. The PNG Development Group expended a great deal of effort identifying compression algorithms that were not protected by patents.

Format:	Tagged Image File Formats (TIFF)
Definition:	TIFF Revision 6.0
Availability:	*ftp://ftp.sgi.com/graphics/tiff/TIFF6.ps*

While TIFF is not as widely seen on the Internet as other graphics formats, it is good to know about because it is the native format of most scanners. That is, the process of scanning an image frequently involves creating a TIFF image, retouching it as needed, and saving it in GIF or JPEG format. TIFF is useful during the intermediate stages because it does not use lossy compression and supports a high number of colors. It is usually not a good choice for a final image because TIFF files tend to be quite large. The file structure that allows graphics professionals quick access to any specific part of a large image takes up more space than either GIF or JPEG, even when using compression.

TIFF is a remarkably flexible format. Version 5 of the specification allows for optional LZW compression, and both version 5 and version 6 can handle multiple color depths (although not all TIFF display programs can understand all the color depths supported by the specification). Because of the continuing uncertainty about LZW's legal status, version 6 does not make use of it, which means that many current graphics programs read and write both TIFF 5.0 and TIFF 6.0.

Another useful feature in TIFF is its support for multipage graphics, making it a common choice for online document delivery systems.

Audio and Video Formats

Faster processors, larger hard disks (not to mention other storage media), and greater bandwidth have made multimedia files more accessible.

In a time not long ago, when a well-equipped desktop computer combined a 40MB hard drive, a monitor displaying 640 × 480 pixels with 16 colors, and a 2400 bits per second (bps) modem, it was neither practical nor especially desirable to work with video files that might take up several megabytes for less than a minute of choppy, low-resolution video. The general expansion of hardware capabilities has made better quality multimedia files a more workable part of desktop computing.

As with image file formats, compression plays an important role in both audio and video formats. The math is simple: a sound file comprised of 44,100 samples per second, with 16 bits per sample on each of two stereo channels—CD quality sound—will use up 44,100 × 16 × 2 = 1,411,200 bits or 172 kilobytes of data per second without compression. Likewise, a small 320 × 200 pixel video clip with 8-bit color running at 15 frames per second would require 320 × 200 × 8 × 15 = 7,680,000 bits or about .91 megabyte of data per second without compression.

As we saw in image formats, the technical quality of a file is measured in several dimensions. For audio, the important characteristics are the sampling rate, or number of times per second the original sound was measured; the number of bits per sample, which indicates the degree to which each sample can match the original sound; and the number of channels, or whether or not the sound is recorded in stereo. A common sound format frequently compared to telephone quality takes 8-bit samples 8,000 times per second on one channel. The compact disc audio format takes 16-bit samples 41,000 times per second on two channels.

Video formats are measured in the same ways as image formats—width and height in pixels and color depth in bits—and also by the number of separate images, or frames, presented per second. Most video files display a maximum of 15 frames per second and may drop some of those if the hardware or software can't keep up. By way of comparison, television signals in the United States display 30 frames per second.

In addition to the compression requirements dictated by working with so much data, another factor is involved with multimedia formats. Within the limits of reasonable system performance, no one really cares how long a graphics program takes to uncompress a JPEG image. A program displaying a video clip created with 15 frames per second, however, must reliably uncompress each frame in one fifteenth of a second. Because of this, compression techniques often require specialized hardware or software to create a compressed file optimized for speedy display. On the other hand, applications like real-time voice or video conferencing cannot take time to optimize their data compression and may either increase their bandwidth requirements or decrease their picture and sound quality as a tradeoff. Because different video applications have different requirements, several formats have a modular design in which developers can choose from among different compression/decompression (codec) services.

Audio Formats

Two main audio file formats are common on the Internet, the UNIX and Macintosh standard AU format and the native Windows WAVE format. Despite their association with specific operating platforms, programs to play both are available for all platforms.

Major Audio Formats

Format: AU or SND

It seems somehow typical of the UNIX community that it cannot even agree on what to call this format. While many computers will understand the Sun Microsystems name of AU, with file extensions of .au, NeXT computers call the same format SND and use the file extension .snd.

Most AU files have a sampling rate of 8,000 Hz on one channel, giving roughly the same quality as telephone connections. The format, however, can support CD-quality stereo sound.

Format: Waveform Audio File Format (WAVE)

Like the AVI video format discussed in the following section, WAVE is a particular implementation of the more-general RIFF (Resource Interchange File Format). RIFF formats are highly modular, meaning that there are few limitations actually built into WAVE. WAVE files commonly support sampling rates of 8,000; 11,025; 22,050; and 44,100 Hz; 8 or 16 bits per sample; and monaural or stereo sound, meaning in effect that they can record anything from telephone quality through broadcast radio quality to CD sound.

Video Formats

Video formats, like audio, have separate roots in the UNIX/Internet, Macintosh, and Windows worlds. Like image formats, they have a division between a format established by a formal standards process and two commercially created formats.

Major Video Formats

Format   Motion Pictures Experts Group (MPEG)
Definition: ISO/IEC 11172:1993
Availability: Not available online

The Motion Picture Experts Group, under the auspices of the ISO, has been working since 1988. Like the JPEG group, the MPEG effort is aimed at creating a compression method; implementing that in file formats has largely been left to others. MPEG actually describes several different compression formats for different needs, corresponding to levels comparable to VHS tape, High Definition Television (HDTV) and low-bandwidth video conferencing.

Format: Audio/Video Interleave (AVI)

AVI is the format used by Microsoft's Video for Windows, which gives it a natural audience on the Net. Like QuickTime, discussed next, AVI can use multiple codecs, meaning that it can be used for relatively high-quality video as well as lower-quality, lower-bandwidth files.

Format: QuickTime
Definition: Inside Macintosh: QuickTime
Availability: Not available online

QuickTime meets several needs. First, it is a flexible video format; like AVI, it provides multiple codecs to meet various video needs. It is also a more general protocol for handling time-specific events. Compared to AVI, QuickTime is able to perform more kinds of tasks, allowing it, for example, to synchronize high-resolution and low-resolution versions of the same movie along with multiple sound files (English and Spanish narration, perhaps).

Compression and Archiving Formats

By this point, the benefits of file compression should be obvious, and many of the formats discussed include one or more compression schemes. Other formats can also benefit from compression, however, and there are a number of very common compression formats in use around the Internet. In addition to compressing files, most compression formats also provide an archiving function of combining multiple files into one compressed file. This makes it easier to distribute multifile documents or software packages. As with other kinds of formats, compression and archiving programs all have a historical emphasis on one computer operating platform, with recent utilities making them usable on other platforms.

The UNIX world usually uses separate programs to archive files and to compress them. The tar (Tape Archive) command is the universal standard for archiving files. Large tar files are frequently then compressed either with the compress command provided with most UNIX systems or with the Gnu's Not UNIX (GNU) organization's gzip program. Gzip addresses a problem mentioned throughout this chapter: compress uses a version of the LZW compression algorithm that, while provided free to the UNIX community, might possibly be unavailable for future development work. Gzip accomplishes the same job with no apparent risk of legal entanglements. Tar and either compression program add their file extensions to an archive name, so it is common to find UNIX software distributed with a name like filename.tar.Z (for compress) or filename.tar.gz (for gzip). Such archives usually need to be retrieved on another UNIX system, first using either uncompress or gunzip, and then extracted from the archive using the tar command again.

The Macintosh world most frequently relies on the StuffIt utility to compress and uncompress files. Freeware and shareware utilities are available to handle StuffIt archives on other platforms.

The DOS/Windows world has had several commonly used archive and compression programs available, but the de facto standard is PKZIP and its companion program, PKUNZIP. Both are available as part of a shareware package; in addition there are several freeware substitutes for PKUNZIP that can extract and uncompress ZIP files.

Bibliography/URLography

Adobe Systems Inc. (1990). *PostScript Language Reference Manual* (2nd ed.). Reading, MA: Addison-Wesley.

Aldus Developers Desk. (1992). *TIFF Revision 6.0*. Seattle: Aldus Corp. [Online]. Available: *ftp://ftp.sgi.com/graphics/tiff/TIFF6.ps*.

Apple Computer. (1993). *Inside Macintosh Quicktime*. Reading, MA: Addison-Wesley.

Berners-Lee, T., and Connolly, D. (1995). *Hypertext Markup Language 2.0*. [Online]. Available: *http://www.w3.org/pub/WWW/MarkUp/html-spec/html-spec_toc.html*

Biehn, T., and Cohn, R. (1993). *Adobe Acrobat Portable Document Format*. [Online]. Available: *ftp://ftp.adobe.com/pub/adobe/Applications/Acrobat/SDK/TECHDOC/PDFSPEC.PDF.*

Borenstein, N., and Freed, N. (1993). *RFC 1521: MIME (Multipurpose Internet Mail Extensions), Part One: Mechanisms for Specifying and Describing the Format of Internet Message Bodies*. [Online]. Available: *http://ds.internic.net/rfc/rfc1521.txt*

Boutell, T., ed. (1996). *PNG (Portable Network Graphics), Version 0.96, Working Draft*. World Wide Web Consortium. [Online]. Available: *http://www.w3.org/pub/WWW/TR/WD-png.html*

CompuServe. (1990). *Graphics Interchange Format, Version 89a*. [Online]. Available: *ftp://ftp.ncsa.uiuc.edu/misc/file.formats/graphics.formats/gif89a.doc.*

Crocker, D. H. (1982). *RFC 822: Standard for the Format of ARPA Internet Text Message*. [Online]. Available: *http://ds.internic.net/rfc/rfc822.txt*

International Organization for Standardization. (1993). *ISO/IEC 11172:1993. Information Technology—Coding of Moving Pictures and Association Audio for Digital Storage Media at up to about 1.5 Mbit/s*. Geneva, Switzerland: Author.

———. (1994). *ISO/IEC 10918:1994. Information Technology—Digital Compression and Coding of Continuous-Tone Still Images*. Geneva, Switzerland: Author.

Kientzle, T. (1995). *Internet File Formats*. Scottsdale, AZ: Coriolis Group Books.

Moore, K. (1993). *RFC 1522: MIME (Multipurpose Internet Mail Extensions), Part Two: Message Header Extensions for Non-ASCII Text*. [Online]. Available: *http://ds.internic.net/rfc/rfc1522.txt*

Murray, J. D., and vanRyper, W. (1994). *Encyclopedia of Graphics File Formats*. Sebastopol, CA: O'Reilly and Assoc.

Unicode Consortium. (1990). *The Unicode Standard: Worldwide Character Encoding, Version 1.0*. Reading, MA: Addison-Wesley.

THE DIGITAL LIBRARY INITIATIVE

COLLECTIONS IN AN ELECTRONIC WORLD

Many libraries and other organizations are out there in the electronic trenches, trying to build digital libraries in preparation for the virtual library of the future. Most notably, six research libraries have developed partnerships that are being funded in a four-year project by the National Science Foundation, the Department of Defense's Advanced Research Projects Administration, and the National Aeronautics and Space Administration.

The intent of this Digital Library Initiative is "to dramatically advance the means to collect, store, and organize information in digital forms, and make it available for searching, retrieval, and processing via communication networks—all in user-friendly ways." These libraries, and their projects, are

- University of California, Berkeley: "The Environmental Electronic Library: A Prototype of a Scalable, Intelligent, Distributed Electronic Library"
- University of California, Santa Barbara: "The Alexandria Project: Towards a Distributed Digital Library with Comprehensive Services for Images and Spatially Referenced Information"
- Carnegie Mellon University: "Informedia: Integrated Speech, Image and Language Understanding for Creation and Exploration of Digital Video Libraries"
- University of Illinois at Urbana–Champaign: "Building the Interspace: Digital Library Infrastructure for a University Engineering Community"
- University of Michigan: "The University of Michigan Digital Libraries Research Proposal"
- Stanford University: "The Stanford Integrated Digital Library Project"

For more information, check the following sites. Both have links to the participating libraries, but the *D-Lib* site also links to other organizations that participate in related projects.

Coalition for National Research Initiatives. (1996, February). *D-Lib, Digital Library Research Projects.* [Online]. Available: *http://www.dlib.org/projects.html*

Digital Library Initiative (D-Lib). [Online]. Available: *http://www.grainger.uiuc.edu/dli/national.htm*

Imaging the Archives

Now Is the Time

Kenneth A. Cory and David W. Hessler

Kenneth A. Cory is assistant professor, Library and Information Science Program, Wayne State University. David W. Hessler *(DWH@SILS. UMICH.EDU)* is professor, School of Library and Information Studies, University of Michigan.

Originally appeared in (1993, issue 1) *Library & Archival Security,* 7–15. Copyright held by Haworth Press.

What Is Imaging? How Does It Work?

Imaging is the application of digital (i.e., computer) technology to the management and manipulation of information in nondigital formats such as paper, photographs, microforms, and voice. By scanning, or frame-grabbing in the case of video stills acquired from motion video, images of correspondence, maps, charts, or drawings are converted into digital files (*1*s and *0*s), that are sent to a computer. Scanned images appear on the computer's monitor. Although high-resolution monitors are desirable for viewing and acting upon one or two complete page images at a time, low-cost VGA monitors can be used effectively to view partial pages.

Index terms are keystroked onto a template. With some systems, the operator can view the document on one side of a split screen while keystroking in the index terms onto a template on the other side. After documents are indexed, the computer is instructed to forward their images to a mass storage medium, usually an optical disk, for long-term preservation. Images can be recalled and viewed on the monitor, printed in hard copy, and transmitted over telephone lines via fax technology.

With flow management software, imaging systems can be networked to permit simultaneous reading or processing of documents. Scholars external to the archive center but connected to a local area network (LAN) can access documents via their personal computers. If a printer with a high-speed interface is also connected, scholars can quickly generate hard copies in their office areas.

In the mid-1980s, imaging vendors concentrated their initial efforts on large applications, such as financial institutions, health care organizations, and the federal government. Currently, as system prices have decreased, managers of medium-sized offices have also invested in imaging. Originally, imaging was sold as a cost-effective alternative to storing files in paper format. More recently, vendors have legitimately demonstrated that their systems have substantially improved customer services by significantly reducing response time to queries. A service justification may likewise apply to archive collections.

Advantages

Transforming Archival Centers into Libraries

Libraries exist to provide access to information. By contrast, archival centers have primarily existed to preserve information. Because of the unique and fragile nature of most archival documents, making information available for extensive scholarly usage, while certainly important, has been a secondary purpose. Undoubtedly, there is something special about holding and reading an archive. Unfortunately, what makes them special also requires that they be used only with stringent restrictions, the most user-unfriendly being that they do not circulate.

Scholarly investigation and resultant publications are thus retarded. A document preserved in digital format, however, can be laser printed and made available to patrons for a nominal charge. This eliminates the demand for photocopies, which must usually be refused because of the potential for damage. Allowing patrons to take home copies of previously restricted documents will eliminate at least one motivation to purloin the archivist's materials. Moreover, digitization makes possible the unthinkable, i.e., external information dissemination of "archives." Imaged documents can be printed and sent to remote scholars, or if facsimile quality reproduction is acceptable, [a] scholar may rapidly receive digitized documents via fax. Imaging creates copies nearly indistinguishable from the originals of rare, expensive, and/or fragile materials that otherwise would not circulate.

After digitization, patrons need never see the original documents. Therefore, and paradoxically, even while it permits library-like usage, imaging will all but eliminate the need for archival security because scholars will work with high-quality facsimiles instead of originals.

External Dissemination to Groups

Imaging will make archives available not only to scholars but to the general public and to school systems. In public institutions, sale of reproductions can generate revenue. One possibility, assuming there are no insurmountable copyright restrictions, is to create optical disks containing information on a specific topic and sell those disks just as a publisher sells CD-ROM disks. Digitized documents can be re-created in a variety of integrated media formats, including text files, graphics, sound, still and motion video, and animation. Therefore, archivists should learn the various options that imaging systems offer for packaging information to suit patrons' needs.

For school systems, new sources of exciting information can become available. At Wayne State University, the main library houses the Folklore Archives, a unique assemblage of documents collected from diverse racial and ethnic groups of the metropolitan Detroit area. Local school teachers who are promoting diversity awareness would be delighted to have printed copies of these currently restricted treasures. As more schools install CD-ROM drives, archivists might consider creating and selling specially selected archives to them on CD-ROM.

Searching and Retrieving

Imaging software permits instant identification and retrieval of individual documents and even of information within documents. Each input document is assigned a variety of descriptors. Dozens of search terms can be assigned to each document, thereby creating multiple access points. For example, in the Greek and Greek-American section of the Folklore Collection described above, holdings are currently described in a booklet containing brief annotations of each collection. These annotations are insufficient for describing the richness of the holdings. Multiple indexing terms, however, would assist scholars to find unsuspected information. In many instances, the existence and relevancy of items appearing in different collections would become evident. For example, a scholar might key in "Kalikantzari (Greek for Christmas)." The scholar would immediately view a listing of all Greek-related documents in the entire collection indexed with that descriptor. Keying in "Christmas" would retrieve documents pertaining to that celebration as practiced by all the ethnic groups.

Inputting search terms usually results in a list of documents from which the user must choose the desired one. As with online public access catalogs, this can be a tedious process. One recent indexing breakthrough, which is highly appropriate for retrieving archives because many of them are in pictorial form, reduces this problem considerably. Now, the user may input indexing terms that serve to retrieve either or both text and thumbnail-sized versions of stored images on the monitor. Then, when the desired document is identified as one of many appearing on the screen, the user can retrieve the right one on the first try.

Full-text searching is possible if the documents are scanned with optical character recognition technology (OCR). Doing this would mean, in a very real sense, that the archive center has exponentially increased its information contents because information that can be found only with painstaking searching, or that may only be found accidentally, is information that is virtually nonexistent. Thanks to imaging, retrieval possibilities that are becoming commonplace in libraries can happen in archival centers also.

Backup Copies of Each Archived Document

Although scanned images temporarily reside on the computer's hard disk, long-term preservation is out of the question because of space limitations, extremely high storage costs, and the inherent volatility of hard disks. Therefore, images are usually stored on optical media. However, the familiar CD-ROM (Compact Disc-Read Only Memory) medium, on which encyclopedias, abstracts, and dictionaries are now available, is not acceptable because they are a read-only, publisher's distribution medium.

The alternative is CD-ROM's close relative, WORM (Write Once Read Many) optical disk, which allows images to be preserved on a local system. At a user's command, images exit the hard disk. An intense laser beam instantly "writes" data to the WORM disk. The laser either heats or "burns" a spot on the disks or it leaves a space to show the basic information signals (1,0) of the binary files. Information burned into the disk cannot be altered. For viewing, a less intense beam reads the signals and re-creates the image on a video screen.

For security purposes, duplicate copies of each disk can be made and stored off-site. At this point, commercial offices may discard their digitized paper documents. However, space saving is not of major importance to archivists because they must retain documents in their original format. Nevertheless, there is a need to provide backup copies that are indistinguishable from the originals. If the Emancipation Proclamation had been digitized before it was destroyed in the Chicago Fire in 1871, perfect reproductions could still be generated.

Reproductive Quality

With imaging, reproductive fidelity is usually excellent and often better than the original documents. Scanners are not sensitive to wrinkles in the paper and faint images are vastly improved by scanning. Even glossy photographs can be replicated with acceptable fidelity, both in black-and-white and in color, through laser and video printing. This is a major advantage of imaging over microfilm. While the latter is the best long-term preservation medium, obtaining clear pictures from microfilmed documents is problematic.

Image Enhancement

Imaging technology can actually improve the readability of orignal documents by "sharpening line edges, removing stains or colored background, removing specks from the background, and filling in broken letters."[1] Digitize George Washington's reports to the Continental Congress, and those reports can be enhanced to look exactly as they did when they were written. Microfilm cannot compete with this ability.

Concerns

The authors, having talked about imaging with several archivists, have noted several common concerns. None are insurmountable.

Preservation

Probably the first objection that an archivist will raise is that the WORM optical disk is not a long-term storage medium. This is undeniably true, but it is a non sequitur. Archivists must not judge optical technology on its preservation merits but on the consequences resulting from its ability to make archives accessible even while affording protection from careless or deceitful users. The major issue is not, in other words, long-term storage. Accessibility and security considerations should take precedence.

Data Reliability

There are no accelerated tests that accurately predict the life span of information on WORM optical disks; therefore, data reliability cannot be guaranteed beyond ten to fifteen years. Nevertheless, images can be transferred from an old disk to a new disk at any time with absolutely no data loss. Data transfer is not expensive, considering that one 5¼″ blank disk containing over 600 million bytes, or about 15,000 pages of images, costs about $200.

In terms of data transfer, optical disks are preferable to microfilm. Digital files copy to other digital storage media without data loss. However, "microfilm loses 10 to 20 percent of its quality when duplicated."[2]

Damage Potential during Scanning

Imaging eliminates the need for photocopies because patrons requesting copies receive facsimiles from a laser printer. This eliminates the probability that a document will be torn, or subject to unacceptable heat, during copying. Scanners, like photocopiers, can damage pages. However, there are flatbed scanners that are very gentle, even to the most fragile of documents. Books, incidentally, need not be disassembled prior to scanning. Overhead scanners with digitizing cameras work perfectly well.

New Information Technology

Because of the rapid advances in information technology, some archivists are reluctant to invest in optical disk technology out of a fear that new developments will render it obsolete. This fear is understandable but unrealistic. Because huge investments have already been made in public and private sector imaging systems, vendors realize that any breakthrough technology must permit affordable migration of data from one technology to another. For that reason, they are creating industry-wide standards for image compression and decompression schemes. In this respect, one should note that the vendors have served both their own and their customer's self-interest by creating devices that digitized data in whatever format it presently exists. Even microforms can now be digitized.

Costs

The hardware cost of building a system is not inexpensive. Single-user, proprietary systems can be purchased from a vendor for prices ranging from under $10,000 to well over $40,000. Some imaging vendors, known as systems integrators, do not sell their own systems, but recommend and assemble application-specific components. In many cases, these special systems can be created for less than an all-purpose system. If networking is necessary, the cost rises exponentially, largely because new sets of complex problems are introduced. Networking problems include the relatively simple ones, such as installing wiring and file servers, and highly challenging problems, such as programming to make the entire system work flawlessly.

Vocabulary Control

Imaging software allows each document to be assigned dozens of descriptors. However, when a large quantity of descriptors are locally created, the problems of vocabulary control are vastly increased. Also, many archival documents are in pictorial format. Because of the voluminous quantities of information in a picture, and the lack of standardization to describe items within a picture, assigning descriptors to pictures is more challenging than assigning descriptors to the text. The demanding nature of these tasks requires that the indexing be done by knowledge engineers, i.e., classification specialists. Employing such personnel, if not already onsite, is expensive.

Conversion Projects Are Disruptive

Preparing documents for scanning (unbinding them, removing staples, keeping them in proper order), scanning and/or frame-grabbing, keystroking in descriptors, putting the original documents back together, and reshelving converted documents is time consuming, may be messy and disruptive, and is expensive. To avoid major problems, archivists are advised to contact a local consultant or an imaging service bureau. They can render advice or even do the entire project.

Data Tampering

Archivists must, of course, be certain that preserved images are not altered in any way. With write-once storage media, undetectable tampering is impossible. However, alteration could occur when an image is stored in the computer's hard disk, either after scanning or retrieval from the optical disk. At that time, portions could be deleted, or new information inserted. The final image could then be returned to the optical disk with the indexing terms pointed to the new image. The original image would remain on the optical disk, but the index would retrieve only the new image.[3] Also, image enhancement can be carried to the point where it is not faithful to the original. Colors, for example, could be changed. Therefore, questions of authenticity may arise. These questions, however, can be easily resolved simply by comparing the electronic image with the original document.

Conclusion

Document image processing is an exciting possibility for archivists. While imaging cannot compete with paper or microfilm for long-term preservation, it can transform archive centers from preservation sites into access-oriented libraries. That would indeed be a radical transformation. The authors predict several fortuitous results. The availability of images of archival documents will generate substantially greater usage of archive centers while the original documents will be secure from theft or damage resulting from usage. Because of the quantitatively increased indexing possibilities that imaging systems allow, and because users will be permitted to possess personal copies of previously restricted materials, scholarly discoveries and publications will undoubtedly occur with significantly greater rapidity. Finally, as library directors know, increased usage tends to result in increased prestige and, ultimately, as users become more numerous, demanding, and collectively willing to support new initiatives, [in] augmented funding.

Notes

1. Donald S. Skupsky, *Recordkeeping Requirements* (Denver: Information Requirements Clearinghouse, 1989), 183.

2. Skupsky, 184.

3. Skupsky, 182.

Editor's note:
For more information about imaging of documents, visit the following site.

Besser, Howard, and Trant, Jennifer. (1995, October). *Introduction to Imaging: Issues in Constructing an Image Database.* [Online]. Available: *http://www.ahip. getty.edu/intro_imaging/home.html*
   This extensive guide to every aspect of doing an imaging project gets down to the real nitty gritty.

Reference in Cyberspace

REFERENCE SERVICES ON THE INTERNET

Judy E. Myers

Judy Myers is assistant to the director at the University of Houston Libraries. One of the developers of Reference Expert, an expert system for reference work, she has written widely on this and other electronic projects. She may be reached as *JM@UH.EDU*.

The possibilities for reference service on the Internet are evolving so rapidly that an Internet reference librarian may need the temperament of an explorer more than any particular type of knowledge. During just the past five years File Transfer Protocol (FTP) was overtaken by Gopher, then both were engulfed by the World Wide Web (WWW or Web). By the time this book is published, the mechanism of the Web will have evolved from a primitive hypertext into a multimedia programmable environment.

Even though the environment is new, we can apply to it the knowledge and skills that are already highly developed in the library profession. By offering reference services on the Internet, librarians have an opportunity to organize and share knowledge and extend services to users we have not reached before.

Serving Individual Users

In most university libraries, perhaps only one in ten of the people entering the library asks a question at the reference desk. Certainly many of the people who do not ask questions don't have one—they have come to study or are searching for something they know quite well how to find. But, just as surely, many library users have questions they do not ask. Many users pick up a printed guide or use our computerized reference aids, but they do not approach the reference desk.

We will find that many of our users who do not ask us questions in person will speak to us by e-mail. Just as many of us communicate by e-mail with people we have never met and might not have had the temerity to approach in person, so might our users like having the same advantages, if only we can make them available.

E-mail gives us one more way to interact with our users and to reach many that our reference services are not reaching now. For librarians, e-mail reference service has several advantages over in-person service at the reference desk. First, questions can be asked from anywhere, at any time. Second, it is easier for us to refer each question to the person best able to respond to it.

Tomorrow, when a critical mass of reference material joins the catalog and the periodical indexes online, e-mail services will become even more important. Many users of our online information and document delivery systems will seldom, or never, come to the library. Our reference service will need to be online because that's where the materials and the users will be.

Libraries may hesitate to offer e-mail reference service out of concern that it will be harder to tell users what to expect. Online, we can't use a pause or a sideways glance to prompt a revised question when a user asks us to write a whole term paper. Online, we'll have to make our service guidelines more explicit. Will users expect an answer in ten minutes, at any hour of the day or night? Will my library in Texas be inundated with queries from Alaska and Amsterdam? To address these concerns, reference librarians can borrow techniques that are already proven to work on the Internet. We can, for example, embed the opportunity to ask a question in a Web page. On the page we can tell the user what to expect, and we can prompt the user to give the information we need to respond.

The Internet already supports an environment in which libraries can provide real-time reference services. The Internet Public Library (IPL) at the University of Michigan School of Library and Information Science *(http://ipl.sils.umich.edu/)* has offered an experimental reference service within a Multi-User Object Oriented environment (MOO). A MOO allows several users to be in the same electronic "space" at the same time. Many MOOs are topic oriented and allow people to gather electronically to discuss interests as diverse as stamp collecting or uncommon diseases. A MOO can have a "floor plan," with rooms dedicated to specific functions (such as discussions of subtopics of the main topic). For example, a library reference MOO could have rooms for service in defined subject areas or for services to certain groups of users, such as students working on term papers.

The IPL MOO is available from the Web address, or by Telnet at *ipl.sils.umich.edu port 8888*. The IPL MOO is an experimental project, staffed on certain dates and for limited hours. The intent of the experiment is to learn how to provide reference service in this environment.

The IPL project has already shown that reference service on a MOO can have limited hours of service. Also, it is possible to limit service to a certain user community by limiting Telnet or log-in rights. However, we can think beyond these limits. Libraries already share cataloging records, and they share their collections via interlibrary loan. Why not share reference services? A MOO could support a joint reference service provided by several libraries. Despite our best efforts, none of us can have specialists in business, chemistry, and government documents all at the reference desk during all of our library's hours of service. But what if we share a MOO with ten libraries in our area?

If we can share services, we can also rethink hours of service. Perhaps within the group of local libraries there are not enough insomniacs to offer service all night, but our colleagues in Amsterdam and London are awake when we are asleep. Perhaps we can work out an agreement to refer our MOO clients to them and theirs to us. My additional thoughts on the ideas on this topic may be found in an article and a conference paper listed in the References section at the end of this essay.

Services by e-mail and multiuser environments can reach one user at a time. (Even though many users can log in to a MOO at the same time, a librarian can answer questions only one at a time!) Many libraries are already taking the next step, by moving their library guides and workbooks onto home pages on the Web. Web pages can showcase the strengths of libraries: our ability to organize information for access and our commitment to public service.

Sharing Our Knowledge

The Internet provides entirely new opportunities for reference librarians to organize and share their knowledge with colleagues and with library users worldwide. In the past, librarians could discuss reference discoveries with a close group of colleagues, develop card files of answers to difficult questions, or publish articles or books. Today, librarians can collaborate on library home pages for the Web. They can create their own home pages on topics of special interest to them, and they can use online discussion groups such as STUMPERS-L to share the answers to difficult questions and the techniques for finding obscure materials. In the future, reference librarians should learn from their colleagues in cataloging (who have not only developed catalogs but have developed ways to share records). We should develop systems and procedures to share our knowledge in a structured way.

But first, we need to develop a structure for the knowledge of reference librarians. Reference librarians now must remember innumerable discrete facts:

When a physics student asks for spectral data, we know to ask if she wants emission or absorption spectra.

When a government student asks for a certain bill, we know to ask if he really wants the bill or the law, and for which government.

We remember that the *World Book* gives the best simple description of why the sky is blue.

The learning curve is endless, and it takes years to become good at the job. It is hard for new librarians to go beyond their predecessors because the real learning is done through a long apprenticeship. Many of us find that our minds have a limited capacity to remember and recall these scraps of knowledge that make up our expertise.

Library catalogs gave us a way to structure and encode the knowledge of the library collection—we don't have to remember what the library owns. But the catalog has given relatively little support to the reference function and is not designed to do so. What is needed is a way to structure and encode the knowledge of reference librarians, so we can share our knowledge. Other librarians need to be able to add new knowledge to the existing body instead of memorizing what is already known.

What would a knowledge structure and a support system for reference service look like? First, if it is to serve users directly, it must be based on the user's point of view. To elicit the user's information need, it must ask questions that the user can answer and that seem sensible. Because many reference questions have a subject, the system should have subject access. However, the reference support system ought to have several starting points: one for people doing term papers, for example; perhaps one for parents wanting simple answers to children's questions (or for the children themselves); and another for people who know they want in-depth information about the interaction between atmospheric conditions and the human physiology that causes the sky to look blue.

Second, a reference support system must ask the right questions to gather the information needed to respond to the user's question. Much work has already been done in describing the reference process and even in designing computer systems to aid users. Articles by Bates and Parrott outline the reference process in a way that has been useful to developers of computer support for reference work. Katz included extensive descriptions and flowcharts of the reference process in early editions of his standard text. Fadell and Myers, Myers, Smith, and Waters describe expert systems and other types of computer programs that have been used to deliver reference service in a number of libraries. (See the References at the end of this essay.)

Third, the reference knowledge structure needs to contain descriptions of the types of information contained in reference works. In 1944 Hutchins noted that to respond to a reference question the librarian needs to ascertain the subject and the kind of information needed. These two do seem to be the primary information types that are required for almost all reference questions. In fact, just these two information types are the basis of the successful Reference Expert program. (See Gunning et al. and Myers in References.) Katz suggests several additional information types that aid in successful responses to reference questions, including scope (how much material is required), time period (current or historical), and format (does the user want a map or a computer-readable file).

Fourth, the knowledge structure needs to contain processes that are specific to certain types of user questions (such as how to trace a legislative history) and decision trees to help with such tasks as selecting the correct index to use for a query of *Chemical Abstracts*.

What would a system built on these principles look like? For the user, it should start with an opportunity to define a question in terms of subject, type of information, extent of material needed, and other elements important to the user. The interface might look like a catalog, with the opportunity for the user to type in terms, or like a Web page with hypertext links, or it might be comprised of several list boxes. To librarians who create the system, part of the "back end" might look like the library catalog and contain a database of descriptions of reference materials. Another part of the back end would contain the decision trees that drive the presentation of questions to the user. Technically, the Web reference support system could be an expert system, a hypertext system plus a database, or a standard computer program.

It would be helpful to be able to include in the MARC record standardized, specific terms for the types of content found in reference works. For example, the present subject heading "Encyclopedias and Dictionaries" may be too broad; the varying and nonspecific terms for periodical indexes need to be standardized. Descriptors for many types of reference materials (such as directories, maps, statistical data, scientific or engineering data) either do not exist or are spread all over the cataloging record.

Over the next few months a new generation of Web programming tools will make it possible for librarians to pursue any of these approaches or to test all of them. A number of expert systems are already in use (see Alberico and Micco, Bailey and Myers, Morris in References), but most of them are not used outside their home institution. When these programs can be moved to the Web, they can be developed collaboratively. Libraries will be able to extend reference service beyond the library building to libraries and users worldwide.

Conclusion

It will never be possible to meet all reference needs with computer-based systems, and that should not be our goal. But just as the automated-teller machine supplements the personal services of our bank, and the library catalog supplements our memory of the library collection, computer-based systems can become an important part of reference service. It is time for reference librarians to learn to organize our knowledge, then to share it instead of duplicating it (as catalogers learned in the 1970s). Once we do that, we can spend more of our time in ongoing dialogues with users who have in-depth questions and with those who need or want personal assistance.

References

Alberico, Ralph, and Micco, Mary. (1990). *Expert Systems for Reference and Information Retrieval.* Westport, CT: Meckler.

Bailey, Charles W., Jr., and Myers, Judy E. (1991). *Expert Systems in ARL Libraries,* Spec Kit 174, Washington, DC: Association of Research Libraries.

Bates, Marcia J. (1979). "Information Search Tactics." *Journal of the American Society for Information Science, 4,* 205–14.

Fadell, Jeff, and Myers, Judy E. (1989). "The Information Machine: A Microcomputer-Based Reference System." *Reference Librarian, 23,* 75–112.

Gunning, Kathleen, Myers, Judy E., and Bailey, Charles W., Jr. (1993). "Networked Electronic Information Systems at the University of Houston Libraries: The IRIS Project and Beyond." *Library Hi Tech, 4,* 49–83.

Hutchins, Margaret. (1944). *Introduction to Reference Work.* Chicago: ALA.

Katz, William A. (1969). *Introduction to Reference Work: Vol. II, Reference Services.* New York: McGraw-Hill.

Morris, A. (1991). "Expert Systems for Library and Information Services: A Review." *Information Processing & Management, 6,* 713–24.

Myers, Judy E. (1992). *Reference Expert: Developing a Computer Expert System for Library Reference Service.* [Online]. Available: *gopher://info.lib.uh.edu:70/00/articles/uhlibrary/myers/prgopher.* The bibliography for this paper is at: *gopher://info.lib.uh.edu:70/00/articles/uhlibrary/myers/prbib.*

———. (1993). "Reference Services in the Virtual Library." *Ninth Texas Conference on Library Automation,* April 2, 1993. [Online]. Available: *gopher://info.lib.uh.edu:70/00/articles/uhlibrary/myers/virtref.* The bibliography for this paper is at: *gopher://info.lib.uh.edu:70/00/articles/uhlibrary/myers/hnd.*

———. (1994). "Reference Services in the Virtual Library." *American Libraries, 7,* 634–8.

Parrott, James M. (1989). "Simulation of the Reference Process, Part II: REFSIM, an Implementation with Expert System and ICAI Modes." *Reference Librarian, 23,* 153–76.

Smith, Karen. (1986). "Robot at the Reference Desk?" *College & Research Libraries, 5,* 486–90.

STUMPERS-L@CRF.CUIS.EDU
   To subscribe, send the message *SUBSCRIBE STUMPERS-L to MAILSERV@ CRF.CUIS.EDU*

Swope, M. J. (1972). "Why Don't They Ask Questions?" *RQ, 2,* 161–6.

Waters, Samuel T. (1986). "Answerman, the Expert Information Specialist: An Expert System for Retrieval of Information from Library Reference Books." *Information Technology and Libraries, 3,* 204–12.

OPACs and More

Steve Hardin

Steve Hardin *(LIBHARD@CML.INDSTATE.EDU)* has worked as a holistic librarian at Indiana State University since 1989. He splits his time between electronic information services and technical services. His publications and presentations cover various aspects of electronic resources and holistic librarianship.

What's Happening?

What happens when you look for library material on the Web? It depends, of course, on the hardware and software at your end as well as the hardware and software at the remote site you're accessing. If you're using a Windows browser like Netscape, you could see a colorful library map with links to the catalog and various special collections. Or, you could see a plain-text Telnet window open, be asked to log on, and be taken to a catalog interface that appears to be no different from something you'd access from a terminal. You may even be prompted to configure an application to handle the display. (Consult the user guides and help screens for your own computer and software to get help with this.) The bottom line is: accessing libraries and related databases on the Web can be a real adventure, with lots of surprises as you make your way through cyberspace. But that's part of the fun!

Personal Preferences

This chapter contains references to some of my favorite Web sites that deal with libraries and related operations. The list, of course, is by no means exhaustive. As much as possible, I've tried to list "metasites," sites that have links to numerous other related sites. (If your favorite site is missing, there may be a link to it in a site I *have* mentioned.) Besides, given the chaotic nature of the Internet, it's a sure bet some of these addresses won't work by the time you read this.

A word about my own Web preferences is in order. Generally, I like sites that keep graphics to a tasteful minimum. I suspect most Web authors and users have a love/hate relationship with graphics. On the one hand, beautiful graphics enhance the appeal of a Web page's layout. A picture is worth a thousand words, and all that. On the other hand, graphics take time to load. A page laden with them can take two or even three times longer to load than a page without them.

If you're using a text-only Web browser, graphics are invisible. One of the cruelest tricks some Web authors play consists of embedding their links within graphics, with no text-only indications as to what the links are. Who uses text-only browsers, you ask? As a matter of fact, I do! An unfortunately timed bout of pneumonia left me using Lynx on an 8088 system with 640 KB of RAM cobbled together at my bedside while researching part of this chapter. This venerable old notebook can't hope to run Windows, let alone a Graphical User Interface (GUI) browser. Frankly, I suspect text-only browsers will be useful for some time for many of us whose personal finances can't keep pace with the latest computing innovations. For all the foregoing reasons, I much prefer Web sites with a minimum of graphics to those swimming in pictures. When I use a GUI browser, I switch off the automatic image-loading option unless it seems the images are important.

I also check for a date whenever I visit a Web site. High-quality sites should display something like "Last updated on 3/1/96" somewhere on their opening page. Knowing when a page was last updated gives you a hint as to how much attention a site's owners are giving it.

One other thing: Does the site include a link to an e-mail address you can use to make comments? The presence of a link tells you someone's interested in what you think of the site. This quality control can lead to a better Web page.

Library OPAC Sites

Let's start with that keystone of electronic librarianship: the Online Public Access Catalog, or OPAC. My favorite site that lists library OPACs is *Hytelnet on the World Wide Web* at *http://library.usask.ca/hytelnet*. The brainchild of Peter Scott at the University of Saskatchewan, this site contains links to library OPACs and other databases available via Telnet around the world. There are even files to help you with the different approaches to searching you'll encounter on various OPACs, depending on the vendor. You can also access this database via anonymous File Transfer Protocol (FTP) at *ftp:// ftp.usask.ca/pub/hytelnet/*.

Prefer a Gopher interface? No problem! Try the *Gopher Tree of Internet-Accessible Libraries* at *gopher://libgopher.cis.yale.edu:70/*. The menus are generally arranged in a geographical hierarchy. This site is an electronic outgrowth of the list compiled by Billy Barron at the University of Texas at Dallas. *Internet Library Catalogs* at *gopher://wilcox.umt.edu/11/Libcats* contains much the same information.

Enter the Web Interface

The sites mentioned previously represent fine ways to keep track of which OPACs are available. But when you connect to the addresses provided, you'll find you're doing little more than a remote search of a library catalog with a dumb terminal. You can do more with the Web, and libraries have begun taking advantage of its hypertext capabilities to mount home pages and catalogs with imbedded links.

One of the best sites I've found to bring together these catalogs is *Online Catalogs with 'Webbed' Interfaces,* maintained by Eric Lease Morgan at *http://www.lib.ncsu.edu/staff/morgan/alcuin/wwwed-catalogs.html*. More than just a collection of library catalogs, this site also provides links to library vendors. If you're thinking about choosing a system for your library, this is a great spot to compare packages. There are also links to electronic text sites such as *Alcuin* and *Alex*. And if you're interested in some of the experimental work involving the Web and the Z39.50 protocol, check out the link to *Z39.50 Gateways*. A new outgrowth of Hytelnet that also links to library catalogs with Web interfaces has been made available by Peter Scott *(http://library.usask.ca/hywebcat/)*; although still under construction as of this writing, it should also be useful.

You can find a large collection of library Web pages at *Libweb–Library Servers via WWW,* available at *http://sunsite.berkeley.edu/Libweb/*. This site may also be used, among other things, to go to bibliographic utilities that are mixed in with the library sites (more later). Also quite useful is the link to *Departments and Schools of Information Studies, etc.* around the world. Some of these pages have links of their own to ERIC and other databases available by Telnet.

While there are scores of remarkable libraries available through the foregoing sites, I must give special mention to the Library of Congress (LC), whose home page is at *http://www.loc.gov*. It sports links to legislative and government information that can make a reference librarian's job much easier. There are numerous links of interest to catalogers, too.

And Now, a Word of Warning . . .

The ability to search hundreds of OPACs around the world is, of course, marvelous, especially to those of us who can remember libraries without computers. Your patrons can take advantage of this ability, too. But they may be disappointed when searches that worked just fine in one library fail miserably in another. For instance, consider call-number searching.

There are several reasons why it should be used with caution, all having to do with cataloging policy in individual libraries. (If you're a cataloger, you can skip the next couple of paragraphs. On the other hand, if you usually shut your eyes and cover your ears when cataloging is discussed, you may find the discussion a useful refresher.)

Often the LC will catalog a new book and assign it a call number. That call number becomes known through records on bibliographic utilities. While many libraries will decide to use LC's call number on their own copies of the book, some won't. For example, most academic libraries in the United States use the LC classification system, while most public libraries use Dewey. A few libraries use other systems. And once you get outside the United States, the possibilities increase.

But there are other reasons for different call numbers, too. Suppose you're a cataloger in a library that has already used the call number LC has assigned to a new book. You now have the choice of reclassifying the item already in your collection (thereby confusing the patrons who are used to finding the item under the call number you've already assigned and making more work for the department that physically attaches call number labels to items in the collection) or going with a slightly different number for the new arrival. Most catalogers, not surprisingly, opt to change the number for the new item. For a variety of reasons, a call number that retrieves a book in one OPAC may not retrieve it in another, even though the book may be there.

Subject headings can be a problem, too. Drabenstott and Vizine-Goetz and others have discussed problems of inconsistency and the difficulty of translating ideas into subject headings. As online searching proliferates, there may well be increased pressure from disgruntled patrons for uniform subject-heading and call-number assignment. But until that happens, a varied searching approach to information retrieval, incorporating call numbers, subject headings, keywords, and other hooks, will yield more hits than one confined to subject headings or call numbers. Make sure your patrons know this, too!

Articles, Tables of Contents, and Bibliographic Utilities

OPACs aren't the only databases related to library work. There are a number of spots on the Web where you can find guides to table-of-contents services and article indexes. Vanderbilt University has a good collection—*Journal Table of Contents Services*—at *http://www.library.vanderbilt.edu/tocs.html*. It covers the services of several publishers and organizations, including *CARL UnCover* at *http://www.carl.org/uncover/unchome.html*. This Web page provides access to the *UnCover* database (also reachable at *telnet:// database.carl.org*) to let you see article citations and tables of contents for nearly 17,000 periodicals. Searching is free; there are fees for obtaining the articles.

The Library of Congress maintains a list of bibliographic utilities at *http:// lcweb.loc.gov/coll/nucmc/utility.html*. You'll find links to Online Computer

Library Center, Inc. (OCLC), Research Libraries Information Network (RLIN), and Western Library Network (WLN). And speaking of OCLC, a visit to *http://www.oclc.org/* is a good investment of time for current and potential users of this service. The site has numerous links of interest to public and technical service librarians. To list just a few:

FirstSearch is available (by subscription only) at *telnet://fscat.oclc.org.* It provides access to ArticleFirst, its article index, and ContentsFirst, an index to tables of contents. You can also search OCLC's WorldCat bibliographic database. A webbed version has recently become available.

OCLC Electronic Journals Online Service provides access to the full text of several dozen journals, with hypertext access to some. It is offered by subscription only.

Tech Services links include information on OCLC's *Technical Bulletins, Dewey Decimal Classification,* and more.

The *Office of Research and Special Projects* link makes for interesting reading, even if you're not involved directly in the research.

The RLIN home page at *http://www-rlg.stanford.edu/rlin.html* has links to information about its bibliographic database, its *English Short Title Catalogue (ESTC),* other databases, and its Eureka and Zephyr interfaces. The Research Library Group home page *(http://www-rlg.stanford.edu/welcome.html)* also contains a link to its *CitaDel* article and document delivery database. The databases are searchable only by subscription.

The *WLN Homepage* at *http://www.wln.com/* (Gopher version: *gopher://gopher.wln.com/*) also features links to information about its products and services, including its online database, CD-ROM products, and Internet services.

Other Online Vendors

If you use DIALOG or DataStar, visit the *Knight-Ridder Information Web Site* at *http://www.dialog.com/.* You can Telnet to the DIALOG service (available by subscription), get help selecting the best database, get the Blue Sheet guides to databases (with nice hypertext links), and get quick information on the various DIALOG commands. You can even look at the *DIALOG Chronolog* in hypertext. For DataStar, you can find information about its databases.

Ovid Technologies has a Web site at *http://www.ovid.com/.* It features good background information for current and potential Ovid users. The Ovid Web Gateway, a Web interface to Ovid, has recently become available.

The *LEXIS-NEXIS Communication Center* at *http://www.lexis-nexis.com/* also has useful information. You can follow a link to Telnet to the information service (for subscribers only) as well as find out more about the database and other LEXIS-NEXIS products and services. There are also links to related companies.

Here's one more: Chemical Abstracts Service (CAS) provides an overview of CAS products and services at *http://info.cas.org/prod.html*. It provides links to Scientific and Technical Information Network (STN) Online (subscription only) as well as to documentation, CD-ROMs, and printed products.

Serials and Texts

Ejournal SiteGuide: A MetaSource at *http://unixg.ubc.ca:7001/0/providers/hss/zjj/ejhome.html* provides links to sites that list journals available electronically. It's maintained by Joseph Jones at the University of British Columbia Library. Note that these sites are not limited to electronic journals; there are also links to print scholarly journals and popular magazines.

Carnegie-Mellon University maintains *The On-Line Books Page* at *http://www.cs.cmu.edu/Web/books.html*. Here you can find links to text collections such as *Project Gutenberg* and to online publishers and retailers.

More Useful Spots

The *Internet Public Library* at *http://ipl.sils.umich.edu/* provides a smorgasbord of electronic resources approximating what you could find in the various divisions of a public library. The graphics provide the "feel" of a real library.

INFOBAHN Librarian: Libraries and the WWW: Selected Resources at *http://www.ualberta.ca/~nfriesen/* contains useful links to a number of library-related sites. One of the most useful to librarians is Barbara Deutsch's *Library Automation on the Web (http://asis_siglan.microsoft.com/libauto/libauto.html)*. It lists "WWW sites of library-related software, library software vendors, and library sites that explain how to use library software found on the Internet." There are resources here for almost anyone who works in a library.

Concluding Remarks

To use a cliché, "we've just scratched the surface" in this chapter. The best way to find sites most appropriate to your particular interests is to search the Web yourself. Here are a few sites to help you get started. See the section on "Searching Cyberspace" in this book for URLs for Web search engines. See "Colleagues in Cyberspace" in this book for more information on electronic lists.

Argus/University of Michigan Clearinghouse: http://www.clearinghouse.net/

TradeWave Galaxy: http://www.einet.net/galaxy.html
Webbed Archie Server: http://hoohoo.ncsa.uiuc.edu/archie.html
Whole Internet Catalog: http://gnn.com/gnn/wic/index.html
World Wide Web Virtual Library: http://www.w3.org/hypertext/
  DataSources/bySubject/Overview.html

Enjoy!

Selected Bibliography

Braun, E. (1994). *The Internet Directory*. New York: Fawcett Columbine.

Drabenstott, K. M., and Vizine-Goetz, D. (1994). *Using Subject Headings for Online Retrieval: Theory, Practice and Potential*. San Diego: Academic.

Krol, E. (1994). *The Whole Internet: User's Guide & Catalog* (2nd ed.). Sebastopol, CA: O'Reilly.

Public-Access Computer Systems Forum. LIBPACS@UHUPVM1.UH.EDU

Web4Lib. web4lib@library.berkeley.edu

WEBCAT-L. WEBCAT-L@WUVMD.WUSTL.EDU

COOL OR WHAT?

QUALITY AND EVALUATION

In the last year or so there have been many calls for librarians to be involved in evaluating Web sites—it is said that this is a function we are perhaps uniquely prepared to perform. Not much has been written yet, though, in the library literature about how exactly we are to do this. Some library-related projects, for example, the Subject Guide Clearinghouse, which originated at the University of Michigan, are selective in what they include. Some other efforts at organizing the Web claim to consider quality in deciding what they list.

The following listings relate to the consideration of quality and the evaluation of Web resources. Possible approaches to deciding criteria for what constitutes quality include not only reading the literature but also seeing what selective sources, such as the University of Michigan Clearinghouse, say about their practices and looking at guidelines such as "UW–Madison Campus Libraries: Web Page Standards and Guidelines," included in this book.

Argus/University of Michigan Clearinghouse. [Online]. Available: *http://www.clearinghouse.net/*

   This is a site that connects to many subject guides on the Internet. The guides must pass through an evaluation process and are generally focused on quality resources.

Collins, Boyd R. (February 15, 1996). "Beyond Cruising: Reviewing." *Library Journal,* 122–4.

   The founder of the InfoFilter project calls for librarian involvement in evaluation, and, more important, provides a sidebar on "Rating the Net."

Ensor, Pat. (1996, January). "Further Big Adventures with Web Organization." *Technicalities,* 1, 3–4.

   In this column, I discussed the University of Michigan Clearinghouse as well as SilverPlatter and Gale attempts to provide Web pointers.

Gale Research. (1996). *Cyberhound.* [Online]. Available: *http://www.cyberhound.com*

A new Gale service aimed at organizing the Web, it is selective in what it includes, and it has an elaborate rating system. Look under *About Cyberhound,* then look for the link for "rating criteria."

The InfoFilter Project. (1995, May). [Online]. Available: *http://www.kcpl.lib. mo.us/infofilter.htm*
This minimalist site has reviews of the sites it includes. Although there are no explanations of InfoFilter, you could look at the reviews to see what is considered in evaluations of quality.

Lycos, Inc. (1996). *Point: It's What You're Searching for.* [Online]. Available: *http://www.pointcom.com/*
Look under "Info" for a lengthy introduction to what Point is all about and how it makes its evaluations.

The McKinley Group. (1996). *Welcome to Magellan!* [Online]. Available: *http://www.mckinley.com/*
Look under "About Magellan," then for the Frequently Asked Questions (FAQ) to learn about how it evaluates sites.

OCLC. (1996). *NetFirst Information.* [Online]. Available: *http://www.oclc.org/ oclc/netfirst/netfirst.htm*
Look in the FAQ for OCLC's mention of evaluation criteria. NetFirst indexers are selective about what is included in the database.

Rosenfeld, Lou. (1996, April). *Get Rich Quick! Rate Web Sites!* [Online]. *Web Review.* Available: *http://webreview.com/96/04/26/webarch/index.html*
This is a hilarous stab at the quality-rating sites on the Web. It ponders what it means to be in the top 5 percent of the Web and has some great points to make about all of these rating systems that are springing up.

Rosenfeld, Lou. (1994, issue 4). "Guides, Clearinghouses, and Value-added Repackaging: Some Thoughts on How Librarians Can Improve the Internet." *Reference Services Review,* 11–16.
Lengthy, thorough discussion of librarians' role in organizing and evaluating the Internet by the founder of the University of Michigan Clearinghouse.

CYBER-CITING

CITING ELECTRONIC SOURCES

Kristin D. Vogel

Kristin Vogel *(KVOGEL@TITAN.IWU.EDU)* is access librarian and assistant professor at Illinois Wesleyan University. For the past four years she has worked on information technology issues and implementation for liberal arts colleges.

As the helpful voice responding over the phone to a desperate researcher at the end of the day, I field questions such as "What page does this article end on? I forgot to write it down," or, "My photocopy cut off the journal name. I know the author and title. Can you help me?" Now I am getting a brand-new question. . . . "I forgot to write down the URL and my paper's due tomorrow! Can you help me?" As reference librarians know, this is another version of the dreaded "How do I cite this?" question. We must be ready to answer this, and we can be.

Reminding ourselves of the purpose of the citation helps keep things in perspective and provides direction in the search for the "documented answer" to *the question*. Scholarship has one primary use for the citation. Readers require a citation to successfully locate the original source. The reader may need clarification or may have doubts about the content. The reader may wish to reconstruct the argument and need each individual part, or the reader may simply have an insatiable hunger for knowledge.

Citations to electronic sources have the dubious honor of aiming at a moving target. There are potential problems due to the constant state of flux in technology and the relative impermanence of electronic documents. A nightmare begins when the source has been

- deleted and may never be found again
- edited and may never be the same again
- moved and may never be found again
- corrupted and may never be the same again

Currently, scholars and librarians are discussing and hotly debating how to handle all of this. Is it okay for the original source to change? Should an archival copy be kept and not be allowed to change or disappear? What are the necessary parts of the citation?

Print Style Manuals

Meanwhile, my phone rings, and in response to my enthusiastic "How may I help you?" the desperate voice on the other end asks "How do I cite this?" I ask what style manual the caller is using, and in reply I hear, "Style? I don't know. Aren't they all the same?" Realizing that I can no longer put off the question, I head to my well-stocked reference collection and begin to peruse the style manuals. In the reference collection there are a few existing style manuals that may help answer this question. With each revision of the major style manuals, additions and changes are made to guide authors in the creation of bibliographies that must incorporate electronic sources.

Publication Manual of the American Psychological Association

First I examine *The Publication Manual of the American Psychological Association* (APA), which contains an appendix on the "Elements and Examples of References in APA Style" and incorporates a subsection on electronic media. I feel encouraged prior to opening the book by the appearance of the notation indicating this is the fourth edition, 1994, and must certainly contain everything that I need. I read the section on page 175 on creating a reference list and anticipate what is included. I find:

> Because one purpose of listing references is to enable readers to retrieve and use the sources, reference data must be correct and complete. Each entry usually contains the following elements: authors, year of publication, title, and publishing data—all the information necessary for unique identification and library search.

I even see an admonishment by Brunner dating back to 1942 that indicates that "an inaccurate or incomplete reference 'will stand in print as an annoyance to future investigators and a monument to the writer's carelessness.'"

In my continuing effort to deduce the APA style, the following information jumps off pages 175–6:

> Because a reference list includes only references that document the article and provide recoverable data, do not include personal communications, such as letters, memoranda, and informal electronic communication. Instead, cite personal communications only in text.

My skin begins to crawl. What does this mean? What is the APA saying about electronic mail? Quickly, very quickly, I flip back a few pages to pages 173–4 and reach the section defining personal communications and find the following:

> Personal communications may be letters, memos, some electronic communications (e.g., e-mail, discussion groups, messages from electronic bulletin boards), telephone conversations, and the like. Because they do not provide recoverable data, personal communications are not included in the reference list. Cite personal communications in text only. . . . Use your judgment in citing other forms of personal communications; networks currently provide a casual forum for communicating, and what you cite should have scholarly relevance.

Indeed, now my skin has jumped off and done a few laps around the building, gone upstairs to share the news with colleagues, e-mailed my brother-in-law, and returned feeling particularly prickly. I take note of the fact that the personal communications definition may include listservs that therefore would be in the text of the paper but would not be included in the reference list and would not be considered to have scholarly relevance. That may be true but, oh, what a can of worms this opens! It is as though a fork in the road has appeared, and I begin gazing through a fog to try to determine which way to go. What's up the road to the north? It looks somewhat like a gravel road with electronic communications being pushed back, relegated to maintaining the status of an "invisible college." To the south? I see a barely discernible trail blazing the way through a jungle that illuminates electronic communications and points to a radical change in scholarship and research. You can tell that someone has gone in that direction, but the road is merely a trail with few directional signs.

Pull back! Pull back! My caller is still on hold, and even if I feel I am on the edge of a new frontier, the metaphysical discussion must wait a little while longer. I need more information! In the APA's appendix on electronic sources, I take note of the examples for online journals, online journal abstracts, abstracts on CD-ROM, software, and data files. I also note the included parts of the citation: author, date, title, and an availability statement that includes protocol, directory, and file name.

Revived somewhat by a 10-second interruption for the population of China, which I'm able to supply reassuringly from a 3-D, acid-free with soy ink, paper book, I return to the style manuals for another bout answering the question, "How do I cite this?"

Chicago Manual of Style

The 1993 *Chicago Manual of Style* is the next manual I investigate. Encouraged, I remember that, while it is establishing rules, "an authoritarian position in favor of common sense and flexibility has always been a fundamental and abiding principle." I also know from browsing the book when it was still on the new-book shelf that "computer programs are given more attention and are augmented with more examples, and guidelines for the citation of electronic documents have been added." I flip to the sections on documentation and discover guides to materials obtained through "loose-leaf, computer, or information service" as well as "computer programs and electronic documents." The examples contained here include two for electronic bulletin boards and imply the inclusion of listservs.

To confirm or refute this, I move to the sections on personal communication. While this section does not mention electronic sources, I do notice statements dictating the citation of personal communication within the text, as opposed to in the bibliography, implying that the sources are unobtainable. I note to myself that this manual indicates that the parts of this citation include author, title, description of source, citation date, and an availability statement including the address for obtaining the item. The inclusion of addresses in this citation appears somewhat vague as there are no examples that illustrate a file obtained via File Transfer Protocol (FTP). I also take down information on how to contact the International Standards Organization that is the guiding entity for electronic source citations for the *Chicago Manual of Style*. This may be helpful in determining how to handle my questions about addresses.

MLA Handbook for Writers of Research Papers

The Modern Language Association of America's *MLA Handbook for Writers of Research Papers* (1995) states in its foreword that

> The rules for citing electronic material that the MLA committee established are not presented as definitive, and they will surely change as the technology and practices governing electronic communication evolve.

Turning to the sections on electronic sources I am first interested to find how MLA handles "personal communication" and so read with interest on page 165 that citations for an "electronic journal, electronic newsletter, or electronic conference document should be similar to one for an article in a print periodical, though there are a few necessary differences." Elements of the citation include author, title, publication date, pages or paragraphs or no pagination indication, medium, name of computer network, and access date. The three final elements are where the primary differences lie.

Reading further on the page, I note that following the examples it makes a direct statement about addresses.

> At the end of the entry, you may add as supplementary information the electronic address you used to access the document. . . . Your instructor may require this information."

Another important section that I peruse is section 4.10.7 titled "A letter, a memo, an e-mail communication, or a public online posting." This indicates that my caller would need to treat a personal e-mail message similarly to a memo and would include it in the works-cited list.

Electronic Style: A Guide to Citing Electronic Information

The final book that I examine is *Electronic Style: A Guide to Citing Electronic Information*. Li and Crane published this manual in 1993, with a second edition in 1996, intending to provide concrete examples of how to cite electronic sources in APA format. APA's fourth edition cites it as the guide for APA-style manuscripts. The parts of the citation included here are author, date, title, type of medium, and availability statement that includes the information on accessing the source again. I notice that there are subtle differences between this style manual and the current version of the APA style manual. It will be important for my caller to evaluate the importance of using the most recent style manual versus the extent of the examples in Li and Crane's manual. From my professional reading, I am aware that a new edition of this book has come out in 1996 and that it includes a section following MLA style as well as revising the section following APA style.

Internet-Obtained Style Manuals

If it were ten years ago, I would be able to stop and provide my caller with the information that I've found. Wait, ten years ago I might not have gotten this question at all! Now, I can't stop with the print reference collection. I must also check the Internet to see what may be available to guide the caller. Several guides to citation styles exist, and I am almost overwhelmed by discovering that nearly everyone has an opinion on citation of electronic sources. Not only does everyone have an opinion, but everyone is now able to electronically publish his or her version of a chosen style manual. After browsing through a number of these, I narrow it down to just a few more-general sites and save the others for later. (For URLs of these sites, see the references at the end of the article.)

APA Publication Manual Crib Sheet

The first electronic style manual that I view is the *APA Publication Manual Crib Sheet* created by R. A. Dewey at Georgia Southern University. This electronic manual provides a digested version of the print manual. I see at first a statement that

> for e-mail, and other "unrecoverable data" use personal communication, for example: (V.-G. Nguyen, personal communication, September 28, 1993). These do not appear in the reference list.

I also find more-specific examples of how to cite sources found using World Wide Web (WWW) browsers and the inclusion of Uniform Resource Locators (URLs) or electronic addresses. This indicates one change from the print APA manual as is indicated by the author's statement,

> The use of URLs is *not* specified in the APA style manual. However, the URL is increasingly recognized as the standard way of specifying addresses for retrievable documents on the Internet.

I will be sure to point out to the caller the uses of URLs in this manual since it includes definitive examples to direct formulation of citations that include addresses.

MLA-Style Citations of Electronic Sources

The second site I visit virtually is Janice Walker's 1995 *MLA-Style Citations of Electronic Sources.* She created it to handle the information she found in her research and to answer her students' "How do I cite this?" questions. I note her suggestion to adapt the punctuation of the MLA style when necessary to eliminate confusion with Internet addresses. The parts of the citation include author, title, title of complete work, protocol and address, and the date of posting or date of citing.

Walker's treatment of electronic personal communication such as e-mail and listservs is equivalent to her treatment of other electronic sources. They would all appear in a citation list. E-mail and listservs do have unique citation styles. For e-mail she states, "The address may be omitted." Apparently written shortly before the publication of the fourth edition of the *MLA Handbook for Writers of Research Papers,* this guide contains some conflicts with the current MLA rules.

Other Electronic Sources

In the characteristic manner of our times, it is possible to find information about a book on the Internet even before print publication. I find two style sheets online titled *Electronic Sources* that illustrate the methods for citing electronic sources used by Li and Crane to update their 1993 book. One style sheet illustrates the revised APA format. The second illustrates MLA-style citations.

Answering the Original Question

When I return the call, I indicate that I have information to help answer the question. I have in front of me a variety of style manuals, and I prepare myself with documentation to back up my answer. I navigate through the call with ease and am able to give the caller confidence that the citation is accurate and that the library is indeed the place to go with these questions!

Future Citation Guides

So, I've answered the question. I've gotten what I needed to provide resources for the caller. Unfortunately, the question doesn't end there. It will come back tomorrow, next week, next month, and next year. Things will continue to change. I've mastered the Gopher citation and the online information service citation. I've learned to think about the analogies between paper and electronic sources to make my way through the style manuals. I've learned that the personal communication sections of the style manuals are just as important as the electronic sources sections. Today I'm working on the WWW citation. What citations will I need tomorrow? Are the basic rules of citations enough to make the transition? What about scholarly relevance? Will it be up to editors, peer reviewers, or serendipity? Looking to the immediate future, there is a development on the horizon that may provide different answers to the question "How do I cite this?" But it may only raise more questions.

ISO Standard 690-2

During 1996, the International Organization for Standardization (ISO) will publish a new standard for citing electronic sources. Due to a renaming of the existing bibliographic citation standard 690 to 690-1, the new standard will be called 690-2. This standard is in the final stages of development. The next-to-last vote was taken in December 1995. With an early count of 95 percent approval, the final vote will likely be positive, and publication will be imminent. The ISO Technical Committee 46, Subcommittee 9 is responsible for the creation of this standard (J. Thacker, personal communication, January 31, 1996). The citation parts include primary responsibility (author), title, type of medium, place of publication, publication date, citation date, availability and access, and, if available, standard number (e.g., ISSN, ISBN). In addition, rules for capitalization, abbreviation, and punctuation are explicitly delineated.

Examples

Realizing that my colleagues could benefit from the work I've done, I put together a quick guide directing them to the resources I've identified and examined as well as including some examples of citations.

Publication Manual of the American Psychological Association

Schönfeld, M. (1995, Spring). Introduction to justifying value in nature [18 paragraphs]. *Electronic Journal of Analytic Philosophy* [On-line serial], (3). Available WWW: Hostname: www.phil.indiana.edu Directory: ejap/1995.spring File: schonfeld.1995.spring.html

The Chicago Manual of Style

Documentation one:

Schönfeld, Martin. Introduction to Justifying Value in Nature. In *Electronic Journal of Analytic Philosophy* [journal online], (spring) no. 3. (1995) [cited 11 February 1996]. Available from WWW www.phil.indiana.edu/ejap/1995/schonfeld.1995.spring.html

Documentation two:

Schönfeld, Martin. 1995. Introduction to justifying value in nature. In *Electronic Journal of Analytic Philosophy* [journal online], (spring) no. 3. [cited

11 February 1996]. Available from WWW www.phil.indiana.edu/ejap/1995/schonfeld.1995.spring.html

The MLA Handbook for Writers of Research Papers

Schönfeld, Martin. "Introduction to Justifying Value in Nature." *Electronic Journal of Analytic Philosophy* 3 (1995) : n. pag. Online. Internet. 11 February 1996.

Optional:

Schönfeld, Martin. "Introduction to Justifying Value in Nature." *Electronic Journal of Analytic Philosophy* 3 (1995) : n. pag. Online. Internet. 11 February 1996. Available WWW: www.phil.indiana.edu/ejap/1995.spring/schonfeld.1995.spring.html

Electronic Style: A Guide to Citing Electronic Information

Schönfeld, M. (1995, Spring). Introduction to justifying value in nature. *Electronic Journal of Analytic Philosophy* [On-line], (3). Available WWW: www.phil.indiana.edu Directory: ejap/1995.spring File: schonfeld.1995.spring.html

APA Publication Manual Crib Sheet

Schönfeld, M. (1995, Spring). Introduction to justifying value in nature. *Electronic Journal of Analytic Philosophy* [On-line], (3). Available http://www.phil.indiana.edu/ejap/1995.spring/schonfeld.1995.spring.html.

MLA-Style Citations of Electronic Sources

Schönfeld, Martin. "Introduction to Justifying Value in Nature." *Electronic Journal of Analytic Philosophy* http://www.phil.indiana.edu/ejap/1995.spring/schonfeld.1995.spring.html (11 February 1995).

Other Electronic Sources

APA style:

Schoñfeld, M. (1995, Spring). Introduction to justifying value in nature. *Electronic Journal of Analytic Philosophy* [Online], (3), 18 paragraphs. Available HTTP: http://www.phil.indiana.edu/ejap/1995.spring/schonfeld.1995.spring.html [1996, February 11].

MLA style:

Schönfeld, Martin. "Introduction to Justifying Value in Nature." *Electronic Journal of Analytic Philosophy* 3 (1995) 18 pars. Online. Available HTTP: http://www.phil.indiana.edu/ejap/1995.spring/schonfeld.1995.spring.html. 11 February 1996.

ISO Draft International Standard 690-2

Schönfeld, Martin. Introduction to justifying value in nature. Electronic Journal of Analytic Philosophy [online]. 1995. no. 3 [cited 1996-02-11]. Available from Internet: <URL:http: //www.phil.indiana.edu/ejap/ 1995.spring/ schonfeld.1995.spring.html>. ISSN 1071-5800.

Fork in the Road

I'm back now at that fork in the road. I've navigated the question. I've helped out my colleague, but I still feel that something's missing. I feel rather alone, yet I sense many colleagues, scholars, and librarians around me. Some are making decisive movements heading in each direction. Others pause, watching and waiting.

I hear murmurs through the fog. There are discussions. Some of them are heated, and some are not. To the north I sense familiarity and a definition of "scholarly evidence." To the south I sense the unknown. It's a trail just beginning. Where does it go? What is the destination?

I realize that no matter what, I'll always remember being at this fork and which way I ended up going.

References

American Psychological Association. (1994). *Publication Manual of the American Psychological Association* (4th ed.). Washington, DC: APA.

Chicago Manual of Style (14th ed.). (1993). Chicago: University of Chicago Press.

Dewey, R. A. (n.d.). *APA Publication Manual Crib Sheet.* [Online]. Available: *http://www.gasou.edu/psychweb/tipsheet/apacrib.htm*

Gibaldi, J. (1995). *MLA Handbook for Writers of Research Papers* (4th ed.). New York: The Modern Language Association of America.

Guernsey, L. (1996, January 12). "Cyberspace Citations: Scholars Debate How Best to Cite Research Conducted on the Internet." *Chronicle of Higher Education, 42,* A18, A20–21.

International Organization for Standardization. (1996). *ISO TC 46/SC 9: Standards for the Presentation, Identification, and Description of Documents* [Online]. Available: *http://www.nlc-bnc.ca/iso/tc46sc9/index.htm*

Li, X., and Crane, N. B. (2nd ed.). (1996). *Electronic Style: A Guide to Citing Electronic Information.* Westport, CT: Meckler.

———. (1995a). *Electronic Sources: APA Style of Citation* [Online]. Available: *http://www.uvm.edu/~xli/reference/apa.html*

———. (1995b). *Electronic Sources: MLA Style of Citation* [Online]. Available: *http://www.uvm.edu/xli/reference/mla.html*

Tannehill, R. S., Jr., (1995, October). "Emerging Standards on the Citation of Electronic Documents: A Status Report." *Information Standards Quarterly, 7,* 1–5.

Walker, J. R. (1995). *MLA-style Citations of Electronic Sources* [Online]. Available: *http://www.cas.usf.edu/english/walker/mla.html*

Civic Cybrarianship

Government and the Information Superhighway Public Lanes

John Shuler

John Shuler *(ALFRED@UIC.EDU)* has been involved in documents work at the University of Oregon, Colgate University, and currently as department head for the Documents, Maps, Microforms, and Curriculum Department at the University of Illinois at Chicago. He has presented and written nationally about documents and is the creator of the electronic reading room for the Department of State.

Whether we choose to be called cybrarians or librarians, the basics of providing government information within most library organizations will remain largely unchanged for the next decade. The "laws" that govern the information superhighway's public lanes will continue to depend upon the tidal flows of popular political and economic philosophy, the broad principles of public administration, and the abiding sensibilities of library practice as well as an understanding of civic responsibility and education. What has changed, often beyond the recognition of most traditional library perspectives, is the economic and technological contexts that support a vibrant government information infrastructure. And it is within these changing contexts that cybrarians committed to the ideals of "government information for the people" must fashion a new rhetoric and purpose for themselves.

These future "public information soldiers," naturally enough, will need to upgrade their technological skills; that is a given for anyone who strives to make a living out on the information byways. On a deeper level, however, public information librarians/cybrarians must give up the bibliographic comforts they derive from "ownership" of separate physical collections and shift to a new paradigm of shared "serviceship" within a larger community of networked resources. This will demand a more active partnership with the many levels of government and other community groups. It anticipates that the heart of the electronic public information enterprise will not be in collecting and managing the traditional "containers" of information created by governments (reports, hearings, studies, prints, etc.).

Rather, the future cybrarian/librarian will serve as a community organizer and educator who will work for a strong, active and particpatory democracy at the local and regional level. In cooperation with other cultural and educational institutions, these cybrarians will create electronic information services and develop information resources that will allow all citizens to participate more fully in government deliberations and decisions. This kind of activity includes regular outreach to and education of citizens about how government works; assisting local organizations in learning how to organize their own information resources and make them available to the wider community; and helping community groups, neighborhood organizations, and government agencies develop standardized and easily accessible public collections of electronic government data. I choose to call this new professional orientation "civic cybrarianship."

The Old Era

Simply put, over the last 50 years, the core concepts that argue for a system of government information distribution and access as a "free" and "public" good (and, some argue, a basic civil right) have lost their traditional hold over many parts of the private and public sectors. Through this perspective, one largely based on the political and social reforms of the late nineteenth-century progressive movements, the government provides subsidies and builds the infrastructure for the diffusion of "public knowledge." This diffusion, in turn, is further enhanced by an array of public institutions (libraries, public schools, community and regional newspapers, a national postal system, public halls and theaters, etc.). These institutions serve as intermediaries between the government and citizens.

However, a succession of revolutions, reforms, and privatization initiatives spread throughout all levels of government around the globe, seeking fulfillment through the promise of a Global Information Infrastructure (GII) in conjunction with the development of National Information Infrastructures (NII). The historic ideal of government information as a public good has been undermined throughout the world, not least of all in the United States. Information Resource Management (IRM) now dominates. IRM, as a concept, considers government information as just one more "commodity" to be created, organized, managed, distributed, leased, sought, sold, or traded in a rational fashion within a free and open market of private or public products and services.

Government agencies that produce information products and services must be careful to avoid unfair competition with the private information sector. Subsidized public information access and transfer must be kept to a minimum, which often includes government efforts to develop public shareware or freeware applications that could make electronic public data more accessible to ordinary citizens. The more radical proponents of this free market perspective envision a vibrant global community of private information providers who draw upon the rich resources of "raw" public data and provide essential civic information to more citizens through the private expansion of the NII. This kind of information environment between citizen and government no longer demands the same intermediaries as those created in the previous century.

A New Era

Henry J. Perritt Jr., in his *Public Information in the National Information Infrastructure,* describes this new, rapidly evolving economic market and argues that any

> government information policy must encourage a diversity of information products and channels, and permit the disaggregation of production so that a variety of product bundles can be offered and assembled through the electronic market. The market also must accommodate the technologically unsophisticated and poor, who should be able to access and use modern technology to obtain basic citizenship information.

He does support some form of minimal level "universal access" and goes on to describe three essential elements that must be considered during the formulation and implementation of these policies. First, for any particular "citizen information bundle," the policy should address how much "enhanced value" should be added by public agencies and how much should come from the private sector. Second, there must be assurances that this citizen information bundle enjoys equitable distribution, specifically identifying which proportion of the information package's delivery costs should be subsidized by the government and which should be determined by forces on the free market. Third, the policy must clearly outline specific and reasonable methods for public agencies to ensure the information package's affordability and accessibility among citizens who have neither the resources nor the ability to obtain the package on their own.

This does not mean, however, that this basic information package will (or should) be available from a single location or service provider (i.e., libraries). According to Perritt, the electronic public information market will gradually form into a kaleidoscope of dynamic relationships among producers, disseminators, and end users. Any effective government policy ". . . must be empirical and evolve from decentralized decision making within broad principles. It also means that some risks of under-dissemination and threats to private markets are inevitable as agencies, private suppliers, and consumers feel their way with new technologies."

The expanding technological capabilities of computers in the last few years add another complication to these economic arguments. The promise of widely available low-cost computers and telecommunication networks is hailed by some as a chance to revitalize the "civic center" of political and social life, especially in the United States. Advocates of this "teledemocracy" consider technology a natural tool to encourage more effective citizen-to-citizen communication on important public issues. They talk of "electronic town halls" and "equal access" to electronic public records. An excellent example of this perspective is in Douglas Schuler's *New Community Networks: Wired for Change*. This grassroots vision of the NII comes into direct conflict with equally compelling counterarguments. These hold that the values of public access and universal service (which includes the lion's share of government information) are best met through the deregulation of the telecommunication industry. This perspective has essentially become the law of the land with the enactment of the Telecommunications Act of 1996.

These revolutions within government information's technological and economic infrastructure not only suggest Perritt's policy shifts but also foreshadow the considerable alterations to the traditional arrangements between governments and libraries. The distinction between government services and government publications has become blurred. In an information environment dominated by print technology, the forms and publications of any public program could be separated, and each would seemingly survive. Indeed, a system of depository libraries could be constructed around knowledge and skills about the publications and, to a limited degree, their contents. The government, in turn, would continue to provide both the service and the publications. In an information environment dominated by electronic data, the quality and quantity of the public service are directly dependent on the value of data exchanged between the agency and the citizen. Publications, in a sense, are no longer needed. The information becomes a highly interdependent, changeable, individualized, and interactive trade between the public and the government or some other third-party service provider.

Therefore, one can no longer speak of tangible government information "containers" (i.e., printed or microformed versions of hearings, reports, studies, debates, etc.) stored on shelves or in file cabinets (and on computer disks or tapes). Rather, we must now speak of access to and services from distant and commonly held "pools" of electronic public information. In the print-dominated model, these "containers" are distributed already "sanctioned" and organized by the public authorities. These authorities determine the length of study, choose the statistical analysis, or select parts of the public testimony they want to use. An individual must extract what he or she needs from the rest of the information in the container. If the information is not in a form or style that suits his or her purposes, the person must process and compare it with data from other containers and then organize and present the distilled information in a fashion suitable to his or her needs.

However, electronic government information remains a raw material to all users who would take from the common "pools." This means the government still ensures the validity of the basic data through its legal authority, but does not determine, or get involved with, how individuals might want to fabricate the data into specific products or services. In a very real sense, the digitalization of government record keeping is driving public authorities from publishing and research. To follow this to its logical conclusion, then, most institutions already involved in depository library or clearinghouse arrangements with governments will find themselves more actively involved in building relationships and infrastructures that demand access to federal information rather than its ownership. This goes beyond "libraries without walls" or "electronic libraries." The profound alterations in the life cycle of federal information created by its digitalization in turn demand new ways of operating from libraries and their host institutions in relation to how they interact with members of their community and with the federal institutions that create public data.

To put it another way, researchers and citizens will create their own unique government information products (or in some cases, services) by combining and merging different elements from a myriad of full-text and numeric databases. It is something that is already happening with or without a system of depository libraries.

An individual can connect to the Government Printing Office's (GPO) official Web site, download a specific passage from a proposed piece of legislation, then locate and capture a few paragraphs from the House of Representatives' official report related to the legislation, and then go on to find and download observations in a General Accounting Office study on the subject. The individual could then leave the GPO Web site, "move" on over to the Census Bureau's Web site, and locate and download statistical information. At no time does the individual need or use a printed document. What is even more sobering, if this individual had Internet access from a home or office computer (with enough experience on how to search the Internet), a library would not be needed as well.

The "Four Empires" of Government Information

Because of these developments, government information, as it is presently managed in libraries, can be divided into four distinct "empires." Each will continue to demand a unique set of technical skills, and seamless integration among the empires will have to come from the professional knowledge and experience of cybrarians. Libraries will remain a natural nexus between extensive scholarly research and federal information. Individuals will continue to demand the ability to transcend "information formats" and "transmission channels." Most descriptions in the popular and professional press paint the information superhighway as a simplistic monorail: electronic data distributed through telecommunication networks. In reality, this road is much more demanding and complex, with different traffic lanes (formats) and speed limits (transmission channels). Therefore, any extensive research involving public information, at least in the foreseeable future, will depend on ready and convenient access to all these traffic lanes. At one level, library collections, data centers, and other information archives are already fulfilling this function of integration and transcendence.

Granted, the public authorities are attempting to create a universal passport through these areas, something they call "Government Information Locator Services" or GILS. As part of the federal role in the National Information Infrastructure, the Z39.50-based GILS attempt to integrate information resources through common standards and search techniques throughout the federal government and to provide assistance in obtaining the information. However, until these technologies and standards are stabilized, libraries will remain the most significant location on the Net for negotiating the different and difficult mosaic of public information products and services.

The First Empire: Paper

The paper empire is going to be with us for a very long time. Indeed, any research requires a significant visit to this realm. The 1994 Sears and Moody guide remains one of the best guides to U.S. federal information resources in this realm.

The Second Empire: Data Disks

The data disk empire is a transitional empire; many of the early disks were either electronic paper products or raw data from mainframe computers. Much of the software was ill-conceived and badly applied. Some of the best developments have been in the areas of CD-ROMs and selected databases, such as those from the Census Bureau. Maxymuk's U.S. federal government CD-ROM volume is a good reference source for this material.

The Third Empire: Electronic Bulletin Boards/Gophers

Electronic bulletin boards and Gophers are fascinating places to visit because they should not have to exist; many people consider them to have been made obsolete by the World Wide Web. Yet they still remain active areas for many sources of government information, some of which are not found in any of the other empires. Bruce Maxwell's *Washington Online* remains one of the best guides to this empire, and the Gopher guide produced by Calvin Boyer at the University of California, Irvine, can be found at: *gopher://peg.cwis.uci.edu:7000/11/gopher.welcome/peg/GOPHERS/gov.*

The Fourth Empire: World Wide Web

In the World Wide Web (WWW) empire, which dominates the current landscape, we are witnessing the final merger of government service and information production. The greatest threat to the concept of traditional government information librarianship comes from this realm. Its interactivity and individual access suggest that it will become the natural successor to many traditional library collections and public services. It is also one of the most confusing empires, since none of the government agencies are building their Web sites in any kind of standardized fashion. As the Web develops, many more home pages will serve as mediation points between the searcher and the official sites, such as those listed under the "General Sources" category. If civic cybrarians must stake a place on the information highway, it should be in the development of these mediation points (what I call "electronic reading rooms"). Users should be able to trust that, if they continue to use the Web site, they will know that someone is responsible for making sure the links work, that all the links are current and really do link to "official" government Web pages, and that there is a chance to leave questions or seek further help.

However, many of the government sites are little more than promotional devices for particular agencies and office holders. In other cases, especially at the local and state level, the information content is just slightly beyond the level of hawking a particular municipality or location as a prime location for business and commercial investment. The following is a selected list of the some of the best examples of this varied evolution on the WWW.

U.S. Federal Government Agencies

GENERAL SOURCES

Government Agency WWW Servers. Available: *http://www.eit.com/web/ www.servers/government.html*

U.S. Federal Government Agencies. Available: *http://www.lib.lsu.edu/gov/ fedgov.html*

The Villanova Center for Information Law and Policy. Available: *http:// www.law.vill.edu/Fed-Agency/fedwebloc.html*

WWW Servers (U.S. Federal Government). Available: *http://www.fie.com/ www/us_gov.htm*

SPECIFIC AGENCIES

Government Printing Office (GPO) Access. Available: *http://www.gpo.gov/*

National Technical Information Service (NTIS)/Fedworld. Available: *http:// www.fedworld.gov/*

Thomas (Library of Congress legislative information). Available: *http:// thomas.loc.gov/*

U.S. Department of Census. Available: *http://www.census.gov/*

U.S. Department of State. Available: *http://www.state.gov/*

Welcome to the White House. Available: *http://www1.whitehouse.gov/WH/ Welcome.html*

U.S. State, Local, and Regional Government Agencies

Arizona. Available: *http://www.state.az.us/*

Delaware Valley Regional Planning Commission. Available: *http://www. libertynet.org/~dvrpc/index.html*

Huntsville, Alabama. Available: *http://www.ci.huntsville.al.us/*

Marin County, California. Available: *http://midas.co.marin.ca.us/*

Oregon. Available: *http://www.or.us/*

State and Local Government Information. Available: *http://www.piperinfo. com/~piper/state/states.html*

International and National Governments

Embassies in Washington, D.C., Area. Available: *http://www.embassy.org/embassies/eep-1100.html*

International Government. Available: *http://gnn.com/wic/wics/govt.un.html*

National Governments. Available: *http://www.yahoo.com/Government/Countries/*

New Zealand. Available: *http://www.govt.nz/*

Taiwan. Available: *http://gio.gov.tw/*

Civic Cybrarians

The transition from paper to electronic formats suggests a whole new relationship with libraries' local communities of users and with the public agencies responsible for producing the information. In the end, success of these efforts will depend on two cooperative strategies: the first aimed at a national and multi-institutional approach and the second through the formation of community information organizations (CIOs) at the regional or local level. Libraries and information centers must become re-fabricators of information, aiding in the creation of products that are designed by users drawing on a wide range of information products. The development of electronic reading rooms as a concept will mean organizing electronic space on a network so that public institutions and citizens can identify, gather, and maintain selected parts of the public information infrastructure.

The several national systems of depository libraries or information centers are no longer effective models of distribution and access for net-worked government information. Instead of building collections based on these relationships, many institutions will need to build alliances and in-frastructures with other peer institutions and create public information management organizations (PIMOs.) Comparable to health management organizations (HMOs), PIMOs would allow for the identification, organi-zation, and support of common electronic records and interfaces de-manded by the public and multiple levels of networked government information.

These organizations would also play a crucial role in the creation of performance benchmarks to identify effective public services measurements and enhance local and regional access to the expanding pools of electronic federal information. In addition, PIMOs would actively work with govern-ment agencies to ensure a minimum level of preservation, access, and pre-sentation for vital public information needed for long-term political, social, educational, medical, and historical purposes. Although these alliances should not, and could not, replace the legal and managerial responsibilities of the public authorities to properly archive and preserve their information, PIMOs could play an important role as intermediary organizations. In other words, these alliances would provide opportunities for government agencies and citizens to explore their common problems and opportunities to maintain an effective public-information life cycle.

At the local level and regional level, these alliances would foster the development of local and regional CIOs. As discussed earlier, the expansion of the GII and NIIs has sparked a comparable increase in the development of local computer networks. However, many of these efforts work in near isolation, and they often find it difficult to locate or develop the necessary technical and professional skills. Even as the numbers of community information networks grow into the hundreds, cybrarians and community leaders must form and maintain partnerships to marshal and mobilize community and government resources and must use their expertise to maintain a common pool of local community information. The express purpose of CIOs, as with the PIMOs, would be to develop an integrated environment of community information resources by working with citizens at the local and regional level. This would include developing specific minimum-level citizen-information packages that would be easily available to a local or regional community. This package would include the most significant economic, social, and political information. Strong local partnerships of librarians, citizen activists, government officials, and civic leaders will leverage the variety of resources and skills necessary.

A key information resource in any community information network is the information produced by all levels of government. Demographic and economic data, employment and business information, and vital statistics as well as information on the works and affairs of government are crucial to the economic development of neighborhoods and communities, the education of children and young people, and the participation of citizens in their local governments and civic affairs. Much of this information, and the knowledge of how to accumulate, disseminate, and provide access to it, already exists in libraries that function as depository libraries for agencies at all levels of government. These libraries can provide a crucial element in supporting and sustaining community projects if they become active partners at the community level.

If these alliances take root, then we would no longer be speaking of a form of librarianship that depends on a format or method of information distribution. From a tradition of ownership to one of serviceship, civic cybrarians would assume a new and empowered role in the next century.

References

Maxwell, Bruce. (1995). *Washington Online: How to Access the Government's Electronic Bulletin Boards.* Washington, DC: Congressional Quarterly Books.

Maxymuk, John, ed. (1994) *Government CD-ROMs: A Practical Guide to Searching Electronic Documents Databases.* Westport, CT: MecklerMedia.

Perritt, Henry H. (1994). *Public Information in the National Information Infrastructure.* Washington, DC: United States Office of Management and Budget.

Schuler, Douglas. (1996). *New Community Networks: Wired for Change.* Reading, MA: Addison-Wesley.

Sears, Jean L., and Moody, Marilyn. (1994). *Using Government Information Sources* (2nd ed.) Phoenix, AZ: Oryx Press.

BEYOND SURFING

SERVING INFORMATION TO OUR PATRONS

Larry Schankman

Larry Schankman is a reference librarian at Mansfield University and is the author of "How to Become an Internet Power User" in *College & Research Libraries News*. He has an extensive set of Web pages, helpful to many subject searchers, at *http://www.clark.net/pub/lschank/home.html*.

Surfing the Internet is fun and can be a pleasant diversion. But surfing is not reference work. In the early years, before Dummy Series books and point-and-click software, information professionals explored the seemingly uncharted ocean of the Internet without a compass. Surfing the Net worked in those days as an effective educational strategy. Farsighted librarians at smaller, poorer institutions realized the Internet, once tamed, could serve as an equalizing force, allowing free access to data and resources previously deemed unaffordable. Nevertheless, many directors and heads of reference during those innocent years considered use of the Net in libraries akin to playing computer games. In stark contrast to the past, the Internet has now evolved into a recognized information asset. But as the amount of online information increases, we need to develop more effective search and retrieval methods. This essay offers advice to librarians on how best to integrate the Internet, and technology in general, into reference service.

Throughout this chapter I assume that readers possess a basic familiarity with the Internet and World Wide Web (hereafter called the Web). If not, most good book stores today are stocked full to the rafters with beginner's books on all aspects of the Internet. For a fairly well-maintained list of Internet books, see Hope N. Tillman's *Internet Bibliographies* at *http://www.tiac.net/users/hope/intbib.html* or Kevin Savetz's *Unofficial Internet Booklist* at *http://www.cis.ohio-state.edu/hypertext/faq/usenet/internet-services/book-list/faq.html*.

The tips, if you want just the gist of this essay, are as follows:

1. You gotta believe . . . the ends justify the means
2. Lead, don't follow, the way into the twenty-first century
3. Train the trainers first
4. Enough with the links, already
5. Where's the beef?
6. Wow to attract, not to distract
7. Librarians gotta know their place
8. Schedule time to check out what's new
9. Plan for the future

You Gotta Believe . . . The Ends Justify the Means

Librarians, we should agree, care primarily about content. Our students and patrons look to us for guidance, not for high-tech entertainment and certainly not for excuses. When faced with a difficult question, we should endeavor to call upon any available resource to provide the answer, regardless of format. Many libraries, however, have to downsize their collections to satisfy declining budgets. Fortunately, expenditures on Internet and online access can pay for themselves over time. As a result, networked libraries can provide patrons information that they would otherwise have to find elsewhere or not at all. If the requested data, speech, historical document, or report happens to be free (at least from a marginal-cost perspective), then so much the better.

Yet, many Internet applications today seem to only muddy the information waters as new crops of smart agents and virtual libraries promise to transform every computer terminal into both library and librarian combined. Unfortunately, too many people equate the latest gimmicks (e.g., bouncing heads in Java, obnoxious little frames in Netscape 2.0, flashing banners that require a gazillion megabytes of memory to load, etc.) with information, though not necessarily with knowledge or understanding.

Should librarians then embrace technology? Yes, for we live in an age where information rules. And regardless of our feelings toward the so-called virtual library, technology now rules information access. If we allow technology to marginalize our profession, not only will we lose our jobs but our patrons will lose the ability to seek compassionate assistance in finding answers for which they quite possibly don't even know the right questions. When our patrons conduct their research at home without a librarian to guide them, who will teach them strategies for efficient search definition, resource selection, and evaluation of retrieved material?

Indeed, if technocrats replace librarians, information content simply evolves into a mathematical formula called "relevancy." By retrieving documents with high counts of a specified word or phrase, especially if the word or phrase appears frequently in the first few sentences, a typical search robot today declares hundreds of undesired documents as relevant.

A search, for example, on the phrase *communication bill* would award the maximum rank of 1,000 to a title such as, "Communication Grid Lock: Newt Refuses Communication with Bill on Proposed Farm Bill." How many patrons of the virtual library will finish their papers on time with retrieval like this? Of course, librarians notice the obvious weakness of these robots: lack of controlled vocabulary and indexing.

Librarians will definitely not become irrelevant in the information age, whether paper is replaced with electronic bits or not. Computers may make very smart machines, but they also make very dumb librarians. The bottom line is our ability to organize and locate appropriate information. As long as librarians are best qualified to help humans ask the right questions or teach users to push the right buttons while asking those questions, our future will remain secure. Nevertheless, we must get off the surfboard and help convert technology into enhanced reference service. If we are unable to actually design the new crop of emerging search and retrieval tools, then we should at least help develop standards and procedures for their use in libraries.

Lead, Don't Follow, the Way into the Twenty-First Century

If your library enjoys blazingly fast, state-of-the-art network connections with graphical programs like the latest versions of Netscape or Mosaic, then consider yourself fortunate and skip ahead to the next section. If, on the other hand, you have no connection, or access the Internet with text-based programs such as Lynx or Gopher, then demand better. Agitate for change, and if money is the obstacle, write a grant to finance a modernization campaign. Though money is tight all over, several small pools still exist specifically for telecommunications and networking. For grant information from the National Telecommunications & Information Administration (NTIA), point your browser to *http://www.ntia.doc.gov:80/otiahome/otiaact.html*. For grants in general, start with the *Grant Writers Assistant HotLinks* to funding resources on the Net (Falling Rock Software) at *http://fallingrock.com/GWA/LINKS/HOTLINKS*. Alternatively, see the Department of Health and Human Services' *GrantsNet* at *http://www.os.dhhs.gov* or via Gopher at *gopher://gopher.os.dhhs.gov:70/11/Topics/grantsnet*.

A winning strategy, from my experience, is to find partners at a library or institution different from your own. Successful projects today must serve a diverse, large mixture of constituents (ideally, citizens who vote). A typical partnership could involve a university and public library district or a special library and a school library. When preparing the budget, be sure to allocate significant monies for training (both for you and your staff), employment of temporary network experts, publicity, and travel for "training the trainers."

Most importantly, state your case to the administration: As employers expect their workers and leaders to function in a networked environment, a networked library is no longer a luxury but a necessity. Change may be understandably fearsome and certainly expected; nonetheless, librarians must soon come to realize that the evolving technology of information is a tiger that will either be tamed or fattened on the carcasses of unemployed bibliophiles.

Train the Trainers First

Now that many libraries feature Internet and other remote information access, a common complaint among all levels of reference staff (professional, support, and student assistants) is unfamiliarity with online resources. Surely we cannot expect patrons to receive help with networked tools if we ourselves are not prepared or willing to assume that responsibility. (And we should not forget that to most patrons, whoever answers a question in a library is a librarian, regardless of status, education, or pay.) Moreover, we can't ensure the success of networked tools in the library unless end users feel confident that they can receive assistance when requested. For them, human compassion and guidance are crucial.

To this end, libraries should prepare for new electronic services by first developing a plan for effective instruction, perhaps with frequent workshops or demonstrations. Later, libraries should publish pathfinders, Webographies, and other guides that not so coincidentally imitate traditional bibliographic materials. Libraries could also benefit from a publicity campaign to encourage usage of (and appreciation for) library services.

Perhaps the low morale and professional anxiety in the face of revolutionary changes in technology result directly from the lack of preparation and training. This is especially true after patrons take for granted the high-tech access and customer service provided by one or two resident "gurus." Administrators, then, should appreciate the absolute necessity for adequate training if they truly wish to enhance the value of public and reference services. Once they accept the need for training, their next philosophical step is to provide release time for faculty and staff to receive training, whether formal or in-house.

One efficient way to bring staff up to speed is to offer one or two convincing introductory demonstrations with hands-on exercises. Afterward, schedule short 15- to 30-minute presentations during regular reference or staff meetings, conducted by the librarians or staff members themselves. These presentations can focus on a new or recently discovered Web site, database, or other useful discovery. Finally, ask reference librarians and staff to create a home page, or at least a well-maintained bookmark file, representing those sites identified as most useful for reference purposes.

Enough with the Links, Already

Nowadays, almost everyone and their cat have Web pages, most of which merely point to the same favored sites, catchy images, or humorous discoveries. In most cases, mirroring an already overcrowded collection of links provides nothing but added confusion. No librarian would consider placing a heavily used reference book in the middle of the circulating collection. Likewise, creating redundant Web pages causes cyber patrons frustration in weeding through an endless sea of entangled Web debris. At times like these, librarians should remember their most intrinsic and invaluable contribution to the information age: the ability to organize and abstract information resources.

Preferably, libraries should mount on their servers unique files and local data, such as campus or community newsletters, archival materials, class schedules, or digitized special collections. In many cases, local resources can include data and text not found elsewhere on the Internet. Rural areas can especially reap the rewards of uploading information that larger, urban institutions care not a fig about, such as local demographic or historical data.

Libraries need not rely on their own resources to produce value-added content. Many local, state, and even federal agencies, often with funds in hand, would benefit richly from a partnership with your institution to serve their information to the public. Many local organizations especially need our services to help distribute important community information. Sadly, such ventures as these rarely occur, and generally for rather needless reasons. Town and gown issues aside, partnerships with owners of unique information make sense for both community development and information development.

Where's the Beef?

When conducting Internet research, patrons want substance. What they might think they need are virtual surfboards to navigate endless layers of menus. Our job is to maximize the ability of users to find what they need quickly and efficiently. We can accomplish this task through a variety of means: instruction, pathfinders, roaming reference coverage, or well-designed Web pages. We also can rely on precedent. When we assist students with bibliographic research, we surely don't escort them to the index area and say, "Try any of these thick books, they all do the same thing." Our greatest service to Net users is our holistic approach to resource management: evaluate it, organize it, and finally, instruct patrons how to best select the right material for their particular needs.

When designed specifically for reference use, Web links should point to the desired file or data, not simply to a home page. The fewer steps required by users to find what they want, the better. Herein lies the power of the browser: the ability to link to a specific file. In fact, links may even point to material mounted on a local hard drive, thus serving as a cheap but effective menu for text files (or multimedia programs capable of running under the new generation of Web browsers). A common frustration for Webmasters is maintaining valid links, as many sites often change their Uniform Resource Locator (URL). New developments, however, do allow for permanent addresses. For one library-initiated solution, see an explanation and demonstration of OCLC's Persistent Uniform Resource Locator (PURL) project, from the *Persistent URL Homepage,* at *http://purl.oclc.org/.*

Libraries that are unable to create their own Web page or Gopher can enhance reference service by maintaining a continually updated (and weeded) bookmark file. All browsers today provide a bookmark function, and most (e.g., Netscape, Microsoft Internet Explorer, Mosaic, etc.) allow the bookmark file to open as the default home page. If you do not know how to edit bookmarks and their source files, read any of the popular Web books on the market or visit some of the Web pages aimed at new users. (See the section at the end of this essay.) Power users may wish to download Netscape's Smartmarks, an enhanced bookmark program from the *Netscape Home Page,* at *http://home.mcom.com/comprod/mirror/index.html.* Bookmark management software, including shareware, is also available from third-party developers.

Another important technique for ensuring that patrons find targeted material is to provide abstracts on library-created Web pages. Most sites simply provide a link with limited description of what the navigator will find once connected. Too often, sites contain exactly what visitors want, somewhere within their structure, but their menus offer no clue as to where a specific data set, document, or file resides. For the library Web page to truly connect users with information, the Web citation should contain not only an abstract but internal links, that is, hypertext references to specific resources beyond the main URL provided.

The U.S. Census Bureau *(http://www.census.gov),* for example, contains a vast treasure trove of valuable data, but from the home page, users can quickly become disoriented. In some cases, desired directories aren't even linked to the top-level pages. Although the *Census Home Page* offers search capability, as do many of the better sites, we can further guide our patrons by pointing out the most useful or anticipated census destinations. Who would figure, continuing this example, that historic county data would be found under the directory for population estimates?

From a service perspective we should treat online resources the same as print. No caring reference librarian would ever look a patron in the eye upon a request for printed 1990 census data, point to the entire census collection, and end the interview with a curt, "There it is." If that particular volume were missing, furthermore, and the librarian advised the hapless demographer to return later (even though the same data were contained in

FIGURE 1   Sample Link

- Statistical Abstract ("Uncle Sam's Reference Shelf")

    One of the premier reference sources for statistics. Categories include Frequently Requested Tables for the most requested data; State Rankings, for statistical comparisons of states; and Economic Indicators for economic and labor data. Sam even allows a Keyword Search of all data sets.

several available resources), we should all recognize a disservice committed against the patron. Why, then, should our Web pages treat customers any differently?

As a demonstration of this concept, see figure 1 for a sample link to the Census Bureau's *Statistical Abstract,* from my *Census and Demographics Page* at *http://www.clark.net/pub/lschank/web/census.html.*

Wow to Attract, Not Distract

The Internet and Web are wonderful tools for distributing information, especially to remote users. But given the virtual tonnage of material in cyberspace, we must assure users that library-built services can quickly identify and locate information. Large and numerous graphics, including baud-busting image maps, can turn users away before their browsers ever load the page. Unless the site served contains important photo or image archives, it is best for reference pages to keep graphics to a minimum. Icons help attract users to particular links, but they should be no larger than 2 kilobytes (2K) to allow rapid transfer of pages.

Currently, many new techniques enhance Web services. Many of these are quite sophisticated and fun, too. But advanced applications such as Java, Virtual Reality Modeling Language (VRML), frames, etc. require more-powerful browsers, computers, and operating systems than many libraries or remote users possess. Information is useless if not accessible. For this reason, libraries should avoid applying new gimmicks to their Web servers just to play the "me too" game. Rather, libraries should concentrate on providing quality information services. Experimenting with gee-whiz designs should not be a function of that service. The old adage, "Keep it simple, stupid," seems to work well for content-enriched Web sites.

One potentially valuable use of Web browsers is their power to present information locally. Library pathfinders and research guides are natural beneficiaries of the Web browser's hyperlink functions, as are several other programs (e.g., Adobe Acrobat, Asymetrix Toolbook, Macromedia Director with its Shockwave plug-in for Netscape, etc.). The advantage of local distribution is the independence from a network or Internet connection. These programs will always be available, offline. The advantage of the browser, of course, is the attractive and organized character of multimedia hypertext. Students and staff, moreover, probably already feel comfortable with the library's browser. Thus, the program will be fairly easy to use. (See my Web page, *Launching Programs and CDs from Web Browsers,* at *http://www.clark.net/pub/lschank/web/launch.html.*)

One example of an appropriate application is my hypertext guide to statistical resources (still a work in progress) at *http://www.clark.net/pub/lschank/web/govstats.html.* The table of contents points the patron to various categories of statistics, such as local and state demographics, social indicators, etc. The resources provide abstracts for both print and Internet resources, with links when available. Listings for print resources also include holdings and location information.

Librarians Gotta Know Their Place

Agreed, we all think we're too busy to take on more work. But librarians can ill afford to let nonlibrarians become the experts on information in nonprint format. And whether or not we like to admit it, electronic content is quickly supplementing, if not replacing, print. The U.S. Government Printing Office (the world's largest publisher by most accounts), in fact, recently announced its intention to publish almost exclusively in electronic format by the end of 1998. Although this timetable may be lengthened, the impact will still be tremendous.

If we shy away from technology, are we also prepared to direct online researchers to the computer center for advice on locating historical documents, statistics, or America's current foreign policy? We should answer no, not for dislike of computer technicians and programmers, but because their training focuses on how and why the Internet works, not on the information content itself. We should also feel inspired by the real opportunity to increase the scope of the collection, even if the materials do not actually reside within the physical confines of the library or campus.

Sadly, though, many designers of search engines, Web applications, and Net-served databases don't realize that libraries are part of the information-science community. Perhaps we could advertise our services more aggressively or initiate more dialogue with developers. What we cannot afford to do is sit back and let teams of programmers design new virtual libraries without librarians present. We should insist that at least some librarians represent our interests and concerns in the development or testing of Web-based search and retrieval tools (e.g., AltaVista, Excite, InfoSeek, etc.). Every library should place a designated representative on university or organizational computer-advisory councils to monitor developments and advocate library interests. In the end, we'll all have better information products that are truly both user friendly and powerful.

But we must also be careful not to get ourselves so caught up in the hoopla of the Internet that we forget our primary task: to enhance information access. We should repeat this mantra to ourselves, especially when we feel the urge to swashbuckle throughout cyberspace aimlessly. Again, the most valuable contribution to the age of information is our historical strength in selecting, cataloging, and teaching. From this traditional base we can transform raw information (electronic bits and bytes) into value-added products. Now, that's a powerful service!

Schedule Time to Check out What's New

Information constantly changes. This should come as no surprise to librarians; however, we must be constantly aware of significant changes, as our patrons want answers, not excuses (e.g., "Well, that site used to be there."). Internet resources are simply another resource to acquire, catalog, teach,

and serve. And should we ignore collection development of electronic resources merely because we can't curl up in bed with them? If economics
students scour the library for historical data on agricultural prices, and if
print sources are inadequate, subject specialists should confidently direct
those students to Cornell University's *Agricultural Economics* Web site
(http://usda.mannlib.cornell.edu/catalog/subject/ag-econ.html) or the *USDA
Economic Research Service* home page *(http://www.econ.ag.gov/)*. Such
subject-specific sites are our tools, and we must be familiar with them to
serve our customers.

But we need not cruise mean streets alone. To help share current awareness, libraries can designate one dedicated cybrarian or form pools of subject specialists to monitor listservs and Internet publications (both online
and print) for new resources. Reference staff can organize an internal discussion list or simply route recent discoveries by either e-mail or traditional
(snail) mail. If the reference desk has a Web browser, the staff could maintain a shared bookmark file for all to use. As bookmark files grow unman-
ageable, one of the staff should weed old links or organize the file by
subject or librarian directories at regular intervals (e.g., once per week). If
this seems too much work for one individual, then perhaps the department
could rotate the duty intermittently so that everyone assumes an equal share
of the responsibility.

Organization of our own time is another crucial necessity for keeping
current. In many cases, we might know of several good online sources of
current awareness but simply forget to check them from time to time. One
solution is to maintain a schedule of weekly or monthly "check-ins." The
list need not be long; just write on your calendar or appointment organizer
the address (URL) of your favorite five sites and browse through them while
at the reference desk, during a break, or whenever you have a free moment
or two. Resources may range from online book reviews to Web journals
featuring new sites of interest to librarians, such as the University of Abertay
Dundee's (UK) *Ariadne,* at *http://ukoln.bath.ac.uk/ariadne/*. A good example of a traditional current-awareness service online is Jim Rettig's online
column, *Rettig on Reference* (formerly published in the *Wilson Library Bulletin*) with monthly reviews of reference books and Internet resources:
http://www.hwwilson.com/retintro.html. (See the last section of this essay
for additional current awareness sites.)

Plan for the Future

Today's technology will become obsolete within another couple of years.
To apply new skills, librarians should keep current with all the latest
developments in networked educational resources. Any librarian who
claims the title "professional" should monitor at least one or two specialized
listservs. Librarians should browse the titles of journals such as *Internet
World, Computers in Libraries, Online,* etc. (See "Check these out Regularly" elsewhere in this book for a list of useful resources, both in print and
online.)

Electronic resource librarians, in particular, should keep a close eye on emerging software and hardware developments. Farsighted librarians may apply for grants to develop their own interactive Web applications or "applets." These short, fully functional programs work directly from client Web browsers. One name to keep an eye on is Hyper-G, the European alternative to the World Wide Web. Even though advanced Web browsers such as Netscape 2.0 and Sun Microsystem's HotJava allow execution of multimedia programs, they still lack the interactive power of Hyper-G and its browsers (Amadeus for Windows and Harmony for UNIX). Unlike the proprietary and complex programming languages required by Netscape and Java, Hyper-G servers use a simpler shareware multimedia program for creating online pathfinders and tutorials. The software, called HM-Card, is quite similar to the Macintosh HyperCard. For further information, links to demos and software, and research papers, see the *Hyper-G Home Page* from the Technology University of Graz (Austria) at *http://hyperg.iicm.tu-graz.ac.at/.*

Another way to ensure our viability is to hire recent graduates with technical training. In many institutions, much to their discredit, the traditional practice is to hire experienced librarians who offer no disruption to the status quo. In the new era of technology and turf battles with technocrats, search committees should shun this business-as-usual hiring practice.

Similarly, library schools must guarantee that their graduates receive the necessary skills for applying current technology to the efficient retrieval of appropriate information. Graduates should be aware of next-generation techniques and programs and should demonstrate that they can share their knowledge and training with both patrons and colleagues, perhaps even providing leadership.

Concluding Remarks

Will the digital library replace librarians? Definitely not. The explosive torrent of emerging access tools and techniques will highlight the value of librarians to organize and manage information. Usage of the Internet will probably increase the demand for our services and elevate our status. In a society of information haves and have-nots, libraries are the only public institutions capable of providing all citizens, especially those without their own technical or financial means, to enter the information fast lane. Libraries have the potential to extend their reach worldwide as global networking centers, if only we make it happen.

Patrons approach the reference desk seeking fulfillment of some kind. They don't particularly care how we help them as long as they feel satisfied as a result. If an online resource gets the job done, especially if it's the only resource available, then we have a duty to give customers what they need. By merely surfing the Net, information seekers will soon discover that they need human guidance to find exactly what they want, especially when lost deep in the bowels of Gopher holes or sticky Webs. In many cases, what they really want will be available in libraries, at least in forms more convenient than huge downloadable files, possibly in a seemingly obscure binary format (e.g., PostScript, Microsoft Word, Adobe Acrobat, dBASE, etc.).

Innovative services and technologies offer us an enriching opportunity to attract new customers and inspire the faithful. By displaying enthusiasm for new techniques and resources, librarians instill in their patrons an excitement about research and libraries. Coached by us, Internet users can discover the awesome power of libraries and information, perhaps like the Cornflakes commercial, "again for the first time."

Power Tools for Librarians Too Busy to Surf

Following, in order by preference, are my ten favorite current-awareness tools for quickly assessing the state-of-the-art in Web management and reference use.

International Federation of Library Associations and Institutions. *IFLA Virtual Library.* [Online]. Available: *http://www.nlc-bnc.ca/ifla/II/docs.htm*
> Excellent page for all the best in electronic library resources with an international focus. See especially their large collection of library and information science electronic resources.

University of California at Berkeley. *Web4Lib Archive.* [Online]. Available: *http://sunsite.berkeley.edu/Web4Lib/archive.html*
> Convenient front-end interface for browsing or searching postings of *Web4Lib,* the discussion list created by librarians for cybrarian Webmasters and others concerned with Web applications in libraries. An especially useful feature is their *Library Web Manager's Reference Center,* at: *http://sunsite.berkeley.edu/Web4Lib/faq.html,* which contains the most helpful tips and discussions from *Web4lib* postings.

Ariadne. [Online]. Available: *http://ukoln.bath.ac.uk/ariadne/*
> Designed as an online, free-current awareness magazine for librarians and information professionals. See especially their Web reviews, at: *http://ukoln.bath.ac.uk/ariadne/checkout/*

Middle Tennessee State University. *Innovative Internet Applications in Libraries.* [Online]. Available: *http://frank.mtsu.edu/~kmiddlet/libweb/innovate.html*
> Links arranged by topics, such as bibliographic instruction, cataloging, digital library projects, and library research guides.

Directory of Scholarly and Professional E-Conferences. [Online]. Available: *http://n2b2.com/KOVACS/*
> Searchable Web version of the venerable list compiled by Diane K. Kovacs and the directory team at Kent State University. For one-stop shopping for actual archives of library-oriented e-mail discussions, along with subscription information, see the Texas State Electronic Library's *Library and Information Science Mailing Lists,* at: *http://link.tsl.state.tx.us/1/.dir/libmail.dir*

Where the Wild Things Are: Librarian's Guide to the Best Information on the Net. [Online]. Available: *http://www.sau.edu/CWIS/Internet/Wild/index.htm*

Virtual cornucopia of good stuff compiled by Marylaine Block of St. Ambrose University. Useful sections include Hot Paper Topics, Important Sites by Major Field of Study, Internet Guides and Resources, Librarian's Gold Mine, and What's New on the Net.

Berkeley Digital Library SunSITE. *Current Cites*. [Online]. Available: *http://sunsite.berkeley.edu/CurrentCites/*

Monthly e-publication of the University of California at Berkeley Library. Indexes more than thirty journals in librarianship and information technology. Topics include computer networks and networking, multimedia, hypermedia, expert systems, artificial intelligence, etc. Citations include abstracts.

WWW "How-To" Resources and Guides. [Online]. Available: *http://lcweb.loc.gov/global/www.html*

Let the Library of Congress be your one-stop shop not just for library needs but for Internet needs as well! This page links to dozens of resources regarding Web management, design, usage, and general know-how.

Scout Report. [Online]. Available: *http://rs.internic.net/scout/report/*

Weekly publication, also available via e-mail subscription. The reports, designed for researchers and educators (serious users, unlike the popular *Net-Happenings* that seems to announce far more frivolous and useless sites than useful ones), are conveniently divided into three sections: Research and Education, General Interest, and Network Tools.

Heriot-Watt University, UK. *Internet Resources Newsletter*. [Online]. Available: *http://www.hw.ac.uk/libWWW/irn/irn.html*

Another online current-awareness periodical, with archive, from the UK. Includes lists of new discussion groups, Web sites, and books about the Internet.

10

I've Grown Accustomed to Your (Inter)Face

Why Can't a User Be More Like a Librarian?

(With apologies to *My Fair Lady*'s "Why Can't a Woman Be More Like a Man?")

Pat Ensor

Originally appeared in (1993, May) *Technicalities,* 10–12. Copyright held by Trozzolo Resources, Inc.

Isn't that what we really want, way down deep in our secret heart of hearts? Don't we all spend our days saying, "It drives me crazy that they always . . ." and "No matter how hard we try, they never . . ."? And, "I don't understand how they can . . ."? What we really want is for library users to be more like library staff.

When we want them to be more like us, what do we mean? We want them to do things the right (our) way. We want them to look for information the proper, correct way. We want them to go through the library systematically, in the proper order. We want them to search a computer the way we think it ought to be searched. We want them to be properly gratified that they found citations to information, even if they can't find the information. We want them to read text on paper or on the screen. We want them not to be satisfied with anything less than all the information on a topic, or the best quality information. We want them to want us to train them to use the library and its computer systems. And, most of all, come on, admit it—we want them to use . . . Boolean operators.

If They Won't Read the Classics,
They Can't Read Anything at All

This professional certainty that we know best for library users is not new, of course. We librarians have had a long tradition of not only presenting people with the so-called best literature of the world and the past, in other words, the writings of dead white men, but of trying our best to limit their reading to those works. We were quite willing to consider ourselves experts in what people should read for their own good.

Fortunately, for my reading pleasure, at least, my local public library branch is long past this stage and is quite willing to support my trashy reading habits to the best of its ability. It offers the classics, but it also offers me my mysteries, horror, and true crime. Librarians, for the most part, and certainly as far as their organized public face is concerned, now profess an unwillingness to decide what people should or should not read. Many of them will even fight for the right to present the public with books that some people find repugnant. Of course, they are limited by their resources to being selective, but the average person entering a public library won't be hounded by a 100-year-old woman waving a copy of *Pilgrim's Progress* at them. (If you are uncomfortable with this image, substitute your own "too close for comfort" stereotype.)

Currently, however, many of us who think of ourselves as modern, enlightened, electronically plugged in and turned on, on the bleeding edge, whatever you want to call it, are just Miss Bun-and-Sensible-Shoes in disguise. We knock ourselves out trying to train electronic information users to find and utilize information in the "right" way, in tune with the limitations of the computer system and with the way we've always done things. We spend endless time worrying about why library users won't fall into line with our system.

TQM and Electronic Information Retrieval

Right, you guessed it. You can't read any article nowadays without Total Quality Management [TQM] rearing its ugly head. But in the case of electronic information retrieval, it might well be more productive for librarians to move away from the professional "we know best" model to the "the client knows what she wants" TQM model. How often do we say, "They never . . ." and "They always . . ." before we realize that we need to adjust our behavior and our systems to what they always, or never, want to do?

If electronic information users want to find just a few on-target items about a topic, we should help them do it by not showing them more databases than they need. If they are disappointed and demanding about not finding end results in electronic form, we should spend no time bewailing their ingratitude, but rather redouble our efforts to get them access to sources that are end results in themselves.

If library patrons do not find the highest quality or most complete information by doing computer searches, how is this different from when they did not have computers available? In the print-index era, most patrons did not even know of the existence of print indexes, unless they were among the small minority of people who actually asked a librarian for help or who invested a great deal of effort in discovering these materials themselves. Even when asked, librarians simply showed them the index, explained its purpose, demonstrated how to use the index, and perhaps helped them find a subject heading. They did not peruse the index listings to help the patron judge their quality, and one suspects the patron did not stay any longer than necessary to get the few citations they needed—certainly not long enough to search all the volumes of the index to see if they had the most complete list of material.

Systems Design and the 500-Result Search

Many librarians who see from day to day the way that users interact with electronic information systems have begun to sound the alarm that these pitiful, helpless waifs are so ignorant of their own best interests that they are actually content to get search result sets with 500 hits. These deluded fools will then actually just start looking through the hits till they find enough that they like and be content with that. They simply are so wrong-headed they will not take a moment to realize that they are using these systems incorrectly. If they just took, oh, half an hour to figure it out, or asked their friendly librarian, they could learn the principles of Boolean logic, and get the right number of results—50 to 100.

Pardon me a moment while I scream. AAAAARRRRGGHHHH!!! There, that feels better. Who decided that 50 to 100 results were about right? The answer is librarians who were experts at searching commercial databases that charged for each result printed out. Those of us who are online searchers have long been guilty of trying our best to reduce the universe of information on every topic that was submitted to us to 50 to 100 citations. We just forgot to explain this to the users who now actually get to do their own searches and are so silly as to think that, since they are not being charged for this process, they can spend a longer amount of time doing it.

To look at it another way, look at the olden, pre–end-user computing days when we showed our patrons to the index tables when they wanted magazine articles. Many of them had fairly broad topics, and say they found about 50 articles listed under the heading we helped them find, in one year. Say then, that the user did what any good researcher should do and checked back about ten years. I think you get the point. And these 500 citations were even harder to deal with since the user didn't have a computer to tell "print out the ones I've marked."

What's wrong with looking at a long list of results until you have located enough of them that suit your purpose? Most databases present results with the most recent first, and nothing says that because the user has retrieved 500 results, she has to look at 500 results. Systems that make it easy to create a result set and browse it are the ones most users like best. If the system does not provide almost transparently easy searching, and there are no outside factors like the user not being able to stay on a database as long as she wants, most users prefer to browse result sets even if they're large. I have even done some research that backs this up—two thirds of 400 users of a NOTIS OPAC (Online Public Access Catalog) indicated they'd rather browse a large result set that has irrelevant citations than a small set with higher relevance but lower recall. (The question was asked in understandable terms, not jargon.)[1] There is nothing wrong with a system that tries to accommodate more than one style of information retrieval since no one solution answers everyone's needs, but there is something wrong with having librarians push everyone to use one particular style of searching.

So let's start dealing with this situation in a realistic way. When it doesn't hurt anything for users to browse large result sets, let them. When it does cause a real problem—not just that you think they're doing wrong, but because they are limited in time or not finding anything they want—let's look at system design, not user design. Instead of trying to teach database users the difficult, nonintuitive searching techniques provided with most databases now publicly available, why not try to use every bit of influence we have to provide them with systems that do not make them do all the work?

What kind of systems would these be? These systems perform automatic Boolean operations without the user having to say "and," and they automatically ignore "stop" words and do the search correctly anyway. They rank results so that the most relevant and current ones appear first, and, if requested, they include synonyms for the words included in a search request. They allow the user to easily say, "Get me more results like this one." For those who like to know why they retrieved the results that they did or want to have more control over the searching process, the system should accommodate this, too. If we were able to provide users with systems like this and they still got results sets of 500, perhaps then we can justify griping.

What Influence?

Librarians can ask for these more-intelligent systems in every way at their disposal—at user group meetings, when comments are requested by vendors, when they are asked to participate in focus groups, when they beta test and conduct trials on products, when they review products, when they have done research that might be useful to vendors, when they develop products along with vendors, and above all they can ask for them with their pocket books. Vendors will sell what we will buy, and we should be spending much more time telling them what we want and less time trying to figure out how to teach users to work around poorly designed systems.

Note

1. Ensor, Pat. *Keyword/Boolean Searching on an Online Public Access Catalog: Patrons and Their Perceptions.* ERIC Document ED 337163. 1990.

Knowbot Explorations in Similarity Space

Martin Halbert

Martin Halbert is head of networked systems at Rice University's Fondren Library; his home page address is *http://is.rice.edu/~halbert/*. He continues to be interested in research to support the idea of "similarity spaces" and has spoken and presented widely on various aspects of electronics in libraries.

Originally appeared in *Thinking Robots, an Aware Internet and Cyberpunk Librarians*. Published by the Library and Information Technology Association. Copyright 1992, American Library Association.

A library conversation in 2010
Participants:

> *Carmen,* a philosophy professor
> *Tamara,* a cognitive science graduate student
> *David,* a reference librarian

Carmen: Tamara, I thought you were going to the library to work on the literature review for your thesis research, not to play video games.

Tamara: Oh! Hi, Dr. Rodriguez, you startled me. But, I *am* working on . . .

Carmen: I'm just your thesis advisor, not your den mother. I'll see you later.

Tamara: No, wait! It really isn't a video game, I'm doing an online search of *Philosopher's Index.*

Carmen: Looks more like you're flying over Mars.

Tamara: No, that "planet" is *Philosopher's Index.* I'm not making this up! That's just how the database looks on this work station . . .

David: How's everything going with the search, Tamara?

Tamara: David, I'm glad you came back! I'd like you to meet my thesis advisor, Dr. Carmen Rodriguez. I was just trying to explain to her that I'm doing an online literature search.

David: That's right, Dr. Rodriguez, she's searching a similarity space visualization of a philosophy database.

Carmen: Hmm. I don't remember online searches looking like video games when I did my doctoral research.

David: These holographic simulations are very new. Would you like a quick demonstration of how it works?

Carmen: Sure, you've piqued my curiosity. Could you tell me first of all what we're looking at? The holographic monitor Tamara is using seems to show the surface of some kind of electronically simulated alien world. And what are the other spherical things that look like psychedelic planets hanging in the black sky?

David: All of them are graphical representations of literature databases. The program Tamara is using can present data in a variety of formats, including this "planetscape" type. The program is called a similarity space visualizer.

Carmen: Hold on, back up and explain a few things. I haven't come to the library for an online literature search in several years, but what I remember getting were reams and reams of paper printouts of citations that matched keywords I gave the librarians. I had to sift through all the irrelevant citations looking for the good ones.

David: If you haven't had a search done for you in the last few years, I think you'll be pleasantly surprised. Online searching has advanced quite a bit lately. One of the main things the new systems are good at is prioritizing the output retrieved in terms of relevance to your query.

Carmen: How do they do that?

David: The new similarity comparison systems can statistically compare the words in the database documents with both your initial query and sample documents that you identify as relevant. Then they produce an output list ranked in descending order from most relevant to least relevant.

Carmen: That sounds pretty complicated. I'm not a computer programmer.

David: You don't have to be. The software handles all the complicated and tedious parts. At most, all you have to do is answer simple yes or no questions the system prompts you with. Here, let me show you a practical example, the search I helped Tamara with today. And let me also introduce you to the search tool we used, which is called a knowbot.

Carmen: A knowbot? What's that?

David: Knowbots are programs that collect information from network databases and organize it for you. Tamara and I created a knowbot this morning to do the literature review for her thesis.

Carmen: I gather that a knowbot isn't a physical robot. But what is it, exactly? How do you make one?

David: The same way you set up a spreadsheet or an electronic mail message on the computer. A knowbot, like a spreadsheet, is basically a collection of data that you use the computer to manipulate and produce new information. A knowbot is a bit more sophisticated, in that it can also make decisions and recommendations for you, like an expert system. In fact a knowbot is really just a kind of specialized expert system that deals with databases accessible through computer networks.

Carmen: Are knowbots intelligent, then?

David: No, certainly not intelligent in the sense that a human is intelligent. However, they can transmit, transform, and store immense amounts of data. Knowbots developed inevitably from the point when computers were networked together and used to store large distributed databases. You need tools similar to knowbots in order to gather and organize information from computer networks. Knowbots grew out of a combination of ideas from network bulletin boards, electronic mail systems, and expert systems.

Carmen: Show me the one you made for Tamara.

David: Do you see this cluster of text windows in the holographic display? That's the knowbot. This window displays all the information on Tamara's query request, starting with the sentence she typed in that framed her information need: "I am writing a doctoral thesis on the historical development of the concept of human rights, with a focus on the philosophical doctrine of heterotelism, and I want to review the literature on the subject."

Carmen: It can understand sentences?

David: The knowbot has a natural-language parser, or program to break down sentences into components that it can analyze. It prompts you with yes or no questions to make sure it has analyzed your query correctly. As I said before, it's important to remember that it really is not intelligent. It can only apply its rules of programming to your query. We refined the query in various ways as we went along, but we started out with Tamara's sentence.

Carmen: I think I understand. What happened then?

David: Then we went to the window of the knowbot that governs network operations and typed in where we wanted the knowbot to search. You can either type in the identifying names for specific databases or pick them from a pop-up menu. Based on topical focus and journal coverage, Tamara and I picked out five databases that we thought would give us the best results. If we had wanted to, we could have picked clusters of databases or entire regions of the network. You usually don't want to tell the knowbot to search entire network regions because of the cost involved in searching through so much data. That brings us to another very important piece of information that goes in the network window, the knowbot's operating budget.

Carmen: What? I have to put it on a budget, like my husband?

David: You sure do. When the knowbot is activated, it will connect to the network systems that you have chosen, translate your query into executable searches on those systems according to their protocols, gather information, and collect it on your work station. Most of the network databases that you will typically want to search are commercial repositories of information and charge fees for providing your knowbot with information. Your knowbot has to know how much money you want to spend on the search!

Carmen: But how on earth would I know how much money would be needed or reasonable to spend?

David: The knowbot has current information about the fee schedules of different database systems and can estimate the cost of a given query. In other words, it can tell you about how much the search will cost.

Carmen: Hmm. But since we're searching so many different databases at once, won't the costs of retrieving all those articles and citations be astronomical?

David: Not at all, because at this point we aren't retrieving the actual information yet, just information about the information!

Carmen: That sounds like it would cost even more money.

Tamara: No, it's like asking a store for a catalog of their merchandise. You haven't bought anything yet, you're just trying to find out if they have anything you want.

David: Right. They may still charge you for the catalog, but not a great deal. After all, they want you to see all the great things they have to offer.

Carmen: Okay. So then what happens?

David: The knowbot "looks through the catalogs." It compares the query you gave it with the documents in the various databases. It finds the documents that are the most similar to your query in statistical terms. It ranks them in descending order and, depending on how much budget it has left, retrieves as many as are affordable of the top candidate documents. These will be the items that are most likely to be relevant to your needs and not just any citations that happen to contain a few keywords you entered.

Tamara: It produces great results. The first time we did a search we retrieved and printed out the top 50 hits. Almost all of them were exactly on my topic. We told the knowbot which ones I liked best. We also told the knowbot about some that weren't useful to me.

David: That's right. An important part of using knowbots for searching is that you can refine the knowbot's understanding of your information needs. After we picked the top five and the worst five items in the first list it retrieved for Tamara, it used the information to statistically modify its profile of her query. After that it didn't make any mistakes that we noticed in ranking its output.

Carmen: That's quite impressive. Now I have a better idea of what you're talking about. But you still haven't explained what a "similarity space" is.

David: One of the things that the knowbot can do is feed data into another specialized program that can graphically represent the characteristics of the databases the knowbot has explored. Graphical representations can show you patterns in the literature that are useful for the researcher to know about. A graphical representation of the similarity relationships of documents in a database is called an SSV for similarity space visualization, or simspace for short. It's a "space" in the sense that the statistical measurements of similarity between documents are represented by spatial relationships. An SSV typically looks like zillions of multicolored dots clustered in clouds or surface shapes. Each dot represents a document in the database. For any given document, the neighboring dots will be other documents that are statistically similar to it. The colors, heights from the surface plane, and other aspects of the graphics can represent other data, but the main idea is that documents that are similar in concepts will be close spatially. Let me reactivate the simspace associated with Tamara's knowbot so you can see an example.

Carmen: It certainly is colorful.

Tamara: I think these simspace graphics are beautiful.

David: I find the simspace visualizer fun to work with because it can transform an enormous amount of data into gorgeous patterns that you can grasp intuitively.

Carmen: So these "planets" are databases indexing different kinds of literature. What a strange concept.

David: The visualizer can represent the similarity data in lots of ways. Those spheres are representations of the five databases that Tamara and I decided to explore. Each representation is a simspace normalized or "mapped" onto a sphere. Some of the spheres are bigger than others because they have more documents than others. Color and "altitude" on the surfaces of the simspace spheres indicate relevance to Tamara's query. Let's take a closer look at one of these simspaces, the little one there that sort of looks like Mars.

Carmen: Hmph. Those other spheres that look like gas giants must contain some of my colleagues' work. You use a joystick to move the view around? I thought joysticks were just for video games.

David: Video games usually involve a lot of three-dimensional movement, and most people are accustomed to using joysticks in that context. We use joysticks when working with simspaces because they are an effective control device. It is sort of fun though, too. . . .

Tamara: Yes, the effect is like flying a spacecraft down to the simspace planets.

David: Would you like to "fly" it, Dr. Rodriguez?

Carmen: Well, now that you've offered, yes! It looks intriguing. How do I make it work?

David: That slider controls your "speed." The joystick handles just like a video game aircraft. See if you can maneuver the view down to the surface of the red "planet."

Carmen: This is fun. Hmm. The surface detail is incredible. What are all the red continents with spiky mountains? This "planet" is actually a database, right?

David: Right, you're currently cruising over the "surface" of *Philosopher's Index,* a database published in Bowling Green, Ohio. The "mountainous regions" are clusters of documents that are more akin to Tamara's research interests than the surrounding "plains." Fly in closer to that region of peaks.

Carmen: The one with the blinking lights? What is that, anyway, a colony?

David: Sort of. Quit laughing, Tamara. Those blinking lights at the peaks are the documents that Tamara retrieved during her first search. The visualizer marks them for future reference.

Carmen: Why are the mountains red, and the flatlands green and blue?

David: When I asked Tamara how to color the landscape, she picked a spectrum in which red means "most relevant" on one end, and blue means "least relevant" on the other end. The color is just another way of viewing the relationships in the database. Red mountains are what she wanted to look for. You could just as easily reverse the graphical representation so that the most relevant regions of the database showed up as purple valleys.

Carmen: Hmm, let me see if I can "land" this spaceship of the mind. Hey! Now that we're near the surface I can see all kinds of . . . objects? What are those things, trees or what?

David: The visualizer is programmed to represent some kinds of documents in special ways to distinguish them. The "trees," as you call them, in this simspace represent review articles. Critiques, overview articles, and other identifiable classes of documents are represented by other distinctive shapes.

Carmen: I see. So how do I actually retrieve one of these documents if I want to read it?

David: Hold down this button on the stick and cross hairs will appear. Center the cross hairs on a surface object, pull the trigger and the system will retrieve the text of that item from the database.

Carmen: Fascinating. So I could investigate why this entire ridge of spiked shrubs is so reddish and therefore relevant to Tamara's needs presumably?

David: Exactly.

Carmen: Let me try the trigger. I wish I could shoot down the arguments of some philosophers this easily. Interesting! This window that's popped up contains . . . what, a citation and abstract?

David: Right. It's from a colloquium on heterotelism, Tamara's main topic of interest. The "shrubs" as you call them must all be citations to articles from this colloquium.

Tamara: And now that spot shows a blinking light, like the others I've looked at. I really think this search will help my thesis a lot.

Carmen: It certainly livens up the process of scholarly research. It also poses an ethical question.

David: What's that?

Carmen: This holographic work station looks pretty expensive. Businesses, research centers, and rich universities like ours may be able to afford this kind of gadget, but what about the average people on the street? When do they get to explore similarity space?

David: You have a very good point there. It's the old question of the information haves and have nots. Information technology is only liberating for those who have access to it.

Tamara: I never thought of that. Now I feel kind of guilty sitting here using this computer.

David: There are a lot of other ethical questions raised by new systems like this. It's easier than ever to pirate information. The database vendors lose a lot of money to software pirates who use knowbots to illegally copy similarity spaces, falsify account information, and other shady activities.

Carmen: I suppose Pandora's technology box never gives you uncomplicated gifts.

Tamara: Well, I still like the searching I can do on this work station.

Carmen: I have to admit, I find the possibilities fascinating. Has anyone used similarity spaces to study patterns of scholarly research and activity? It strikes me that you could use these visualizations to study all kinds of patterns in the literature. For instance, does a paradigm shift look like a cresting wave on a simspace beach?

David: Now you're beyond my expertise. Why don't you log on and find out?

Notes

The idea of similarity spaces was inspired by a presentation by Scott Deerwester at the 1991 annual conference of the American Library Association. His presentation involved the use of a NeXT work station to graphically show clustering properties of citations in terms of similarity. Although he did not use the term "similarity space," and his graphical representations were not much like what I have described in this dialogue, his presentation nevertheless inspired in me the strong belief that graphical representations of database properties are a wave of the future.

For an excellent discussion of the general concept of similarity space (the more traditional term in information retrieval research is "Vector Space")

see the classic textbook *Automatic Text Processing* by Gerard Salton (Reading, MA: Addison-Wesley, 1988), chapter 10.

For a more abstracted and advanced discussion of the problems of similarity analysis, see the book *Multidimensional Similarity Structure Analysis* by Ingwer Borg and James Lingoes (New York: Springer-Verlag, 1987).

SEVEN BUTTONS

A USER-FRIENDLY, PATRON-APPROPRIATE TECHNIQUE

Rebecca Owl and Robert Morgan

Rebecca Owl is at Idaho State University and Robert Morgan is at Eastern Montana College.

Originally appeared in (1994, August) *Audiovisual Librarian,* 220–2. Copyright held by Aslib, Association for Information Management.

Libraries make a significant contribution in their role as bridge between breakthrough and application. Scientific and medical advances may languish for years before becoming available to the professional community unless the fresh information is effectively and quickly transmitted to those most needing it. Further, this transmission needs to take into account the specific needs, desires, and talents of their clientele.

In a university library setting, faculty and students may often find themselves in the geographic proximity of this new knowledge, but the library lacks a clear mechanism to call their attention to the material and, more important, to create a successful transmission for the important information.

A library, moving into the technology of a postmodern world, may begin employing certain attention techniques borrowed from advertising. Large electronic billboards of the kind normally found in hotels and bars to share baseball scores may be used to flash updates on newly acquired materials offering breakthroughs in various fields. In such a setting, the patron might then, once aware of the subject via the billboard display, step up to speak the subject into a microphone and push one of the buttons for a user-friendly, patron-appropriate information transmission.

The buttons are listed and numbered in order of increasing convenience to the patron.

Button Number 1 Once pushed, the original journal articles or technical books containing the breakthrough material appear. Copyright or other fees are charged to the patron or library, depending on the budget.

> *Other Alternatives:* List of journal citations, list of original technical books.
>
> *Down side:* Many faculty and students don't care to follow the jargon typical of technical sources. For them, button 2 might be better.

Button Number 2 Pushing this button produces books and articles written specifically for the public, ones that might be also found in book stores or on the bus at the end of the day. These are much more readable.

> *Other Alternatives:* List of same books and articles, some discount coupons.
>
> *Down side:* This still involves reading, something many in the university community would prefer not to devote so much time to. Of course, we also still sacrifice living trees. On to button 3.

Button Number 3 This button will produce a more colorful and inexpensive version of the information: full color comic books (e.g., *Classic Comics*).

> *Other Alternatives:* Listing of same plus library lottery opportunity.
>
> *Down side:* Some might feel this approach lacks prestige or thoroughness. Still not interested in reading for very long, they push number 4.

Button Number 4 Following the depression of this button, the patron receives copies of articles on the subject derived from the supermarket checkout newspapers (*Enquirer, Examiner,* etc). These are, of course, much more immediately involving.

> *Other Alternatives:* Listing of same plus opportunity to buy moon land before the rush.
>
> *Down side:* It has been alleged that these sources lack credibility, accuracy, decency, and oral hygiene (but not imagination). Any observer of the postmodern library knows many patrons really never developed much interest in reading of any kind. For a TV generation, depressing this button might still be depressing. On to button number 5.

Button Number 5 Tickling this button produces MTV-style videotapes on the breakthrough subject, materials most libraries increasingly stock in their media center. This allows the receptive trance state unique to TV monitors to do its educational work, even allowing hands free for chips and romance.

> *Other Alternatives:* List of videos with discount coupons for over the weekend and proportion ratings for violence, nudity, coherent dialogue.
>
> *Down side:* Still requiring concentration and possibly subtracting much valued time from other television or Nintendo. Button number 6 offers a more personal approach.

Button Number 6 Some time and money has been devoted in progressive libraries to special facilities for the physically challenged (less so for educationally or morally challenged). By hiring drama students, engrossing live readings and reenactments may illustrate the material for all patrons. Pushing the button provides a map and entry ticket for this service. For many, being read to is much better than reading for oneself.

> *Alternatives:* Interactive readers draw the listener into the material through dance, music, art, or body massage.
>
> *Downside:* Although reading is no longer needed by the patron, time and effort is still involved. We can do better.

Button Number 7 Poking this last button produces the key and map for a private library alcove stocked with comfortable bed and earphones. The patron then takes a welcome timesaving nap while incorporating the critical information as sleep-learning. This combines the acquisition of knowledge with a wellness approach to health.

> *Other Alternatives:* Couples may wish to use this technique while sharing affection: a fun way to stay on top of the field.
>
> *Downside:* Research is equivocal on this form of learning. Worth trying though.

We are working on further buttons, even more attuned to today's post-modern electronic generation. Reader suggestions are welcome.

11

Do You Mean the New Online or the Old Online?

One World Linked by the Universal Machine

Barbara Quint

Barbara Quint is editor-in-chief of Information Today, Inc.'s *Searcher: The Magazine for Database Professionals* and a long-time searcher. Her Internet address is *BQUINT@NETCOM.COM*.

Originally appeared in (1995, October) *Information Today*, 6–8. Copyright held by Information Today, Inc.

Charles Babbage and his programmer, Ada Lovelace, outlined the design of the "Analytical Engine" in the early nineteenth century. They dreamed of a machine that could perform any and all mechanical functions. In the twentieth century, John Von Neumann developed the architecture that produced the universal computer. Although historians say Von Neumann never saw the work of Babbage or Lovelace, his accomplishment resembles their dream plans. Break any complex physical action down into its component mechanisms. Program the computer to perform the repetitive tasks. Customize the interface to suit the problem. There you have the Universal Machine, a single machine that can perform any mechanical function from adding and subtracting to cooking a good cup of coffee, from sending a spaceship to the moon to telling time.

So here we are in the last few gasps of the twentieth century. At present, the Universal Machine seems to be the computer and its friendly peripherals.

By the way, remember when people used to use the phrase "twentieth century" as a kind of moral or aesthetic club with which to threaten dullards, as in "Oh, honestly, this *is* the twentieth century"? I always loved the reply a supporting character gave to such a dismissal in the Billy Wilder movie, *Sabrina,* "Twentieth century! Humph! I could pick a better century out of a hat—blindfolded!" No matter what the next century holds, I doubt

its title will have the same cachet. "Come on, this *is* the twenty-first century," just doesn't scan somehow. Too many syllables. And, "Really, this *is*
the third millennium," doesn't do it either. Millennial references depress
everyone. Too massive a reminder of the narrow scope of human mortality,
I suppose. Besides, is anyone really sure when the next millennium starts?
Is it 2001 or 2100 or what? A case of multivitamin supplements should get
most of us to the year 2001, but that other one could be a stretch.

Converging Technologies

All asides aside, where is that Universal Machine today? Where will it take
us tomorrow? Actually, two "universal machines" have converged, with a
third one only a heartbeat away. The computer, with its ability to manipulate information input to produce new output, has melded with the Internet, to produce a universal knowledge machine. And now multimedia technology—television, video, movies, etc.—is rushing to join. The rise of
universal interfaces, whether Windows or Mac GUI (Graphical User Interface) interfaces or the popular Netscape or Mosaic Internet browser, ho-
mogenizes the presentation of information even further. If we hurry, this
century will close on the stunning technological achievement of the development of an integrated technical tool that offers a common and universal
access to all (or almost all) human knowledge.

Do any of you Trekkers out there remember that scene in one of the
Star Trek movies (I can never keep the numbers straight, the one with the
whales) where the crew returned to the twentieth century? Kirk needed a
few brilliant calculations. Scottie turned to a nearby computer and started
asking questions—out loud. Imagine his chagrin when the darn thing
wouldn't answer! The audience laughed at the scene. Do any of you really
believe that Trekker conventions in the year 2025 or 2010 or maybe even
2005 will laugh at the idea of expecting a machine to understand and reply
in speech? That's almost as silly as doubting whether the twenty-first century
will host Trekker conventions.

Look at the Internet component of the Universal Machine. The first AR-
PANET-networked computers went operational in 1969. It was only in 1983
that they adopted the TCP/IP [Transmission Control Protocol/Internet Pro-
tocol] protocol. Someday when you misplace your remote-control zapper,
watch the credits at the end of TV news shows. Most of them now carry
Internet addresses. Just today I saw an Internet address and a Web URL
[Uniform Resource Locator] for a local humane society's pet placement
show. (Can you really e-mail a kitten?) Considering how much most people
rely on electronic communication—phone, fax, e-mail—for ordering objects,
one might consider UPS and FedEx the three-dimensional form of "hard
copy" delivery. Fax has taken over most of the two-dimensional delivery.

The convergence of machinery is as awesome as the massive increase
in information created and carried on the Net. Think about the concept of
the client-server architecture—Your Machine, My Machine, Our Machine,
The Machine. Experienced professional searchers all have funny stories to

tell about end users who don't understand the differences between a database provider and a database service, between a source and a system. "So this guy says to me, 'Well, if an average search costs $25, could you search just one database for $5?' and I asked him, 'Which one?' and he says, 'DIALOG.' What a hoot!"

No one's laughing any more. One Internet access provider account can get anyone onto the Net and from there, a browser and a credit card can get you about anywhere else in the online universe. Novices and current nonsubscribers to commercial services might take a little longer to reach their target, but with time and money, they could have the same access as anyone else.

At this point, about the only barrier to The Machine's total dominance is the distraction of entertainment. People still want to watch television more than to work with a computer. A recent survey published in *Interactive Age* indicated residents of homes with computers and televisions spent about equal times with each. What happens when the television becomes a computer? Already the proliferation of cable channels has created a flow problem that will probably require a computer to solve. *TV Guide* has opened an electronic service, you'll be happy to know.

How long before computers dominate the delivery of entertainment as much as they are coming to dominate the delivery of information? Say you're working hard on The Machine, while you listen to some music in the background. The music doesn't suit your mood, so you may have to turn to the radio and start fiddling with knobs or else get up and go through your CD collection. Then suddenly you remember! No problem. Just click out of workplace and onto the Net and over to the music/radio section to pick the category or even the tune of your choice. Click back to your work as the Net feeds the SoundBlaster program. "Music hath charms to soothe a savage breast."

The Machine, The Company, The Library, The . . .

Convergence also affects the institutions that serve the users. The line between publishing and telecommunications and computers continues to melt away. All content providers can now reach the Internet's mammoth audience fairly cheaply and reasonably easily. That puts pressure on the traditional commercial search services—or it will when the content providers can figure out a reliable way to collect money for their products. Frankly, solving the problem of money collection should come pretty quickly, I would reckon. It also puts pressure on traditional publishers to produce a diversified product line. This could explain West Publishing's decision to stop going it alone.[1]

Some sectors of the database industry face particular challenges. Ironically, information professionals as a group are among them. After years of being the only reliable way to reach online information, new classes of end users—which may include the corporate librarians' bosses—now think they can go it alone. After all, they have a Windows interface and an Internet address. What more could it take? It would be funny if it weren't so painful. Still, top-notch information professionals have begun converting from handlers of data to bookers of data. In days gone by, rich men's chauffeurs probably converted to car sales or became garage owners after Ford's model Ts and model As filled the roads, and automobiles stopped being rich men's toys.

Vendors that traditionally market to and through information professionals have begun to change their strategies. Two leading vendors, in particular, have been forging alliances, developing products, and acquiring companies; this seems to indicate a long-term survival strategy that answers the question, "Is there life after libraries?" If libraries go under, these vendors do not intend to go down with them. Instead they may supply a centralized information-delivery service with branches that could substitute and ultimately turn into The Library. OCLC had targeted public and academic libraries. This year they introduced a complete document-delivery service supporting their EPIC and FirstSearch online service. If you have a citation, OCLC can deliver it.

Knight-Ridder Information, Inc. [KRI], seems to have a similar grand strategy. They have a deal to supply retail searches on demand through DialSearch and through a wide expansion of their document-delivery capabilities with the acquisition of CARL. Recently they brought a substantial minority interest in Teltech, a library outsourcing operation. KRI president, Pat Tierney, will be on Teltech's board. Teltech recently got the contract that outsourced General Electric's libraries. How long before KRI becomes The Library for corporations and agencies as OCLC moves in on more-traditional libraries? [See "OPACs and More" elsewhere in this book for URLs of online vendors.]

Because I am an information professional, such developments leave me in something of a quandary. I don't like seeing friends and colleagues (not to mention myself) at risk. On the other hand, if centralized information services can deliver better, faster, cheaper data (two out of three will do), then they should get the business. Still, I have some real questions about letting vendors make ultimate decisions on the acquisition of critical information. When a company or a client employs an information professional, they have some assurance that the professional works for their interest first. What are the chances that "house brokers," intermediary searchers working for specific vendors, will tell customers that the answers to their questions lie in databases on competitor services? And where are the economics of scale in outsourcing? Wouldn't they lie in serving multiple companies in an industry, to maximize the return on present skills and resources by producing similar answers to similar questions for similar clients? If I got the contract for GE's libraries, for example, wouldn't it make sense to go after Westinghouse's libraries next? But what happens to critical areas of privacy and proprietary protection when the same company serves competitors? Law librarians bemoan the death of some leading law firms' libraries recently. How on earth could one guarantee fully protected confidentiality of legal services with outsourced legal research?

Of course, one could depend on end-user information services entirely. You know, if libraries or information professionals ever had a vicious bone in their bodies—which, of course, none of them do—this could get pretty funny, in a sinister kind of way. Always supposing we have the pensions or golden handshake funds to keep us alive long enough to watch the show, it ought to be a real scream observing know-it-all amateurs as they try to find the right information at the best price with nothing more than a short training in Windows navigation and in an Internet browser. How did Texas Guinan put it all those years ago? Oh, yeah. "Hello, suckers!"

The most digitally committed executives would be wiser to keep their librarians, even if they decide to get rid of the libraries. To paraphrase the Scriptures, "The race is not always to the swift nor the battle to the strong nor the knowledge to the expert—but that's the way to bet."

On the other hand, the best way to reveal one's expertise may be to rely upon its value in new environments. Maybe corporate librarians should go to work for the outsourcers. At least, they would finally work for employers who appreciated and understood their skills and performance. Perhaps information brokers and consultants should head off into the Net to bring order out of the chaos but with a personal touch. Designing services would offer more opportunities for entrepreneurial accomplishment.

It's a brave new world we live in, a brave new "one world" linked by the Universal Machine.

Note

1. "West Publishing Bankers to Explore Opportunities." (1995, October). *Information Today,* 1.

There's Nothing New Under the Sun

Or, All New! All Improved! It's Online Searching!

Pat Ensor

Originally appeared in (1993, March) *Technicalities,* 7–8. Copyright held by Trozzolo Resources, Inc.

Hi, it's the late sixties, and I have this great database of stuff that we put together for the members of our society, Dirty Joketellers of America. Yeah, we put it on a mainframe computer, and now we can search it by topic, sexual orientation, audience level, critical review—it's called SMUTLAF. You know, we'd like it to be available more widely, and I think we can make some money off of this.

We don't have the data communication structure to support a whole bunch of people dialing into this thing, though. And it would be a bad trip to get into this whole marketing thing. Plus, the way it works is even tough for the staff to figure out; how could we explain it to a bunch of other people?

Huh? Duolog? What's that? You mean, they put these tapes on their computer, organize them, set up dial-in, and let people search them the same way they search a bunch of other databases? And they market it? And we get some of the money? Wow, groovy, what's the catch? We probably don't get much of the money, I bet, but it would probably be worth it to avoid the hassle. You know, you hate to put all this work into something and not have a bunch of people use it.

The Eighties: The Next Meaningful Step

Hi, I'm Larry; I'll be your systems programmer for today. CD-ROM? Yeah, I've heard of it. If a reference librarian has heard of it, I've heard of it. I thought you were into online searching, though, like with Duolog? Yeah, I know, it's tough to use so only people with training and experience can do it right. It's on a mainframe and it's command-based, so how can you expect the average library schlub to do it?

I agree, what really makes that a problem is how they charge you an arm and a leg for every second you're on there, plus charges for how much information you get out of it. No way an amateur could use these things at a decent cost. And the telecommunications aren't all that fast or dependable. Mmm, I'm convinced it's got problems. And you think CD-ROMs will solve them?

Okay, you want us to get our own copy of SQUIDBIB, a complete bibliographic database on squid and octopi. We do use that one an awful lot, I know, but we have to have a microcomputer we can put this on out in the public, plus it will have to have a CD-ROM player attached to it. Those things run about $1,000, but I bet the prices will drop soon. At least CD-ROMS aren't pay-as-you-go, though—how much is this one annually, $1,500, was it?

You got it, as far as I'm concerned. And I know these things are supposed to be easier to use, since they can take advantage of microcomputer interface capabilities and they've been designed for the average Jane Q. Public to search. And I guess there won't be any telecommunications problems; the things are right there, all the time. But will you reference librarians be able to handle this computing stuff day to day? Not all of you did online searching, but now this is something that will be right out there in public, every day, and don't think you're going to call me every time there's a question. Okay, okay, if you think you can do it, let's go ahead.

Network CD-ROMs? It'll Never Work

Yeah, this is Larry. I heard you were talking about the possibility of networking those ten CD-ROM work stations we've got. I don't know, I've heard people who really know say that just doesn't work, the CD-ROM drives are just too slow. Well, I guess we could get some of those new, faster kind, but that'll cost us, plus we'll have to get hardware and software to do the networking, and it don't come cheap.

Isn't it working well enough, just having the separate stations? We systems people work really hard on keeping those going. Service problems, huh? I guess it's a problem that only one person can use one database at a time. I heard you had to buy another copy of SQUIDBIB last month. And you have fifteen databases now, with only ten stations. Some of those databases have more than one disc, too. You have to keep taking discs in and out; yeah, I sure do know it's a problem that they keep getting dirty and scratched—we have to clean 'em all the time. And I know a disc got stolen last year.

Okay, we're already setting up a local area network in the library, so I'll look into what's involved in networking the CD-ROM stations. On your end of things, you know you'll probably have to pay more for each of those databases to network them? And we don't know how many people will be able to use them at once without getting bad performance out of the databases, let alone how many users the CD-ROM vendors will allow at once. And they'll still all use different searching interfaces. You know, wouldn't it be great if online searching could work like this, with the fixed, affordable price, reliable connections, and be really easy to use? 'Cause that's what we're doing here, starting to become our own online vendor.

Load *What* Locally?

Load tapes of databases locally? Now we're really getting into the online business! Why do you think databases vendors set up these big companies to take care of this stuff? Oh well, of course, we can do it, I'm not saying we can't. But those things don't come locally loaded, you know! And they don't come with their own software either. Do you know how much disk space they take up, too? There's no way we can ever load all the ones you'd want.

Have you talked to anybody about the costs of these things? Well, on the software, up front, we're talking $80,000 to $100,000, plus ongoing costs. I can't even estimate disk storage costs till we've decided which databases, for how many years of coverage, and whether we'll have abstracts or not. Each database will have an ongoing charge, too, and some of them are pretty steep and have crazy ways of determining fees—per terminal, or some such nonsense.

I guess it would really be preferable to CD-ROM networks for patron service for some of the most used databases, though. We could buy database-loading software that would look just like our OPAC, so it would make it a lot easier for the users. And the mainframe can support dial-in access really easily, whereas it's a little tougher for the CD-ROM network. And for some strange reason, database producers will deal with dial-in access to loaded tapes with no problem, while they don't even seem to comprehend the word "dial access" occurring anywhere near "CD-ROM." And maybe search performance will be better overall on a mainframe, although don't bet the farm on that one. Well, it's just like all these changes we've been going through, if you can get the money together, I guess we can do it.

The New Online?

Oh, no, you don't! I've seen you coming now! You're not talking me into anything else that has anything to do with computers and periodical databases! We spent tons of money, worked hundreds of hours, we ran out of disk space months ago, and I can only regenerate indexes by shutting everything down and chanting spells at midnight on Halloween! We're getting poorer and poorer response time, and we still haven't talked everyone out of searching the word "squid" on SQUIDBIB! It's 1994; can't we see our way to some better solution because I can't add any more databases!

I know we've been working on connecting our CD-ROM network to the OPAC, but I still don't think CD-ROM is a long-term solution. Yeah, I know "long-term" means six months, but still . . . I'm starting to remember the good old days of online searching. What was it lacking—ease of use and choice of interface, fixed price, and high-quality telecommunications. If we could just figure out a way to get over those things but not keep hundreds of separate copies of SQUIDBIB all over the country; I mean, that's more calamari research capability than the world needs.

Z39.50? Sure, I know about that. Hey, that's an idea; I know our automation vendor is working on making the OPAC interface compliant with Z39.50. Now, if the people that produce SQUIDBIB would just do that. . . . They are, huh? So we could access a copy they maintain through our OPAC, they're used to getting paid a fixed price for unlimited usage, and we wouldn't have to keep a copy of it here. Yeah, I know we might have telecommunications problems, but they're a heck of a lot more powerful today than they used to be. And, like I said, it's not like we don't have problems searching it with it loaded here.

I like it, but it sure sounds like online searching with most of the kinks worked out. Yeah, it'll do, till the next big thing comes along. . . .

Editor's note: Although he should receive no blame for this piece, some of the thoughts were inspired by conversations with Tom Wilson, Head of Systems, University of Houston Libraries, whose article "Zen and the Art of CD-ROM Network License Negotiation" appears later in this book.

Consumer Online Services

Yes, consumer online services is what many of our users and most of the media mean nowadays when they refer to "online services"—Prodigy, America Online, Microsoft Network, etc. Librarians have not tended to stay very up-to-date on developments with these services since, with a few exceptions, libraries did not really find very good ways to use them in their operations. We need to be much more aware of them for two reasons: more and more of our "wired" users will be getting a lot of information this way, and some of these online services have big effects on the "browser wars." So here are the home pages of the major players and a few sites for staying current.

Online Company Home Pages

These tend to describe services, provide an access into the service for those with accounts, include a sampling of content, and give subscription information.

America Online. (1996). *America Online*. [Online]. Available: *http://www. aol.com/*

CompuServe. (1996). *CompuServe*. [Online]. Available: *http://www. compuserve.com/*

Genie Online Services. (1996). *Genie Services Home Page*. [Online]. Available: *http://www.genie.com/*

Microsoft Network. (1996). *MSN Welcomes You to the Internet!* [Online]. Available: *http://www.msn.com/*

Prodigy Services Company. (1996). *Prodigy Services*. [Online]. Available: *http://www.prodigy.com/*

News and Commentary

Egelhof, James. (1996). *Why AOL Sucks.* [Online]. Available: *http://www.cloud9.net/~jegelhof/*

Finley, Tom. (1996, February). *America Online: Why Should You Not Support It?* [Online]. Available: *http://www.en.com/users/tfinley/*
Wanna read openly biased information about America Online and find out what all the fuss is about? Wanna ponder how some people need to get a life? Check out the above two sites.

Seidman, Robert. *Seidman's Online Insider.* [Online]. Available: *http://www.clark.net/pub/robert/*
This is a genuine news source devoted exclusively to consumer online services and appearing weekly.

To keep up to date on what is coming out about consumer online services, check Yahoo as follows: *http://www.yahoo.com/Business_and_Economy/Companies/Computers/Networking/Online_Services/.*

Many of the Web publications cited in "Check These Out Regularly" (previously in this book) also include news about consumer online services.

It's Time Once Again to Ask [Alternate] Dr. Internet!

1. What's the deal with "Silicon Snake Oil"?

In 1990, Cliff Stoll wrote a quirky little book called "The Cuckoo's Egg," which turned out to be a surprise hit. NBC was even poised to make it into a movie of the week (starring Bruce Boxleitner and Cheryl Ladd), but the production fell through at the last minute. Network executives wanted to change the title to "Dark Desires: Profile of a Spy Tracker" but Stoll stood firm on the original title. NBC abandoned the project and PBS picked up the option for an episode of NOVA—for a substantially reduced fee.

Embittered by the experience, Stoll turned against the Internet, successfully albeit reiteratively attacking some of the more hyperinflated claims made about it. A repeated criticism in his new book "Silicon Snake Oil" is that the Net allows many people to act as authors but has few people acting as editors, as can be observed in this column. One wonders, though, what Doubleday's excuse is.

(Readers should note that historical research like this can be hard to verify with complete certainty. The "Cliff's Evil Twin" theory cannot be entirely ruled out.)

2. What are SLIP and PPP connections?

SLIP and PPP are two mechanisms for demonstrating that you need a faster modem. With Father's Day coming up, I invited my family into Dr. Internet Labs to demonstrate modem speed in downloading some Web pages laden with extraneous graphics (a keyword search for "Netscape enhanced" usually turns these up). The speed of the PPP connection left us plenty of time to discuss the merits of 28.8k modems versus neckties and aftershave.

The difference between the two is that SLIP is only inadequate for IP connections, whereas PPP is insufficient for multiple networking protocols.

3. What is the Clipper chip?

Earlier this year, the America's Cup team from New Zealand licensed Computer Associates' Clipper database software for help in designing their keel. To optimize performance, CA rewrote parts of the program in firmware, creating the now famous Clipper chip. Concerned that a niche market was developing, Microsoft immediately announced plans to include keel design software in the next version of Microsoft Office.

Novell, whose own Corsair program let Dennis Conner down so badly, claimed that Microsoft's entry into yacht design was anticompetitive and asked the Department of Justice to investigate. The Justice Department discovered that most electronic messages in the highly secretive yacht-design industry are encrypted and insisted that the government impose a common encryption system that would protect data in general but would allow the government to hold a decryption key.

The future of Clipper encryption is uncertain; due to the race results, New Zealand's government would hold the key for at least the next three years.

4. The online industry seems to be taking after the larger computer industry in the way larger companies consume smaller ones. What will be the next big buyout?

Oracle will purchase Delphi, combining forces to create a new online service that can answer any question. However, early beta tests indicate that the answers, while technically correct, will be subject to whatever interpretation the questioner wanted in the first place.

Tune in next time for Ask Dr. Internet—
"I have a master's degree . . . in
Internet!"

Dr. Internet, Master of All Knowledge
Benedictine On the Rocks With a Twist
No official connection to Dr. Science

Editor's note: [Alternate] Dr. Internet is channeled by
Thomas Dowling, who holds copyright on these effusions. You can find his contact information in his chapter on "Multimedia File Formats," which is more serious. At least, I think it is.

Anyway, you can find more wisdom of [Alternate]
Dr. Internet at *http://chehalis.lib.washington.edu/dri*

12

Cyberspace Needs Technical Service

CATALOGING THE INTERNET

ISSUES AND VIEWPOINTS

Judy E. Myers

Judy Myers is assistant to the director at the University of Houston Libraries. One of the developers of Reference Expert, an expert system for reference work, she has written widely on this and other electronic projects. She may be reached as *JM@UH.EDU*.

This essay elaborates on my belief that, in the electronic age, libraries should stick with their core tasks but may perform them in new ways. Some of the components of this belief are

- In the electronic age libraries can, and should, continue to perform their core functions of describing materials and arranging them for use.
- Just as there are many types of printed material that libraries do not typically acquire or catalog, libraries should not try to catalog everything on the Internet.
- Libraries do not have to do the whole job of organizing Internet materials for access. In the past libraries ceded the opportunity to catalog periodical articles and other types of material. As a result, periodical indexing companies and other agencies stepped in, and over time libraries have developed mature, established relationships to share the task of providing access. Many agencies have an interest in facilitating access to materials on the Internet, but the relationships have not been worked out.
- Search engines and automatic indexing have their place as access tools, but they cannot replace classification schemes, controlled vocabularies, and thesauruses.
- The objective of cataloging will come to focus more on access than description.

At first, we use any new technology with the mind-set of the old. Cataloging can, and should, evolve beyond the constraints of drawers of printed cards, the current MARC format, and the current generation of online catalog systems.

Should Libraries Catalog the Internet?

There are several arguments against cataloging the Internet. Here are some of them.

There is a huge amount of material on the Internet, more than we have ever sought to deal with by cataloging.

Much of it would not be collected by libraries if it were on paper.

Maybe we won't have to do it. The commercial sector may provide access to Internet materials by indexing them, just as it indexes periodical articles.

Perhaps there will be a breakthrough in computer searching technology that will obviate the need for cataloging or indexing.

Some of the arguments in favor of cataloging items on the Internet are

There is a huge amount of useful information on the Internet, and libraries need better access to this material.

Librarians have the knowledge and skills to do the job.

The Internet has caught the public interest. By adding value to it, we can attract users to libraries.

What Has Stayed the Same?

The Internet has some features in common with earlier grass-roots explosions in the distribution of information, from the broadsides printed on portable, itinerant presses in the late 1500s through the photocopied samizdat of the twentieth-century Soviet Union, the author-distributed preprint and technical report gray literature, and transmissions over low-power radio and community-access television channels.

The Internet contains materials like all of these and more. It contains electronic broadsides; books and articles not acceptable for publication for political, social, or economic reasons; preprints; technical and government reports; and discussions. It contains materials that emulate print publications, such as electronic journals and the *CIA World Fact Book*. Materials that are not typically widely circulated in print or broadcast media reach a much broader constituency on the Internet—such materials range from resumes of academic geologists to sale notices from car dealers.

What Is Different?

When dealing with Internet material, libraries still make decisions on acquisition, cataloging, and retention. However, they make these decisions in a different order, and the decisions have different meanings.

First, collection development is different. When a library places an Internet terminal in a public area, that library has made an implicit decision to acquire all of the freely available material on the Internet. However, libraries can decide to improve access to certain materials by cataloging them, by linking to them explicitly on a Web page, or by providing access to third-party indexes or search mechanisms.

When a library makes a traditional cataloging record for an electronic item available to its users, that library has in effect made an explicit decision to "collect" the item. Regarding material on the Internet, when a library decides what to catalog, it is, in a sense, deciding what to collect. Libraries can decide not to catalog certain materials or whole classes of materials. This is a collection-development decision, but it is expressed as a cataloging decision, not an acquisitions decision.

Retention decisions are also different in the electronic environment. When a paper item is acquired, it typically requires little attention until it deteriorates due to use or time. In the electronic world, if a library decides to catalog an item on the Internet, the library must also decide whether to store a copy of the file on a local computer or to rely on having it available elsewhere.

The Internet is an Alice-in-Wonderland world in which items may not be what they seem. In the next moment they may be something other than what they were, may be somewhere else, or may have vanished. It is beyond the scope of this paper to provide a full treatment of the issues of retention of electronic information, but here is a partial list of these issues:

- copyright and licensing laws and agreements to allow libraries to retain electronic copies for preservation purposes
- cooperative agreements to allow libraries to share the responsibility for preserving electronic material
- commitments to migrate the material to new formats when the old ones become unsupportable
- development and widespread acceptance of methods of authentication (to ensure that a document is as the author intended)

Approaching the Issue

At first view, the Internet seems entirely too large, complex, and mutable to catalog. It would involve a great deal more work than any library could do, and materials are of so many types.

The first thing to realize about the Internet is that it is not necessary for libraries to catalog everything. Many of the items and events on the Internet are not the sorts of things that are typically acquired by libraries, and we need not feel compelled to catalog them.

The Internet may be compared to particle physics from the 1920s through the 1980s, a time when many new types of particles were being discovered and classified. If we choose to do so, librarians can play a useful role in describing the types of particles on the Internet and creating a taxonomy of them so that they may be thought of as sets of similar materials. Such a taxonomy would help libraries decide what to collect, what to catalog, and what priority to give to cataloging. A librarian collecting materials in literature would be helped by being able to search for the available electronic journals, news groups, publisher's catalogs, and home pages of scholars in the field without having all of these types of material jumbled together. And, just as some libraries today collect comic books, orange-crate labels, and theater posters, some libraries will choose to collect and catalog materials that most libraries do not. It would help to have different kinds of materials identified by type on the Internet, whether or not most libraries collect or catalog them.

The second thing to realize about the Internet is that libraries are not the only players in this game. Companies and other groups outside libraries have already developed search tools and indexes to assist in the large task of making materials on the Internet easier to identify and retrieve. To a large extent, these outside groups are working independently of libraries and of one another in pursuit of their individual interests, and they will continue to do so. New indexes, search engines, and Web browsers are continually being introduced. Librarians are being included in the work of some standard-setting bodies and information providers. At first contact librarians often consider the access proposals of these outside groups to be naive. The nonlibrary groups, in turn, typically appreciate library classification systems and subject thesauruses but see the descriptive cataloging system as amazingly overwrought.

Third, over the past quarter century libraries have developed a marvelous capacity to set cooperative standards and to share the work of creating bibliographic records. Also, librarians know how to structure access to large bodies of knowledge. These can be invaluable contributions to the use of electronic information, just as they are for print. Our profession can contribute a unique capability to the task of bringing groups together to find ways to organize access to materials on the Internet.

More About the Players

Many efforts are under way to prepare for cataloging in the electronic realm. Several of these efforts are outlined in this section.

A committee of the International Federation of Library Associations and Institutions (IFLA) is developing a draft of the functional requirements for descriptive cataloging of electronic publications. The draft specifications will be forwarded for review to national libraries and other organizations that develop cataloging standards. The intent is to determine which descriptive elements are not needed for electronic materials and what new elements would be useful. For example, for an electronic item it might be useful to know the encoding scheme for the text (such as American Standard Code for Information Interchange [ASCII], HyperText Markup Language [HTML], PostScript, or Acrobat), and the format of any graphic, full-motion, or sound content. This would tell a library or a user what kind of computer program is necessary to view (or hear) the item. It might also be useful to know if the item has an index or a searchable archive (as do the messages posted on many Internet discussion lists) and where this index or archive is located.

OCLC, Inc., is conducting an Internet Resources Cataloging Project (InterCat) in which a group of volunteer libraries is applying conventional cataloging processes to Internet resources. (See the Ensor article cited in References.) One goal of the project is to see how libraries select Internet resources for cataloging. The cataloging records created by the contributing libraries were available for a trial period from OCLC on its World Wide Web. The catalog featured hot links from the catalog records to the items themselves.

Another OCLC project, NetFirst, moves beyond the information contained in traditional cataloging records and beyond the one-at-a-time selection methods of items to be cataloged. Significant features of the project include the following:

Items are identified by an automated process that finds new materials.

Information about the item is collected by the automated process. This information is reviewed by an editor who decides if the item meets the selection criteria.

Descriptive information about the item is drawn from the header of the computer file instead of being created by a descriptive cataloger.

Items are reviewed automatically to verify that they are still active and available.

Additional information about the InterCat project and NetFirst is available at the OCLC Web site, *http://www.oclc.org.*

The Association for Library Collections and Technical Services (ALCTS), which is part of the American Library Association, has established a Task Force to Define Bibliographic Access in the Electronic Environment. The Task Force, which is to report its findings in mid-1997, has a very broad charge: to lead in defining access and bibliographic control mechanisms for information in electronic form and to communicate those mechanisms to the users, producers, and organizers of electronic information. The Task Force Web page *(http://www.lib.virginia.edu/alcts)* contains a wealth of background information, project descriptions, and position papers.

Some material has appeared in the literature that expands on this topic. A 1993 article by Caplan conveys the complexity of the intellectual task and the interlocking nature of the discussions between the various groups involved. A bibliography by Bailey includes additional articles on this topic. A recent article by Weihs provides an update on some existing projects. (See the References section at the end of this essay.)

There are, of course, players other than libraries in this endeavor. Their products are of two basic types, indexes and search engines. Commercial indexing services have played a major role in providing access to periodical articles in libraries, and they expect to find a way to offer services in this new arena. New indexing services, such as Yahoo *(http://www.yahoo.com)*, have sprung up to serve the Web. Indexes are constructed by humans and are based on the meaning of words and terms and on a thesaurus or a classification system that gives shape to knowledge.

Search engines, such as Archie and WebCrawler, are computer programs that inspect all or parts of the headers or contents of electronic items to find words that match a user's search query. Search engines can use a variety of means to reduce the number of irrelevant items retrieved. These means can include synonyms, truncation, fuzzy logic, and other techniques for refining a search, but they cannot be based on meaning. They cannot, therefore, substitute for the human intelligence that is embodied in a good index or a well-applied classification scheme. Because they cannot understand the meaning of a text, they cannot gather texts of similar meaning when the meaning is expressed in different ways.

Just as the various methods of searching have different strengths, different points of view can also contribute to the description of a work and to its placement in a context of meaning and scholarship. Authors provide titles, indexes, and abstracts, each with the point of view of the creator of the document. Librarians place a work in a context of human knowledge. Librarians may not have the depth of knowledge of the field that the author has, but they have an objectivity that the author cannot have. Scholars in the field can place the work in another context: in relation to other specific works that define a field of knowledge. At present, scholars do this by citing the work of others or by writing survey articles or books. In the online environment, it would be possible to express this level of relationship as commented links from one work to another.

Drawers of Printed Cards

Just as early horseless carriages looked like horse-drawn carriages, down to the sockets for buggy whips, so in this early era of online records we are bound by our history of card and book catalogs and by our present experiences with online catalog software and cataloging codes that have not kept up with the possibilities of present mass storage and computer processing.

Today we can add twenty or thirty subject headings to a record without having to file a single card. Because the call number no longer implies a shelf location, we can classify an electronic resource in both Dewey and LC if we believe that will help users place it in a context of other materials. Perhaps it is not necessary in all cases to provide a comprehensive description of an Internet resource if the item itself is available with a mouse click on the catalog record or if the catalog record has been made a part of the electronic work itself. But we cannot make these changes until we have come to accept them ourselves. And once we are ready to change, we must work within the decision processes of agencies that design and approve cataloging codes and formats to gain widespread acceptance.

In the electronic realm of the World Wide Web, in which users can move from one document to another by clicking on a link within the document, it makes sense to reexamine our subject thesauruses and our classification schemes. The ERIC thesaurus is a good example of a thesaurus designed for computer searching. Most of the subject headings in the thesaurus are accompanied by lists of broader subjects, narrower subjects, and related subjects.

Conclusion

The Web is teaching us anew that information is not self-organizing. Librarians know how to organize information for access, and we can apply our knowledge to the Web just as we have applied it to paper. One of the wonders of librarianship is that the public at large has no idea that libraries do this. Editorials in the computer press express hope that the next generation of Web browsers will make the Web into an orderly place in which it is easy to find what is wanted. This will not happen; it is the work of knowledgeable human beings to select material and put it in a useful arrangement.

One handicap we have is that the library community is large and tends to move slowly. We have had little competition for the task of cataloging books. Many library bodies are responding with commendable rapidity to the opportunities created by the Internet. However, our movement seems slow compared to the pace of growth and change in the Internet itself.

Our great strength is the ability of this large library community to cooperate. If we can move quickly to get the standards and agreements in place, and if we can work with the other players in this game, librarians can apply their ability to share the work of cataloging electronic materials, just as they do for print.

References

Bailey, Charles W., Jr. (1995). "Network-Based Electronic Publishing of Scholarly Works: A Selective Bibliography, Section 2.6.1, Cataloging, Classification, and URLs." [Online]. *The Public Access Computer Systems Review.* Available: *http:/info.lib.uh.edu/pr/v6/n1/lbcat.htm*

Caplan, Priscilla. (1993). "Cataloging Internet Resources." [Online]. *The Public Access Computer Systems Review.* Available: *gopher://info.lib.uh.edu:70/00/articles/e-journals/uhlibrary/pacsreview/v4/n2/caplan.4n2*

Ensor, Pat. (1995, November). "Libraryland Organizes the Web: an Unnatural Process?" *Technicalities*, 9–11.

Weihs, Jean. (1996, April). "Solving the Internet Cataloging Nightmare." *Technicalities, 4–6.*

How "Helathy" Is Your OPAC?

Terry Ballard

Terry Ballard is automation coordinator at the New York University School of Law Library. He has written a number of articles about the Internet and automation; one of them gave rise to this list of words that tend to be misspelled in OPACs (Online Public Access Catalogs), which many libraries have used to do maintenance on their databases. Terry may be reached at *BALLARDT@TURING.LAW.NYU.EDU.*

The original article, of which this is an outgrowth, can be found in (1992, June) "Spelling and Typographical Errors in Library Databases: One Library's System for Rooting out Spelling Errors," *Computers in Libraries,* 14–19.

This list started as a byproduct of a keyword inspection of the online catalog of Adelphi University in 1991. Early in the process, I found that words appearing more than once in the Adelphi catalog were almost always found in other OPACs of similar size or larger. Since then, I have added some words as I found them. This particular version of the list integrates material from a confirming study performed at the University of North Florida by Bob Jones. Words that only appeared once in the Adelphi list that had multiple hits in the UNF catalog have been added to the "Medium Probability" section.

High Probability Misspellings

Acquistion	Communites	Intergral	Psychanalytic
Adminstration	Comtemporary	Internatonal	Questionaire
Analyis	Curriculm	Krushchev	Reponses
Associaton	Decisons	Linquistic	Reseach
Assoication	Developement	Literatue	Responsiblity
Behaviorial	Ecomomic	Medival	Seventeeth
Bibiography	Ecomonic	Occurence	Techique
Britian	Educaton	Ofthe	Techiques
Characterisitics	Eduction	Pantomine	Univeristy
Commerical	Hisory	Philosphy	Universty
Committe	Inroduction	Psychanalysis	Withdrawl

Moderate Probability Misspellings

Activites	Developmemt	Institue	Phildelphia
Administation	Develpment	Instructiion	Philosopy
Afairs	Devlopment	Instutution	Physcial
Agression	Dictonary	Intergovenmental	Plannning
Alcholics	Disabilites	Internatinal	Politcal
Applicatons	Dissertion	Internatonal	Politican
Apprasial	Divison	Langauge	Pratice
Artic	Educaion	Lanugage	Presidental
Artifical	Educatiion	Libray	Prespective
Asociation	Eductation	Logitudinal	Problms
Assocation	Eigth	Massachusset	Pscyhology
Biograhy	Eigthteenth	Matematical	Psychoanlytic
Biograpical	Encyclopdia	Mexica	Psychosical
Buddist	Environnmental	Musuem	Psycological
Challange	Estabishment	Nationl	Publiations
Characterisitcs	Evaulation	Nietzche	Pyschological
Chidlren	Facilites	Ochestra	Quide
Childern	Facsimilies	Opera (zero	Realtions
Citicism	Febrary	instead	Relatoinhip
Clincial	Foreward	of O)	Rememberance
Commitee	Frontierthe	Opportunites	Rennaissance
Commmittee	Governement	Orgaization	Reportof
Consitution	Helath	Organiation	Residental
Consitutional	Historial	Organizatin	Revolutinary
Contemporay	Histoy	Orgin	Rrelations
Contempory	Hospital	Orhcestra	Scienes
Contributon	Iindustrial	Perpective	Selction
Decisionns	Indentification	Persepectives	Selectd
Develoment	Infomation	Philadephia	Severly

Sevice	Sufficent	Thehistory	Unsre
Sevices	Supression	Tommorrow	Unsrer
Spainish	Techinques	Toyko	Virture
Stablization	Televison	Transporation	Workship
Statisitics	Temperment	Troubador	
Stuggle	Tendancies	UnitedSttes	

Editor's note: For practical advice in how technical services staff can use the Web, check these out:

Scheschy, Virginia. (1996). *Technical Services and the Web.* [Online]. Available: *http://www.library.ucsb.edu/untangle/scheschy.html*

Stewart, Barbara. (1996, April). *Top 200 Technical Services Benefits of Home Page Development.* [Online]. Available: *http://tpot.ucsd.edu/Cataloging/Misc/top200.html*

This is an excellent guide, filled with ideas and links to useful resources.

Do You Have a License for That?

Electronic Data Pricing

Or, Through the Looking Glass

Pat Ensor

Originally appeared in (1992, May) *Technicalities,* 9–11. Copyright held by Trozzolo Resources, Inc.

Author's/Editor's note: Although the industry has changed practices somewhat to conform more closely with what is called for in this article, there are still many exceptions to the rule!

Alice brushed back her long yellow hair, straightened her blue dress, and entered the library. Immediately her attention was drawn to a shelf of periodical indexes with a sign on it, saying "USE ME." As she drew a book from the shelf, she was startled to hear running footsteps behind her. "No, no, you can't do that!" said a short man with an unaccountably tall hat, pulling the volume from her hand. "We've reached our permitted limit on the number of index users!"

Alice looked around and saw no one else using the indexes. When she remarked on this, the little man snapped, "They're using some in the next building, of course. We'll have a call when your turn comes."

"There are a lot of volumes here. Can't I use some of the older material? You own it, you can let me use it," pleaded Alice.

"We don't own these, we're just leasing them. In fact, we had to return anything older than fifteen years last month," grumbled the librarian. "It was just as well, since we had to pay a fee for each volume we had, in addition to the fee we still pay for each person who might ever want to use the indexes, and the fee for each building where we take a volume."

Alice thought for a moment and said, "But these are history indexes—can't you keep the old ones? And you have to pay for anyone who might use them?—Most people on this campus won't want to. Oh well, as long as I'm waiting, do you have that index I saw at Cheshire University that focuses on Victorian England?"

"Oh no," said the librarian, "Cheshire has much more money than we do, and they negotiated a private contract with those publishers. They can't let anyone know what they paid. Those publishers never quote prices, so we figure if you have to ask, it costs too much."

At that moment, an imperious-looking woman wearing a dress covered in red hearts came up behind the man in the tall hat and said sharply, "She can use the index now, but did you tell her she has to pay each time she looks up a term? And every time she writes something down?"

Alice, upset, said, "How much does that usually cost?"

"It depends on how good you are at coming up with the right term, doesn't it?" noted Mrs. Queen.

"Isn't the library supposed to pay for that sort of thing?" asked Alice plaintively.

Mrs. Queen looked down her nose and said, "I suppose that would be nice, but we put all our money into those," indicating a pile of graven stone tablets that Alice had not previously noticed. "Perhaps when the publishers feel that they've been adequately compensated for them, they'll drop some of these charges. But by then, they'll have thought of something new to charge for," Mrs. Queen remarked, then turned away.

Alice left the library and decided she would have to go and rent a video about Victorian England. At least she would know up front how much that would cost.

The Point

Electronic information costs much more than print information. You don't own most CD-ROMs, you lease them. Online vendors don't provide fixed pricing. Publishers fear that with each new mode of information they provide that they will lose more than they gain. (In that case, why introduce them?) All of this is just intended as a reminder of what we as librarians have agreed to live with as the ground rules we would laugh at if applied to printed information.

No, I don't think publishers are charitable concerns—in fact, their lack of charity has been proven beyond a doubt! I know that if a firm couldn't hope to realize a profit from a service or product, no one would ever get the benefit. Yes, I understand that both costs and benefits of electronic information are higher than for print information. In fact, I love electronic information. I just want to give more of the library's users a chance to get in on this love affair. I want an orgy of electronic information!

Principles of Electronic Information Pricing

Publishers don't need me to tell them that one of the main principles of pricing is to charge what people will pay. But beyond that, since the marketplace makes decisions about whether or not the initial price for electronic data is too high, I want to add into the mix what I consider the most important and successful principles of pricing: predictability and fairness. Most libraries have as their goal maximizing use of their resources to facilitate patron access to needed information. These two principles can best help them do it, while making them love, and buy more products from, those publishers who follow the principles.

The Problem with FirstSearch

I want to state up front that I do not hate OCLC's FirstSearch; I think it is an excellent usable interface to a number of popular online databases at an affordable price. They are also doing an excellent job of marketing it. If you want more basic information, read a favorable review in February's *Information Today* by Mick O'Leary.[1]

I think, though, that so far OCLC has missed the mark of providing real predictability in pricing. FirstSearch's interface is menu driven and about as usable as a Boolean-based front end could reasonably be but still encounters the problems of Information Access Company's now-defunct Search Helper and H. W. Wilson's Wilsearch interfaces. That is, the patron who walks up to one of these systems may be able to figure out the mechanics of searching, but the system does not help them very much in formulating their topic, understanding the relationships between the different concepts contained in the topic, and conceptualizing the data that they are accessing.

In practical terms, and this was definitely the case with Search Helper, the average patron needs to perform several searches, perhaps as many as six to eight, to be satisfied with output. FirstSearch charges for each search statement entered, not for each session or every ten results or whatever. Say your library bought 500 searches, which will cost $.90 each. Say it also became popular enough that you had about five users per day, maybe a conservative estimate if it becomes really popular. After all, I bet your CD-ROMs get a lot more use than that. At 30 searches per day, you'd be done with your searches in about three weeks. Of course, OCLC allows you to purchase larger blocks than this, at a lower cost per search, but the question is, how many will be used? This is not fixed pricing.

Ah, you say, we can charge the patrons for the searches; OCLC has methods that facilitate this. Whatever the ethics of the fee vs. free situation, no service that charges the user can provide true electronic information access. It's just another specialized service like traditional online searching that causes overhead for the library and does not truly help all the patrons. Besides, who among us wants to volunteer to sell those passwords?

RLIN [Research Libraries Information Network] has recently announced that Brigham Young University and Rutgers University are testing a system called CitaDel, developed by RLG [Research Libraries Group] to be accessed through the RLIN system. Part of CitaDel will include the chance to subscribe to certain databases, such as ABI/Inform and Ei Page One (from Engineering Information), for a fixed fee based on simultaneous users at an institution. This sounds like a step in the right direction, perhaps really moving toward allowing online access to replace wasteful local loading of tapes.

Word is that OCLC is considering true subscription pricing for FirstSearch, and undoubtedly their current subscribers will help them gather the costing data to help them decide whether this service is possible and how much the fees should be. They should be further encouraged to provide these options, allowing truly predictable pricing.

Local Database Licensing

What is fairness in licensing of data CD-ROMs or tapes? I don't know, but I know what is not fair when I see it. Data vendors are (mostly) for-profit businesses, but I expect them to price their data based on costs to produce it plus the intrinsic value of the data plus a reasonable profit margin. If they charge an additional fee for something, I expect the fee to be based on the realistic additional benefit my users are getting from new access to the data. If I am paying for eight people to use the data simultaneously, it does not seem reasonable to pay more if they are going to be dialing up to the data or if they are in the next building, as long as they are "my" patrons.

There has been extensive discussion of this issue on the Public Access Computer Systems List (PACS-L at *UHUPVM1*) on Bitnet. I couldn't express all this better than Judy Koren of Technion Libraries in Israel who said,

> MultiSITE licensing, in my opinion, should be covered by multiUSER licensing. If I've paid for 10 users to access the database simultaneously, I don't understand why it's the database producer's business whether they're sitting in my library, an office on my campus, or 100 miles away. The 10th will get in, even if s/he's coming from Timbuktoo [*sic*], and the 11th won't, even if s/he's sitting next door to the database machine.

The only caveat I would give to this is that I understand data vendors' prohibitions on sharing data with other institutions since those other institutions probably would have bought a separate copy of the data if they were not sharing it. I only ask, again, that vendors be reasonable, and not prohibitive.

Simultaneous-User Pricing

What's the most reasonable way to price data access? Base it on simultaneous authorized users allowed to search the data. Not on the number of terminals, since they are not all accessing the same database at the same time, and not on the number of students or citizens, since they are not all interested in the same database.

Steve Ifshin, information services manager at CD Plus, has written a paper on "Concurrent User Licensing." In it, he states,

> The licensing practice of choice, concurrent user licensing, will enable growth in usage and, consequently, revenues without imposing onerous, if not impossible, tasks on management. . . . The site/entity licensing model reflects the costly, highly centralized environment of the mainframe computer, which assumes large numbers of users searching on non-intelligent (i.e., "dumb") terminals. Today's microcomputer-based local area networks are based on a growth model in which processing may be distributed on both workstations and servers. This modular approach requires that modular pricing be seriously considered. The approach assumes that a system, its users and the activity of those users can grow, and that this growth can be accommodated by standard, easy to understand and easy to administer pricing.[2]

Hip, hip hoorah! The more vendors who believe this and implement it, the better for libraries and the information industry. I think most librarians would find it reasonable, and the vendors will not lose out. Think about it—if I put a database on my wide-area network going all over the campus, the vendor does not have to charge me some arbitrary fee for it. I cannot possibly make this database available using the same tiny number of simultaneous users I had for use within the library. When I add users, they'll make more money than when I put the database on a LAN [Local Area Network], but they'll make it in a way that seems reasonable to the library and will get them more customers. Those vendors who adopt this pricing model should market it aggressively; I guarantee they'll get a good response. And maybe Alice will come back to the library.

Notes

1. O'Leary, Mick. "Database Review: FirstSearch Takes the Lead." (1992, February). *Information Today*, v. 9, 11–14.

2. Ifshin, Steven L. "Concurrent User Licensing." (1991). New York: CD Plus.

Zen and the Art of CD-ROM Network License Negotiation

Thomas C. Wilson

Thomas C. Wilson is the head of the Systems Department at the University of Houston. He is the editor of *Telecommunications Electronic Reviews,* a publication of the Library and Information Technology Association (LITA) of the American Library Association. He has written and spoken widely about technology issues. He may be reached at *TWILSON@UH.EDU.*

Originally appeared in (1990, issue 2) *The Public-Access Computer Systems Review, 1,* 4–14. (It can be located at *gopher://info.lib.uh.edu:70/00/articles/ e-journals/uhlibrary/pacsreview/v1/n2/wilson.1n2.*) Copyright held by Thomas C. Wilson.

Editor's note: This article is comparatively old and was written in reference to CD-ROM databases. However, the concepts contained in it are still essentially true, and they are applicable to electronic information available for subscription through any avenue.

Multi-user access is one of the fastest growing areas of the CD-ROM marketplace. Since several library sites have tested the merger of multiple technologies to build such networks, clearly it is technologically possible to provide either in-house or remote networked access to some CD-ROM databases.

As with many experiments in library automation, the technological hurdles that must be overcome belong to the first stage of the process and, complicated though they may be, do not represent the totality of the problem. License agreements represent another challenging area in the universe of CD-ROM networking. The first indication of the complexity at hand is the lack of standard methods for initiating, negotiating, or determining such arrangements. Each vendor is likely to produce a unique license agreement and, in some cases, is likely to have different arrangements with each institution, regardless of the similarity of their network environments.

CD-ROM network license agreements are also frequently extensions of or riders to existing single-use agreements, not separately designed legal documents. This situation is further complicated by the implied separation of licenses for data and licenses for software. Additionally, some agreements require that the established relationship be held in confidence, thereby limiting customers' ability to learn how others have handled specific licensing dilemmas. It is clear that this segment of the information industry has not fully matured.

End-users, network managers, database producers, and product vendors all approach licensing issues from different perspectives. Even within these groups opinions, policies, and procedures vary greatly. It is also the case that none of these groups have a corner on clarity or sensibility. The issues are often fraught with philosophically opposing motivations, but that is not to say that compromises cannot be made. This paper will outline several descriptive categories of CD-ROM network license arrangements available in the marketplace at this time and will attempt to examine and clarify some of their pitfalls.

Context of CD-ROM License Agreements

To establish a context for CD-ROM license agreements, it may be helpful to view them as an outgrowth of two other related types of licenses—commercial microcomputer software licenses (e.g., dBASE IV, Lotus 1-2-3, and WordPerfect) and large-scale database licenses (e.g., Current Contents, INSPEC, and Magazine Index). In the former, it is use of the software that is granted under certain stipulations, primarily concerned with the number of users, work stations, or program copies. In the latter, similar concerns remain; however, since software is an entirely separate entity that is purchased or leased from another vendor, the primary limitation is on access to or use of data.

CD-ROM products represent a combination of software and data. As such, one would expect that the process of licensing would be straightforward in terms of dealing with a single entity (e.g., database producer, vendor, or jobber). Frequently, this is not the case, since the CD-ROM marketplace is filled with a variety of combinations of data gatherers and compilers, software developers and marketers, publishers, and product vendors and jobbers, each with some involvement in the process.

It may also be helpful to understand that most current CD-ROM database products are extensions of online files. While there are a growing number of products that followed a different development path (e.g., Microsoft Bookshelf), most of the products of interest to large-scale centralized information centers are and will be databases that have been previously available in some online format or have existed in machine-readable format for other purposes (e.g., preparation for traditional print publishing).

The major implication of this developmental history is the role that database producers play in CD-ROM network licensing. The role is somewhat schizophrenic in that, while they certainly want users to gain access to the valuable knowledge stored in their particular databases, database producers also want to recover the cost of producing the databases and, if they are a commercial company, to make a profit. The latter economic concern inherently limits CD-ROM networking to customers for whom the cost of access to the data is less than its applied value.

Since distributing data in CD-ROM format may reduce the demand for online access to equivalent files, many database producers are leery of providing broad-based access to CD-ROM products in a local environment, particularly when "local" means a campus-wide LAN [Local Area Network] with dial-access capability and connections to wide-area networks. By behaving in this manner, database producers frequently present a somewhat inconsistent image to institutions that wish to license CD-ROM products for network access.

Categories of License Agreements

The result of this complex scenario is that a variety of network license arrangements exist in the marketplace. Two general issues are involved in these licenses, restrictions and pricing.

Restrictions

Typically, a CD-ROM network licensing agreement will indicate the legal network location or the legal number of registered users, simultaneous users, or work stations on the network. If the agreement is numerically oriented, the method of measuring these users or work stations may vary but usually will stipulate the exact number or specify ranges within which the network must operate.

Registered Users. Some license agreements identify by name the individuals who are permitted to have access to a particular product. While an arrangement such as this may work in an organizational environment where information needs are clearly and fairly predetermined, most libraries and information centers would find this type of agreement unacceptable since most do not identify users individually in terms of utilizing particular resources.

Number of Work Stations. License agreements that limit the number of network work stations are more amenable to standard library practice. It is possible to identify honestly how many work stations have access to a network, provided there is no gateway, bridge, or dial-in access to that network. However, this restriction is problematic for libraries that wish to provide convenient access to clients from homes and offices through dial-in or wide-area network strategies. In many cases, it would be difficult or impossible to count effectively the total number of work stations having access to the network. Furthermore, since the method of counting has financial implications, it does not make sense to assume that every work station that has access to every resource on the network will use every resource on the network.

Number of Potential Users. A variant of limiting the number of work stations on the network is restricting the number of potential users on the network. This number is even more difficult to count than the total number of work stations on an open network. Fortunately, the number of potential users has not been a common restriction with CD-ROM networking. It is found more frequently in mainframe-oriented database license agreements. But it may become an issue with CD-ROM licensing. Aside from the practical impossibility of determining this number, such an approach also confuses potentiality with reality. If faced with this type of restriction, it may be wiser for librarians to seek other databases with more-realistic license agreements.

Simultaneous Users. Stipulating the number of simultaneous users of a product is another common CD-ROM network license restriction. Simultaneous use is defined as the use of a specific product at the same time; it is not measured by simultaneous disc access or keyboard activity. If a user enters a CD-ROM product, the user will be counted as one user until the user leaves that product entirely. This method is based on the assumption that, through the network software, access to any given resource can be limited to a set number of simultaneous users. This type of arrangement establishes a maximum number of simultaneous users, regardless of the number of work stations on the network. Restrictions of this sort appear to be approaching a happy medium between identifying specific users on one extreme and paying for universal access on the other. In an arrangement such as this, institutions also retain the freedom to expand the size and nature of a network without the necessity of renegotiating licensing agreements with each vendor, providing the number of simultaneous users remains the same.

Network Location. Some CD-ROM network licensing agreements stipulate a spatial restriction rather than a numeric one. In this category, the licensee may have any number of work stations on the network as long as they all reside in the same physical building and no access is granted beyond the physical building housing the network. This is actually fairly common in CD-ROM network licenses, although it is quite rare for commercial software like Lotus 1-2-3. Frequently, this is an additional stipulation along with one of the other licensing restrictions mentioned above.

While this restriction eliminates external access, it does grant high levels of freedom within a given physical space. License agreements with restrictions such as this become more complicated in cases where libraries house computer equipment in separate buildings (e.g., computing centers, branch libraries, and out-buildings). Clearly, this is an area requiring attention in order to make CD-ROM networking a realistic option in many libraries.

User Affiliation. Many single-user CD-ROM license agreements carry a restriction that stipulates that only individuals who are affiliated with the licensing organization may have access to the product. Since libraries rarely require that users identify themselves before using information resources, this license restriction is problematic for both single-user and multi-user settings. Once this situation is expanded to include remote access, the ability to monitor the relationship between user and organization becomes less controllable.

Pricing

Just as the restrictions placed on licensees vary greatly, so do the pricing structures for networking CD-ROM databases. In general, there are four categories.

No Additional Fee. Some vendors will permit licensees to mount their CD-ROM databases on a local area network without incurring additional cost. Surprisingly, there are several companies that have pursued this pricing scheme. Certainly it does encourage those who can afford to install a LAN to do so using these vendors' products. Usually this type of pricing scheme is married to the physical-building restriction mentioned above, effectively limiting the scope of the network while still providing multi-user access.

Base Plus Percentage. All CD-ROM databases have a base purchase or subscription fee. To network some products requires an additional charge figured as a percentage of the base fee. These percentages typically range from 50 percent to 100 percent (i.e., twice the base price), but they can exceed 100 percent. The agreement typically stipulates a range for the number of users or work stations. For example, two to ten users or work stations on the network might be charged at base plus 50 percent, while eleven to twenty users or work stations might be charged at base plus 100 percent.

Base Plus Fixed Fee. This category is a variant of the previous one. Instead of the additional cost being figured as a percentage of the base, it is a set fee per user or work station. These users or work stations may be counted in a variety of ways: registered users, simultaneous users, potential users, permitted work stations, or total work stations. For example, if a network permitted five simultaneous uses of a given database, the cost would be base plus five times the additional fee. These fees range from $20 or $30 to several hundred dollars per user or work station.

Separate Structure. In some cases, the pricing structure for CD-ROM network licenses is completely different than the pricing structure for single-user licenses for the same product. The price range for multi-user access is usually significantly higher.

Combinations of Restrictions in License Agreements

Given that there appear to be six categories of restrictions and four pricing schemes, statistically there could be up to twenty-four different combinations of licensing arrangements considering just these two factors.

In reality, there are probably even more possibilities, since individual database producers or vendors may include variations on these themes. It is no wonder that the existing CD-ROM networks tend to be limited to relatively few products or multiple products from the same database producer or vendor. Implementing a larger LAN that provides access to a wide array of CD-ROM resources may require difficult negotiations and may result in a myriad of agreements, each with its own unique limitations.

Conclusion

Out of this rather complicated matrix, is there one clear option that could serve in all situations? Probably not! In fact, it is the existence of options in the marketplace that suggests that different libraries and database producers have different needs and desires. Having a variety of combinations of restrictions and pricing schemes permits more libraries to consider CD-ROM networks than if there were only one solution. However, the variety occurs at the global level (i.e., as one considers all vendors and producers). If any single vendor or producer is examined, the results are likely to include one or, at most, two options.

Despite the already complex nature of CD-ROM licensing agreements, more flexibility is needed from producers and vendors. For libraries to buy into networking arrangements, database producers and vendors must not view libraries as one monolithic entity. What works in one instance will not work in another. It would be helpful to have several options from each vendor or producer to create solutions that are truly effective.

Restrictions and pricing schemes are necessary components of the symbiotic commercial relationship between database producers and libraries, but alternatives that facilitate the operational management of LANs are more likely to succeed. Short of this end, CD-ROM networking will remain limited in scope, not necessarily because of the cost entailed, but rather because of the difficulty in managing multiple resources with unique and binding license restrictions.

PRESS 1 FOR VENDOR RELATIONS

Nancy Buchanan

Nancy Buchanan *(NBUCHANAN@UH.EDU)* is the coordinator of electronic resources at University of Houston Libraries. She has written and spoken extensively about electronic information resources and has been conducting Internet training for more than three years.

Editor's note: A presentation based on parts of this paper was given at the 1996 North American Serials Interest Group meeting.

This is one of those things they don't teach in library school. We learn how to search databases; we learn about the organization and indexing of electronic information; we learn about library systems; we learn machine-readable cataloging. But we don't learn that librarians spend a lot of time dealing with electronic-product vendors, much less how to interact with them. And any library with a reasonable amount of electronic resources will have to deal with vendors. If you're one of the people who will be doing this (sounds better than "has to do this"), grounding yourself in a few "whats," "whos," "whys," "hows," and a very important "when and where" can help.

What? What Do You Mean by "Vendor Relations"?

What does the term *vendor relations* mean? It's the way in which you work with the representatives of companies who sell electronic products; ideally, it means establishing a positive, beneficial working relationship with these companies and representatives.

What kinds of things fall under the general heading vendor relations? All kinds of good things. More importantly, all kinds of necessary things. Your relationship with a vendor includes

- getting information about potential products and services
- arranging for vendor visits and demonstrations

- arranging for evaluative trials of products
- negotiating contracts and licenses
- purchasing or subscribing to products
- dealing with training and documentation for products after they are acquired
- dealing with maintenance and support for products after they are acquired

Who? The Players

Staff who deal with certain aspects of vendor relations vary by library. Some libraries prefer to have only one person deal with vendors. This is not the best arrangement, since it is unlikely that one person will be the best to discuss and interpret information on all fronts. Some libraries split these responsibilities between individuals, possibly with one person taking the lead position and others called upon when specialized knowledge is needed. When the responsibilities are divided, the important thing is for all involved to understand who is dealing with what aspect and to communicate to the others involved what he or she is doing. After all, serials staff may not be amused to learn that a reference librarian without the proper authority has signed a subscription agreement with a vendor, but serials staff members also probably don't want to field sales calls or arrange for trials. In this piece, I will be using *you* to refer to anyone involved in vendor relations. "You" know who "you" are.

Your counterparts on the vendor side are not so easy to describe. Who the representatives are and what roles they play in their companies vary drastically. Some vendor representatives are employees of the company they represent, paid on salary or commission or a combination. Others are independent contractors who work on commission only. Some representatives work out of a main headquarters or regional office, while some work out of their homes.

Regardless of which model the representative fits into, one common denominator usually holds: a company has one, and only one, individual designated as the primary sales (as opposed to account or technical) representative for a product in your library. Some companies apportion their representatives on a geographic basis. ("You're in Texas? Then your rep is . . .") Others divide them on a product basis. ("Do you want to talk to someone about our online databases? Then you need . . . Oh, you want CD-ROM products? Then it's . . .") Others divide their contacts by the type of institution. ("Are you an academic, public, or corporate library? A nonprofit, gee, I don't know who your rep would be. Let me check.") And yes, some companies combine two or even all three of these schemes. Sometimes just identifying your representative is the hardest part of the relationship. Getting the right person is a very important step. But be warned: once you have the right person, he or she may not be the right person for very long. Some companies change representatives quite frequently, due either to personnel turnover or to a change in how representatives are assigned.

Why? What's in It for You and the Vendor?

Let's be blunt. You and the vendor are out to use each other. But that's not a bad thing. A good relationship between a vendor and a library benefits both parties. One of the world's true win-win situations.

What's in it for you and your library? Your life will be easier. Need quick information, an instant response, someone at the company to investigate something for you?—all these are easier to get if you have established a relationship with your vendor representative. Can you get these things without an established vendor relationship? Yes, but quite possibly not as easily. You will have to deal with customer service, where you can get basic information but not personalized service or in-depth problem solving, or you will have to take the time to find out who your representative is and establish initial contact. Do you want notification of new products and features, advance word on price changes, and the like? Also easier to get with good vendor relations. So your life is easier, and the benefits to your library are obvious. As an added bonus, you might also get on a Christmas card list.

What's in it for the vendors? The better relations they establish with a library, the easier it is for them to communicate the information they want to communicate to that library. And once a company's got its foot in the door, the reasoning goes, the easier future sales will be. Astute vendors are also concerned about their client's relationship with a product after the product is in use. The better the postsale experience, the happier with the company the library is, and (they hope) that much more likely to acquire more of the company's products (and not drop the ones they have).

How? Rules for Library-Vendor Relations

I'll skip the simple rules. If you haven't learned by now to be polite, return phone calls, treat others with respect, etc., it's probably too late for you. Just remember to apply these to vendors as you would to others. And take heed of these additional rules for library-vendor relations.

Rules for You

Let the Vendor Understand Your Context, Needs, and Expectations. An important part of getting what your library needs from a vendor is letting that vendor know where you are now, where you want to go, and what kind of products and services you need to reach your goals. It sounds simple, but it's easy to forget. When a vendor has an understanding of your library's current electronic setup, he or she will have a better idea of the level and types of products and information in which you're interested. (Translation: you should hear more about the products you actually care about and less about the ones you don't.) There's nothing like having a vendor try to sell you on an archaeology database when you're at a university without an archaeology or anthropology program or explain to you what "LAN" stands for when you've got one in the next room.

Don't Assume You and the Vendor Speak the Same Language. We in library land know we use jargon, but we think we know what we mean by it. *We* may, but many vendors do not. Or worse, they have different definitions of the words we use. It's easy to think you know what the vendor is saying, for the vendor to think he or she knows what you are saying, and for neither one to really understand the other. My nominations for the words that are most likely to be used differently by vendors: *site, facility, organization, institution, network, local area network, remote access, dial-in, Internet, authorized user, registered patron,* and *in-house use.*

Real-Life Vendor Story #1

In my library's quest to have useful and up-to-date resources, we decided to reevaluate the electronic encyclopedia we provided on our library network. A quick call to the distributors of the CD version of a major print encyclopedia determined that it did, indeed, have a network version available. We received it for a trial but had to return it without even testing it. Its "network version" required that the search software be installed on every work station from which a patron might use the product (for our library, more than 100). After returning the product, accompanied by a letter explaining why we could not consider it, I received a call from the vendor. He did not understand why this product was unacceptable in our network environment, repeatedly stressing "but the CD can be put on a network." Experiences like these provide one benefit: they teach new questions to ask. I have since found one other product (an Internet client for an online database) whose producer has a similarly warped definition of *network;* this "networkable" product can run on a network if it is installed on each work station that accesses the network.

Provide Feedback. Providing feedback benefits both your library and the vendor. If you want a product to change in some way, the first step is communicating this to the vendor. If you do not let the vendor know you want something to change, how do you expect the company to know? Feedback benefits the vendor company by giving them honest input that could improve their product. And feedback does not stop after your initial evaluation. Feedback should continue as long as your library continues to use the product. Don't be discouraged if not every company and representative takes your comments as seriously as you wish they would. The ones with the determination to improve their products will.

Explain Your Decisions. When you decide whether or not to get a product you've been evaluating, be sure to explain your decision to the vendor. This helps the vendor to better understand your needs and, in the case of a negative decision, provides feedback to the company that can be taken into account in product decisions. If you want a company to understand that your library has a serious problem with its product, pricing, or licensing, giving this as the reason for not purchasing the product is the most powerful way to communicate this message.

Don't Threaten Unless You Mean It. When you're not getting what you want or are having serious problems with a product, it's very tempting to threaten to not buy or to cancel a product or a service. But don't do this unless you mean it! This is not a good time to bluff. Why not? Because if your bluff is called, you've lost all future power such threats might have held and probably the opportunity to have this and other concerns taken seriously. Let a vendor know such-and-such is a serious problem, that it might prohibit you from acquiring the product, that your library is very concerned (and say all of those in a suitably serious tone of voice), but don't threaten unless you're ready to carry out your threat.

Real-Life Vendor Story #2

In the early years of my library's involvement with electronic resources, we subscribed to two databases from a company. When we received the products, we discovered a significant security breach that would allow patrons to access directories they shouldn't be able to. We communicated to the company that this was a very serious problem and, if not fixed, would result in us returning the products. The problem was not fixed, and we returned the two databases. Less than a year later, the company came out with a new version of their search software. One of the advertised improvements was the elimination of the security hole. The company told us that our library's identification of this problem as the reason for the returned products (and the serious concern this demonstrated) was the main reason they recognized this as a major problem that should be addressed in the new software. We then resubscribed to the two databases. (This incident also led us to the strict technical evaluation now given to all electronic products before acquisition.)

Don't Promise Unless You Mean It. It's okay to let a vendor know you're interested in a product, that you'll be seriously considering a product, or that you'll probably evaluate a product in the next year, but it's not okay to lead a vendor on. The ethics of this are dubious, needless to say. It can also put the vendor representative in a very bad position because he or she probably regularly reports to the company about potential sales. Your behavior has put the representative who took you seriously in a bad position with his or her company and, possibly, supervisor. Putting a vendor in such a spot is not only unkind, it buys you no good will.

Ask Questions. Use vendor representatives as information resources. Ask them for updates on products and services. If they don't provide a service or feature you want, inquire about it on a regular basis. Along with getting you the most up-to-date information, this conveys your serious interest. When you call to ask about one issue, you may be happily surprised to get information on another one.

Real-Life Vendor Story #3

When I called the supplier of an end-user online service to inquire about one issue, the representative took a moment to ask me about a fax she'd recently received. The service supplier had started sending her statistics on usage by her customers. She didn't know what to do with this information. Since my library used this service and she had me on the phone, she thought she'd ask me if I thought the statistics might be useful to the subscribing libraries. Needless to say, I said yes. Now we get our usage statistics (whose nonexistence we had previously bemoaned) on a monthly basis. You never know what unexpected benefits an inquiry will bring.

Provide Documentation of Problems. The best way to get a vendor to take a problem seriously is to document problems. A record of how often a problem occurs is more effective than the assertion that "it happens all the time." A screen of garbled characters makes much more of an impact than a verbal description of the problem. For some problems, this is the only way to accurately convey the situation.

Rules for Them

You can probably guess that I really wanted to call this section "Why Do Vendors Do That?" But my calmer side prevailed. Nonetheless, here are some rules I'd really, really like to see all vendors follow:

Answer Questions. A good representative will always answer any questions you have. If the representative does not know the answer, he or she will find out and communicate the information to you. Alternatively, the representative will refer you to another person in the company who can answer your question. (Ideally, the representative will have the appropriate person call you.) If your questions go unanswered or take an unreasonably long time to answer, this could indicate the level of service you will receive after you acquire the product. After all, when you are in the consideration phase is probably when the vendor is most interested in impressing you.

Give Advance Warning of Big News. Why do so many vendors not provide advance warning of significant price increases, changes in price structure, major product changes, and the like? If it's good news, why not advertise it? If it's bad news, I much prefer to be able to plan in advance. Time to change database reference cards, alert library staff, figure out where that extra $3,000 will come from—why wouldn't I want that? This trait is especially annoying in representatives who call to plug a product the library doesn't subscribe to, but in the same conversation don't mention the big change coming with next week's update of the product we do subscribe to. I assume vendors don't like to spread bad news any more than the rest of us, but I view representatives who give advance warning of negative changes with more respect (even though I may also tell them what I think of the change).

Discuss Products and Clients with Technical Support. Don't be surprised if your representative is unaware of any problems you have with his or her products, even if you have engaged in extensive discussions with the company's technical support department. Many companies have a solid wall between customer service and technical service that puts libraries' fabled public/technical services divide to shame. Not only could your representative be unaware of the nature of your problem, he or she probably has no idea you even have a problem. If dealing with a technical service department does not solve a problem, bring your representative into the equation. It's his or her job to keep you happy with the product, and guaranteeing it works is the best way to do that. From the vendor perspective, it's also the best way to ensure that you stay interested in other products from the company.

Leave More Information on Cold Calls. With more and more companies getting into electronic resources, a technique that many are adopting is cold calling. If you answer the call, you can easily deal with the representative. However, if the vendor gets a receptionist or your voice mail, you often get a message from a person you don't know with no clear indication of what product or (in extreme cases) company is involved. I don't know why some vendors do this. Does a sense of mystery lead to a higher rate of returned calls? I am most likely to return a cold call if I know what the product is and if it's one in which I'm interested. (Confession: cold calls are when I sometimes break my "always return calls" rule.)

(An Important) When and Where

Negotiating Contracts and Licenses

Yes, you can negotiate! A vendor's contract or license is not the last word. It's just what the vendor wants you to agree to. Now that you've seen it, let the vendor know what you want him or her to agree to. The license and contract stage is the most important place for vendor relations.

What can you ask for? Ask for anything you want, with the understanding that you may not get it. But you won't get anything if you don't ask. Whether a contract or license is the kind that both parties sign or a standard printed license that comes packaged with a product, you can try to change it. Sections you might want to change include the following topics.

Terms of Payment. These can include dates payment are due, the time between invoice date or receipt and payment, and the time between product shipment or receipt and payment. Always check these in a contract. Sometimes they must be changed to comply with an institution's policies or, for public institutions, a state's policies.

Place of Litigation. Most contracts specify in which court litigation will occur, if any arises. Most contracts specify the company's home state. Some institutions require that this be changed to the institution's home state.

Terms of Remote Access. This is tricky, since many companies use different definitions of *remote access*. Some mean dial-in only, some mean on-campus only, some mean password-protected only, etc. Make sure that the definition in the license covers the method you use to provide remote access. If the contract requires you to make security provisions, make sure the ones you have in place are encompassed by the contract's wording.

When you secure changes in contracts or licenses, always get them in writing. This can take several forms, including clauses that are struck or changed and initialed by all parties, addendums, or a letter from a company official specifying the changes. Don't accept verbal changes or "I know it says *X*, but we really don't care if you do *Y*." These are not binding, and such understandings can be easily forgotten after a sale is made and are rarely passed on to others in the company or to the next representative who takes over your account.

And in Conclusion . . .

That's it! You know what, who, why, how, and the most important where and when. Now it's up to the best teacher of all, experience. And I guarantee that each vendor interaction has the potential to be a memorable learning experience.

Standards Is Good

INFORMATION STANDARDS

In a world where everyone wants to connect, standards are of increasing importance. Standards for interoperability are what lie at the heart of the Internet and the Web. There are official standards and unofficial ones, ones that are propagated by nonprofit organizations and ones that become "industry standards," ones that are actually called standards and ones that are called protocols. TCP/IP (Transmission Control Protocol/Internet Protocol) provides the underlying standard layer for most of the communication on the Internet. HTTP (HyperText Transfer Protocol) is the standard that underlies the Web. HTML (HyperText Markup Language) is also based on a standard; it is a form of SGML (Standardized General Markup Language). All of these standards allow different computers to understand each other and carry out transactions. (For more information on these standards and protocols, see the essays on these topics and on organizations elsewhere in this book.)

One of the most prominent standards in the U.S. library world has been Z39.50, a standard for information retrieval across different systems. Developed by the National Information Standards Organization (NISO), it allows compliant systems to interoperate in such a way that a searcher on one information system can use the "local" searching capabilities to query a database that is made available using another information retrieval software program. This is already in use between many library catalogs. For example, if I have the right software on my Innovative Interfaces catalog, I can use it to search the Library of Congress database, which is also Z39.50-compliant. But I will appear to be using the Innovative Interfaces OPAC (Online Public Access Catalog) software. The system I am searching would not have to be another OPAC; the online system FirstSearch, for example, is Z39.50-compliant, so I could search it using Innovative Interfaces.

Z39.50 is on its third version, and a group of implementors meets quarterly and is always working on the next version of the standard. A fairly large body of literature has been built up on this standard, especially in the context of the library world. Many of the other standards and protocols are of much more widespread interest in the networking world. For more information on Z39.50 and other library-related standards, check out the following:

Ensor, Pat. (1994, November). "Z39.50 at the Turning Point." *Technicalities,* 13+.

——. (1992, July). "Z39.50—What It Is and What It Means, or, I'll Have My Data Call Your Data." *Technicalities,* 10–12.

> Yeah, I know, I wrote these, but I did try to write approachable and understandable explanations of Z39.50, which has not necessarily been the aim of other writers on this topic.

Faxon. *Library and Publishing Standards.* [Online]. Available: *http://www.faxon.com/Standards/StandardsMenu.html*

> Faxon is the maintenance agency for the Serial Item and Contribution Identifier (SICI). The company is also concerned with the standard for Electronic Data Interchange (EDI), a standard that is of interest throughout the business world. Faxon maintains this section on its Web site that has links to standards organizations worldwide as well as links related to SICI and EDI.

National Information Standards Organization (NISO). *Information Standards Quarterly.* $70, free to NISO members. Available from NISO at P.O. Box 338, Oxon Hill, MD 20750-0338.

> The official NISO newsletter provides ongoing information about NISO and International Organization for Standardization (ISO) standards efforts, with many updates about topics related to information standards.

International Organization for Standardization. *Welcome to ISO Online.* [Online]. Available: *http://www.iso.ch/welcome.html*

> ISO provides an excellent connection to standards-making bodies all over the world. Actions of ISO directly affect standards worldwide, since standards such as Z39.50 aren't much use if they don't make international connections. For information especially of interest to the library world, look in the section on technical committees, then check for listings about the Joint Technical Committee (JTC) 1, which covers information technology, and Technical Committee (TC) 46, about information and documentation.

Kelly, Mark. (1996, May). *Internet Searching with Z39.50.* [Online]. Available: *http://pages.prodigy.com/ZUPN84A/z3950.htm*

> A well-organized site, it gives links for using Z39.50-based mechanisms to search for information. It also includes general links about Z39.50, places for downloading Z39.50 software, Z39.50's interactions with other standards, and international standards relating to Z39.50.

Library of Congress. (1996). *Z39.50 Maintenance Agency Home Page.* [Online]. Available: *http://lcweb.loc.gov/z3950/agency/*

> The official Z39.50 page is full of information. Here is the official register of implementors, information about the Z39.50 Implementors' Group (ZIG), the list of official object identifiers, and a copy of the standard itself. There is also information about planning for Version 4, a list of

links to other information about Z39.50 on the Web, and papers by implementors on various implementation issues.

Michael, James J, and Hinnebusch, Mark. (1995). *From A to Z39.50: A Networking Primer.* Westport, CT: Mecklermedia.

This work by two of the "Grand Old Men" of Z39.50 development is the most authoritative book that has appeared on the topic.

National Information Standards Organization. *NISO Home Page.* [Online]. Available: *http://www.niso.org/*

This home page tells much more about NISO than it does about standards, but here you can see what the current standards development efforts are. Maintenance agencies for some existing standards are listed. We can hope that they build this site up more.

Schwarz, Michael, and Bowman, Mic. (1996, May). *Distributed Indexing/ Searching Workshop.* [Online]. Available: *http://www.w3.org/pub/WWW/ Protocols/9605-Indexing-Workshop/*

Available at the site is a document with the papers from this workshop, which happen to be a treasure trove of advanced information about Z39.50, including "Z39.50 and the Web," "Z39.50 and Multinational/ Multilingual Environments," and "Z39.50 and Navigating Digital Collections."

Waldstein, Robert. (1995). *Z39.50 Resources—A Pointer Page.* [Online]. Available: *http://ds.internic.net/z3950/z3950.html*

The page gives a narrative about Z39.50 that includes links to much useful information; it includes information about profiles and about organizations that have Z39.50-compliant software packages available.

Uniform Resource Names

A Progress Report

William Arms

William Arms is chair of the D-Lib Forum, sponsored by the Corporation for National Research Initiatives (CNRI). Other contributors of information to this chapter are Leslie Daigle (Bunyip Information Systems, Inc.), Ron Daniel (Los Alamos National Laboratory), Dan LaLiberte (National Center for Supercomputing Applications [NCSA]), Michael Mealling (Georgia Institute of Technology), Keith Moore (University of Tennessee), and Stuart Weibel (OCLC).

This article first appeared in (1996, February) *D-Lib Magazine* (online), available: *http://www.dlib.org/magazine.html*. It can be located at *http://www.dlib.org/dlib/february96/02arms.html*. Copyright held by CNRI.

The development of networked information requires reliable ways to name resources on networks. The Internet community has adopted the term *Uniform Resource Name* (URN) for a name that identifies a resource or unit of information independent of its location. URNs are globally unique, persistent, and accessible over the network.

The concept of universal names has been warmly embraced by the networking and library communities, but convergence on the details proved difficult until recently. During fall 1995, however, members of the principal groups that are actively working in the field reached outline agreement on most of the major topics. The main characteristics of this agreement are described in this paper.

The catalyst for the recent progress was a meeting in October 1995 hosted by Keith Moore at the University of Tennessee. Invitations were sent to every group that had a current Internet draft on this subject. The URN groups represented are listed at the end of this report. This meeting was followed by a series of discussions including informal sessions at the December meeting in Dallas, Texas, of the Internet Engineering Task Force (IETF).

Convergence is important because many people who manage large collections of online information have been reluctant to commit to using any form of URN during a period of flux. The present consensus has two major results:

Users who wish to give permanent names to online resources can now plan to incorporate URNs from existing naming schemes in documents, indexes, and online systems. They can be reasonably confident that future developments of the URN framework will not force them to reformat or otherwise modify existing URNs.

The implementation of this framework will remove the concern that using a particular name scheme might affect longevity or the future usefulness of assigned URNs. The framework allows continued support for existing URNs, through other resolution systems if one name scheme ceases to be supported in its original form. Thus users who assign names within any of the agreed-upon schemes are assured against obsolescence.

This report summarizes the emerging consensus. A strength of the framework is that it allows different approaches to be pursued, and the framework has the ability to evolve over the long term. Naming is a complex issue and the groups are interested in URNs for a variety of different reasons. They bring different philosophies and different technical approaches. Their implementations range in scope and complexity. It is therefore encouraging for the community that they have reached general agreement and are working together to find technical solutions to the outstanding questions.

Background

A good introduction to URNs is Internet RFC [Request for Comments] 1737, *Functional Requirements for Uniform Resource Names,* by Karen Sollins and Larry Masinter, December 1994.[1] The following is an extract from their introduction. It describes the function of URNs and, in particular, how they differ from the Uniform Resource Locators (URLs) used by the World Wide Web.

A URN identifies a resource or unit of information. It may identify, for example, intellectual content, a particular presentation of intellectual content, or whatever a name assignment authority determines is a distinctly namable entity. A URL identifies the location or a container for an instance of a resource identified by a URN. The resource identified by a URN may reside in one or more locations at any given time, may move, or may not be available at all. Of course, not all resources will move during their lifetimes, and not all resources, although identifiable and identified by a URN will be instantiated at any given time. As such a URL is identifying a place where a resource may reside, or a container, as distinct from the resource itself identified by the URN.

The RFC concentrates on the relationship between a locator (URL) and a persistent name (URN), but naming questions arise in many other contexts. For example, the Resource Cataloging and Distribution System (RCDS), developed in the Computer Science department of the University of Tennessee, uses URNs to support cataloging, replication and caching (for high availability and fault-tolerance), and authenticity and integrity assurances using digital signatures. The paper "A Framework for Distributed Digital Object Services" by Robert Kahn and Robert Wilensky, May 1995, also identifies persistent names assigned to objects in repositories as a key component of a framework to manage intellectual property on networks.[2]

A class of names with some characteristics similar to URNs are the domain names (such as *andrew.cmu.edu*), used to identify computer systems on the Internet. Domain names are supported by a well-tuned computer system, the Domain Name System (DNS).[3] Several URN implementations build on domain names and DNS.

URN Requirements

RFC 1737 lays out functional requirements for URNs. It also makes recommendations about the form that such names might take. An updated version of RFC 1737 is under discussion, but, with some important clarifications, the following list of requirements has been widely accepted.

Global scope: A URN is a name with global scope that does not imply a location. It has the same meaning everywhere.

Global uniqueness: The same URN will never be assigned to two different resources.

Persistence: It is intended that the lifetime of a URN be permanent. That is, the URN will be globally unique forever and may well be used as a reference to a resource well beyond the lifetime of the resource it identifies or of any naming authority involved in the assignment of its name.

Scalability: URNs can be assigned to any resource that might conceivably be available on the network, for hundreds of years.

Legacy support: The scheme must permit the support of existing legacy naming systems, insofar as they satisfy the other requirements described here. . . .

Extensibility: Any scheme for URNs must permit future extensions to the scheme.

Independence: It is solely the responsibility of a name issuing authority to determine the conditions under which it will issue a name.

Notice that these requirements focus on the URN but make no assertions about the resource that it identifies. A URN may be globally unique and last forever without any guarantee that the resource identified by the URN is unique or permanent.

Resolution

To use a URN, there must be a network-accessible service that can map the name onto the corresponding resource. This process is called "resolution."

Frequently, the resolution system will return the current location of the resource or a list of locations. RFC 1737 concentrates on the case of a URN that resolves to a URL, but a URN can resolve to any network resource or service. For example, in RCDS, a URN may resolve to one or more location-independent file names (LIFNs), which can themselves be considered a specific type of URN. In the Kahn/Wilensky model a URN, known as a "handle," resolves to the name of the repository that holds the resource. In other contexts, a URN may resolve to a data structure containing meta-information about the resource.

The URN Framework

This section describes the URN framework that has emerged from the discussions of the past few months. Although many details remain, the level of agreement is promising.

General Principles

Naming Schemes and Resolution Systems. The framework distinguishes between naming schemes and resolution systems. A naming scheme is a procedure for creating and assigning unique URNs that conform to a specified syntax. A resolution system is a network-accessible service that stores URNs and resolves them.

Independence between Naming Schemes and Resolution Systems. A naming scheme is not tied to a specific resolution system. Any resolution system is potentially capable of resolving a URN from any given name scheme.

URN Registries. Since naming schemes and resolution systems are conceptually independent, mechanisms must be created so that the user of a URN can discover what resolution systems are able to resolve the URN. This is called a URN registry or simply a registry.

Multiple independent naming schemes and resolution systems are anticipated. Although the maintainer of a particular URN resolution system may also wish to maintain a registry, it is important to realize that registries and URN schemes are conceptually independent of one another. Any registry is capable of registering resolution services for any URN scheme, and a client may wish to consult multiple registries when attempting to resolve a name.

Syntax

The URN implementors have agreed on the following syntax, with one outstanding difference of opinion; opinions differ whether the leading characters "urn:" should be part of the name. This syntax is acceptable in all proposed naming schemes and resolution systems. There are many details that need to be discussed (for example the precise character sets allowed in URNs).

The following are examples of URNs:

urn:hdl:cnri.dlib/august95
urn:lifn:some.domain:anything-goes-here
urn:path:/A/B/C/doc.html
urn:inet:library.bigstate.edu:aj17-mcc

Notice that the syntax of a URN explicitly indicates the naming scheme by including a naming scheme identifier, "hdl," "lifn," "path," "inet," etc. This is followed by a colon and a string that has a syntax defined by the specific naming scheme.

As can be seen from the examples, the different naming schemes use different formats. Some naming schemes divide the name into two parts, a naming authority followed by a unique string, which is assigned by the naming authority. Thus the handle "cnri.dlib/august95" consists of a naming authority, "cnri.dlib," followed by a unique string, "august95." The path URN "/A/B/C/doc.html" consists of a naming authority (or path), "/A/B/C," and a unique string, "doc.html."

The Internet community is developing a general framework of Uniform Resource Identification (URIs), of which URNs are a component. The URI framework was originally outlined in RFC 1630.[4] Under the proposed framework, each participating naming scheme is a URI as defined in the RFC.

Management of Naming Schemes

The long-term value of URNs requires the naming schemes to be well managed. Initially, a small number of schemes are under development. Hopefully, a small number of high-quality naming schemes will be added in the future.

The criteria for an acceptable URN scheme will be outlined more formally as the URN framework is defined. They are likely to include a requirement that each naming scheme must have a verifiable management system to ensure the integrity of the naming scheme and of the URNs within it. This includes the process for assigning unique URNs within the naming scheme. It must also make sure that there is at least one resolution system able to resolve the names.

Those URN schemes that include naming authorities (e.g., handles, paths) will determine the names of the authority names themselves. Thus, it is possible that different organizations may get the same naming authority string under different naming schemes.

URN Registries

A URN registry is a network service that stores data about URN naming schemes, naming authorities, and resolution systems. A registry provides two types of service. It may provide rules for extracting the naming authority from URNs in a particular naming scheme. In this case, the first step of the URN resolution service may be to provide information on how to find the naming authority in the URN string. The second function is to know which resolution systems are capable of resolving a given URN from the name scheme and, when appropriate, the naming authority.

The concepts of URN registries and resolution systems are not tied to any specific computing system or set of software. This is important since URNs are intended to be valid for long periods of time, much longer than any computer system can be expected to last. The format of data to be stored in a registry is currently under development. It has been given the working name NAPTR ("Naming Authority PoinTeR"). In practice, it is probable that several URN resolution systems will include URN registries, but every registry need not hold full information for all naming schemes. One proposed implementation is a modified version of DNS. Another uses the handle system.

Flexibility within the URN Naming Schemes and Resolution Systems

This report emphasizes the areas where the various URN developments are converging on a common framework. In a number of key areas, the URN implementors have carefully agreed to support flexibility rather than to enforce unnecessary conformity.

The value of a naming scheme or a resolution system depends upon a number of assertions. Are the names unique? Can a resource have many names? Can it change? Is it guaranteed to exist? What is the retention scheme? Does a URN resolve to untyped data, typed data, entity-attribute pairs, a URL, the address of a repository, etc.? Within the general URN framework, such assertions about names, semantic decisions, and management issues may be enforced by the naming scheme or the resolution system, or they may be left to external systems. Variations in these important areas will give the schemes their distinctive features and will determine which are most suitable for specific application areas. The objective of the URN framework is to encourage wide flexibility within a stable system of naming and resolution.

URN Implementors

The following projects were represented at the University of Tennessee meeting in October 1995 and have continued to work together to reach agreement on the URN framework.

Resource Cataloging and Distribution Service (RCDS)[5]

This work is led by Keith Moore, Shirley Browne, Stan Green, and Reed Wade of the University of Tennessee. Its aim is to provide transparent replication along with integrity/authenticity assurances and [to] alleviate the problem of huge demand for some random network resource.

The Handle System[6]

This work is led by David Ely and William Arms of the Corporation of National Research Initiatives. It is based on the ideas in the Kahn/Wilensky framework.

x-dns-2[7]

This is a scheme developed by Paul E. Hoffman of Proper Publishing and Ron Daniel Jr. of Los Alamos National Laboratory. As the name implies it is based on the Internet Domain Name System (DNS).

URN Services[8]

This is a proposal by Keith E. Shafer, Eric J. Miller, Vincent M. Tkac, and Stuart L. Weibel of OCLC. It focuses on the syntax and functions of URNs.

Path URN[9]

This is another scheme that makes use of DNS. It has been developed by Dan LaLiberte and Michael Shapiro at the National Center for Supercomputing Applications.

Whois++[10]

Several groups are working towards using Whois++ as an Internet Directory Service. Work done by Michael Mealling of Georgia Tech and Patrik Faltstrom and Leslie Daigle of Bunyip Information Systems, Inc., focuses on the distribution of URN resolution data and maintenance responsibility in a global publishing environment.

Notes

1. *http://ds.internic.net/rfc/rfc1737.txt*

2. *http://WWW.CNRI.Reston.VA.US/home/cstr/arch/k-w.html*

3. *http://ds.internic.net/rfc/rfc1035.txt*

4. *http://ds.internic.net/rfc/rfc1630.txt*

5. *http://www.netlib.org/utk/projects/rcds/*

6. *http://WWW.CNRI.Reston.VA.US/home/cstr/handle-intro.html*

7. *http://www.acl.lanl.gov/URI/IDs/urn-x-dns-2.txt*

8. *http://www.oclc.org:5047/oclc/research/publications/shafer/urn/draft-ietf-uri-urn-resolution-01.html*

9. *http://union.ncsa.uiuc.edu/~liberte/www/path.html*

10. *ftp://ftp.bunyip.com/research/urnthots.txt*

SGML Documents

A Better System for Communicating Knowledge

David Stern

David Stern is director of Science Libraries and Information Services at Yale University in New Haven, Connecticut. His research involves electronic retrieval and transmission of data, focused primarily on scholars' work stations. He is currently involved in the development of end-user search systems for both local and remote hosts.

Originally appeared in (1995, Spring) *Special Libraries*, 117–24. Copyright held by Special Libraries Association.

Editor's note: One illustration and reference to it have been omitted, and sample text in other illustrations was altered to preserve the copyright of the original examples.

What Is SGML?

SGML (Standard Generalized Markup Language), also referred to as ISO 8879, is an international markup standard that provides a basis for identifying both content and display factors for all types of media. A standard Document Type Definition (DTD) layout using predetermined fields and conventions has been created for each media-type document (e.g., periodical article, book chapter, etc.). SGML document records are machine independent and therefore quite favorable for search, manipulation, display, and data transfer operations across networks and platforms.

Figures 1 and 2 demonstrate that standard SGML records are composed of tagged fields and data. There is a standard protocol used for arranging hierarchies of content (title, headers, chapter, etc.) and identifying alternative data types (images, audio, video, cited references, etc.). These field delimiters allow for complex searching, sorting, manipulation, analysis, and display. The primary limitation to this type of information system is the creativity of the database designers.

FIGURE 1   Sample SGML file

```
<Title>SGML Documents: A Better System for Communicating
Knowledge<\Title>

<Authors>David Stern<Authors>
<Address>(lt>Yale University
New Haven, CT
<\lt><\Address>
<Intro>
<P>
The use of SGML-based (Standard Generalized Markup Language) documents
and databases can provide enhanced access and display capabilities. . . .
Particular emphasis will be placed upon possible enhancements to the currently
limited print-display imitation of most current electronic journals.<\Intro><\P>

<Subcode>Accession numbers:<\Subcode>

<Body>
SGML (Standard Generalized Markup Language), also referred to as ISO 8879,
is an international markup standard . . .
<\Body>
```

FIGURE 2   Sample SGML file

```
<letter>
<sendinfo>
<address>Physics/Astronomy Library
University of Illinois
Champaign, IL 61801<\address>
<\sendinfo>
<recinfo>
<receiver>Special Libraries<\receiver>
<address>1700 Eighteenth Street, NW
Washington, DC 20009<\address>
<\recinfo>
<date>29 March 1994<\date>
<content>
<salu>Dear Editor,<\salu>

<para>
Please consider the following manuscript . . .
<\para>
<\content>
<vale>Sincerely,<\vale>
```

Examples of data types include standard hypertext links (used for accessing online help, definitions, images, and citations), value-added nondisplayable data (such as caption and image descriptions), editor comments, subject hierarchy codes, and post-dissemination comments and revisions.

Database Structure

The maximum usefulness of a system is ultimately determined by the quality and accessibility of the individual data elements. To a large extent, database record formats determine the retrieval power of a system. There are a variety of record formats that can be used to store data. Some primarily provide page layout (display) data while others contain structural (content) data that may be used for additional purposes. This section is a review of some of the major information formatters and their characteristics.

Markup Languages

A markup language should handle data in a document for both the physical layout of the data and the content description. One set of conventions could mark both presentation and content. Powerful front-end software could be developed to handle any data stored in this generic format. The data could be transmitted over the Internet as packets of related data and recomposed when received by the client software. In this way, users could easily transfer both the simple presentation of the data across a variety of hardware platforms and provide for enhanced manipulation of the intellectual content.

Markup languages allow for the tagging of data elements in a document into logical content sections (such as titles, headers, paragraphs, captions, etc). These elements have specified characteristics, such as font size, margins and spacing. Less time needs to be spent on composition (e.g., lists of items with equally spaced and numbered items) and therefore, more time can be spent on the author-added intellectual data (e.g., imbedded added-value data such as caption descriptions, subject hierarchies, and other searchable, enhanced content factors).

PostScript is a popular markup language containing many timesaving display conventions. It also allows for the integration of nontext data. However, PostScript requires proprietary print driver software. The sharing of data across platforms is seriously hampered when such requirements are imposed.

The TeX markup language, which is used by mathematicians and other scientists requiring complex equations, charts, and graphs, is no longer proprietary; however, there are a variety of versions in the publishing world, each with nonstandard conventions. Conversions, for example, from standard TEX to RevTeX or LaTex, can be quite time-intensive and exasperating when one simply desires to display a preprint manuscript identified via the Internet. Slight macro differences can create unreadable files.

Text Formatters

These tools provide primarily text-reproduction capabilities. They can be quite easy to use, as the complex display instructions are handled in the background. Standard options are preprogrammed, but special options such as tables, charts, and special characters require specific definitions that may be time-intensive to create.

The most common text formatters are word processors. The more recent WYSIWYG (What You See Is What You Get) variety has made manuscript preparation quite painless and has therefore transferred the creation of final documents to the researcher rather than [to] a secretary or an editor. Unfortunately, there are a variety of limitations to these basic text formatters. Many incompatible word processors on the market have nonstandard protocols for text display that make sharing files cumbersome (although the introduction of Rich Text Format [RTF] output has made the transfer easier). Even conversions from previous versions of the same word processors can create difficulties, especially in the area of macro definitions. Most also do not handle nontext data very well. The emphasis on display often limits the ability to embed nondisplayable remarks and links to other items that may be helpful for advanced searching and retrieval.

Desktop Publishers

Desktop publishers allow the integration of text and graphic images in a simple cut-and-paste approach. The behind-the-scenes manipulation of various document types makes display layout and composition relatively straightforward. Standard desktop publishers such as PageMaker are somewhat expensive and require practice and exploration in order to create professional output. Each desktop publishing software package has its own internal commands and therefore the raw database is not transferable. This emphasis on customized output markers makes the production of sophisticated printed material possible for nonspecialists but creates a limiting database in terms of shared search and retrieval uses.

Complex Search and Retrieval, Analysis, and Display Engines

The following section will discuss the relationship of the data structure to the searching, retrieval, and manipulation possibilities in an enhanced information tool.

The development of highly defined data documents allows for very sophisticated manipulation of entire knowledge-information systems. Added-value data elements such as descriptive caption data and hierarchical subject links allow for much more powerful searching of full-text databases. The creation of formatted and ranked results from within specific data fields (such as tables, charts, and graphs) means researchers can develop new data products themselves. Over time, a researcher could create new customized "virtual databases" or "electronic journals" from a variety of sources. Think of automatic "journals" being delivered to your mailbox each week based on predetermined search strategies. With the right software, such as Mosaic or Panorama, a researcher could also receive integrated media items in this way.

Many current online journals tend to base their product on word-processed files and simply reproduce the original paper format. They may incorporate bitmapped images to display non-ASCII text. Some forward-thinking information tools such as the CORE [Chemistry Online Retrieval Experiment] and Current Clinical Trials in Medicine electronic journals are now produced from more powerful basic formats such as SGML documents. The results are more user-oriented interface options such as hypertext links to images and other citation and on-screen connections to logical portions of the text such as introductions, methodology, and conclusions. Selective searching replaces simple browsing in this enhanced environment.

Making SGML Systems Work

Early experiments have shown that SGML-based systems provide enhanced user options. This next section will explore areas that need to be explored in order to fully implement this approach.

Challenges to implementing SGML-type sophisticated data manipulation and display systems include

- a lack of standardized knowledge information systems and databases
- a lack of access to useful advanced search/manipulation software (what is available is not user-friendly and easily networked)
- limiting Internet network transmission capabilities
- copyright restrictions

Creation of SGML-Based Knowledge Information Systems and Databases

Conversion routines for previously generated documents in other formats, and author interfaces for original document creation, need to be enhanced and distributed for wide acceptance of the SGML standard to occur. There are currently many publisher and research groups working on the development of SGML-based databases. Among the most advanced groups are the American Physical Society and the American Mathematical Society, which have developed online journals available via the Internet from SGML archives. Other example systems would include the Perseus Greek history CD-ROM project, the CORE online chemistry journal project located at Cornell University in Ithaca, NY, and the WORM database by Bruce Schatz, and now at the University of Illinois in Urbana–Champaign, Illinois.

The migration to SGML documents involves changes in routines and thought processes. Any change in paradigm involves the discomfort associated with attempting to understand and accept new methods and ideas. A primary responsibility of learned/professional societies, educational institutions, and corporations is to counteract this resistance—to promote new opportunities through education, encouragement, and requirements (when necessary). All organizations would benefit greatly by convincing authors to provide enhanced manuscript data. Once the members are well along the learning curve, they will undoubtedly see the long-term benefits of their new actions. A possible scenario could be a future in which third party indexers (such as IEE [Institution for Electrical Engineers], which produces the INSPEC database) may be replaced, and their profits may be redirected, depending upon the degree of standardization required when authors and in-house editorial staffs assign subject codes and keywords.

Enhanced Search/Manipulation Software

Significant improvements need to be made in natural language searching with GUI [graphical user interface] interfaces, in forms-based search screens, and in the refinement of query statements using post-search relevancy analysis. Mead's FREESTYLE and Dialog's TARGET are examples of natural language interfaces. The North Carolina State University library *(http:// ncsulib4.lib.ncsu.edu/drabin/niso_forms)* has an example of a forms-based system. The ability to manipulate search results (be they text, image, or integrated media) will become standard in the future. A standard interface for discipline-wide resources is needed so users will not have to learn multiple interfaces for the various products that are currently being developed (such as TULIP [The University Licensing Program], CORE, Right Pages, OCLC's Guidon system, etc.). The competing and confusing situation in CD-ROM interfaces cannot be allowed to continue. A scalable navigational system must be developed; the journal image approach is not feasible on the interdisciplinary scale.

Display Software

Networked display software needs to be enhanced to handle a wider variety of data types with better resolution than currently available. Mosaic and Netscape only handle HTML [HyperText Markup Language] (a less-sophisticated SGML format) and still have problems with decompression of certain items. The quality of screen images will have to rival that of print sources before users can seriously rely on the Internet for primary data transmission.

Data Compression

The efficient transfer of large numbers of data packets across the Internet requires much better compression techniques than what is available today; especially for bitmapped images and color video.

Network Capabilities

The bandwidth (carrying capacity) of the Internet needs to be upgraded to all nodes in order to avoid bottlenecks at gateways. There is already a noticeable slowdown in Internet transmission speed with the increased use of WWW [World Wide Web] browser software.

Copyright Considerations

The exclusivity and proprietary nature of copyrighted material, even with fair use exemptions, seems to directly conflict, in some cases, with the cooperative distribution techniques afforded by the networked environment discussed in this article. Changes in the interpretation of laws and regulations, changes in the pricing schemes for access to data documents, and/or migration away from commercial distributors may be necessary in order to guarantee access to material intended for educational purposes.

Future Implications

With the development and spread of true information/knowledge transfer systems as described above, very little preparation time will be necessary for the display and transfer of data, thereby significantly lessening the present journal production lag-time and reducing costs while providing an enhanced product. Undoubtedly, there will be new challenges to face. As collaborated databases are created by researchers, librarians, and users, there will be a need for interface standards, although there will always be a need for subject-specific customization of products.

The ability to attach later revisions and reader comments to an original document introduces new archiving and security concerns (beyond the static peer review scenario) to this dynamic medium. Also, the creation of multiple database clearinghouses and gateways between document delivery services will certainly bring the copyright issue to the forefront.

The large-scale adoption of the SGML standard for information storage and delivery will certainly result in better access for users. More specific and enhanced retrieval, more standardization, lower cost, and quicker distribution are some of the benefits to be gained. It is time to move from full-text displayable databases to added-value enhanced knowledge information systems. Librarians can be involved in the collaboration process through active participation or excluded from the creation of these new information tools through passive resistance. It is up to our profession to recognize and act at this early stage of the paradigm shift.

Suggested Readings

Bryan, Martin. (1988). *SGML: An Author's Guide to the Standardized General Markup Language*. Reading, MA: Addison-Wesley.

Goldfarb, Charles F. (1990). *The SGML Handbook*. New York: Oxford University Press.

Mangan, Katherine S. (1991, September 18). "Perseus Helps Students See Links Between Aspects of Ancient Greece." *Chronicle of Higher Education,* A26.

Wu, Gilbert S. K. (1989). *SGML Theory and Practice.* London: British Library Research and Development Department.

Editor's note: Another good recent reference is

Van Herwijnen, Eric. (1994). *Practical SGML.* 2nd ed. Boston: Kluwer Academic.

For information on the Web, see *http://www.yahoo.com/Computers_and_Internet/Software/Data_Formats/SGML/*

15

So, You Want to Be a Cybrarian?

Technologies Change Organizational and Occupational Structures

Librarian, Cybrarian, or ?

Barbara Best-Nichols

Barbara Best-Nichols *(BARBARA.BEST-NICHOLS@REICHHOLD.COM)* is information resources administrator at Reichhold Chemicals, Inc. She is very active in the Special Libraries Association and has done presentations on careers for librarians.

"We've come a long way, baby" was a popular slogan a few years back. While it does not pertain to careers in library science or the information profession, it is certainly very appropriate to the changes occurring in the profession.

We live in an ever-changing world! To thrive, or even exist, we must change with it. The field of library and information science is a dynamic one within our society. As we continue our progress through the post-industrial age, the field of information use continues to be a driving force affecting the way we live, work, communicate, conduct business, and learn.

Technological change continues to have an impact on the very manner in which traditional librarians and information professionals carry out their responsibilities. During the 1800s, the technology of the period was "hand-writing." Indeed, several major library schools taught library handwriting. Included was consistency in letter size, slant, blackness of line, and spacing. We progressed from the electric pen, which was favored by Melvil Dewey, to the typewriter. Around 1876, Dewey and others held the opinion evidenced by Theodor Schuchat when he said that "the librarian's role was believed to be akin to that of a genteel hostess who would elevate the manners and tastes of the guests in her parlor, who were expected to be mannerly and grateful for her tutelage."

Along came the computer and automation age. Mechanization of library procedures started in the 1950s and '60s, with real advances taking place during the '70s through '90s. Through all of this, the role of librarians was also changing.

Librarianship Defined

An examination of new career paths for librarians can only be undertaken if we know the existing or historical definitions for a librarian. Harrod's defines *librarian* as

> One who has care of a library and its contents; the work includes selection of stock, its arrangement and explorations in the widest sense, and the provision of a range of services in the best interests of all groups of users. Coordination of activities, setting of priorities, evaluation and other managerial tasks are an essential part of the work. Involvement in the community served, whether public, academic, private, or any other context is also of great importance.

Yet another definition describes a librarian "as a professional member of a library staff who performs custodial, bibliographic, or administrative duties of a library."

Using either of the definitions and compared with the role described by Schuchat, we have truly "come a long way, baby." The career path of the librarian has changed from that of a parlor hostess with excellent handwriting to one who performs a variety of tasks, not the least of which is performing "custodial . . . duties of a library."

Computers, a Valuable Utility

With the advent of online systems, librarians could retrieve reference information, obtain citations, catalog materials, and request materials, all online. Librarians/information professionals were now able to obtain information more expediently. The constant manual searching of reference tools or other print materials was no longer required.

If the mainframe was the revolution, surprise, surprise, there was an evolution! The microcomputer was introduced, software developed, and networks conceived and implemented. Standards were introduced to allow various makes, models and types to communicate with each other. Libraries were integrated; catalog librarians no longer had to spend long hours searching authority files or filing catalog cards. Online Public Access Catalogs (OPACs) with circulation modules were introduced. Circulation librarians no longer had to manually flip through cards to determine when a book was due, place a recall/hold, or send an overdue notice.

Rapid succession of innovations in computing and networking has certainly created organizational change and new occupational structures. The combination of advanced computer technology, networking and the Age of Information has given birth to the Information Superhighway, the Internet, cyberspace, and cybrarians.

And We Are Called . . .

Many of the cybrarians carry out the same functions as librarians; that is, they select, arrange, coordinate, evaluate, and disseminate information. The traditional roles are handled simultaneously with the electronic roles. Yet there are growing numbers of information professionals whose roles and careers are changing. These changes in many instances have required a great deal of self-examination, professional scrutiny, and intellectual debate. What will the role of librarians be in the twenty-first century? Will everybody be called cybrarians? What new titles are forthcoming? How will jobs or positions be performed? Will end users be so attuned to locating information themselves that they will not need librarians or cybrarians? What will we do differently?

It is important to know how cybrarians see themselves. A request was made of "solo" librarians through the Solo Librarians Listserv:

> Hi fellow librarians and cybrarians.
>
> I need your help. I have been asked to contribute a paper for publication on the role of cybrarians. . . . How many of you consider yourselves to be cybrarians? Why? How have your traditional roles changed? What do you consider to be alternative career choices for librarianship in a networked, virtual, superhighway environment?

Solo librarians provided the following responses to four questions. These responses denote their cyberspace roles, responsibilities, and changes.

How many of you consider yourselves to be cybrarians?

- Cybrarian is used to define a librarian who uses the Internet for library purposes. I fall into the role of cybrarian. I have the role of webmaster. (B. Mattscheck, personal communication, April 30, 1996)
- Most of my work is computer-related, bulk of information resides in CD-ROM and online databases, over 80 percent of materials budget is committed to electronic service. (M. Melaugh, personal communication, April 30, 1996)
- I spend increasingly more time on the "net." . . . I've had a ball discovering all sorts of useful websites (*sic*) governmental, industrial & academic. . . . I teach people how to get started searching electronically. (N. G. Washburne, personal communication, April 30, 1996)
- I became a cybrarian in 1988. I got the opportunity to operate . . . an electronic library. I am an online researcher and Internet

consultant; again, a cybrarian. (T. B. Chadwick, personal communication, May 2, 1996)

■ I handle all Internet activities, . . . patrons come to me if they have a listserv they'd like to join or need to exchange e-mail with a client. I download all e-mail, sort into . . . mailboxes for patrons, print out anything patrons have requested and route printouts, this is for low volume listservs. Access is on one machine. (J. Friedman, personal communication, April 23, 1996)

■ I have never had a job in a "real" library. The company I'm working for sent me for my masters in "information studies." . . . I spend a lot of time online, either on the Internet, or on DIALOG. (E. Thomas, personal communication, May 1, 1996)

■ Yes, I consider myself to be a cybrarian, I have feet planted firmly in both paper and virtual worlds. Sign over door reads "Virtual Library Spoken Here." (L. MacMorris, personal communication, April 30, 1996)

Why?

■ The Internet is just one of the tools I use to provide information to my organization, it replaces some print publications. It is useful as a source of information for snapshots of current events/economic/business events for Asian and Latin American countries. Its greatest use is as a means of communication and help with tough reference questions through e-mail or listservs. (B. Mattscheck, personal communication, April 30, 1996)

■ We help in administering the e-mail system, we have a deep understanding of the company's business and departments and are better able to keep up with changes in names and directions of the company. . . . We help with weeding of our main company server. (M. Melaugh, personal communication, April 30, 1996)

■ Electronic availability of information . . . has enormously changed the pace and accessibility of information. I can give/get vital articles within minutes to hours. I am extremely comfortable on the "net." (N. G. Washburne, personal communication, April 30, 1996)

■ All of my resources for answering questions and doing research are online. (T. B. Chadwick, personal communication, May 2, 1996)

■ I arrange access. (J. Friedman, personal communication, April 23, 1996)

■ I work out of my home for the company. I spend a lot of time online, my research includes historical information on companies, products, different chemicals and their uses, and just search and retrieval of journal articles. (E. Thomas, personal communication, May 1, 1996)

How have your traditional roles changed?

■ My role is still in revolution, I have the opportunity to interact with people throughout the organization that I might not regularly contact. Technology has allowed me to develop skills as Intranet Webmaster. There is a great appreciation of the search skills of librarians, they can find information more quickly. . . . I see the traditional librarian become more visible as a teacher, how to get to the good places, how to keep up with a fluid environment and as an evaluator (what are the good places) and sources of information as opposed to data. (B. Mattscheck, personal communication, April 30, 1996)

- The mainstays of a traditional library are minuscule here, our book and periodical collections compose less than 15 percent of the budget. (M. Melaugh, personal communication, April 30, 1996)
- I remember how awful it was searching SCI [Science Citation Index] with a magnifying glass, and waiting weeks for interlibrary loans to get here. I believe there will always be a need for printed materials, hard copy archives, . . . but I cannot imagine doing without electronic capacities ever again. (N. G. Washburne, personal communication, April 30, 1996)
- No books, except for a few reference and online documentation; no purchasing or acquisitions, except online accounts; no circulation hassles; no shelving, very little cataloging. [I] concentrate on helping people find the information they need, doing the reference work and research that I love doing. (T. B. Chadwick, personal communication, May 2, 1996)
- There are times when I will go out to the local public and university libraries for articles and info, but most of the time I search and have the article sent. I do order books for the company, and my office houses all bound periodicals and proceedings for the company. I very much enjoy the freedom of what I do! We are a small firm . . . everyone works out of their home. We stay in contact by phone/fax/modem and e-mail. I guess we might be considered pioneers of this information age! (E. Thomas, personal communication, May 1, 1996)
- Resource areas have expanded. I download the Federal Register table of contents daily and e-mail to my customers. I query Commerce Business Daily for business opportunities. I send out electronic newsletters, I purchase books, publications, and archival reports online. (L. MacMorris, personal communication, April 30, 1996)

What do you consider to be alternative career choices for librarianship in a networked, virtual, superhighway environment?

- The most obvious role to me for a librarian is in the organization of the amorphous Internet/Intranet. As a corporate librarian, I can serve as a guide to the best of the Net for my organization's purposes. I can also help to develop internal nets that organize corporate information. The attention to detail and persistence of a traditional librarian will go far in turning data into information and filtering out the extraneous items. (B. Mattscheck, personal communication, April 30, 1996)
- I see huge opportunities for librarians, that is, organizers and retrievers of knowledge and information in helping the organization of

electronic knowledge. Any company with PCs, client/server technology, Internet access, e-mail, or groupware could conceivably provide a great opportunity for someone with library skills to help organize. What makes us good at these tasks . . . is the fact that through our reference work, we are so in touch with our company's business and departments. (M. Melaugh, personal communication, April 30, 1996)

- I didn't start out to be an Internet consultant. When I became a cybrarian, I used Dialog, Datastar, STN [Scientific and Technical Information Network], etc. and other online commercial information services. I started using the Internet in 1991 as yet another information resource and, as often happens, became the organization's and my librarian colleagues' guru on the Internet. More and more of my online research is being done on the Internet, and now I'm designing Web pages, promoting Web sites and doing content development. (T. B. Chadwick, personal communication, May 2, 1996)

- I would consider myself a real "virtual" librarian, since there is no real "library" setting for this job. (E. Thomas, personal communication, May 1, 1996)

- Acquaint staff to Internet searching capabilities. Immediate access to full-text newspapers, financial research and in-depth literature. Independent researcher for writers and speakers. (L. MacMorris, personal communication, April 30, 1996)

As indicated in the responses by librarians/cybrarians, information is more accessible and requires reference experience, attention to detail, and other qualities. As we explore alternative career choices for librarians, we might ask ourselves are we being too premature? A 1995 article in *The National Business Weekly* by Gabrielle Solomon very clearly states that there is a market for librarians. The headline for this article reads "The Information Revolution Spurs Demand for Librarians." It continues

Controversy and excitement may not be the first words that come to mind when discussing librarians' careers. Nevertheless, the library profession today is a veritable hotbed of paradoxes. Technological advances are spurring demand for Internet-savvy professions. . . . The spread of computer networks and databases has made a range of information more accessible to individuals, yet finding and evaluating this data often requires an expert touch; the demand for skilled librarians is strong and expected to stay that way.

It would certainly seem to suggest that librarians should not be in too big a hurry to find other career choices. It also suggests that librarians must "make a good argument as to why they're instrumental to the product"— the product being information. However, in making this argument, it is incumbent on librarians to be good at what they do.

The organizational researcher must be an Internet-savvy professional with highly refined skills; she must use those skills to locate not minimal information but as close to "all" information as possible. Once the researcher has this information, she must be able to analyze it, repackage it, and disseminate it. These roles, while they were performed in the past using print-based materials, are taking on new meanings in our electronic environment.

Descriptions of Alternative Careers for Librarians

Abstractors Extract, index, and abstract information from cyberspace, in-house computer systems, print materials, and other sources and produce Intranet or Internet products, CD-ROM products, or other electronically available resources.

Analysts Take information extracted from cyberspace, online searches, annual reports, and other sources and analyze it, compare it to user needs, and interpret and synthesize it for best use by clients.

Brokers Contract for profit with others to provide an information-based service, may include reference work, information retrieval, document delivery, file organization, database management, data entry, human resources, or other tasks.

Collection Developers Evaluate, analyze, and monitor technological developments and make recommendations or decisions on the types of resources to make available to clients. Resources may be software, hardware, services, and print sources.

Consultants Advise and make recommendations and suggestions in a variety of areas including the best manner in which to retrieve, analyze, make accessible, and store information and how to provide services based on that information.

Creators Design front-end engines for search retrieval; create multimedia software; combine information to form new information; develop simple methods for accessing information; design Web pages; write copy; provide, conceive, and develop training tools for in-house use.

Database Managers Create databases, maintain the integrity of data in databases, and design practical, user-friendly programs for ease of end-user access.

Database Set-Up Contractors Requires multiple platform experiences. Contract with clients to set up database programs, perform installations, troubleshoot, train, and possibly be responsible for turnkey systems.

Developers Develop libraries, information centers, and centers of knowledge or other information-based areas. Focus is on consolidating internal and external information into a readily available, easily usable source.

Digital Technologists Integrate computers, publishing, broadcast media (including radio, television, telecommunications), print, and graphics in a manner accessible for home or business use. May be entertainment, technical, or business based.

Digitizers Convert printed materials, sound, and video into digital formats for applications on computers, CD-ROMs, optical imaging, electronic publications, and related materials.

Disseminators Collect, organize, repackage, and distribute information to clients. May consist of internally generated information or externally produced materials. Service may be for repeat clients or specific-project clients.

Entrepreneurs   Obtain, analyze, synthesize, repackage, and reproduce information for a fee or provide services or access to contract customers. Customer base may be individuals, corporations, companies, libraries, governmental agencies, or others.

Evaluators   Take information from a variety of sources and evaluate it for use based on client requirements, goals, missions, and standards. Evaluation may be for quality, accuracy, timeliness, relevance, or suitability.

Graphics Designer   Design graphics or graphic user interfaces for the electronic environment.

HyperText Markup Language Coders   Provide HTML coding to materials for electronic access.

Internet Security Analysis   Monitor and analyze Internet networks for security breaches. Includes careful monitoring of port access, firewalls, Local Area Network/Wide Area Network access and related entry points.

Interpreters   Take information from a variety of sources, including cyberspace, and translate it into a form more suitable for client use. May include simplifying, analyzing, rearranging, and writing reports.

Journalists, Electronic   Write for electronically produced publications. Also, order, produce, and redistribute cyber information into easily readable contents and context.

Knowledge Workers   Gather and use information to increase efficiency at performing specific or general tasks. Also, train others to retrieve, order, and use information to meet customer needs.

LAN Administrators   Maintain LANs containing information-based materials such as communications, CD-ROMs, e-mail, relational databases, financials, etc.; loading, purging, and troubleshooting.

Learning Facilitators   Train internal or external clients to access, retrieve, manipulate, and use electronic information, hardware, and software. Ensure organizational needs are in line with learning requirements, select and evaluate appropriate training vehicles/services, and evaluate performance.

Market Researchers   Extract subject-specific information from sources (electronic and nonelectronic) and provide it in a format specified by the internal or external customer.

Navigators   Locate cyberspace information in a timely and accurate manner. Successfully manipulate data to obtain the correct response and turn it into usable information.

Negotiators   Communicate with vendors and providers to obtain goods, information, and product customization and to resolve licensing issues or establish collaborative efforts or joint ventures.

Organizers   Locate, organize, maintain, and chart accurate records of the manner in which information can be found in cyberspace and disseminate the most accurate methods for retrieval. Organize and prepare print materials in electronic formats, that is, CD-ROM, optical imaging, etc. Organize, arrange, or classify print materials for easy access.

Project Managers   Plan, organize, and implement information-based projects, including supervision of staff performing the tasks.

Records Managers Collect, classify, archive, and ultimately destroy important organizational documentation. Documentation may include historical, financial, personnel, technological, photographic, or other materials relevant to the operations of an organization.

Repackaging Specialists Retrieve, analyze, interpret, reformat, and repackage information according to specific customer requirements.

Salespersons Sell information-based, library-oriented services, equipment, publications, materials, or information.

Strategists Locate, retrieve, analyze, and interpret information and present it for inclusion into reorganization, reengineering, long-range planning, or other strategic-change programs.

Systems Administrators Ensure electronic access to a variety of internal and external computer networks, databases, or CD-ROM configurations; program. Requires knowledge about emerging technologies, expertise in hardware and software capability and, possibly, certification in several platform areas.

Team Leaders Lead teams in the gathering, analysis, and dissemination of information by business units, technical teams, executive teams, and others who require information for effective decision making.

Team Members Work on multiple, cross-functional organizational teams; accurately, quickly, and properly present information for immediate and effective use.

Trainers Requires retrieval expertise. Train colleagues (internally and externally) in the use of information-based technologies or electronic information access, equipment, searching techniques, and analysis. Guide colleagues on the use and applications of information to achieve organizational goals.

Virtual Librarians Work in a non-self-contained, nontraditional library environment. Receive information from clients electronically, retrieve information via the Internet or other online services, and transmit retrieved information electronically to clients.

Webmaster Design, using text and graphics, World Wide Web home pages internally in a company or on a contractual basis. Update pages and maintain them overall.

Conclusion

While it is true that technological advancements have affected our society and the manner in which we now access information, I am not sure it is true that we must create new titles for the jobs that we, as librarians, perform. I believe that we not only have the skills, but also that we have proven that we can effectively operate huge storage and retrieval systems. Although technological change has an impact on the very manner in which traditional librarians and information professionals carry out their responsibilities, this is not unlike our progress from using pen/ink, electric pens, typewriters, to word processors and computers. We are committing words, drawings, or diagrams to some medium that can be retrieved and used by others. As librarians, many of us are performing many of the functions listed in the alternative career descriptions. We naturally assume these roles because to do so enhances our ability to deliver information to our respective customers and increases the value of the information to them.

Being a cybrarian is not a new phenomenon; online searchers could rightly have been called cybrarians some thirty years ago, when the very first online databases were introduced. Did we not sit at computers and retrieve, extract, or locate information via remote locations—locations that crossed air space via phone lines? Is not this air space the same as the newly coined term "cyberspace"? Have we not always analyzed, interpreted, disseminated, and manipulated information for our clients? How different is this from the analysts, evaluators, disseminators, or interpreters described? Have we not always trained end-users or others within our organizations to use searching tools, installed software, maintained records, or served as managers? How different is this from the knowledge workers, trainers, system administrators, records managers/archivists, or project managers/team leaders defined earlier?

As we continue to adapt to new technologies, refine skills, and make information available in the best format for our clientele, it is important to remember that an individual who has a degree in library and information science, who retrieves information, whether electronically or in print, and who manipulates and disseminates it, nine times out of ten is still a librarian.

As technologies change organizational and occupational structures, are we librarians, cybrarians, or something else?

References

The Economist. (1995). *A Survey of the Internet: The Accidental Superhighway.* [Brochure]. New York: Author.

Heilprin, Laurence B. (1995). "Science and Technology: From Prescientific Times to the Present." *Journal of the American Society for Information Science, 48,* 574–8.

Hing, Li. (1984). *Dictionary of Library and Information Sciences.* New York: K. G. Sauer.

Holt, Glenn E. (1996). "On Becoming Essential: An Agenda for Quality in Twenty-First Century Public Libraries." *Library Trends, 44,* 545–71.

Prytherch, Ray, comp. (1995). *Harrod's Librarians Glossary.* Brookfield, VT: Gower.

Schuchat, Theodor. (1970). *The Library Book.* Seattle: Madrona.

Solomon, Gabrielle. (1995, April 30–May 6). "The Information Revolution Spurs Demand for Librarians." *National Business Employment Weekly, 33.*

Young, Peter R. (1994). "Changing Information Access Economics: New Roles for Libraries and Librarians." *Information Technology and Libraries, 13,* 103–14.

What Is Cyberspace?

Michel Bauwens

Michel Bauwens, European Special Librarian of the Year 1993, recently founded his own company, Cybrarian, Inc., to advise on the transition to virtual libraries. He may be reached at 4, Korte Van Peltstraat 2018 Antwerp BELGIUM; Telephone: 32-3-238.33.63; e-mail: *mbauwens@innet.be*

Originally appeared in (1994, April) *Computers in Libraries,* 42–8. Copyright held by *Information Today.*

There are quite a few definitions of cyberspace. Ermel Stepp calls it "the space of interactive computational possibilities, where computers and their contents are available to users of any participating computers, anywhere."[1] It is clear that such a cyberspace already exists today. On the other hand, Michael Benedikt defines cyberspace as "a globally networked, computer-sustained, computer-accessed, and computer-generated, multi-dimensional, artificial or 'virtual' reality."[2] Such a cyberspace clearly does not exist yet, although it may be said that "islands" are being built that fit that model. To resolve the tension between these definitions, it can be useful to distinguish between certain levels of cyberspace, or phases of its emergence. What is common to both definitions is that cyberspace is the space we are "in" during computer-mediated communication.

> *Level 1* is then simply the mental map that we have of the information landscape when we are using our computers to find information or to communicate with others. Everyone with a PC and modem participates in it.

Level 2 comes into being when we actively communicate with a machine or another human being through the mediation of a computer. E-mail and bulletin boards are examples of cyberspace islands of this nature, whereas the Internet is already such a global space, although it is not yet fully multisensorial or three-dimensional.

Level 3 will be attained when that latter stage has been reached. Then, we will have a parallel world existing next to the physical world that will actively engage all our senses, though it will consist of data alone.

Is such a level 3 cyberspace the same as virtual reality [VR]? W. Lambert Gardiner makes a useful distinction.[3] Both are media, he says; that is, they mediate between the objective world and the subjective mind. However, we have different ways of looking at the world. Perceptually, we see the world as a collection of things. VR is a window to see such a world (though artificial); it therefore has to deal with things in an accurate way. We also conceive of the world through concepts and abstractions. Cyberspace is a mirror of these conceptual maps, captured by the computer in order to simplify our understanding of complex situations. Thus, different laws and conditions will apply according to the point of view of those who will make full-immersion, three-dimensional worlds, depending on their intention to make artificial realities or maps to knowledge.

It is also useful to distinguish cyberspace from the more encompassing mediaspace. After all, we've been using electronic media for a long time now. Think of televisions and telephones. Mediaspace is a passive medium that merely communicates signals from A to B. Cyberspace is in some ways "conscious" of your presence. Unlike a book, a computer "knows" that you are reading it. This is what we call the objective criterion. There is also a very important subjective criterion, which has to do with our sense of place. When you're using the telephone, you're simply talking to another human being, using a seemingly passive communication tool. However, on the Internet, a BBS [bulletin board system], or in VR, you're clearly "entering" a shared space.

Thus, in cyberspace, it is you who enters the computer's realm, while in mediaspace the technology becomes ubiquitous and invisible, and it is more of a case of technology entering into our realm. This is why cyberspace will evolve into virtual reality, while mediaspace will evolve into augmented reality. In the latter, computers disappear into the physical surroundings, which become enhanced by embedded intelligence. Perhaps both technologies will strive for supremacy.

The following must be clearly understood: cyberspace, even in its phase 3 variety, is not a fad and is not science fiction. You are using it today and will be using it even more tomorrow. It is the logical outcome of the process of virtualization that affects everything in our society. Cyberspace is therefore unavoidable and something we have to position ourselves toward.

The Virtualization of Everything

The quest of humankind is to replace the realm of necessity by a realm of freedom. In very simple terms, it means that we want to replace what we have to do with what we want to do. Thus, we have developed tools that are increasingly productive in manufacturing our basic necessities. One basic law in this process is that matter is more expensive than energy and that energy is more expensive than information. We produce more and more, using ever fewer resources to do so, and this process is a function of our knowledge. It is this process where matter is increasingly being replaced by information that we call virtualization. In agricultural society, matter was being transformed with physical tools and manual labor; in industrial society, matter was being transformed by machines driven by energy; in information society, matter is transformed by machines driven by intelligence, that is, robots.

To take an example, look at the productivity gains involved in the production of papyrus, printed books, and the one electronic book that can be instantly reproduced to a mass audience of millions. In our postcapitalist society (Drucker), competitiveness is now dependent on applying knowledge at all stages of production, and value creation is a matter of intellectual capabilities and mental labor, enhanced by computers (extensions of our minds) and robots (extensions of our bodies). The maxim "it is cheaper to move information than people or things" explains the growth of cyberspatial tools. Information and knowledge have to flow rapidly in order for the collective intelligence of the organization to be applied, and this can only be done through the intermediary of computers. Virtualization therefore also means the process whereby what is critical and vital for an organization is increasingly taking place through the mediation of computers.[4]

We speak of virtual offices when cyberspace is used for intracompany communication, for instance, by teams working on a certain project (virtual teams); we speak of virtual corporations, when cyberspace is used for intercompany communication. Virtual corporations are pools of talent across companies and organizations, configured together through cyberspace; virtual communities are groups of people exchanging ideas in cyberspace. Such communities are increasingly common, witness the 60,000 U.S. BBSs with 12 million users and the millions who use the Internet. Hans Moravec states that "it is possible to anticipate a time, a few decades hence, when people will spend more time in remote (telepresence) and virtual realities, than in their immediate surroundings, just as today most spend their time in artificial indoor surroundings, than in the great outdoors."[5]

Cyberspatial Tools and the Virtual Library

We can conclude that virtualization means that every piece of information, produced everywhere in the organization, is accessible from anywhere, anytime. This definition leads us naturally to a discussion of the concept of the virtual library.

Information professionals already encounter a variety of cyberspatial tools. First, our traditional online databases now have to be included in our professional cyberspace. We will use them to retrieve general, published information. An increasing amount of original primary material will be available, while it is becoming increasingly simple and economical to digitize printed information in-house and to integrate internal and external databases. However, when we do need contextual information, which is available only through experts, we need the second level of cyberspatial tools, which do not only allow for information retrieval (i.e., human-machine communication), but also people-to-people communication. This is where e-mail comes in (within and without the organization), but also the listserv-based mailing lists, bulletin boards, and computer conferencing systems. Level 3 tools also allow for cooperation in virtual offices (groupware), eventually in real time. Finally, the top-level cyberspatial tools will offer telepresence or immersion technologies. Levels 1 and 2 are regularly used today, [and] level 3 is slowly making an entry in major corporations. . . . Corporations are indeed acquiring groupware technologies for intracompany communication, while internetworking (through the Internet or private networks) is extending that model of cooperation across companies.

The virtualization as discussed above (i.e., 1. the replacement of matter by information; 2. the growth of computer-mediated communication; and 3. universal access to information) affects libraries, hence the growing discussion of the concept of the virtual library.

Different degrees of virtuality should be distinguished:

> *Level 1:* electronic access (OPAC [Online Public Access Catalog]) but real library in the background. This corresponds to the first phase of library automation.
>
> *Level 2:* electronic access to virtual collections but with delivery of real documents (i.e., UNCOVER). This level can be attained today.
>
> *Level 3:* electronic access to virtual collections consisting of electronic documents. This level can already be experimented with in limited collections.

Some commentators distinguish virtual libraries from electronic libraries. A library is defined as a selection of published documents, organized and made available for a defined user population. Thus, there are local electronic libraries, which are the electronic equivalent of a real library. Such a local collection is a stepping stone to a virtual library (i.e., global access). On the other hand, the Internet does not yet have the necessary organization and access tools, though growing parts are being cataloged in such a way. In that sense, the existing virtual library is a stepping stone to a global electronic library.[6]

At BP Nutrition the physical library was abolished, and we opted instead for a level 2 implementation of the virtual library concept, basing ourselves on the following premises: (1) The secondary material (abstracting and indexing services) is available online with few exceptions; (2) the primary material (original documents) is available online (a minority) or through regular document delivery channels; (3) the remainder, mainly gray literature, is difficult to identify and is available only through the producer. However the last-named collection can be digitized in-house after acquisition.[7]

We combined a very comprehensive system of current awareness services in order to send pointers to customers based on the material available online, while requested items were ordered through rapid document delivery. Thus, just-in-case collection building was replaced by just-in-time delivery. A large variety of customized newsletters were produced, according to the just-for-you publishing concept with the help of appropriate information refinery software. For research purposes we used a combination of databases and internetworking tools. The whole gamut of professional communications could be handled from our own desktops.

The results of using cyberspatial tools in this way were quite encouraging: increased productivity (400 percent; i.e., replacing four staff members while providing better service); increased customer satisfaction (as evidenced by information audit and BP Information Prize); elimination of time needed for postprocessing procedures by 70 percent; lower costs (the annual budget was reduced by 30 percent for three consecutive years); and most importantly, vastly enhanced job satisfaction (the "fun" factor went up by a factor of 7 percent).

Other librarians (i.e., cybrarians) have made similar attempts to move toward level 2 virtual libraries. We refer to the professional experience of Barbara Denton of Sematech; Lera Chitwood of Motorola; Toni Emerson of HIT Lab; Alice Cihon of SpencerStuart; and probably quite a few others as well.

At this stage, level 3 experiments require large-scale organizational commitments. We are referring to such endeavors as Carnegie-Mellon's "Mercury Project." Level 3 electronic libraries (local access only) are being attempted by, for instance, Ann Ramsden at De Montfort University (UK).

The Role of Cybrarians Today and Tomorrow

Our own experience, and reports of similar endeavors, along with reflection, have inspired an attempt to redefine our professional role. The concept of library and librarian is clearly linked to a physical building that stores material objects (books). The term is not appropriate for an information professional who no longer works in such a building and who does not handle books, but uses cyberspatial tools for retrieving and disseminating information. We prefer to call such a librarian, one who navigates cyberspace, a cybrarian, an altogether more appropriate and necessary concept.

In our Cybrarian's Manifesto[8] I also argued for a new organizational model. I wrote that the traditional central libraries are becoming obsolete and that they could be replaced, at least in organizational contexts, by a network of cybrarians strategically located throughout the organization, wherever and whenever they are needed. This idea is based on our current capacity to be location independent. [We can work from] wherever there is a PC with modem, and soon there will be wireless portables (i.e., "the

library without roofs"). It is thus possible to "hot-desk" close to our customers, wherever they are moving to.

Such close physical proximity allows human bonding and intimate
knowledge of our customer's needs. It is, of course, also possible to move
"virtually" through the groupware environment and to be assigned to the
perpetually reconfigured virtual teams. The vision here is of the cybrarian
as a kind of information counsel who would be responsible for information
consultancy, just as the legal counsel is responsible for matters of law.

The Manifesto defined three crucial tasks for current cybrarians. The first,
infomapping, means keeping track of internal knowledge resources, be it
experts, teams, or databases. True groupware tools make this process organic by allowing the appropriate knowledge to emerge spontaneously on
the basis of need. Nevertheless, building more formal tools such as directories of expertise, and facilitating and organizing the accumulated knowledge, remains a necessity.

The second task, outsourcing management, means keeping track of external expertise and farming out specialized or routine tasks to external
information providers. (This is also a form of virtualization.) In this era of
increasing specialization, no single individual or organization can master all
skills in-house; as knowledge workers, routine is our deadly enemy. Thus
routine should be rigorously eliminated, automated, or farmed out.

Networking is the third and crucial task of being connected through the
electronic and professional networks. It is the basic premise for making all
the rest possible.

Does all this mean that central libraries will/should disappear altogether?
No, a small core of support staff may be needed. But they will be in the
real sense the periphery, supporting the central core of networked cybrarians. This situation could be achieved today.

Cybrarians should certainly aim to facilitate this change to virtual libraries
and computer-assisted communication and cooperative work. After all,
these are technologies of freedom that empower the end-user, democratize
the workplace, and make information available to our customers regardless
of rank and location. This is why I suggest the following motto for cybrarians: "One organization, one (networked) library, one cyberspace." One
organization because all the information produced in the organization belongs to (all in) the organization; one (networked) library because the information produced from any location should be available from anywhere
(with a proviso for confidentiality and privacy); and one cyberspace because the exchange of knowledge should happen in one electronic com-
mons. This is not so much a utopia as indeed a requirement for companies
if they want to survive in the information age.

But what about tomorrow? What will our future role be in the light of
these developments, that is, the unstoppable emergence of cyberspace?

It has been the historic task of librarians to make the explosion of print
materials accessible by organizing that knowledge. Libraries have performed this job very well. We are now witnessing a very similar situation,
with an explosion of electronic information resources. Although computer
scientists have started building navigation tools such as Archie and Gopher,

cataloguing, classification, indexing, and abstracting will need to be performed by this new breed of librarians, that is, cybrarians.

It must be said, however, that we will have to give up our traditional aim of comprehensiveness. The notion has been proposed of setting up "centers of excellence" for each discipline, if a core of valuable material becomes accessible. The rest of the material will have to be made accessible by the skillful use of automated information retrieval tools.

I believe that we can safely predict that the growth of knowledge in cyberspace will always outpace the capability of end-users to monitor it. Hence, a continuing role of cybrarians is to navigate this data ocean professionally and act as a guide for others, "mapping" cyberspace as it were. This argument for our role in external cyberspace is valid in our internal groupware environments as well.

It has been said that the defining problem of the information economy is too much information, just as the defining problem of industrial society was the problem of the scarcity of energy. Techniques are being developed to deal with this problem: namely, information filtering to stop too much data from coming in; information visualization to identify patterns in huge amounts of complex numeric data; and content analysis to extract meaning from huge amounts of textual data.

We should have a role in all of these techniques, particularly in the latter, which is the most resistant to automation. But even with such techniques, further help will be needed. Cybrarians at the point of entry of the data may wish to use their human intelligence and analytical skills to "flag" particularly important documents. This is an important role, for our users have only limited time and attention, and they will appreciate a qualitative filtering. To paraphrase Bruce Sterling: "in the information economy everything is plentiful, except our attention."

Cybrarians located at the center of cyberspace will design the maps to make the knowledge accessible, playing a role as editorial system operators. A special task will be the building of virtual electronic reference rooms for use by the subject specialists, teams, departments, and so on. It will be our task to stock these reference rooms with appropriate material just as we did in the old-fashioned libraries.

Finally, cybrarians at the end of the datastream will have the task of consolidating the knowledge for future use. This means cleaning out the discussion threads on the online forums before archiving them. This activity is being carried out by the Technical Information Centers at Buckman Labs. Let us not forget that finding the right piece of information will still be a challenge, so all the roles discussed above should be seen in addition to our traditional role.

Furthermore, even in an age of overload, pockets of information poverty will persist. This may mean not having the material means to purchase information—hence the need for public cybraries (on Free-Nets, for example) where we can guide the public and the "informationally disadvantaged." It may mean having the means but not the technical skills to use computers or retrieve information; thus, there will be a continued need for training and advice. It may mean receiving wrong information through manipulation of censorship. In this struggle against information aristocracy in support of a digital democracy, cybrarians can play a politically important function.

Cyberspace is also a place for human interaction and community building. Computer-mediated communication creates new networks, that is, virtual communities. Thus, there is a need for civility, that is, netiquette. These virtual communities, which include organizational cyberspaces, will need virtual guardians. I deem cybrarians more appropriate for this role than, say, the IT [Information Technology] department.

Toward Cyberology

Cyberspace will also be a field of study for a new breed of information scientists whom we may want to call cyberologists. Cyberspace will influence our profession, and this should certainly be examined. Cyberspace also influences the organizations we work for. How does it influence efficiency, prejudice, writing styles, and, most importantly, organizational behavior and structure?

David Ronfeldt of the Rand Corporation[9] has very appropriately coined the term *cyberocracy,* that is, "a form of organization that has a well-developed cyberspace, conducts many key activities through it, and is structured as though its cyberspace were an essential factor for the organization's presence, power, and productivity." He adds that "what may distinguish cyberocratic elites is that they will tend to define issues and trends in informational terms, and to look for answers and solutions through their access to cyberspace and their knowledge of how to use it to affect behavior."

The emergence of cyberspace will profoundly affect our society. It exemplifies major contemporary trends. One is commoditification, and the other is democratization. Everything becomes a commodity to be traded, including information. Cyberspace, where everything is reduced to the common denominator of bits and bytes, represents the possibility of commoditifying our intellect and communication to an unprecedented extent. How will this tendency be moderated by the barter and gift economy that is so typical of today's Internet?

With regard to democratization, our modern society has made cultural consumption and production possible for ever larger masses of people. Many have commented how CMC [Computer Mediated Communication] reduces the barriers of gender, race, and hierarchy, allowing new layers of the population to participate in shared discourse. This democratization has a price, however, in the sense that although it offers new insight and unlocks creativity, it may also lower the overall quality of discourse. We can therefore predict that elites will find ways to restrict access to certain fora, but overall cyberspace will open new vistas of participation.

Finally, not only should the effects of cyberspace be studied, but also it should be examined on its own terms. What are its geography, weather, and climate like? What are its metaphysics? What will it mean to humankind to live in a world of pure simulation and artifice, where everything that seems real is just pure data? I believe these speculations to be valid, and right now they seem to be the almost sole domain of science fiction writers. This problem requires serious scientific study as well.

I do consider such cyberology a form of information science, however, as indeed cyberspace consists of nothing but data. And just as cybrarians are today's librarians, cyberologists should be tomorrow's information scientists. The historic task of cybrarians consists of carrying out the process of virtualization of libraries and knowledge; that of cyberologists will be to understand the process.

Notes

1. Ermel Stepp. "The Virtualization of Institutes of Research," *The Arachnet Electronic Journal of Virtual Culture* 1:6 (1993). To retrieve, send e-mail to *LISTSERV@KENTVM.KENT.EDU* with command: GET STEPP V1N6.

2. Michael Benedikt. *Cyberspace: Some Proposals, in Cyberspace: First Steps* (Cambridge, MA.: MIT Press, 1991), 199–224.

3. W. Lambert Gardiner. "Virtual Reality/Cyberspace: Challenges to Communication Studies," *Canadian Journal of Communication* 18:3 (Summer 1993): 387.

4. Ibid.

5. Hans Moravec. "Pigs in Cyberspace." In: *Thinking Robots, an Aware Internet, and Cyberpunk Librarians* (Chicago: Library and Information Technology Association, 1992), 83–98.

6. Roland Hjerppe. "Libraries of the Future: Real and Virtual." In: *Opportunity 2000: Under-*standing and Serving Users in an Electronic Library* (Essen, Germany: Universitatsbibliothek Essen, 1993), 83–98.

7. This aim was not achieved owing to the managed exit situation of BP Nutrition.

8. Michel Bauwens. "The Emergence of the 'Cybrarian': A New Organizational Model for Corporate Libraries," *Business Information Review* 9:4 (April 1993): 65–7. (Cited in PACS-L as Cybrarian's Manifesto.) Michel Bauwens, "Corporate Cybrary Networks: An Idea Whose Time Has Come," *Internet Business Journal* (June/July 1993): 25–8.

9. David Ronfeldt. *Cyberocracy, Cyberspace, and Cyberology: Political Effects of the Information Revolution* (Santa Monica, CA: Rand Corporation, 1991).

Using the Internet for Promoting Your Skills and Services

Two Basic Techniques

Michael Strangelove

Michael Strangelove is CEO and founder of Strangelove Internet Enterprises (SIE, Inc.), Canada's oldest full-service Internet advertising, publishing, and training company. He is the publisher of the *Internet Business Journal*. More information may be found at *http://www.phoenix.ca/sie/publish/paradigm/author.html*.

Originally appeared in (1994 Spring) *Business & Finance Division Bulletin*, 25–8. Copyright held by Special Libraries Association.

Editor's note: The points made in this chapter apply not only to those trying to market services over the Internet but also to the cybrarian who would like to get involved in professional development.

Over the past twelve months, the Internet has captured considerable attention within the mass media. Perhaps due to the Clinton administration's focus on information technology as the key to global competitiveness, the Internet has quickly established itself as a prominent feature within the landscape of popular culture. Soon, the Internet will take its place within the storehouse of the "common knowledge" of modern life. Alongside other unremarkable items such as the television, telephone, facsimile, VCR, and microwave oven, the mystery that is the Internet will be explained, accepted, adopted, embraced, and finally integrated into the architecture of the mundane.

What makes the Internet such a critical tool for the information professional is the almost banal, but nonetheless real, truism that we are living in the midst of the Information Age. Everything critical to Western civilization rests upon information. The creation, legitimation, and propagation of information informs and directs all structures of modern existence: democracy, religion, careers, personal identity, even our sexuality depends upon the flow of information.

Information informs and creates us much in the same way that DNA orchestrates the structure of life. One infinitesimally small change to the DNA chain and the results can be as dramatic as they are unpredictable. So it is with Internet. By gradually moving us away from a paper-based society, by altering the way information flows and is accessed, by massive participation in the Internet, the Net stands to have an all-encompassing impact on the way the business community and the information professional access and disseminate information.

All this points to the naked fact that the Internet is without question the single most powerful and effective tool for promoting the expertise of an individual professional and his or her services. Simply put, because of the global Internet, never before has it been possible to communicate to so many with so little effort or expense. The interactive, communal nature of the Net uniquely enables the two most important aspects of marketing: name recognition and word-of-mouth advertising.

The Internet will establish product or personal name recognition quickly and efficiently largely as a result of its sheer size. On some Internet online conferences there are as many as two hundred fifty thousand participants (news.answers), and it is not uncommon to find groups numbering in the thousands. Prior to the dawn of this Internet age, reaching such focused audiences was beyond the reach of the individual information broker or small business.

Expanding Your Personal Network

Tapping into the power of the Internet and using it to expand your personal network of colleagues and potential clients is as simple as talking. Talking, that is, in low ASCII, by using electronic mail as a communication tool and entering into conversations on the Net. There are over 8,000 online conferences on the Internet, and these online conferences are extremely efficient means of obtaining answers to your clients' (or your own) questions.

As many of the Internet online conferences are populated by researchers, academics, scientists, technical experts, and other professionals, it is a simple matter to join a conference relevant to your information needs and post questions to the group(s) for discussion. People on the Internet have one thing in common—they love to talk. After a few days, or even a few hours, you will have a variety of informed answers and intelligent leads to build upon.

The only difficulty in using online conferences as a networking tool is in identifying what groups are available. This can be done through the growing number of Internet resource directories available in print, such as the *Directory of Electronic Journals, Newsletters, and Academic Discussion Lists* (available at *http://www.n2h2.com/KOVACS*). Online conferences can also be identified through keyword searches using the

Internet tool Veronica, which searches Gopher archives. Another trick for locating appropriate online conferences is to subscribe to one close to what you are looking for, and then ask the group what other conferences are available in your area. The Internet is always its own best help desk.

Give Information Away for Free—Gain Clients

By engaging in conversation within online conferences, you stand to promote the name recognition of yourself or your company, product, or service. Along with simply talking, one technique for increasing name recognition involves regularly posting quality information to online conferences. These informational postings can take the form of book reviews or newspaper and article abstracts. Better still, when a discussion within a group touches upon your area of expertise, write a thoughtful overview of the issues and make it available to the online group. This will go a long way to keeping your name in the minds of prospective clients.

Another effective technique involves writing an overview of a business topic and referring the reader to your service or product for complete information. I have seen many such e-mail "infomercials" posted to online conferences that introduce the reader to business letter writing techniques, speaking and presentation tips, marketing strategies, management issues, and much more. The ideal, nonobtrusive method is to wait until the conversation comes around to your knowledge areas and then post an appropriate loss leader on the subject. This ensures that you are not seen to be engaging in unsolicited e-mail advertising—a definite violation of Internet etiquette.

If you write skillfully and make frequent informative postings to as many appropriate online conferences as possible, you will quickly become a household name within the Internet community. Prolific and intelligent Internet contributors also stand to build a reputation of expertise.

Internet Enables Word-of-Mouth Advertising

Once you have established yourself as an expert in the eyes of the Internet community, then you are in a position to benefit from another exceptional dynamic of the Net—word-of-mouth advertising (or more precisely, word-of-e-mail). Good news, good information, and a good reputation almost overnight will traverse the global Net and saturate this info-hungry community. You will experience the effect of giving away valuable information for free when potential clients begin to contact you from the 90 plus countries reached by the Internet. Your biggest danger of Internet marketing is getting more business than you can handle.

Postscript: The Real Meaning of the Internet Advertising Phenomenon

When it comes to the issue of Internet-facilitated advertising, the Internet will never mean the same thing to large corporations as it does to the world of information professionals and small- to medium-size enterprises. The key difference between small business and the corporate world is access to national and international markets through advertising. Until the arrival of the Internet as a business communication tool, small businesses and many information brokers never had access to affordable global marketing capability—exorbitant advertising costs represented the final barrier to growth. The high costs of traditional means of advertising have served to ensure that small businesses rarely grow beyond local markets. Now that the commercial Internet has come of age, the privileged access to global audiences previously held by the corporate world can no longer be counted on to ensure market domination. Privileged access to international audiences has been effectively and permanently broken by the rise of Internet entrepreneurs.

Whereas the largest mergers in history are occurring as a result of multinationals jockeying for position of dominance over the InfoSuperhighway, a quiet paradigm shift marked by the evolution of multimedia, bi-directional Internet advertising is quietly and swiftly growing. In the middle of this decade, the corporate world will experience a rude awakening when it finally discovers that tens of thousands of small businesses are gaining an increasing share in the international delivery of products and services due to the empowering effect of Internet-facilitated advertising. With an ever-increasing percentage of the economy and job creation tied to the rise of home-based business, there exists the distinct possibility that the balance of power may shift from inefficient, slow-moving corporate bureaucracies to highly adaptive telecommuting entrepreneurs and virtual partnering collectives.

The Internet as a communication system is historically unique in many aspects; its size, growth rate, decentralized structure, and multicultural character. At the very time in history when we are witness to the rise of the Internet, we are also faced with the globalization of markets and cultures. This generation is also witness to an unparalleled return to home-based businesses and cottage industries. The economic significance of small businesses is occurring at the very time that the Internet is able to empower small businesses to effectively compete in the international market.

In the midst of this information age, both the medium of information is changing (paper to digital), and the centralized control over the mass distribution of sanctioned knowledge is eroding (the second Gutenberg revolution—every computer on the Internet is a potential printing press serving a global audience). Information and the knowledge it yields is power, and today we are witnessing the beginnings of a fundamental change in the nature of information, the flow of information, and the control over information. The linchpin of all these forces is the Internet and the new marketing opportunities it represents.

16

Cyberfuture

NANOTECHNOLOGY

THE LIBRARY OF CONGRESS IN YOUR POCKET

Roberta Wallis

Roberta Wallis, information systems analyst, Research Libraries of the New York Public Library, was chair of the LITA Imagineering Interest Group, 1992/93. She may be reached at *RWALLIS@NYPLGATE.NYPL.ORG*.

Originally appeared in (1992) *Thinking Robots, an Aware Internet and Cyberpunk Librarians*. Copyright held by the Library and Information Technology Association of the American Library Association.

Once upon a time, back in the technological dark ages of 1965, a ten-year-old-girl was taken on a tour of the campus computing center of a major university. She was witness to an amazing sight: a large room filled floor to ceiling and wall to wall with a mainframe computer with lights and knobs and dials, cooling systems and screens, printers and keyboards. She had no way of knowing then that the rudimentary accounting that huge machine was capable of would turn out to be quite primitive a short while after.

Ten years later, in 1975, she was a student at the same university, taking a course in computer programming. She struggled with writing code in gibberish that only the computer could understand, producing a stack of punched cards to turn in at the counter and then waiting interminably to receive the results of her efforts from a line printer, only to find out that somewhere in that stack of cards there was an error in her code, and she had to start the process over again. She bought her first pocket calculator about that time for $85; three months later the same model cost $20.

Another ten years went by, to 1985, and she was working at that university. Now, she had a computer on her desk that was not much larger than a portable television set. She could produce technical documents on the computer, which eliminated the hours of cutting and pasting and typing pages over, which had been necessary with a typewriter. She could track her department's budgets and grants and therefore maintain better control of expenditures, rather than waiting for the university's accounting department to send statements once a month. She could dial into her university's library to search the catalog, and she could communicate with her boss in Switzerland via BITNET. She was also enrolled in another programming class, this time studying a high-level structured programming language, which meant that she could write her programs using English words and divide the program into modules that could easily be changed or used elsewhere. The power, speed, and memory of that desktop computer far exceeded anything that the producers of the big mainframe in 1965 imagined. It meant that the computer in her office could use a simple graphical user interface and that the computer in the programming lab could utilize a compiler to translate her English-language code into machine language that the computer could understand.

She doesn't yet know what she will be using in 1995, but chances are it will be a descendant of what is available to her now in 1992: hard drive storage in small boxes with capacities of hundreds of megabytes, RAM in the tens of megabytes, speeds approaching 50 megahertz. She now has access to laptop computers that have many, many times more power and storage capacity than that huge mainframe of twenty-seven years ago. She can do complicated accounting or financial analysis, statistical analysis, desktop publishing, multimedia, databases, hypertext, animation, telecommunications, and more. And while the power of computers has increased exponentially, the ease of use has also increased. Now there is no need to know programming languages or cryptic commands: the graphical interface found on a Macintosh or a DOS-based PC running Windows 3.0 makes the computer accessible to almost anyone.

This is, of course, a familiar story. Most of us can tell similar accounts of how we have followed technological growth through its shrinking. And this has not been limited to computer hardware: we have seen the same growth in capacity and physical shrinking in computer storage media, from the 500 kilobyte 8-inch floppy disks of a few years ago to 2 megabyte 3½-inch floppies to 700 megabyte CD-ROMS to small digital-tape cartridges that hold gigabytes. Other types of information technologies have also evolved in this way: television sets that were once huge consoles with vacuum tubes and a black-and-white screen can now fit in your pocket complete with a 2-inch color display.

There is every reason to believe that this trend of miniaturization will continue. As scientists and engineers continue to refine production methods and make more sophisticated components, we will see further miniaturization of the products we use now, old products made better, and new products made possible through this micro-engineering. The laws of nature, however, will eventually limit how much smaller products or components of products can be made using current techniques. The point will come when it will simply not be possible to make things any smaller through this top-down approach to manufacturing.

A new science has been born that may solve this problem, as well as many other problems previously regarded as unsolvable. That science is called molecular nanotechnology, defined as "thorough, inexpensive control of the structure of matter based on molecule-by-molecule control of products and byproducts; the products and processes of molecular manufacturing." (Drexler, 1991, 19) *Nano* means one-billionth, as in one-billionth of a second (nanosecond) or one-billionth of a meter (nanometer). In the world of molecular manufacturing, we will think in terms of nanomachines and nanomotors, and in the world of its products we will speak of nanocomputers and nanomedicine. The challenge of research in nanotechnology will not be how to make things smaller, the top-down method, but how to make molecules and collections of molecules larger, a bottom-up approach.

Human beings have always tried to control the environment (i.e., matter) around them, but until recently have only been able to do so in a crude and visible fashion. It is a bit staggering to think of being able to control and manipulate matter at the molecular level, but in fact scientists have been doing just that for a number of years. Chemists have been able to build larger molecules, and biotechnologists have been able to manipulate genes and proteins (hence, genetic engineering and protein engineering). Molecular modeling through the use of computers is already firmly established, and more recently the techniques of virtual reality have enabled researchers to don gloves and goggles and actually walk around the image of a molecule and to maneuver two molecules together (molecular docking). (Rheingold, 14–15)

Nanomachines that are used for molecular manufacturing can already be found in nature, most prominently RNA and DNA, as well as enzymes that contribute to cell repair and reproduction and to the fabrication of proteins. And we already have man-made molecular machines such as artificial antibiotics that are "programmed" to seek out specific disease organisms and destroy them. The next step will be accomplished when scientists can manipulate the same molecules in different ways by changing inputs or stored instructions. Custom-built molecules that can process information and fabricate or manipulate other molecules can be used to assemble other molecular machines and could replicate themselves, just as in nature. Primitive nanoassemblers could build better assemblers, which could build even better assemblers, which could build a wide variety of products and accomplish a wide variety of tasks, which could alter the way that we live! The idea of molecular entities both reproducing themselves and also behaving as building blocks not only has models in nature but also in computer science. Many of us by now have had some experience with computer viruses that are usually premised on some form of self-replication. Researchers already write computer programs that have only the purpose of writing other, more-advanced computer programs. Using tools to build better tools is an ancient tradition.

Nanocomputers might not be products of silicon and solder molecules: naturally occurring molecules can be induced to change state back and forth, acting as a switch, through pulsing laser light or minor electrical charges. Trillions of such molecules, whether natural or synthetic, could form a nanocomputer that would produce unimaginably vast storage and processing capabilities.

Nanotechnology was first proposed as a field of endeavor by the Nobel Prize winning physicist Richard Feynman when he suggested that someday it would be possible to put the entire twenty-four volume *Encyclopaedia Britannica* on the head of a pin. He demonstrated that theoretically, at least, such a feat was possible. "Biological systems can be exceedingly small, but they can do all kinds of marvelous things," said Feynman. "They can manufacture various substances, store information and walk around. Consider the possibility that we too can make an object very small that does what we want." (Ghosg) Some of what Feynman predicted has come true. With the invention by IBM researchers in Switzerland of the scanning tunnel microscope (STM) in 1979, it is possible to look at molecules, even atoms, and also to place them in precise positions. In April 1990, a team in the IBM Research Division placed thirty-five xenon atoms in a precise pattern and spelled out the letters "IBM." The logo was 60 billionths of an inch wide, or 13 millionths of the diameter of a human hair. (Wendy Woods)

In nanotechnological circles, the name that is most widely known is that of K. Eric Drexler, an MIT graduate and visiting professor at Stanford University. Drexler has written a number of technical journal articles and books on the subject including *Engines of Creation* and [with Peterson and Pergamit] *Unbounding the Future: The Nanotechnology Revolution*. (Nontechnical readers who wish for a better understanding of the subject are encouraged to read the books in reverse order of their publication. The latter text serves better as a general introduction, and the former is more detailed and abstract.) In both books, Drexler proposes a number of potential benefits of this new technology, some of them mind-boggling. He is also careful in both books to point out the potential hazards of molecular manipulation, some of which are not too hard to imagine. Several ideas follow.

The Environment. Drexler suggests that molecular manufacturing will leave no waste and therefore no pollution. Molecules can be devised that will clean up the toxic wastes and other ground and water pollution produced in the twentieth century. Other molecules will be able to consume the excess carbon dioxide in the atmosphere and solve the problem of the greenhouse effect and holes in the ozone layer. Products made through nanotechnological means could be disassembled and therefore recycled. Molecular manufacturing will need to consume little to no natural resources and will use very little energy. Forest land and plains that have been cleared for lumber or for farming and grazing could be quickly restored.

Medicine. Nanorobots could be injected into the bloodstream and consume fatty cells or plaque in the walls of the blood vessels. They could also repair cell damage caused by cancer or AIDS. They could rebuild severed limbs and organs. Nanomedicine could reverse the effects of aging; we would not be able to live forever, but we could live a very long time (though, as Drexler points out, after several decades of bad TV we may long for the peace of the grave). Nanomouthwashes could eliminate gum disease and tooth decay. Nanomachines could act as security guards and attack any foreign entity in the body. And all could be programmed to leave the body through normal elimination when their work is complete.

Manufacturing. Almost any product we now use and many that we have never thought of could be made through molecular manufacturing. Materials would be stronger, more durable, very inexpensive, and could even be "smart" enough to self-repair tears or fraying. Factories with smokestacks would be a thing of the past. Housing, food, clothing, appliances, all would be cheap, abundant, and flawless.

Transportation. Lightweight and fast spacecraft could be made inexpensively, and space travel could be available to anyone. Molecular tunneling machines could rapidly and at low cost create thousands of miles of tunnels underground, paving the way for a national or international subway system with trains that could operate at aircraft or spacecraft speed. Automobiles, for those who still wanted one, would be very cheap, very light, and very safe. They would burn clean, inexpensive fuels very efficiently at high mileage. They could be loaded with all the luxury options anyone could ever want and still be easily affordable.

Computers and Information Technology. A desktop computer composed of trillions of nanocomputers would possess more power and speed than all of the world's computers of today put together. Nanocomputers could make possible three-dimensional images so realistic that they could be photographed. The virtual reality technologies of today and the near future would seem primitive compared to those made possible by nanocomputing. Research being done now into ubiquitous computing could lead, through nanocomputers, to a scenario much like we see in the TV series "Star Trek" and "Star Trek: The Next Generation" in which one needs only to speak and the computer will respond to requests for information, for changes in temperature and lighting, for food, and so on. Advanced computing problems posed by artificial intelligence and hypertext systems would be easily solvable and in turn would contribute greatly to the easy use of nanocomputers. Cables resembling string could be run anywhere and would enable one to hook into a worldwide data network. Small devices the size of a pocket calculator could readily contain the information and knowledge of every volume in the Library of Congress.

There are, of course, negative uses to which this technology could be applied. It is important to keep in mind that, like money, any technology is neutral and should be seen as a tool. Like money, tools and technologies have no inherent good or evil built into them. It is the purposes to which we apply these tools that are good and evil, and since we human beings are fallible creatures, we have to safeguard against possible abuses. Military and intelligence applications come immediately to mind. Economic domination could be another danger. Any scenario that enables one person or group of people to have power and control over another has to be considered. Other hazards might include too much leisure and too much abundance: Would we just get lazy and fat, or would we use our wealth and time constructively? Would some problems that nanotechnology may not be able to solve, such as overpopulation, get worse because of it?

Because of the newness of the technology and the potential hazards it presents, there are many in the scientific community who argue that nanotechnology is neither possible nor desirable. Some of these arguments merit further discussion, and others are the products of naysaying. The specifics will not be covered here, but suffice it to say that there are also a great many highly respected researchers who take Drexler's claims very seriously and believe that nanotechnology is not only possible but inevitable. Research in nanotechnology is under discussion and in some cases under way in companies such as IBM, Du Pont, and AutoDesk (one of the five largest software companies in the U.S.). A number of universities have also begun research programs with MIT leading the way. Japan has established highly visible programs at three research institutes and has at least five projects under the sponsorship of ERATO (Exploratory Research for Advanced Technology Organization). (Drexler, Peterson, and Pergamit, 1991, 112)

Where might librarians and information technologists fit in this rather fuzzy picture? First, it is safe to assume that information-related occupations will continue to be important in such a world. Second, the possibilities of information and knowledge being available ubiquitously, whether by pocket libraries or access to worldwide data networks or by very powerful desktop computers, may lead us to examine not only our current roles but how those roles could be expanded. For one example, there are some in the education and information worlds today who propose that the existence of pocket calculators obviates the need for students to learn manual methods of computation—as long as the student can learn to use the calculator, doing arithmetic by hand is not really necessary. (This in no way implies that mathematics should become obsolete—concepts and theories still need to be taught.) Let's extrapolate that notion to the pocket library: If a student can have all the world's knowledge in her pocket, why should she spend twelve or sixteen or twenty years of her life memorizing facts and figures? This in no way is meant to imply that education should become obsolete, but the emphasis could be on using education to teach students how to think, guiding them in creativity, and encouraging their curiosity and enthusiasm for learning. Librarians could play a much more direct role in the educational process by acting as guides through all that information in the pocket and might even replace traditional teachers.

For the technologists, the opportunities for shaping telecommunications and computing in a nanotechnological world are endless. It is up to us to ensure that new information technologies will serve not only our needs and the needs of our immediate colleagues but also the needs of all people, similar to our profession's commitment to access to information. The quantity of information stored in pocket libraries and desktop computers will require that the information and knowledge be organized in a useful manner. Even if hypertext links are used, someone has to determine what those links are. Worldwide and ubiquitous data networks will mandate policy discussions far exceeding anything we are facing with the NREN [National Research and Education Network]. Some estimates predict that we will begin to see real progress and even products from nanotechnology in the next five to ten years. We must become knowledgeable about the implications of nanotechnology for our profession, and, as we have done with other issues such as access to information and the NREN, we must be sure that our voices are heard and that our expertise is included in the development of critical decisions along the way.

References and Recommended Reading

Dewdney, A. K. "Nanotechnology: Wherein Molecular Computers Control Tiny Circulatory Submarines," *Scientific American* 258:100–4 (January 1988).

Drexler, K. Eric. *Engines of Creation* (Garden City, NY: Anchor Press/Doubleday, 1986). [The text of this book is on the World Wide Web at *http://reality.sgi.com/whitaker/EnginesOfCreation/*]

Drexler, K. Eric, Chris Peterson, and Gayle Pergamit, *Unbounding the Future: The Nanotechnology Revolution* (New York: Morrow, 1991).

Erickson, Deborah. "Not Biochips? There May Yet Be Computers Made with Organic Molecules," *Scientific American,* 263:136–8 (November 1990).

Garfinkel, Simson, and K. Eric Drexler, "Critique of Nanotechnology: A Debate in Four Parts," *Whole Earth Review,* 67:104–13 (Summer 1990).

Ghosg, Pallab. "Profit on a Pin Head: When Physicist Richard Feynman Dreamed of Putting the Encyclopaedia Britannica on the Head of a Pin, He Gave Birth to the Science of Nanotechnology," *Management Today,* 140–1 (September 1989).

Rheingold, Howard. *Virtual Reality* (New York: Summit, 1991).

Roland, Jon. "Nanotechnology: The Promise and Peril of Ultratiny Machines," *The Futurist,* 25:29–35 (March–April 1991).

Saffo, Paul. "Think Small (and Mechanical)," *Personal Computing,* 13:219–21 (September 1989).

Woods, Kenan. "The Micro Frontier," *PC-Computing,* 2:147–50 (September 1989).

Woods, Wendy. "IBM Ushers in Age of Nanotechnology," *Newsbytes* (April 7, 1990).

Editor's note: For Web-based information, see the following:

Kwang, Lim Hwee. (1996). *NanoLink.* [Online]. Available at *http://sunsite.nus.sg/MEMEX/nanolink.html*

Morgan, Sean. (1996). *Sean Morgan's Nanotechnology Pages.* [Online]. Available at *http://www.lucifer.com/~sean/Nano.html*

Reference Services in the Virtual Library

Judy E. Myers

Judy Myers is assistant to the director at the University of Houston Libraries. One of the developers of Reference Expert, an expert system for reference work, she has written widely on this and other electronic projects. She may be reached as *JM@UH.EDU*.

Originally appeared in (1994, July/August) *American Libraries*, 634–8. Copyright held by American Library Association.

I'm delighted to bring you this report from the future. Once I returned to 1994, I discovered that *everyone* wants to hear about the year 2000. When *American Libraries* first contacted me, I posted a note on the network asking library users to think back and tell me what surprised them on the way to the year 2000. Here is some of that electronic correspondence:

Hi, Judy,

I didn't expect the change to come so quickly. *J.W.*

Dear J.W.,

Many people were surprised when the journal publishing industry collapsed in the mid-1990s. I guess we should've expected it, but that's hindsight for you. Looking back, it's hard to imagine how we got into that situation. Faculty members gave away their intellectual product, and then our libraries paid excessive fees to buy it back. In the year 2000, most scholarly journals and technical reports are online for free.

Scholars and researchers never really wanted much—just lots of people to read their articles and recognition for their work. For a hundred years, journals met this need. But then, prices rose, circulation dropped, and authors' needs weren't being met anymore. As soon as online journals and reporting forums reached a critical mass, researchers jumped to them.[1] They're happier now, and so are we.

Back in the '80s and early '90s we starved our book budgets and service programs to feed the journal monster. Since then, we've had a hard time regaining our credibility as an information service. *Judy*

Judy:

Back in '94, I wouldn't have imagined a library could be so easy to use. *Mike*

Dear Mike,

Ah, yes. We did make libraries hard to use back then. In an even earlier time, libraries were easy to use. Can you remember your small public library? In mine, the service desk was right up front as I walked in. The card catalog was over to the right. The book stacks were around the walls. The books were arranged by the Dewey Decimal System, which we all learned in school. The librarian could recommend a good book on just about anything.

By 1994, all that had changed. First, we expanded the library beyond human scale. Somewhere along the way we decided that big libraries had to own as much as possible. Then the card catalog and the periodical indexes disappeared into computers. It was hard to tell which computer did what. Once you figured that out, it was even harder to find what you wanted. Remember those command-driven searches, where you had to type "a=" or "aut"? Remember *Boolean* searching? Looking back, it seems crazy.

What's happened to bibliographic control in the year 2000? It hasn't disappeared: we've just moved it behind the scenes. After all, to enjoy a stage play, you don't need to see the ropes and pulleys that move the sets. Inspired by the way Macintosh computers moved the operating system out of the way, we designed systems to take advantage of human abilities: to visualize, to search a space, to follow a path.

In 1994, we had clues to these future interfaces in several well-designed hypertext products and in the work of Tony Buzan[2] and Ed Fox,[3] who showed us visual, manipulable search spaces and fuzzy searches. Here's an example that's loosely based on their work. When I started working on this paper, I entered this search:

Reference service in the virtual library

Here's what the search returned:

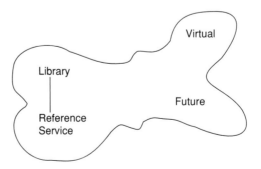

Let's see. The computer is telling me "Library" is a broader term than "Reference Service." There may be no direct connection between

"Reference Service" and "Virtual," but maybe I can get there through "Future."

If I point within the outlined search space, the computer will display the citation that's closest to it. If I point at "Virtual," I get: *Report from Virtual Reality World*. Well, that's not quite it.

I'll try the little bump between "Virtual" and "Library"—the computer displays Nina Matheson's article "The Academic Library Nexus."[4] Aha, that's closer to what I want. What's the little bump between "Reference Service" and "Future"?—Ah, here's a report from a workshop on *The Future of Reference Service*. I'll draw a circle around that to get the related citations. I'll dump those into my computer and clean them up a bit, and put them in the bibliography for this paper.

In 1994 you've got search interfaces that appeal to lotto players. If a search fails, you start over and pick another set of words. I don't think lotto is popular because people like dead-end searches; it just shows we'll try almost anything to win a million dollars. A search space, on the other hand, appeals to more basic human skills. Humans would have evolved just fine without lotto, but we've always needed to find our way from place to place. *Judy*

Hello, Judy,

I used to avoid the reference desk because I worried that my question was stupid or that I might be misunderstood. I hardly ever saw the same person twice at the desk, so I'd have to start over from scratch every time. Often the person at the desk didn't help very much.

For some reason, when I send an e-mail message to the help desk, I don't worry that my question might be stupid. Sometimes the help desk staff sends my question to the expert system, and sometimes I hear from a person. If I need help with a search process, I get to work with the same person all the way through. You answered one of my questions, Judy, and you've helped me find a lot of information on computer languages. Sometimes I call you on the phone, but it's almost always a follow-up to talk we started on e-mail. *Juan*

Hi, Juan, it's good to hear from you,

We were having pretty serious problems on our side of the reference desk, too. In our largest libraries, the ones that were already hardest to use, we pulled in the librarians from science, from sociology, from government documents, and we centralized reference service. I wasn't likely to be at the desk when you came with your question about computer languages. We were handling a wide range of questions at a fast pace. We worried a lot about burnout, and we were frustrated because we knew we weren't doing a very good job.

Now, the staff at the help desk takes a first look at incoming e-mail questions. They route some to the expert system or the hypertext search guide. Some go to research advisors who can work with you throughout your research process. We also refer questions to faculty members or other outside experts. I'm a lot more satisfied with my job because I get to follow through on your questions. I feel a lot better about my quality of service, too. *Judy*

Dear Judy,

I don't need as much help with the library as I used to because I can ask questions of my friends in my online discussion groups. *Chien*

Dear Chien,

When you ask us a question, electronic discussion groups help us, too. As a computer science librarian in 1994, if someone asked me to recommend a book on using pointers in the programming language "C," I could have used various tools to find some; but I didn't know anything about "C."

Today, I still don't know much about "C," but I can get help from my colleagues in my computer-reference discussion group. We specialize in different areas of computer science.

I don't want to keep answering the same questions over and over. So I'm training a neural network to handle this. I'll put it on the Net, where it'll join many similar resources. For example, our math faculty has posted a whole database of good math books for learning particular topics.

Today, librarians have time to learn more about the content of books and electronic publications because we *share* our knowledge instead of *duplicating* it. This is very similar to what happened in cataloging in the 1970s, when we began to share cataloging records instead of creating them over and over in each library. We reference librarians have gone back to the kind of work we did before the information explosion, working with real people to meet real information needs. *Judy*

Dear Judy,

I am in the third grade. I really like having the library in my computer at school. My mother told me when she was my age her parents would drive her all over Houston to find things in libraries. Sometimes she never did find out what she wanted to know. We are working with kids at other schools to measure acid rain. We get information from scientists and from the library right here on KidsNet. *Hillary*

Dear Hillary,

Did you know that school children began to measure acid rain in 1992 and to share their findings on KidsNet?[5] Back then, I felt sorry for people who didn't work in a library because it was so easy for me to look up anything I wanted to know. Now, people can use electronic information anywhere they are. *Judy*

Judy,

I'm a civil engineer. I used to work in an office. I had to interrupt my work to go to the library. I felt like I never got anything done. Now the information I need is online. I've discovered I don't need the office either; I was just using it to store stuff. Now I do most of my work in the field. *Emily*

Dear Emily,

Now that information is electronic and phones are cellular, information can be anywhere you are. Even in 1994, cellular communication was growing faster than most people expected, and the airwaves were getting full. To free up more bandwidth for telephones, we moved almost all of the TV transmission to cable, just as Nicholas Negroponte predicted we would.[6] *Judy*

Correspondence from 1994

In addition to bringing those letters from library users in the year 2000, I asked some of you in 1994 what you wanted to know about the future. Here are some of your questions:

Dear Judy,

What were the biggest changes in your job? *Kathleen*

Dear Kathleen,

I think the biggest change is that we recognized the difference between hard and soft information. As Francis Miksa said, soft information leads to personal growth and enlightenment. Hard information answers questions.[7] To find hard information, we need a way to explore, and we may want a trail guide or a consultant.

For a while, libraries focused on ways to find hard, factual information, the kind in reference books and technical journals. We emphasized information retrieval. We developed systems for finding answers—the "trivial pursuit" aspect of libraries. And we judged ourselves largely on how well we did this small part of our role.

Soft information is about what knowledge can do for the person internally, not what the person with knowledge can do to the outside world. Soft information isn't retrieved, it's fitted—to the needs of a particular time. To help users with soft information, we need to do more than index it. We need to be willing to make judgments of others.

We can think of three levels of involvement with users. At the first, most abstract level, we organize materials. We classify and index. We may never see the people who use these services. At the second level, people ask us to meet particular needs. This is the one-time, ready-reference function. At the third level, the most personal one, we have ongoing dialogues with users. We guide them through multistep processes. We encourage and advise them as they learn and explore.

By 1994 we were delivering most of our first-level, organizing services with computers. We'd started using reference expert systems and hypertext to computerize the second-level, identification services. As we turn over to computers more of the hard tasks of organizing and identifying, and remembering details, we have more time for soft tasks that humans do best. *Judy*

_____

Dear Judy,

How is online information indexed? *Heather*

Dear Heather,

Our search tools have evolved from ones you had in 1994, Gopher and Archie and WAIS [Wide Area Information Server] and Mehitabel— oops, I don't think you had Mehitabel quite then. It's used to classify the *materials* on the net.

The LC classification has become much more important as a search aid. The LC subject headings aren't used much anymore because they aren't designed for computer searching. Some subject heading systems are designed for computer searching—for example the ERIC Thesaurus. It's hierarchical, with broader and narrower terms. It has links across the branches to related terms.

Actually, the subject headings *are* still used, but they've been melded with the classification. The broader and narrower terms in the subject headings give us more branches for our search paths. And, related terms from the subject headings give us links to nearby branches of the class system.

We use the classification system differently in 2000. In 1994, we'd give a physical book only one call number because we could put it in only one place on the shelf. In 2000, we still use a primary call number for the shelf location, but we give books and electronic materials several more call numbers. We use these numbers to generate a search environment for online searches. Of course, we show users the words that describe the class, not the numbers.

Then we can start with a term or concept and find related materials by moving up and down the class system. When we find one source we like, we can use it as a model to find others with a similar whole set of call numbers. Or we can pick out one of the secondary call numbers and use it to move across the class system to another branch of the class number tree.

Here's an example: *Godel, Escher, Bach,* by Douglas Hofstadter. The primary call number is QA 9.8, Metamathematics. But it's about much more than that. So in the year 2000 it's also classed in Philosophy, Consciousness, and Artificial Intelligence. I can ask the Catalog to find more books and articles with this whole *set* of class numbers. Or I can ask for books kind of like this, but with more on human intelligence. Then I'll be over in the Psychology part of the class system, in the BF's. *Judy*

––––––––––––––––

Dear Judy,

What happened to ownership of collection? Does your virtual library reach a wider population? *Marilynn*

Dear Marilynn,

We've quit thinking of "our collection." Many computers at the University of Houston are hosts for electronic articles and preprints. Information is distributed from small computers everywhere. We find it on the net. Our library archives material from the campus sites and many others. We cooperate with other libraries to replicate archives at multiple sites to reduce the risk of loss. Digital information is archived on discs that look very much like your CD-ROM's, but they're made of glass.

We've also pretty much quit thinking of "our users." In 1994, libraries already had cooperative agreements for interlibrary loan, and we've just extended that idea. It's easy to tell whether an electronic user belongs to your service area, and some groups of libraries have cooperative agreements to exchange services and settle up at the end of the year. But there's very little of that; most libraries just help the people who ask. In the early 1900s we thought of libraries as a public good, available to all. We've returned to that model and extended it to most parts of the world. *Judy*

––––––––––––––––

Dear Judy,

What's your work day like? Where do you work? *Kathleen*

Dear Kathleen,

I still work at the reference desk several hours a week. From my office I can log on for duty at the electronic help desk. I check the incoming e-mail questions and select ones I want to work on. The help desk monitor assigns the questions that aren't snapped up voluntarily. During the day I check my e-mail and phone mail often because I have follow-up questions and discussions with the people I've helped.

People I'm working with drop by, sometimes just to see me in person, sometimes to show me something. I work more at night and on weekends because there's lots of demand then, but usually I don't come to the library on those days. I do most of my night and weekend work by e-mail at home. *Judy*

––––––––––––––

Dear Judy,

What happened to the library? Is it still there? *Richard*

Dear Richard,

Physical libraries are still here. Information has become virtual, but people haven't. They still need a place to study and reflect—a place to learn as individuals, instead of as part of a mass.

When we finally realized that libraries couldn't own everything (and shouldn't try), some libraries moved the little-used books and the old print journals to remote storage to make more room for people. In fact, libraries are better places for people, now that we've quit using them to warehouse all possible snippets of fact. We still buy plenty of books, in electronic form and in paper. The book is a marvelous technology for telling extended stories and making overarching statements. Books will be around for a long time.

The virtual space of the library has a physical interface. There was a time when the physical interface helped us to use the library, then there was a time when it didn't. Now we have another generation of physical interfaces based on information spaces and search processes, not on right or wrong searches. Libraries in 1994 were based on information, organization, and assistance. In the year 2000, they still are. *Judy*

––––––––––––––

Well, that's the end of the mail file. Now it's up to you. You can create this future. Or maybe a different one. Hey, I may get back to the year 2000 and find you've changed my job! There's more to time travel than I thought. They tell me my luggage is in Atlanta. In 1997.

Notes

This article is based on a paper presented at the Ninth Texas Conference on Library Automation in Houston, Apr. 2, 1993.

Thanks to Brian Lassinger of the Houston Public Library for suggesting using the LC subject headings to enrich the classification scheme. Thanks to my University of Houston colleagues Pat Ensor, Marilynn Green, Kathleen Gunning, and Heather Moore for their questions. The other correspondents are fictitious. The format of this paper was suggested by Bruce Tognazzini's *Tog on Interface*, Addison-Wesley, 1991.

1. Gary Taubes, "Publication by Electronic Mail Takes Physics by Storm," *Science,* vol. 259, Feb. 26, 1993, 1246–8.

2. Tony Buzan, *Use Both Sides of Your Brain,* New York: Dutton, revised edition 1983. Buzan presents a technique of mapping as a method of arranging paths to understanding.

3. Ed Fox demonstrated a three-dimensional interface for a real library online catalog at the 1991 ALA Annual Conference. The interface featured a 3-D search space that you could grab with the mouse and rotate in space.

4. Nina Matheson, "The Academic Library Nexus," *College and Research Libraries,* vol. 45, no. 3, May 1984, 207–13.

5. "The Future Is Now/The New ABC's," *PBS Innovation Special,* broadcast in Houston on Mar. 4, 1993.

6. "Communications, Computers, and Networks: How to Work, Play and Thrive in Cyberspace," *Scientific American,* vol. 265, no. 1, Sept. 1991. Articles by Vinton Cerf, Nicholas Negroponte, Alan Kay, and others.

7. Francis Miksa, "Information Access Requirements: An Historical and Future Perspective," in Joe A. Hewitt, ed., *Advances in Library Automation and Networking,* vol. 2, 1988, 45–68.

CYBERPUNK

INFORMATION AS GOD

Milton T. Wolf

Milton T. Wolf is the director for collection development at the University of Nevada, Reno. He has written more than 60 publications in different fields, was the founding editor of *Technicalities,* and has written for *The New Encyclopedia of Science Fiction.* He was coeditor of *Thinking Robots, an Aware Internet, and Cyberpunk Librarians* and of the December 1995 issue of *Information Technology and Libraries* on "The Information Future."

The "consensual hallucination" about the deification of information began right after World War II when it became apparent that giant computers, like ENIAC, were instrumental not only in the successful war effort but also in the "Command, Control, Communications" process around which Big Brother and Big Government were organized. The advent of the microprocessor personal computer and the subsequent growth of the Internet dramatically democratized the exchange of information by liberating individuals from the centralized tyranny of mainframes—and their owners. Information freedom became an issue of cultural importance and a contested nexus for the New World Order.

The Global Information Business found itself at the focal point of this new "wired" world of digital technology where corporations, governments, and plugged-in citizens were jostling each other for a piece of frontier territory in this newly created manifest destiny. Like the Wild West, many aspects of the cultural fabric were woven into a new social tapestry, including two heretofore diverse communities: librarian/information specialists and science fiction writers/readers—who found they had much more in common than they might have thought.

Strange Bedfellows?

Like librarianship, science fiction found itself at the center of things, sloughing off its traditional image of purveyor of galactic space opera and becoming a voice for a new mode of awareness in an increasingly technological world of constant change. While many of us would admit that we are unable to stay abreast of the tremendous scientific discoveries and technological innovations of our time, we are far less prone to say that we are also ignorant of advances in literature. Yet many would be surprised, if not disturbed, to learn that in the most recent edition (1988) of the *Columbia Literary History of the United States* under the section "The Fictions of the Present," it lists science fiction as "arguably the most significant body of work in contemporary fiction," citing it "as a major literary genre" and one of the "most significant new directions in recent American fiction."

Science fiction shares with postmodernism a keen interest in the powerful, perhaps evolutionary, effects that computer technology and information systems (including biotechnology) are having on human beings. While most of the Industrial Revolution technologies expanded human muscle power exponentially, the introduction of the computer, commercially available since 1951, enhanced the province of the human mind and significantly commodified data.

If, as some scientists and philosophers suggest, the fundamental materials of the universe are matter, energy, and information patterns (or intelligence), then the human race, once again, is not as unique as it purports to be. The idea that information, like energy or matter, is a quantifiable entity that can be manipulated at will forms the basis of cybernetic information theory. In fact, to many people in the artificial intelligence field, humans and computers are but two species in the genus of information-processing systems. Digitally encoded information has become recognized as a resource like energy. It provides the matrix, like the philosopher's stone, for a brave new existence: a potential transcendence of the "biology barrier"!

Cyborgs Arise

Cyberpunk science fiction (SF) was quick to recognize the implications of this new *Weltanschauung*. It visualized information as the sea we swim (or drown) in, and it understood that humans are rapidly melding into their machines, that human destiny may well be that of cyborgs. (*Cyborg* is short for "cybernetic organism": a self-regulating human-machine system that can be mechanically or biologically enhanced—or both!)

Since many of us are already in the initial stages of cyborg growth, adding artificial limbs, breasts, pacemakers, implanted optics, and biosensors at a steadily increasing rate, we should have little trouble understanding the cyberpunk term of "morphing" the body. The fusion of robotics and medical engineering with its bionic prosthetics is already here, so what role do we expect from our advancing cyborg evolution? Whether this intimacy with our technology is a boon permitting longer lives, perhaps even downloading minds and cloning new body parts, or whether humanity will become mechanized, unfeeling golems without souls is moot. The real horror of cyberpunk SF is not death or even mass destruction but dehumanization.

Jacking in the Meat

If we eventually do physically "jack in" to our computer enhancements and zip virtually down the digital infobahns, what part of our humanity do we gain? or lose? Liberated into an information matrix, will we spurn the physical altogether, content to exchange pixels of a brave new cyberspace unfettered by the continuously decaying lump of protoplasm that brought us to "meat" consciousness? As we "disappear into our machines," to quote Hans Moravec, melding mind and machine and genetically morphing our body to overcome our "biology barrier," what remains human? if anything? Or, to paraphrase Pogo, perhaps we have met the enemy and the technology is us!

Cyberpunk SF attempts to address such questions. Taking *cyber* from the aforementioned "cybernetic organism" and splicing it to *punk* from 1970s rock music terminology, generally meaning "young, rebellious, and alienated," cyberpunk emphasizes technology's impact on gratifying human desires. Cyberpunk characters readily replace parts of their body; customize the color of their eyes, hair, and skin; and escape the "meat" reality by "jacking into" cyberspace where they can project their disembodied consciousness into virtual reality landscapes inhabited by computer-modified simulacra as well as artificial intelligences whose only existence *is* in cyberspace.

New Bad Future

Cyberpunk tends toward the dystopian, using the backdrop of a "New Bad Future" set often in a monstrous urban sprawl draped in a polluted natural environment. Easily extrapolating from the present social tensions and contradictions, cyberpunk posits a government/corporation that controls and monitors all (dis)information channels and cybernetic technologies, ruthlessly hunting down any infiltrators of its vast data banks. While information may want to be free to spontaneously mix and match, to express constantly changing algorithms of potential knowledge, bottom-line outcomes prefer stable, patented, monopolized situations—and passive consumers fat with bread and circuses!

The word *cyberpunk* first appeared publicly in the title of a story by Bruce Bethke in the November 1983 issue of *Amazing Stories*. The noted SF editor/critic Gardner Dozois then used it to describe a new subgenre of

SF that was aborning in the early 1980s, but it was William Gibson's *Neuromancer* (1984) that rightfully is credited with popularizing the concept, especially of cyberspace as a "consensual hallucination," a merging interface between human and machine. Gibson was one of the first to recognize the vital importance of information to the New World Order and the future global village(s).

Interrogating the boundaries of a near-future humanity that employs technological enhancements to the "meat" such as artificial intelligence, prosthetics, neural jack implants, and other intimate computer-driven accessories (including sexual ones), Gibson's seminal book *Neuromancer* provided a dystopian futurology and the Big Brother conventions that have become the stock-in-trade of cyberpunk and provide the haunting atmosphere of such movies as *Blade Runner, Robocop, Running Man, Outland,* and *Total Recall* (which featured another cyberpunk computer technology: virtual reality).

Hacking the Dream

While Aldous Huxley and George Orwell were star-class worriers more concerned with totalitarian governments, cyberpunk's turf became the mean streets and hacker underground where technology, especially computer/information technology, is wedded to the meat puppet to "crack" into the ill-gotten digital treasury of globalized (if not galactic) multinational-corporate capitalism.

Technically augmented to surf the digital data banks, the cyberpunk hero/heroine generally lives in a moral vacuum created by a society controlled by the corporations, for the corporations and of the corporations. The Have-Nots far exceed the Haves, who truly see the Have-Nots as expendable meat puppets. The cyberpunk hero/heroine often dresses in leather, wears mirrorshades, does tailored drugs, and has a technically enhanced body, usually consisting of at least a neural jack that directly interfaces with the computer. The cyberpunk protagonist is basically a console cowboy or a cyborg appendage to a sophisticated computer deck, having a Hemingwayesque code of honor that creates its own private sense of duty.

Gumshoe Progenitors

Harking back to the classic private eye detectives of Raymond Chandler, Dashiell Hammett, or James M. Cain, the cyberpunk hero/heroine gives the impression of a Sam Spade or Philip Marlowe who, for all the sentimental finales and the almost frenetic use of drugs, electronic highs, and the dazzling technology of cyberspace, lives a life of drab, quiet desperation, waiting for the next information trip, the next out-of-the-body experience.

In cyberpunk (which is strongly influenced by Japanese products and culture) the console cowboy/ninja hacker surfs out onto the worldwide electronic Net seeking "data," which can be put to use/sold. "Hacking" (breaking into information banks) is a metaphor for civil disobedience. Convinced that corporations and other power bases, legal and illegal, control the thoughtless dumping of technological innovation upon the masses, cyberpunk fiction posits that the street will find its own uses for technology, different from and counterproductive to what the "Man" has in mind.

Given the current corporate worldwide downsizing, massive layoffs of workers, and government gridlock, cyberpunk found a ready market of paranoid anxiety about a "gentler and kinder" future. Unlike those who would, Luddite-like, attempt to return us to some pastoral bliss, cyberpunk marshals the technology against the forces of social and environmental degradation, reminding us that the price of liberty *is* eternal vigilance—and a faster PC!

New World Plantation

Cyberpunk fiction has, in large measure, served as a blueprint for creating cyberspace by providing the vocabulary, the phrases and metaphors, and the inspiration. Fiction doesn't have to wait for scientists to prove theories and engineers to construct the tools. Imagination alone is sufficient to bring people together—even if it's only a dream or "consensual hallucination." Many people understood that the world had changed socially and economically, that the old regime no longer represented the future, that in cyberpunk a new vision, not necessarily brighter but perhaps truer, was aborning. International business was the new world order, for better or worse, and nationalistic governments everywhere were merely overseers, of different stripes, for the New World Plantation!

Proto Cyberpunk

Almost from its inception with Mary Shelley's *Frankenstein,* SF has reported and extrapolated on the potential effects of science and technology upon the hairless ape, attempting to understand its evolution and destiny. The hybridization of human and machine has been a longtime concern of SF, and the ancestors of cyberpunk SF are easily discerned in works like Bernard Wolfe's *Limbo* (1952) with its prosthetic ironies and body mutilations; the novels of William S. Burroughs, especially *The Soft Machine* (1966) with its drug-induced biological Fantasias; and the many pessimistic stories of Philip K. Dick, especially his *Do Androids Dream of Electric Sheep?* (1968), which was made into the noir cyberpunk movie *Blade Runner* (1982).

Other cyberpunk prototypes can be found in John Brunner's *The Shockwave Rider* (1975), which depicts a world manipulated and monitored by sophisticated high-tech surveillance communications that makes privacy an almost antisocial act. Influenced by Alvin Toffler's *Future Shock* (who called SF the "sovereign prophylactic against future shock"), Brunner's main protagonist "worms" the worldwide network with a panache that would make a cyberpunk hacker proud indeed! And much of the Internet technology and its social impact had been extrapolated in SF long before its actual appearance in Vernor Vinge's *True Names* (1981), which depicts the world of MUDs (multiuser dungeons) and MOOs (multiuser object oriented), with perceptive cautionary warnings about the psychological and social consequences of cyberspace (mis)identities.

Cyberpunk SF became a media event right after the publication of *Neuromancer* (one critic referred to it as "the romance of the neurons"), which Gibson subsequently made into a trilogy by continuing and expanding the saga with *Count Zero* (1986 UK) and *Mona Lisa Overdrive* (1988). His novel *The Difference Engine* (1990 UK), coauthored with the unofficial cyberpunk spokesperson and political polemicist Bruce Sterling, used the SF trope of alternate history to examine what might have happened to Victorian England (and the world) if the computer had been brought to its present technical sophistication by Charles Babbage. Dubbed a "steampunk" novel, the outcome is no less dystopian than the near-future venues of the *Neuromancer* trilogies—perhaps because the "meat" can't be transcended weighted down with data!

Bruce Sterling, however in his own works, like *Schismatrix* (1985), outlines a future space-traveling posthumanity divided into two camps: the Shapers who are bioengineered, and the Mechanists, who augment their bodies with robotic parts. The politics of a highly computerized and networked future, where humans seek cyborg augmentations and/or bionic morphing, is a perfect platform for Sterling's rhetorical forays into social planning. Like Gibson, he can't seem to shake the suspicion that artificial intelligence may dominate people in the future, forcing us into a technological intimacy that ultimately absorbs our humanity and reduces us to bits and bytes. In a cosmic irony, the "couch potato" becomes the "mouse potato" becomes the "plug-slug," jacking away existence in an interactive environment that takes "virtual" to the philosophical level of "death-in-life"!

Bruce Sterling also assembled the first significant anthology of this SF movement, *Mirrorshades: The Cyberpunk Anthology* (1986), and became one of its more ardent expositors. While cyberpunk saw technology as both liberating and limiting, it also posited an extreme individualism that is at odds with centralization of authority. More importantly, cyberpunk stirred the SF pot, serving up new clusters of ideas, pushing the relevance of SF "right in your face." It also stimulated other respected SF writers like Greg Bear, Pat Cadigan, and Orson Scott Card to produce works that took cyberpunk into account.

Cyberpunk Fertilization

Other fields felt the influence of SF cyberpunk as well. Music, art, philosophy and postmodernist fiction all were affected by it and returned the favor. The intersection of SF cyberpunk with postmodernism was indicative of the continued narrowing of territory between SF and mainstream literature and was the substance of the critical work *Storming the Reality Studio: A Casebook of Cyberpunk and Postmodern Science Fiction* edited by Larry McCaffery (1991).

Under the intense media eye of modern journalism and its concomitant commodifications, cyberpunk as a movement mutated quickly, so much so that the initial midwives and delivery-room attendants (William Gibson, Bruce Sterling, Lewis Shiner, Pat Cadigan, Rudy Rucker, John Shirley, et al.) quickly (by the beginning of the 1990s) pronounced the original patient dead. But the mutation(s) found fertile minds waiting, and while the movement was dead, the central metaphors were alive and well—and breeding across both reality and literary lines like a pluralistic New Age virus.

The Cyberpunk Canon

The number of books and stories to use cyberpunk conventions is legion, for it became a booksellers' and media term more than a literary designation. Nevertheless, there have been an unusually high number of remarkable efforts to sustain the momentum, the inquiry, about the Age of Information and what it portends. Certainly David Brin's *Earth* (1990) is a tour de force projection of the possible ramifications of our present information technologies, especially the social, political and economical outcome(s) of a highly networked world where "neighborhood watch" takes on a whole new digital meaning. Countering the usual cyberpunk pessimism, Brin, schooled in astronomy and applied physics, believes that humans are capable of more wisdom than folly.

Although it was accused initially of being a "phallocratic" movement, many women have found cyberpunk a valuable forum to address gender issues. Pat Cadigan early on in *Synners* (1989) made the mean streets of our decaying "burbs" a place to rock the reader's neurons with the interface blues, suggesting that viral artificial intelligences may be even more immoral than their meat ancestry. For artificial intelligence the sins of the fathers may be revisited with a vengeance indeed!

And former corporate lawyer Lisa Mason, in *Arachne* (1990), made it clear that "getting with the program" calls into question the Progammer, particularly the self-generating, genderless ones of artificial intelligence. Mason envisions a future where online becomes a time sump that drains away the "meat" trying to keep up with made-for-cyberspace agents who don't need to rest. Her digitally enhanced protagonists, diseased with information overload and data burnout, remind you of librarians trying to comprehend the newest in a never-ending line of software releases made by user-friendless nerds.

Neal Stephenson in *Snow Crash* (1992) creates a library and a librarian (sometimes called a "knowbot") who inhabits *only* a sophisticated digital information world that peels back reality like a multilayered brain scan. Hacking in this future world is not an optional talent, it is a survival skill in a world where manipulation of info *is* everything! In a future where privatization of government is a Republican's dream, the Library of Congress and the Central Intelligence Agency are combined into the Central Intelligence Corporation, whose only business is Big Business. This is cyberpunk with tongue in computer and cheek in reality!

In *Mother of Storms* (1994) John Barnes projects a near-future world (ala the TV miniseries "Wild Palms") where virtual reality media personalities deliver chills, thrills, and spills right into the nervous system of a plugged-in worldwide audience of voyeurs whose passivity and appetite for violence and sexual stimulation has been properly whetted by decades of television soaps, and the "under-the-counter" videos of media creations like John Wayne Bobbitt and Tanya Harding. And, of course, Barnes's black market provides a type of invasive "information wedge" that makes today's "snuff" films tame indeed!

For another good read about the possible implications of virtual reality technology, check out Alexander Besher's *Rim* (1994) in which entire cities are trapped inside VR, where computer games literally suck you in, and where the hero attempts to save the world from its virtual self. This is cybernoir with a vengeance: consciousness-processing served up like sushi! And taking the dedicated "digiterati" one step further, Greg Egan in *Permutation City* (1994) reduces everything to the information common denominator where virtual clones live in virtual worlds reporting back like so many virtual Alices in Wonderland. In this fictional philosophical inquiry, Egan posits an information hall of mirrors that questions the reality of reality!

SF from its inception has been a disturber of the literary peace. In retrospect, it hardly seems coincidental that SF was born at about the same time as modern science. SF became a medium to examine and to extrapolate change and to caution people. It emphasizes alternatives and, most subversive of all, the imagination.

Technology is not the only concern of SF. It is the possible uses to which technology may be put. Technology is neither good nor bad, but humans are an uneasy mixture of the two. The human race with its tool-making proclivities has been constructing an "artificial environment" to protect itself from nature's indifference from the very first whimper. Any cry for a return to some idyllic pastoral scene of bucolic innocence and cosmic harmony fails to comprehend that, short of the mythical Garden of Eden, the evolution of human life has largely been a violent struggle with the natural elements and each other.

Red in Tooth and Claw

SF has shown that harmony with nature, which is not congruent with culture, is neither desirable nor possible. The very essence of humankind, the toolmaker, is the birth of the "artificial," that is, that which did not exist before in nature. Whether this constitutes cosmic hubris (as depicted in *Frankenstein*) or cosmic creation (as depicted in innumerable SF terraforming stories) is moot, but the cultural journey is exceptionally, per-haps quintessentially, a "real" series of accomplishments in the "artificial" (both in art and science). Sentimental longing for some idealized pastoral existence is the mark of intellectual bankruptcy, slouching not toward Beth-lehem but extinction. Human transcendence is *not* conditioned on rejection of technology! But our existence may well depend on the uses to which we put it.

Be assured, many of the now accepted explanations of reality will change. It may be that nature is a complicated message, an information algorithm about all manner of things. But if we agree with everything every-body else thinks, we risk not seeing a possibly critical perspective. Toler-ation of different ideas may be a survival strategy for the species. New ideas can erupt (and generally do) outside of convention and the sacred texts. If technology and science collide with dogma and doctrine, perhaps a new transcendental path is being cleared. Perhaps cyberspace, where data, facts, and information are all around us, is a new dispensation, a new time and space for the highly adaptive hairless ape.

Cyberpunk Bibliography

Like any other bibliography, there is no escaping the subjectivity of the composer. While there are numerous directions that any reader could take, what is proposed here is a list of books that, if read, would give a person with no former knowledge of the field a general overview of SF cyberpunk written by American and British authors. That said, it must be remembered that SF cyberpunk overlaps other genres, especially postmodernism and fantasy, and that authors seldom feel restricted to make neat categories and pigeonholes for themselves to roost in.

And, while this is a bibliography only of books, the monthly publication *Wired* is good place to keep up on some of the aspects of cyberculture, an outgrowth of cyberpunk as an art form.

Cyberpunk Fiction

Acker, Kathy. ([1988] 1989). *Empire of the Senseless*. New York: Grove.

Barnes, John. (1994). *Mother of Storms*. New York: TOR.

Bear, Greg. (1985). *Blood Music*. New York: Arbor House.

Besher, Alexander. (1994). *RIM: A Novel of Virtual Reality*. New York: HarperCollinsWest.

Brin, David. (1990). *Earth*. New York: Bantam.

Bury, Stephen. (1994). *Interface*. New York: Bantam.

Cadigan, Pat. ([1989] 1991). *Synners*. New York: Bantam.

DeLillo, Don. (1985). *White Noise*. New York: Viking.

Effinger, George Alec. (1987). *When Gravity Fails*. New York: Arbor House.

Egan, Greg. (1994). *Permutation City.* London: Millennium.

Gibson, William. (1984). *Neuromancer.* New York: Berkley.

———. (1986). *Count Zero.* New York: Arbor House.

———. (1986). *Burning Chrome.* New York: Arbor House.

———. (1988). *Mona Lisa Overdrive.* New York: Bantam.

———. (1993). *Virtual Light.* New York: Bantam.

Gibson, William, and Sterling, Bruce. (1991). *The Difference Engine.* New York: Bantam.

Mason, Lisa. (1990). *Arachne.* New York: Morrow.

Milan, Victor. (1985). *The Cybernetic Samurai.* New York: Arbor House.

Rucker, Rudy. (1988). *Wetware.* New York: Avon.

Shirley, John. (1985). *Eclipse.* New York: Bluejay.

———. (1987). *Eclipse Penumbra.* New York: Warner.

———. (1989). *Total Eclipse.* New York: Warner.

Simmons, Dan. (1989). *Hyperion.* New York: Doubleday.

Stephenson, Neal. (1992). *Snow Crash.* New York: Bantam.

———. (1995). *The Diamond Age.* New York: Bantam.

Sterling, Bruce. (1980). *The Artificial Kid.* New York: Ace.

———. (1985). *Schismatrix.* New York: Arbor House.

———, ed. (1986). *Mirrorshades:* The Cyberpunk Anthology. New York: Arbor House.

———. (1988). *Islands in the Net.* New York: Morrow.

Swanwick, Michael. (1987). *Vacuum Flowers.* New York: Morrow.

Varley, John. (1992). *Steel Beach.* New York: Ace/Putnam.

Vinge, Vernor. ([1981] 1984). *True Names.* New York: Blue Jay.

Williams, Walter Jon. (1986). *Hardwired.* New York: T. Doherty Associates.

Proto-Cyberpunk

Brunner, John. (1975). *Shockwave Rider.* New York: Harper & Row.

Burgess, Anthony. (1962). *A Clockwork Orange.* New York: Norton.

Burroughs, William S. (1966). *The Soft Machine.* New York: Grove.

Chandler, Raymond. (1939). *The Big Sleep.* New York: Random House.

Delany, Samuel R. (1968). *Nova.* Garden City, NY: Doubleday.

Dick, Philip K. (1968). *Do Androids Dream of Electric Sheep?* New York: Ballantine.

Hammett, Dashiell. (1929). *Red Harvest.* New York: Vintage.

———. (1930). *Maltese Falcon.* New York: Vintage.

Herbert, Frank. ([1966] 1978). *Destination Void*. New York: Ace.

Mailer, Norman. (1948). *The Naked and the Dead*. New York: Rinehart.

McElroy, Joseph. (1977). *Plus*. New York: Knopf.

Pynchon, Thomas. (1973). *Gravity's Rainbow*. New York: Viking.

Spinrad, Norman. (1969). *Bug Jack Barron*. New York: Walker.

Wolfe, Bernard. ([1952] 1985). *Limbo*. New York: Carroll & Graf.

Scholarship

Broderick, Damien. (1995). *Readings by Starlight*. London: Routledge.

Clute, John, and Nicholls, Peter, eds. (1993). *The Encyclopedia of Science Fiction*. London: Orbit.

Dery, Mark, ed. (1994). *Flame Wars: The Discourse of Cyberculture*. Durham, NC: Duke University.

Elliott, Emory, ed. (1988). *Columbia Literary History of the United States*. New York: Columbia University.

Kroker, Arthur, and Cook, David. (1986). *The Postmodern Scene: Excremental Culture and Hyper-Aesthetics*. New York: St. Martin's.

McCaffery, Larry, ed. (1991). *Storming the Reality Studio*. Durham, NC: Duke University.

McHale, Brian. (1987). *Postmodernist Fiction*. London: Methuen.

Porush, David A. (1985). *The Soft Machine: Cybernetic Fiction*. New York: Methuen.

Puschmann-Nalenz, Barbara. (1992). *Science Fiction and Postmodern Fiction: A Genre Study*. New York: Peter Lang.

Slusser, George, and Shippey, Tom, eds. (1992). *Fiction 2000: Cyberpunk and the Future of Narrative*. Athens: University of Georgia.

Tabbi, Joseph. (1995). *Postmodern Sublime: Technology and American Writing from Mailer to Cyberpunk*. Ithaca, NY: Cornell University.

Librarians and the Cyberfuture

Miller, R. Bruce, and Wolf, Milton T., eds. (1992). *Thinking Robots, an Aware Internet, and Cyberpunk Librarians: The 1992 LITA President's Program*. Chicago: Library and Information Technology Association.

Wolf, Milton T., and Miller, R. Bruce, eds. (1995). "Special Issue: The Information Future." *Information Technology and Libraries, 14,* 215–69.

INDEX

Pat Ensor *(PLENSOR@UH.EDU)* is the head of information services at the University of Houston Libraries. She was previously coordinator of electronic information services at Indiana State University and reference librarian at California State University, Long Beach. Ensor has published and presented widely on electronic information topics. She edited *Information Standards Quarterly* and the "CD-ROM Librarian" section of *Computers in Libraries*. She is currently book review editor of *Telecommunications Electronic Reviews* and edits a book series called *Key Guides to Electronic Reference*. Ensor is a long-time columnist for *Technicalities* and the author of *CD-ROM Research Collections* as well as several other CD-ROM–related books.